What is Money?

This volume provocatively rethinks the economics, politics and sociology of money and examines the classic question of what money is. Starting from the two main alternative views of money, as either a neutral instrument or a social relation, *What is Money?* presents a thematic, interdisciplinary approach which points towards a definitive statement on money.

Bringing together a variety of different perspectives, this work collects the latest thinking of some of the best-known scholars on the question of money. The contributors are Victoria Chick, Kevin Dowd, Gilles Dostaler, Steve Fleetwood, Gunnar Heinsohn, Geoff Ingham, Peter Kennedy, Peter G. Klein, Bernard Maris, Scott Meikle, Alain Parguez, Colin Rogers, T. K. Rymes, Mario Seccareccia, George Selgin, Otto Steiger, John Smithin and L. Randall Wray.

The book will be of interest to students and researchers in political economy, monetary policy, the history of economic thought and Post Keynesian economics.

John Smithin is Professor of Economics in the Deparment of Economics and Schulich School of Business, York University, Canada. He is the author and editor of many works on economic issues including *Controversies in Monetary Economics (1994), Macroeconomic Policy and the Future of Capatalism (1996),* and *Money, Financial Institutions and Macroeconomics (1997).*

Routledge International Studies in Money and Banking

1 Private Banking in Europe
Lyn Bicker

2 Bank Deregulation and Monetary Order
George Selgin

3 Money in Islam
A study in Islamic political economy
Masudul Alam Choudhury

4 The Future of European Financial Centres
Kirstem Bindemann

5 Payment Systems in Global Perspective
Maxwell J. Fry, Isaack Kilato, Sandra Roger, Kryzstof Senderowicz, David Sheppard, Francisco Solis and John Trundle

6 What is Money?
Edited by John Smithin

What is Money?

**Edited by
John Smithin**

London and New York

First published 2000
by Routledge
2 Park Square, Milton Park, Abingdon, Oxon, OX14 4RN

Simultaneously published in the USA and Canada
by Routledge
270 Madison Ave, New York NY 10016

Routledge is an imprint of the Taylor & Francis Group

Transferred to Digital Printing 2006

© 2000 John Smithin, selection and editorial matter;
individual chapters, the contributors.

The right of John Smithin to be identified as the Author of
this Work has been asserted by him in accordance with the
Copyright, Designs and Patents Act 1988

Typeset in Baskerville
by Curran Publishing Services Ltd

All rights reserved. No part of this book may be reprinted
or reproduced or utilised in any form or by any electronic,
mechanical, or other means, now known or hereafter
invented, including photocopying and recording, or in any
information storage or retrieval system, without permission
in writing from the publishers.

British Library Cataloguing in Publication Data
A catalogue record for this book is available
from the British Library.

Library of Congress Cataloging in Publication Data
A catalog record for this book has been requested.

ISBN10: 0-415-20690-1 (hbk)
ISBN10: 0-415-40707-9 (pbk)

ISBN13: 978-0-415-20690-7 (hbk)
ISBN13: 978-0-415-40707-6 (pbk)

Contents

List of figures		vii
List of tables		viii
List of contributors		ix
Acknowledgements		x

1 **What is money? Introduction**   1
JOHN SMITHIN

2 **'Babylonian madness': on the historical and sociological origins of money**   16
GEOFFREY INGHAM

3 **Modern money**   42
L. RANDALL WRAY

4 **The property theory of interest and money**   67
GUNNAR HEINSOHN AND OTTO STEIGER

5 **The credit theory of money: the monetary circuit approach**   101
ALAIN PARGUEZ AND MARIO SECCARECCIA

6 **Money and effective demand**   124
VICTORIA CHICK

7 **The invisible hand and the evolution of the monetary system**   139
KEVIN DOWD

8 **Aristotle on money**   157
SCOTT MEIKLE

9	A Marxist theory of *commodity* money revisited STEVE FLEETWOOD	174
10	A Marxist account of the relationship between commodity money and symbolic money in the context of contemporary capitalist development PETER KENNEDY	194
11	Menger's theory of money: some experimental evidence PETER G. KLEIN AND GEORGE SELGIN	217
12	Dr Freud and Mr Keynes on money and capitalism GILLES DOSTALER AND BERNARD MARIS	235
13	The disappearance of Keynes's nascent theory of banking between the *Treatise* and the *General Theory* COLIN ROGERS AND T. K. RYMES	257
	Index	270

Figures

9.1	Types of exchange	183
11.1	Convergence path for base model (ten agents, ten goods)	224
11.2	Effects of changes in the number of agents	225
11.3a	Convergence paths with changes in the number of agents (twenty agents, ten goods)	225
11.3b	Convergence paths with changes in the number of agents (forty agents, ten goods)	226
11.3c	Convergence paths with changes in the number of agents (eighty agents, ten goods)	226
11.4	Effect of changes in the number of goods	227
11.5a	Convergence paths with changes in the number of goods (twenty agents, five goods)	227
11.5b	Convergence paths with changes in the number of goods (twenty agents, ten goods)	228
11.5c	Convergence paths with changes in the number of goods (twenty agents, twenty goods)	228
11.6	Effects of changes in scale	229
11.7a	Convergence paths with changes in scale (ten agents, ten goods)	229
11.7b	Convergence paths with changes in scale (twenty agents, twenty goods)	230
11.7c	Convergence paths with changes in scale (forty agents, forty goods)	230
11.8	Effects of focal point on time to convergence	232
11.9	Effectiveness of focal point	232

Tables

7.1 The stages of development of the monetary system under
    laissez-faire   153
11.1 Simulation results   223
11.2 Focal point simulation results   231

Contributors

Victoria Chick, University College London, England.

Gilles Dostaler, UQAM, Montreal, Canada.

Kevin Dowd, University of Sheffield, England.

Steve Fleetwood, Lancaster University, England.

Gunnar Heinsohn, University of Bremen, Germany.

Geoffrey Ingham, Cambridge University, England.

Peter Kennedy, University of Abertay-Dundee, Scotland.

Peter G. Klein, University of Georgia, USA.

Bernard Maris, University of Toulouse, France.

Scott Meikle, University of Glasgow, Scotland.

Alain Parguez, University of Franche Comté, Besançon, France.

Colin Rogers, University of Adelaide, Australia.

T. K. Rymes, Carleton University, Ottawa, Canada.

Mario Seccareccia, University of Ottawa, Canada.

George Selgin, University of Georgia, USA.

John Smithin, York University, Toronto, Canada.

Otto Steiger, University of Bremen, Germany.

L. Randall Wray, Jerome Levy Economics Institute, Annandale-on-Hudson, USA.

Acknowledgements

Chapter 8 by Scott Meikle, 'Aristotle on Money', originally appeared in *Phronesis* vol. 39: 1 (1994). It is reprinted with minor editorial changes by permission of Brill Academic Publishers, Leiden, The Netherlands.

1 What is money?
Introduction

John Smithin

From a commonsense point of view, economic activity in the capitalist or market economy is all about money: making money, earning money, spending money, saving money, and so forth. It is true that recent changes in computer technology have led to discussions of a 'cashless society' or 'virtual money'. However, it is fairly obvious (except perhaps to writers of 'op-ed' articles in the popular and financial press) that this is a change of form rather than substance. All that is implied by a cashless society is that it is possible to envisage a payments technology which makes no use of bits of paper and small metal discs. However, the cashless society is hardly 'moneyless', far from it. The purpose of e-business or e-commerce is also to 'make money', exactly as before. Indeed, under capitalism new technology would not be introduced at all if it could not be made 'to pay' in the traditional sense.

A much more serious issue, intellectually, in terms of arriving at a scientific understanding of the economic system, is that orthodox economic theory, the theory on which we were all 'brought up' in the words of Keynes (1936: 1), has had a persistent tendency to deny the importance of money and monetary factors in determining economic outcomes, despite the apparent evidence of our senses. This goes back to a time long before anybody had thought of computers. The essence of the economic thought of the classical economists, such as Smith (1981 [1776]), Ricardo (1973 [1817]), and Mill (1987 [1848]) was their indignation at what they perceived to be the errors of their mercantilist predecessors, including the idea 'that wealth consists in . . . gold and silver' (Smith 1981 [1776]: 429), or in other words, the money of the day. And this attitude has persisted to the present day. As is stated by Dostaler and Maris (Chapter 12 of this volume) 'orthodox economics wanted to create a science that ignored money', and every economist is familiar with the catchphrases and slogans which express this point of view, such as 'money is neutral' or 'money is a veil'. Underlying this perspective is the view that economics deals fundamentally with the so-called 'real' exchange of goods and services, as opposed to the accumulation of financial resources. As Yeager has recently expressed it, in a volume which nonetheless stresses the importance of monetary disequilibrium, '(f)undamentally, behind the veil of money, people specialize in producing particular goods and services to exchange them for the specialized outputs of other people' (Yeager (1997 [1986]: 217). This is a proposition which is virtually unchallenged in the textbooks and journal articles of contemporary neoclassical economic analysis, and which naturally leads on to a viewpoint which de-emphasizes the importance of money in the evolution of actual economic outcomes, except precisely in disequilibrium situations. The latter, however, no matter how serious the consequences may be in the short-run, are held not to permanently affect the underlying real economic equilibrium.

At a more formal level, and as discussed by Rogers (1989), Schumpeter, in his classic *History of Economic Analysis* (1994 [1954]) made the important distinction between 'real analysis' and 'monetary analysis' in the history of economic thought. Real analysis operates on the assumption that all the important features of the economic process can be understood in terms of the barter exchange of real goods and services, and their cooperation in production. In monetary analysis, however, the fact that employment and production decisions depend on expectations of monetary receipts relative to money costs, and, in general, that the reward structure of the whole society depends ultimately on monetary receipts and monetary disbursements, is taken seriously. In other words, money, and in particular the cost of acquiring financial resources (the rate of interest), is an integral part of the economic process. For our purposes, the significance of Schumpeter's distinctions is that almost all mainstream economic analysis since the time of Adam Smith has been orientated to real, rather than monetary, analysis. One exception would obviously be Keynesian monetary production, but the so-called 'Keynesian Revolution' ultimately failed to have a lasting impact on the majority of academic economists and policy-makers. This was due to both theoretical flaws in the *General Theory* itself (see Rogers and Rymes, Chapter 13 of this volume), and a variety of historical, political, and sociological factors, which I have discussed elsewhere (Smithin 1990, 1994, 1996).

However, in spite of the eclipse of Keynes's thought, and stepping back from the ubiquitous influence of contemporary textbook orthodoxy, there are a number of fairly obvious reasons for questioning the validity of the underlying neutral money assumption. The first is the frequency with which problems in the real economy have been accompanied by, or coincided with, disruptions and crises in monetary conditions, and the twists and turns of monetary policy. Monetary matters have been at the very centre of the debate about real world economic and political problems from the original 'Great Depression' of the 1890s (the very existence of which is, significantly, denied by some contemporary scholars on the basis of revised statistical evidence), through its much more serious successor in the 1930s, then through the stagflationary era of the 1970s and the recrudescence of the business cycle in the 1980s, and up to and including the recurrent currency crises of the 1990s. Moreover, it is presumably this general impression which has instinctively led many of the most important names in economics to devote such a large part of their energies to money and monetary matters, including Keynes, Hicks, Hayek and Friedman in the twentieth century. This point remains valid, even if a number of those devoting themselves to money (Friedman, for example) eventually arrived at a real rather than a monetary analysis, in the sense defined above (Smithin 1994). An even more compelling argument, however, is that if money really does not matter it would be impossible to explain why the social control and production of money and credit continues to be the subject of such ferocious political debate. Why is it important to the financial interests, for example, that central banks should be independent (i.e., not subject to democratic control)? Why do participants in the financial markets in Wall Street hang on every word uttered by the Chair of the Board of Governors of the Federal Reserve System in congressional testimony? And what is the significance of the contentious social experiment of the 'single currency', the Euro, currently underway in Europe? (See Smithin and Smithin 1998 and Parguez 1999.)

In a recent paper (Smithin 1999), I argued that two fundamental issues in monetary theory were the exogeneity or endogeneity of the money supply in the system under consideration, and whether the Wicksellian notion of a (non-monetary) 'natural rate' of interest (Wicksell 1962 [1898]) is a meaningful concept. Orthodox or mainstream monetary theory with its insistence on monetary exogeneity and a basically non-monetary theory of interest was taken to be at one extreme. Conversely, it was argued that a more viable or realistic theory for the monetary production economy would reject both exogenous money and the existence of a mythical natural rate. In other words, the jettisoning of these assumptions is necessary for the correct analysis of what Ingham (Chapter 2 of this volume) calls 'capitalist credit money'. There is, however, clearly a prior question to both of these analytical problems, which is how the social constructs of money and credit come into existence in the first place.

It is the premise of this volume that the answers given to the analytical questions in dispute will be closely related to the views taken on the prior issue of the role which money plays in the economy. This is coupled with the historical/logical question of how capitalist institutions, in particular the basic concept of production for the market, specifically for monetary reward, came to exert such a dominating influence in our social life.

Although it will be seen that not all of the contributors whose work is represented here would agree with this point of view, the starting point of the original call for papers was that two main approaches to the issues could be identified. The first was one version or another of the mainstream view which focuses on money's role as a medium of exchange, and asserts that money arises as an optimizing response to the technical inefficiencies of barter. The classic account which is usually cited is that by Menger

(1892), and the tradition has persisted to the present day in such contributions as Jones (1976), Kiyotaki and Wright (1989, 1993) and almost every textbook. In this view, the development of money must presumably make some difference to the economic system at the time it is first introduced, in terms of improving the efficiency of exchange and reducing transactions costs. However, it is held (somewhat inconsistently?) that once the concept is firmly established, subsequent changes in the monetary variables do not impinge on the underlying barter exchange ratios. The whole approach is therefore consonant with, and leads to, concepts of neutral money, money as a veil, natural rates of interest, fixed quantities of money, and so on. In short, it leads directly up to an essentially real analysis of economic phenomena in Schumpeter's sense.

The other main line of approach begins with what Ingham (1996) has called the 'social relation' of money. Starting with the basic concept or idea of money, and the development of specific social rules, mechanisms, and institutions regarding money creation, the suggestion is, in effect, that markets, exchange, even capitalist production itself, are the consequence, rather than the cause, of the development of the notions of money, price lists, and credit. From this point of view, the textbook story about money emerging spontaneously from some pre-existing natural economy based on barter exchange is rejected as being both historically and logically inaccurate. Rather than money emerging from the market, the suggestion is that if anything the converse is true. Some writers have focused on what Hoover argues has been 'traditionally regarded as the weak sister of the famous triad', that is, '[the] unit of account' (Hoover 1996: 212). Interestingly Keynes for one explicitly stated that, '[m]oney of account, namely that in which debts and prices are *expressed*, is the primary concept of a theory of money' (Keynes 1930: 3, original emphasis). However, on a wider view presumably a money of account would be just the starting point for a more complete description of the development of the social structure of monetary practice, which would also include the development of standardized means of (final) payment denominated in the unit of account and the development of secure credit relations (see Ingham, Chapter 2 of this volume).

The main point is that these alternative views on the logical and historical development of monetary concepts ultimately lead to the view that money, or at least the price of money (the rate of interest), 'enters as a real determinant in the economic scheme' (Keynes 1936: 191), and away from neutral money, exogenous money, and 'natural rates' of all kinds. In other words it leads to a more genuinely monetary analysis, of which Keynesian monetary production is itself one prototype.

In addition to, and frequently overlapping with, the two broad streams of thought identified here, there are ongoing debates on the nature of money within the confines of particular analytical traditions, such as the Austrian, Marxian, and Post Keynesian traditions (Dow 1985). Whatever view is ultimately taken on the merits of the various positions in detail, the basic point that different opinions on the key analytical and policy questions will depend on the underlying views taken on the role of money in the economy and the social structure must surely survive. This is inescapable, as soon as it is accepted that there is more than one way of looking at these issues.

Mention of the textbook functions of money highlights another difficulty which seems endemic in most discussions of monetary theory. The textbook triad (medium of exchange, store of value, unit of account) has in itself tended to structure and limit the discussion in a variety of ways. Among these are attempts to define money as simply that which fulfils each of the three functions in any given society at any point in time, an approach which inevitably comes to grief as financial innovation proceeds. In the early twentieth century the academic journals were filled with discussions on whether the checkable demand deposits of commercial banks should count as money. That issue having been decided, during the debates over monetarism in the 1960s and 1970s, the issue shifted to precisely which deposits in which financial institutions should be allowed to count, M1 versus M2 versus M3, and so on. Financial innovation and deregulation have obviously proceeded even more rapidly in the past twenty-five years, making the search for a unique monetary aggregate which fulfills textbook requirements even more futile.

An opposite temptation suggested by the textbook triad is to question whether the different functions logically need to be bundled together in the same asset or set of assets, and whether it is possible to design a coherent system in which the monetary functions are separated. This viewpoint also questions whether such a system would function more efficiently than the current one, and which of these alternatives would have evolved in the imagined ideal natural economy. Comprehensive discussions of these issues are to be found, for example, in Cowen and Kroszner (1994), Greenfield and Yeager (1983, 1989), and Selgin and White (1994).

Finally, there are the debates on which is the most important or significant of the different functions of money, and (perhaps even more importantly to contemporary economic theorists) which is the most capable of being modelled with the requisite degree of formalism. For example, both the search models discussed earlier, and cash-in-advance models based on the original suggestion of Clower (1967), try to model formally the medium of exchange function, while overlapping generations of models following Samuelson (1958) focus on money as a store of value, as do portfolio choice models in the tradition of Tobin (1958). For an overview of the neoclassical literature see Walsh (1999); or, in a more accessible treatment Laidler (1993); and for a reasoned critique see Hoover (1996). Frequently however the debates over the usefulness or otherwise of the formal models boil down to the assertion that they each emphasize one of the monetary functions at the expense of the other(s), and, as mentioned, the unit of account aspect invariably seems to be on the back burner.

As is demonstrated in a number of the contributions in this volume, a major weakness of the textbook triad approach is that it draws attention away from the hierarchical nature of monetary systems in practice. Even if there is a multiplicity of media of exchange in any given monetary system, there invariably seems to be a unique asset which constitutes the medium of (final) settlement or medium of redemption in the given social setting. This corresponds to what is described as base money in the mainstream literature, or *valuata* money in the chartalist or state money approach discussed by Wray (Chapter 3 of this volume). Dow and Smithin (1999) have argued that a hierarchical system is in some sense fundamental, and that a logical prerequisite for a functioning system of monetary production is that the medium of (final) settlement and the unit of account are unambiguously united in the same asset, even in the presence of a multiplicity of actual exchange media. Only in these circumstances does taking a long position in the production of goods for sale in the market become a feasible or viable proposition.

It is clear from both current practice and historical example that various exchange media other than the final medium of settlement can arise, but by definition they attract less confidence, and must be related to the ultimate means of payment in some way, such as by redemption pledges. This results in the notorious fragility of credit-based systems in periods of crisis, when the reliability of the substitute media has been called into question for some reason. In the typical banking system the substitute media, after all, consist simply of the balance-sheet counterparts on the liabilities side to the credits which have been granted on the prospect of future income, sales, or profit.

Another key issue is whether the ultimate reserve asset is in relatively fixed supply (e.g. if it is a commodity such as gold). It is clear that monetary systems in which the reserve asset is not in fixed supply will operate in a different fashion from those in which it is. In the former, supplies of the reserve assert can be readily increased whenever the issuing institution itself is willing to make loans of some kind. Hence the emergence of the 'pure credit economy' (Wicksell 1962 [1898], Hicks 1989), in which the money supply becomes 'fully endogenous'. The interest rate on the 'loans' granted by the issuing institution then becomes the main instrument by which the reserve asset is rationed, rather than any quantity principle. Furthermore, as mentioned earlier, control over the monetary instruments and the monetary institutions which operate them, becomes one of the main 'contested terrains' in the struggle for political control and supremacy in the society (Parguez 1999). In the contemporary era of electronic money, these points should be even more clear than formerly.

Each of the authors whose work is represented in this volume has made a number of distinguished, and in many cases provocative, contributions to the debates sketched out above. A wide range of points of view and different schools of thought is represented, some of which are in broad agreement with the type of argument put forward here, while others tend to the opposite, or least a different, direction. Each contributor was asked to set down her or his current position on the key question of the role of money in the economy and society, in order to provide the reader with authoritative statements of as many as possible of the alternative arguments and theories. It is hoped that the cumulative effects of the work presented here will be to clarify the issues in dispute, suggest directions for further research, and, at a minimum, provoke some re-examination of the fundamental assumption of neutral money which underlies much of contemporary economic theory.

In Chapter 2 Geoffrey Ingham makes the case, as he has done in previous work, that money is most usefully seen as a socially constructed (and continually re-negotiated) category, and is constituted by social relations between the monetary and other economic agencies in the society. Serious implications for the social control and production of money, and for the impact of changes in monetary variables on the so-called real economy would immediately follow. Ingham approaches the issues from the perspective of a sociologist, and makes a number of references to classic writers such as Simmel, Durkheim, and in particular Weber. However, in earlier work (Ingham 1998) he has also made the point that neither the orthodox economics nor the orthodox sociology of the present day have really got to grips with subject of money, since the academic disciplines split to follow their different paths after the *Methodenstreit* at the end of the nineteenth century. The sociologists ceded the field to the economists (presumably on the grounds that money is pre-eminently an economic subject), but as has been shown, the prevailing tendency among the economists was also to relegate the discussion of money to a very low order of priority. It would seem, however, that any unified social science worthy of the name must at some point seriously confront what has always been, and still is, one of the key social institutions in everyday life.

Unlike their mainstream colleagues, the charge of neglecting money could hardly be made against economists of the so-called 'neo-chartalist' school. Chapter 3 is contributed by L. Randall Wray, who is one of the leading figures of this school, and has set out the main principles in a recent book (Wray 1998). Wray would not disagree with Ingham that money is a social relation, but he is quite specific as to the nature of that relation. Modern money is pre-eminently state money, and the liabilities of state central banks acquire the status of *valuata* money or base money because of the coercive power of the state, and in particular its ability to levy taxes on its citizens payable in its own currency. This is a modern revival of the views of Knapp (1924), the originator of the state theory of money, and Keynes (1930), who both used the term 'chartal' in describing money. The approach is also known as the 'taxes drive money' view. An important implication, which I believe would also accepted by a number of the other contributors, is that control over the monetary system in this sense *enables*

8 *John Smithin*

a wide range of public policy initiatives, which need not be restrained by essentially self-imposed financing constraints, such as the need to balance the budget. This type of reasoning, of course, lay behind the once-popular 'functional finance' version of Keynesianism, associated with Lerner (1943), which has now been abandoned by economic orthodoxy. Wray and his colleagues would similarly argue in favour of an ELR (employer of last resort) programme, operated by governments, who, on this view, should be concerned only with the substantive benefits of such a scheme, and not with essentially spurious worries about whether such a proposal can be 'afforded'.

Chapter 4 contains an exposition by Gunnar Heinsohn and Otto Steiger of their own 'property theory' of interest and money. There is clearly a good deal of affinity between their views and those of the previous two authors (see, e.g., Heinsohn and Steiger 1989) and perhaps also on some policy questions. None the less, there are also important differences. For example, on questions such as the ultimate genesis of money. Heinsohn and Steiger argue that money can only arise in societies based on the institution of private property, and that it is created in a credit contract when property is encumbered and collateralized. The rate of interest is therefore interpreted as a 'property premium', that which must be given up when property is encumbered. This, the authors stress, is an immaterial yield which exists as a result of the legal/social relations in the society, it is not the same as a physical yield resulting from the actual possession of resources. This view of money can then be applied to a variety of theoretical and policy issues of the monetary economy. For example, in their paper, the authors discuss the unfolding of the typical business cycle in these terms. Their work has attracted a good deal of attention, as well as much controversy, in the German-language literature, as witnessed, for example, by the critiques of Betz and Roy (1999) and Laufer (1998). Their contribution here provides an accessible English-language version of the theory.

The next chapter, by Alain Parguez and Mario Seccareccia, also deals with a theoretical approach to monetary economics and monetary institutions which has perhaps been more widely discussed in continental Europe than in the North American and other English-language literature (Graziani 1990, Deleplace and Nell 1996). They provide an exposition and explanation of the 'theory of the monetary circuit', or TMC. On this view, money is quite simply the by-product of the balance sheet operations of financial institutions or 'banks', which, in the particular set of social relations which have evolved to create the monetary economy, play a well-defined role in the sequence of transactions necessary to set production in train and create new wealth. Debts are created to allow private firms, or the state itself, to begin the production process by acquiring the necessary financial resources. These debts can then be reimbursed if the debtor can acquire a sufficient quantity of the banks's own outstanding liabilities (e.g.,

Introduction 9

by the sale of output) not only to repay principal plus interest, but also to generate a monetary profit. The conditions which are necessary to complete the circuit in this way then generate the core theoretical propositions and policy positions which flow from the approach. Parguez and Seccareccia also relate the circuit approach to other versions of monetary theory, including the neoclassical barter-exchange theory, and two heterodox approaches, post-Keynesian theory and the neo-chartalist theory discussed above. They conclude that the so-called horizontalist version of Post Keynesian theory (e.g. Moore 1988, Kaldor 1986, Lavoie 1992) is the closest to circuit theory, compared with that of the rival structuralist wing which remains closer to the views expressed in Keynes's *General Theory*. On the difference between the views of horizontalists and structuralists, see also Rochon (1999). The authors also identify a number of similarities of outlook between the neo-chartalist position and the circuit theory, with the exception, perhaps, of the emphasis that the former places on taxes.

Chapter 6, contributed by Victoria Chick, deals specifically with the role of money in the Post Keynesian theory of effective demand. She makes explicit what has often been left implicit, that in Post Keynesian theory an increase in effective demand, the driving force of the system, is always understood to be accompanied by an endogenous increase in the money supply. The monetary/financial system therefore plays a crucial enabling or accommodating role, if not a causal one. As in the previous chapter by Parguez and Seccareccia, Chick also addresses the relationship between Post Keynesian monetary thought and that of other heterodox schools, including the circuit school. It is argued that in practical situations the methods of financing spending decisions are more varied and complex than is recognized in some of the simpler theories, and therefore that the extent of any economic expansion must be influenced by the outcome of the financing decisions.

It will be evident the first few chapters of this volume all deal with one version or another of aheterodox approach to the role of money in the economy. However, in chapter 7 there is a change of tack and Kevin Dowd provides an authoritative statement of the more widely-accepted argument that money emerges from an initial situation of barter via the optimizing response of individual agents, guided by the 'invisible hand' of the market. As most of the contributors to this volume obviously take a different view, I am most grateful to Dowd, and also to Peter G. Klein and George Selgin, who contribute a piece on the Mengerian theory in chapter 11, for allowing their work to appear in this forum. In my view, this exchange of ideas, and the detailed presentation of alternative points of view, is essential in furthering the academic debate. In addition to a thorough exposition of the market-based theory, Dowd also makes the interesting argument that the historical accuracy *per se* of the competing theories is not really the main point at issue. Even if money and monetary institutions did not in fact evolve in the sequence usually described in the textbooks, the logical/theoretical demonstration that they *could* have done so is still important. It shows that the spontaneous emergence of a market-based monetary order, without intervention by the state, is a least a theoretical possibility or benchmark. If such an order can also be shown to have desirable welfare properties (to use the standard economic jargon), then it can reasonably be the basis for policy advocacy, for example, in favour of 'free banking' or *laissez-faire* in the financial services industry (Dowd 1996). One imagines, however, that a number of the other authors in the volume would question whether a regime of capitalist monetary production is feasible on this basis (see Dow and Smithin 1999).

Chapters 8 to 13 each contain the name of a major thinker or thinkers on monetary issues in their titles, and are arranged in a rough chronological order on that basis. In Chapter 8 Scott Meikle discusses Aristotle's views on money. Classical Greece was clearly not a monetary production economy in the sense in which Keynesian writers and others use the term. Nevertheless, Meikle shows that many of the same ethical and analytical issues which have concerned later writers were already present in Aristotle's work.

Chapters 9 and 10 are both concerned with the modern Marxist approach to money, and are intended by their authors, Steve Fleetwood and Peter Kennedy, to be complementary. Both authors address and seek to resolve the difficulties for classical Marxian theory which are apparently posed by contemporary forms of money, which are all more or less insubstantial, consisting of electronic money, paper money, token coins, and so forth. The difficulty which this poses for Marxian theory is that Marx conceived of money as a commodity (in the standard Marxian sense), and, moreover, as a special commodity which has emerged as the 'universal equivalent' (e.g. gold). So, in ways which (ironically) are reminiscent of the problems of the orthodox real-exchange theory (with all due allowances for differences in terminology and philosophical perspective), the Marxian theory also is in danger of being perceived as anachronistic. Fleetwood and Kennedy both seek to dispel this view.

The other main feature of Marxian monetary economics, of course, is its own version of the circuit, M–C–M' (see Meikle, Chapter 8 of this volume). The capitalist production process is seen as transforming an initial amount of money, M, into commodities, C, and then into a presumably greater 'value' of money, M´. It seems to me that many of the issues at stake can be condensed into the question how this is supposed to happen. The simple answer given by many of the credit-based endogenous money theories discussed earlier is that monetary profits must be generated by *money creation* over and above the initial costs of production. This is why, for example, so much attention is paid to the role of government budget deficits in sustaining aggregate demand, and why surpluses are perceived as a danger. One sector or another must be continuously willing to go into deficit in order to generate monetary profits, and, as a practical matter, the most likely candidate is the public sector. However, as is well known, this is not the route taken by classical Marxian theory. The latter involves a 'real' theory of exploitation in which employers extract surplus value, defined in terms of labour power, from the workforce. As Fleetwood and Kennedy discuss, there are therefore basically two potential responses to contemporary financial developments for Marx-inspired theory. One is to develop a credit-based theory of exploitation (with similar mechanisms to the other credit-based theories discussed) which is informed by Marxian social theory, but nonetheless abandons the original commodity theory of money. Some scholars have moved in this direction, and Fleetwood and Kennedy provide references to the literature. The second is to affirm the essential validity of Marx's original analysis of money, capitalism and exploitation, which then implies that modern developments must in some way represent a disempowerment of the original value relation. Money (as originally defined) is seen as losing its power to structure the relations of production. In other words capitalism, as analysed by Marx in a historically specific setting, must be undergoing a metamorphosis. This is the case made by both of our contributors, who focus on the theoretical and practical aspects respectively.

In Chapter 11, Peter G. Klein and George Selgin seek to provide experimental evidence, via computer simulations, for Menger's rather different commodity theory of money. As with Dowd's contribution in Chapter 7, the objective is to discover the logical conditions under which a unique commodity money could emerge as a generalized medium of exchange from an initial state of barter. More can be learned about the viability of the original Mengerian theory by varying the experimental conditions, such as changes in the number of agents and changes in the number of goods. The authors conclude that convergence on a single exchange medium can occur theoretically, even if the agents have a very limited amount of information at the outset.

Gilles Dostaler and Bernard Maris, in Chapter 12, look at money from a diametrically opposed perspective, and focus in particular on the psychological aspects on the role of money in the social order. Such ideas as the irrational love of money, greed, and the urge for accumulation for its own sake, are certainly widely discussed in popular culture, and are constant themes in myth and folklore. However, they have only rarely featured in economic literature. Most economists shy away from such topics, because of their (psychologically-based?) desire to construct a rational science. The authors point out, however, that interestingly enough, at least one famous monetary economist, Keynes, sometimes adopted an approach to money and capitalism which was very close to that of Freud, and that the two thinkers (who were near contemporaries) had a reciprocal effect on the development of each other's thought in small, but important, ways. It is therefore legitimate to speak of a 'Freudo-Keynesian' concept of money, which would have very different implications for the conduct of economic and social policy than the more orthodox notions of rational choice.

Finally, in Chapter 13, Colin Rogers and T. K. Rymes discuss two important issue in monetary economics, one old and one brand new. The first concerns the theory of banking which Keynes put forward in his *Treatise on Money* (1930). This had famously disappeared by the time of the *General Theory* in which 'technical monetary detail falls into the background' (Keynes 1936: vii). The authors argue that this omission was very much to the detriment of the latter book. They also discuss developments in modern payments systems in which regulatory and technical change have created a situation in which the net clearing balances of the major banks and near banks (the 'direct clearers' in the Canadian institutional conntext), can be kept at effectively zero on average. Central bankers can none the less control monetary policy via interest rate changes, as they are still able to set the ultimate penalty rate on negative balances (the bank rate or discount rate), the rate which they would pay on any positive balances, and the spread between them. These instruments, together with the continuing ability to put the system as a whole into an overall negative position if needed, are sufficient to influence rates in the inter-bank market (the overnight rate in Canada), and thereby the whole complex of rates tied in to this key indicator. Nonetheless, as the authors point out, it is possible to interpret this '*modus operandi* of the bank rate' (Keynes 1930 1: 166) as a system operating without a traditional monetary base or 'nominal anchor'.

Presumably, the existence of a unique *valuata* money, combining the attributes of unit of account and means of (final) settlement (in this case the liabilities of the central bank) would continue to be important as the lynch-pin of the system, because otherwise there could hardly be a penalty for falling into a negative settlements position. However, it is evidently impossible to think of this system operating in terms of quantitative changes in the monetary base feeding through to the broader aggregates via some kind of money multiplier. Instead the system works precisely through the central bank controlling interest rates, which leads in turn to productive agents in the economy deciding whether or not to become indebted to the banking system, and the wide variety of consequences which flow from such decisions.

The connection to Keynes is the argument that the banking theory of the *Treatise* anticipated this kind of world, and provided a starting point for the type of monetary theory which would be relevant in the new environment. According to Keynes 'it is broadly true to say that the governor of the whole system is the rate of discount' (Keynes 1930 2: 189). Rogers and Rymes argue that economic theory would be more advanced today if Keynes had retained the banking theory of the *Treatise* in his *General Theory*. In particular, the relevance of changes in banking activity for both real rates of interest and real economic growth would be much better understood. On the latter points see also Smithin (1994, 1997, 1998).

It should be mentioned finally that in the course of preparing this volume, it was discovered that the title *What is Money?* was anticipated as long ago as 1913 in a little-known article by W. Mitchell Innes, published in the *Banking Law Journal*. Several of the contributors to this volume have studied Innes's arguments and make reference to his article. The coincidence of titles is perhaps not all that surprising. Rather more so is the content of Innes's argument, which not only provides a concise summary of the traditional commodity-exchange theory of money, and criticizes it on logical and historical grounds, but also proposes an alternative credit-based theory of money. In other words, the actual subject matter of Innes's contribution also anticipates the concerns of the present work. I hope that contemporary readers will feel that each of the contributors has finally taken up Innes's challenge to thoroughly re-evaluate what he called 'the fundamental theories on which the modern science of political economy is based' (Innes 1913: 377), and collectively have made some progress towards the construction of a more relevant theory of the role of money in the capitalist economy for the twenty-first century.

References

Betz, E. and Roy, T. (eds) (1999) *Geld, Zins und Eigentum in der Geldwirtschaft: Beitrage zum symposium uber Heinsohns und Steigers 'Eigentum, Zins und Geld'*, Marburg: Metropolis.
Clower, R. W. (1967) 'A Reconsideration of the Micro-foundations of Monetary Theory', *Western Economic Journal* 6: 1–9.
Cowen, T. and Kroszner, R. (1994) *Explorations in the New Monetary Economics*, Oxford: Blackwell.
Deleplace, G. and Nell, E. J. (eds) (1996) *Money in Motion: The Post Keynesian and Circulation Approaches*, London: Macmillan.
Dow, S. C. (1985) *Macroeconomic Thought: A Methodological Approach*, Oxford: Blackwell.
Dow, S. C. and Smithin, J. (1999) 'The Structure of Financial Markets and the "First Principles" of Monetary Economics', *Scottish Journal of Political Economy* 46, 1: 72–90.
Dowd, K. (1996) 'The Case for Financial *Laissez-Faire*' *Economic Journal* 106: 679–87.
Graziani, A. (1990) 'The Theory of the Monetary Circuit', *Economies et Sociétés* 24, 7: 7–36.
Greenfield, R. L. and Yeager, L. B. (1983) 'A *Laissez-Faire* Approach to Monetary Stability', *Journal of Money, Credit, and Banking* 15: 302–15.
—— (1989) 'Can Monetary Disequilibrium be Eliminated?', *Cato Journal* 9: 405–21.
Heinsohn, G. and Steiger, O. (1989) 'The Veil of Barter: The Solution to "The Task of Obtaining Representations of an Economy in which Money is Essential"', in J. Kregel (ed.) *Inflation, Income Distribution and Capitalist Crisis: Essays in Memory of Sidney Weintraub*, New York: New York University Press.
Hicks, J. (1989) *A Market Theory of Money*, Oxford: Clarendon Press.
Hoover, K. D. (1996) 'Some Suggestions for Complicating the Theory of Money', in S. Pressman (ed.) *Interactions in Political Economy: Malvern After Ten Years*, London: Routledge.
Ingham, G. (1996) 'Money is a Social Relation', *Review of Social Economy* 54, 4: 243–75.

—— (1998) 'On the Underdevelopment of the Sociology of Money', *Acta Sociologica* 41, 1: 507–29.
Innes, A. M. (1913) 'What is Money?', *Banking Law Journal* May: 377–408.
Jones, R. A. (1976) 'The Origin and Development of Media of Exchange', *Journal of Political Economy* 84, 4: 757–75.
Kaldor, N. (1986). *The Scourge of Monetarism* (2nd edn), Oxford: Oxford University Press.
Keynes, J. M. (1930) *A Treatise on Money* (2 vols), London: Macmillan.
—— (1936) *The General Theory of Employment Interest and Money*, London: Macmillan.
Kiyotaki, N. and Wright, R. (1989) 'On Money as a Medium of Exchange', *Journal of Political Economy* 97, 4: 927–54.
—— (1993) 'A Search-Theoretic Approach to Monetary Economics', *American Economic Review* 83: 63–77.
Knapp, G. F. (1973 [1924]) *The State Theory of Money*, New York: Augustus M. Kelley.
Laidler, D. E. W. (1993), *The Demand for Money: Theories, Evidence and Problems* (4th edn), New York: HarperCollins College Publishers.
Lavoie, M. (1992) *Foundations of Post-Keynesian Economic Analysis*, Aldershot: Edward Elgar.
Laufer, N. K. A. (1998) 'The Heinsohn-Steiger Confusion on Interest, Money and Property', mimeo, University of Konstanz, June.
Lerner, A. P. (1943) 'Functional Finance and the Federal Debt', *Social Research* 10: 38–51.
Menger, K. (1892) 'On the Origin of Money', *Economic Journal* 2, 6: 239–55.
Mill, J. S. (1987 [1848]) *Principles of Political Economy*, ed. W. Ashley, New York: Augustus M. Kelley.
Moore, B. J. (1988) *Horizontalists and Verticalists: The Macroeconomics of Credit Money*, Cambridge: Cambridge University Press.
Parguez, A. (1999) 'What Canada Has to Learn from the European Economic and Monetary Union', paper presented at a conference on The Economics of Public Spending: Debt, Deficits and Economic Performance, Laurentian University, Sudbury, Ontario, March.
Ricardo, D. (1973 [1817]) *The Principles of Political Economy and Taxation*, ed. D. Winch, London: Dent.
Rochon, L.-P. (1999) *Credit, Money and Production*, Cheltenham: Edward Elgar.
Rogers, C. (1989) *Money, Interest and Capital: A Study in the Foundations of Monetary Theory*, Cambridge: Cambridge University Press.
Samuelson, P. (1958) 'An Exact Consumption-Loans Model of Interest With or Without the Social Contrivance of Money', *Journal of Political Economy* 66: 1002–11.
Schumpeter, J. A. (1994 [1954]) *History of Economic Analysis*, London: Routledge.
Selgin, G. and White, L. H. (1994) 'How Would the Invisible Hand Handle Money?', *Journal of Economic Literature* 32: 1718–49.
Smith, A. (1981 [1776]) *An Inquiry into the Nature and Causes of the Wealth of Nations* (2 vols), ed. R. H. Campbell and A. S. Skinner, Indianapolis: Liberty Fund.
Smithin, H. and Smithin, J. (1998) 'Spolecna mena: nove moznosti, nebo hrozba?', *Novy domov* August.
Smithin, J. (1990) *Macroeconomics After Thatcher and Reagan: The Conservative Policy Revolution in Retrospect*, Aldershot: Edward Elgar.
—— (1994) *Controversies in Monetary Economics: Ideas, Issues and Policy*, Aldershot: Edward Elgar.

—— (1996) *Macroeconomic Policy and the Future of Capitalism: The Revenge of the Rentiers and the Threat to Prosperity*, Aldershot: Edward Elgar.

—— (1997) 'An Alternative Monetary Model of Inflation and Growth', *Review of Political Economy* 9, 4: 395–409.

—— (1998) 'An Alternative Monetary Model of Inflation and Growth (Revised Version)' paper presented at a conference on Functional Finance and Full Employment, New School for Social Research, New York City, April.

——(1999) 'Fundamental Issues in Monetary Economics' in S. G. Dahiya (ed.) *The Current State of Economic Science*, Rohtak: Spellbound.

Tobin, J. (1958) 'Liquidity Preference as Behaviour Towards Risk', *Review of Economic Studies* 25: 65–86.

Walsh, C. E. (1999) *Monetary Theory and Policy*, Cambridge, Mass.: MIT Press.

Wicksell, K. (1962 [1898]) *Interest and Prices*, New York: Augustus M. Kelley.

Wray, L. R. (1998) *Understanding Modern Money: The Key to Full Employment and Price Stability*, Cheltenham: Edward Elgar.

Yeager, L .B. (1997) *The Fluttering Veil: Essays on Monetary Disequilibrium*, ed. G. Selgin, Indianapolis: Liberty Fund.

2 'Babylonian madness': on the historical and sociological origins of money

Geoffrey Ingham

Introduction

Following initiation into the 'Sociog' tribe (Leijonhufvud 1973), I lived for many years among the 'Econ', working as an underlabourer on what was referred to as the 'social context' of economics. During this time, I became interested in London's capital markets and asked some of the 'Econ Bigmen' for guidance (Ingham 1984). I wanted to know, in simple terms, what money was. They seemed amused by my naivety and explained that money, as such, was not really as important as common sense might suggest. But, I was not convinced, and lacking a thorough grounding in microeconomic analysis, found it difficult to accept the counter-intuitive 'neutral veil' conception. General equilibrium theory's inability to provide an essential place for money in its formulations was even more puzzling (Hahn 1982). I dropped the matter for quite a time.

When I eventually returned to money, a much more congenial Post Keynesian literature was available.[1] It led me back to Schumpeter (1994 [1954]); but more importantly, I also discovered the first two chapters of Keynes's *A Treatise on Money* (1930) and, subsequently, what he referred to as his 'Babylonian madness'. For five or six years in the 1920s, Keynes studied metrology and numismatics in a search for the historical and logical origins of money in the ancient Near East civilizations.[2] At times he thought the enterprise to be 'purely absurd and quite useless'; but, none the less, 'became absorbed to the point of frenzy'.[3] However, his instinct was surely sound. This method of inquiry, I shall argue, leads to a better understanding of money than pure theory, supported or otherwise by fanciful historical conjecture.[4]

Keynes was also aware of the rich body of work on money that the German historical school had produced around the turn of the century.[5] By the 1920s, however, this had been more or less expunged from the growing economic orthodoxy, and even Keynes's flirtation with the historical and sociological approach to money was short-lived. As he was implicitly aware, it sat uneasily with his classical economic education. However, a clearer conception of money's essential properties and its role in the economic process requires the rehabilitation of this kind of perspective, which has lain dormant outside not only mainstream economics, but also modern sociology (Ingham 1998b).

Money in orthodox economic analysis

Two basic methodological tenets in mainstream economics, consolidated after the theorists' victory in the *Methodenstreit*, have prevented the development of an adequate conceptual framework for the understanding of money (Ingham 1996b, 1998b).[6] The first is the retention of the model of an essentially barter exchange economy in 'real' analysis in which money is *essentially* a commodity (Schumpeter 1994 [1954], Rogers 1989, Smithin 1994); and the second, the methodological individualism of the rational utility maximization model. Within this paradigm, an acceptable theory of money has come to be one which does not violate the above canons.

Money as a convenient medium of exchange

The metatheory of the 'real' economy that underpins (neo)classical analysis is concerned exclusively with money as a *medium of exchange*. The other functions (unit of account, means of payment, and store of value) are taken for granted or assumed to follow from the medium of exchange function. As either a commodity itself, a medium of exchange can have an exchange ratio with other commodities; or, as no more than a symbol or token, it can *directly* represent 'real' commodities. In this conception, money can only act as a 'neutral veil' or 'lubricant'. Money is not an autonomous economic force – it does not make a difference – rather, it merely enables us, according to Mill, to do more easily that which we could do without it.[7]

Real analysis and, ultimately, the equations of general equilibrium models are not, as it is generally supposed, purely the results of the axiomatic-deductive method. The 'real economy' abstraction actually derives from an inaccurate historical conception of a small scale, pre-capitalist 'natural economy' or the 'village fair'.[8] In this model, economic activity is seen to involve routine spot trades in which media of exchange can be readily taken to be the direct representation of real commodities – that is, as their 'vehicles' – by the continuously transacting economic agents. The natural economy does not possess a complex social-economic structure; it is essentially simple barter with a monetary veil.

This restricted view of money, and, indeed of economic activity in general, creates a number of problems. In the first place, I shall argue that taking all other functions of money (money of account, means of payment/settlement, store of abstract value) for granted, is not only unwarranted, but also diverts the theoretical focus from fundamental questions regarding the actual social processes by which money is produced and the problematic relationship between money and goods is socially enacted.[9] Second, the narrow concern with media of exchange has created difficulties in understanding modern capitalist credit money, in which special signifiers of debt (promises to pay) issued by states and banks, become means of payment and stores of abstract value.

In their preoccupation with the theory of the value in exchange of the 'money-stuff' of actual media of exchange, the nineteenth century commodity exchange theorists and their neoclassical heirs appeared to have missed the central importance of money of account. This is evident, for example, in Edgeworth's parable of the two men taking a barrel of beer to sell at the races, by which he provided a neat illustration of the assumptions that underlie the view of money as a neutral veil over real exchange. As the men become thirsty on their journey, one of them asks the other if he may buy a share of the beer with the only threepenny piece they have between them. As the day gets hotter, both men become thirstier and the transactions multiply. Eventually, the velocity of circulation of this 'vehicle' of a single coin, as it passes from one to the other, is able to finance the sale of the entire barrel (quoted in Robertson 1928). It is interesting to note the contrived equilibrium conditions of symmetrical, dyadic trade in the example. It is more important to realize, however, that the transactions – symmetrical or not – could have been recorded in *money of account* to be settled at a later date by an acceptable means of payment.

Following Keynes's 'Babylonia' and the German historical school, I shall argue that money of account is the pivotal element of monetary practice.[10] Money of account is the *essential* means by which price lists are constructed and multilateral, inter-temporal exchange is made possible. Markets, such as the Champagne Fairs of the late Middle Ages, demonstrate (Boyer-Xambeu *et al.* 1994) that actual money-stuff is not required for the immediate transactions, and Edgeworth's beer carriers ought really to have known this. Only monetary practice in the sense of an abstract system of accounting ('book money') and an agreed means of payment to effect an eventual settlement is needed. If the latter is universally acceptable so much the better; but extensive and complex monetary practice (as opposed to barter) involving price lists and debt contract, denominated in abstract value, is possible without it: as, for example, in eighteenth century Boston.[11] Indeed, there are compelling reasons for agreeing with Keynes (1930: 3) that 'Money of Account . . . is the primary concept of a Theory of Money' (see also Keynes 1982: 252–5, 1983: 402; Hicks 1989). However, money of account cannot simply be assumed to be the spontaneous outcome of 'truck, barter and exchange': the very idea of money needs to be explained. And the economic theory of pure exchange, based as it is on a basic dyadic model of rational utility maximizers, is incapable of providing an explanation.

A second major problem with this restricted view of money as a medium of exchange in a natural or real economy is the difficulty in adequately

Historical and sociological origins 19

conceptualizing capitalist financing. In the natural/real economy of spot transactions, there is no investment in a 'money wage or entrepreneurial economy' (Keynes quoted in Smithin 1994: 2). Indeed, it is ironic that the neutral veil conception achieved its fullest expression at the very time that modern capitalist credit money became firmly established. As Schumpeter implied, orthodox analysis is unable to conceptualize this form of money without considerable intellectual contortion:

> saving and investment must be interpreted to mean saving of some real factors of production . . . such as buildings, machines, raw materials; and though 'in the form of money', it is these physical capital goods that are 'really' lent when an industrial borrower arranges for a loan.
> (Schumpeter 1994 [1954]: 277)

It was precisely this impasse that Keynes sought to break, especially with his radical conception of socially constructed credit money:

> there is no limit to the amount of bank money which the banks can safely create provided that *they move forward in step*. The words italicised are the clue to the behaviour of the system . . . Each Bank Chairman sitting in his parlour may regard himself as the passive instrument of 'outside forces' over which he has no control; yet the 'outside forces' may be nothing but himself and his fellow-chairmen, and certainly not his depositors.
> (Keynes 1930: 26–7)

We shall return to this central issue of money as a system of social relations based on power relations and social norms. Here, I simply wish to underline that this conception differs radically from economic orthodoxy's fixation with the actual forms of 'money-stuff' as commodity-objects and 'commodity-bundles', or as symbols directly representing these. A solution to the question of how a promise to pay could function as both a universally acceptable means of (final) payment and store of value has remained intractable within the confines of the theoretical assumptions of real analysis. Such an approach utterly fails to recognise that money *necessarily* consists in *social relations* between economic agents and between them and a monetary 'authority'. I shall argue, first, that all monetary systems, including commodity-money, are social systems which construct the way to 'move forward in step', and second, that capitalist credit money is a qualitatively distinct form in which money-stuff itself is essentially the social relation of the promise to pay.

Explaining money's existence

Money's existence, narrowly conceived as a medium of exchange, is explained in orthodox economics as the outcome of individual rational

20 *Geoffrey Ingham*

utility maximization. Whether or not it is acknowledged, Menger's (1892) formulation has provided the basis for all subsequent attempts in modern neoclassical analysis to establish the logical origins of money in these 'microfoundations' (see, for example, Jones 1976). Both the original version and more recent variants are, however, seriously flawed logically. As I have argued in detail elsewhere, the microfoundations of money are not merely 'weak' (Smithin 1994: 14), but non-existent (Ingham 1996b).

When attached to the nineteenth century evolutionary perspective, Jevons's sensible observation that money overcomes the inconveniences of barter that occur in the absence of a 'double coincidence of wants' implies a crude teleological functionalism.[12] However, Menger's attempt to avoid this logical problem, by arguing that the origin of money was the unintended consequence of individual rationality in holding stocks of the most tradeable commodity in a barter economy, merely posed another question. The existence of non-commodity or token money presented him with the paradox that money was 'in the common interest', but conflicted with the 'nearest and immediate interests of contracting individuals' in that they 'should be ready to exchange his goods for little metal discs apparently useless as such, or for documents representing the latter' (Menger quoted in Jones 1976: 757). Modern neoclassical economics has taken up the challenge by attempting to establish that holding money brings various types of transactions cost reduction for the rational maximizer. (Jones 1976, see especially the survey in Hoover 1996). However, these approaches must presuppose what they set out to explain; that is to say, at the very best they can only demonstrate that it is economically rational for the individual to hold money once it is in existence and widely accepted.[13] Modern neoclassicism is unable to explain its own interpretation of the problem of the logical origins – microfoundations – of money, exclusively as a medium of exchange.

Means of payment and store of abstract value

In his rigid attachment to commodity-exchange theory, Menger was adamant that the means of (final) payment was not a distinct function. Indeed, in arguing his case, he insisted that money had only one function as a medium of exchange.[14] There is a tendency to use the two functions interchangeably, but the distinction is an important one that helps to distinguish different types of economic transaction.

In the small, continuously operating, spot trades system of the natural economy, abstract purchasing power in the form of money (as the means of payment) need not be held for any significant length of time. However, as Hicks and others have pointed out, the most significant transactions in existing modern (as opposed to 'real') economies are not spot, but involve contract and deferred (final) payment or settlement (Hicks 1989).[15] Keynes's Babylonia had led him to the same conclusion: 'Something which

Historical and sociological origins 21

is merely used as a convenient medium of exchange on the spot may approach to being Money . . . But if this is all, we have scarcely emerged from the stage of Barter' (Keynes 1930: 3). In short, money is uniquely specified, first, by being a measure of value/unit of account and, second, by the capacity to store abstract value in a universally accepted form that enables it to act as a means of payment (see also Hicks 1989).

In the simple realm of lubricated barter, holding money as a store of abstract value for the spot trades is scarcely necessary. The *theoretical* specification of these empirical features of the natural economy in general equilibrium theory is achieved with the assumptions of foresight, rationality, and by the bracketing of time. But as some of the theory's astute adherents, such as Hahn, have realized, the result is the same: money as a store of abstract value is made redundant.[16] In sharp contrast to this (neo)classical conception, Keynes and others have insisted that rationality is limited not only by ignorance, but also by radical uncertainty. Future information is not amenable to probabilistic treatment. Rather, we simply do not know and do not have the means of knowing. In these typical and normal circumstances, Keynes argued that money – as a means of payment that is also a viable store of abstract value – links the past, present and future. The problem of the social reproduction of the economy is taken care of by 'tradition' in the natural economy, and it is simply not an issue in a timeless Walrasian world.

Money – as a store of abstract value – *makes possible the reproduction and continuity of economic life* in a complex, actually existing capitalist economy. In this role, money is anything but neutral and the dislocation of the real economy follows hard on the heels of any perturbation of the social relation of money. It has not proved possible to incorporate this essential property of money as a temporal transporter of abstract value, and the consequences of this property, into orthodox microeconomic analysis. For example, the very title of Samuelson's (1966 [1958]) work – 'An Exact Consumption-Loan Model of Interest *With or Without The Social Contrivance of Money*' (emphasis added) – betrays the serious logical problem. In other words, this method was unable to specify why money, as opposed to any other functionally alternative asset, performs as an intergenerational store of value.

Two quite distinct issues have always been entangled in the orthodox approach. First, how does money achieve its definitive property as a widely accepted means of payment? The simple answer, as Keynes argued, following the chartalists, is by fiat. The second question is more challenging and recalcitrant: how does fiat money actually become a viable store of abstract value? Within the framework of neoclassicism's methodological canons, explanations become locked into exactly the same kind of circularity that we encounter earlier in the microeconomic explanations for holding media of exchange. Money is a means of payment because it is a store of value, or vice-versa. Furthermore, as we have just noted, microeconomics cannot specify why more adequate stores of value do not become 'money'.

'Money-stuff' and the social relation of money

Mainstream economic conceptions of money cannot account for money's essential properties. First, no explanation is sought or given for the *idea* of money: that is, money of account. Second, it has not proved possible to explain the existence of media of exchange, means of payment, and stores of abstract value in terms of the model of the individual rational utility maximizer. Within a framework that focuses exclusively on commodity–commodity relations (exchange ratios) that are produced by individual calculations of utility, money-stuff can be nothing other than a special, but perplexing commodity, as Clower (1984) for example was forced to conclude. However, the orthodox emphasis on quantities or stocks of money-stuff that flow or circulate at a varying velocity entirely misses the fact that a commodity or its symbol becomes money *because it is a social relation* (Ingham 1996b; see also Hart 1986, Dodd 1994, Leyshon and Thrift 1997).

Money is a social relation in three closely related senses. First, money – as a social institution – is produced by non-market agencies and does not obey the economic 'laws' of the production and exchange of commodities. While we may freely produce the goods to exchange for a particular money-stuff in order to purchase other goods, we may not directly produce our own private money in response to demand.[17] The creation of money, as a unit of account and means of payment, is assigned to specialized *legitimately sanctioned* agencies – states, banks and so on – and its supply is strictly regulated. Commodities, such as precious metal, became money because they were 'counted' by those who 'counted'. They were thereby transformed into coin by means of a complex social structure which in medieval Europe, for example, comprised the sovereign, mints, moneyers, money-changers, merchants and bill-issuers. The 'moneyness' of commodity-money lay not in the exchange value of the precious metal, but in its socially constructed 'promise to pay' (see the general analysis in Boyer-Xambeu 1994). In short, commodity-exchange theory did not provide an adequate explanation of commodity money. Nevertheless, the concepts of this theory – quantity, circulation and so on – were to provide the basis for the effort in mainstream economics to understand forms of dematerialized capitalist credit money, and in the process the original error was compounded.

Second, monetary exchange consists in a social relation and is qualitatively different from the pure exchange – or barter – of economic theory. In the most general terms, money is not simply a veil over such exchange, but consists of structurally distinct social relations. As Simmel argued, this is the case with respect to commodity and non-commodity forms of money. The nature of the money-stuff is of secondary significance in the dynamics of monetary exchange.

> [M]oney is only a claim upon society. Money appears so to speak, as a bill of exchange from which the name of the drawee is lacking . . . The liqui-

dation of every private obligation by money means that the community now assumes this obligation to the creditor ... [M]etallic money is also a promise to pay and ... it differs from the cheque only with respect to the size of the group which vouches for its being accepted. The common relationship that the owner of money and the seller have to a social group – the claim of the former to a service and the trust of the latter that this claim will be honoured – provides the sociological constellation in which money transactions, as distinct from barter are accomplished.

(Simmel 1978 [1907]: 177, 174–9)

Holding that all money consists in claims and obligations directs attention to the fact that it is *constituted by social relations* and cannot be fully understood outside them. In other words, it may be argued that all money is best understood as credit (Schumpeter 1994[1954]: 320–1, Hicks in Smithin 1994: 25), which is a social relation. Barter exchange of commodities, whatever the complexity of the system, is essentially bilateral; but, monetary relations are trilateral.[18] Transacting agents are themselves unable to produce a universally acceptable money at will. Monetary exchange, unlike exchange in general, involves a third party of those authorities that may legitimately produce money. It has been the fundamental error of economic orthodoxy to subsume monetary exchange under the general rubric of pure dyadic exchange.

Third, modern capitalist money-stuff itself now consists in nothing more than a symbol or signifier of states' and banks' promises to pay. As we have seen, commodity money, as opposed to bullion, also consists in a social relation. Over the past five hundred years, almost all money-stuff, if that is still an appropriate description, has become nothing more than this. Modern credit money consists in the expansion or contraction of credit (social) relations expressed in double-entry form in the accounts of the state and the banking system.

The essential nature of money has become clearer with the stripping-out of its material form to leave its structural framework as a social system which accounts for value (money of account), provides an agreed means of payment, and attempts to regulate the relationship between what is seen as the quantities of money and goods, and thereby produce an acceptable store of abstract value. I shall return briefly to the implications of looking on money in this way in the last section. First, we must take up the road from Babylon and explore the historical and sociological foundations of money in a little more detail.

The historical and sociological origins of money

Keynes's amateur numismatic analysis of the ancient Near East led him to the conclusion that money is uniquely specified, first, as a money of account and, second, as a means of payment and store of abstract purchasing power (value) (Keynes 1930: ch. 1, 1983: ch. 5, 1982: ch. 2). The elaboration of this argument involves establishing the 'logical origins' of money in the concept of money of account, then locating the latter's actual historical and social conditions of existence. I shall suggest that the concept of money of account, which enables the construction of price lists and accounting for credit-debt relations, is the function of certain fundamental properties of social structure. Society itself is the analogue on which its based.

We need to explain how the social relation of money enables symbols and tokens to become acceptable stores of abstract value and means of payment. To repeat: all money has a fiduciary character (Dodd 1994); that is to say, in a fundamental sense all money is credit (Simmel 1978 [1907], Schumpeter 1994[1954], Hicks in Smithin 1994), and this is a social relation (Ingham 1996b).

These general conditions of existence – that is to say, the social bases of money of account, acceptable means of payment, and store of abstract value – should be seen as comprising money's sociological 'origins'.

Money of account

It is a telling failure of economic orthodoxy that money of account has been 'traditionally regarded as the weak sister of the famous triad (means of exchange, store of value, unit of account)' (Hoover 1996). This basic conceptual *lacuna* stems from the underlying theory of exchange. In their eagerness to establish that value can only be established by means of exchange, economic theorists of the late nineteenth century did not pursue the question of precisely what pre-conditions were assumed in a *theoretically coherent* model of multilateral market exchange. The problem within the microeconomic paradigm is how to specify theoretically the transformation from the real exchange ratios between goods, established on the basis of individual subjective preferences, to the price lists of the fully-fledged invisible hand market. Without a money of account, exchange ratios are only easily established between pairs of commodities in dyadic exchange; that is to say, pure barter (as opposed to payment in kind) can only be bilateral. The central question is whether money of account can, without the existence of other conditions, arise out of bilateral barter? Is it reasonable to think that price lists might spring spontaneously from barter?

In the Mengerian myth, it should be noted, the holding of stocks of liquid commodities does not in itself result in the use of price lists. As Walras realized, a theory of the movement from barter to complex multilateral exchange could only be constructed with the use of a *deus ex machina*. The '*tatonnement*' can only begin with an opening price, denominated in a '*numéraire*' and announced by the 'auctioneer'. This recourse to *ad hoc* categories and theoretical devices betrays a general failing of orthodox economic theory. Neoclassical economics operates with 'a theory of "pure exchange" that is unable to specify the analytical boundaries of a *market*' (White in Swedberg 1990: 83, emphasis added).

This problem has been addressed in scholarly depth by the numismatist Grierson. First, he argues, as did Keynes on the basis of his Babylonian *excursus*, that money of account is fundamental: 'Unless the commodities used for exchange bear some relation to a fixed standard, we are still dealing with barter [because] [t]he parties in barter-exchange are comparing their individual needs, not *values in the abstract*' (Grierson 1977: 16–19, emphasis added). For example, the tobacco used as a medium of exchange in seventeenth century Virginia only became money when its value was fixed at three shillings a pound (Grierson 1977: 17). However, the standard of value determined by weight – the exchange value of the money-stuff – is not the important issue. It is rather 'countability' that transforms the 'commodity' (*qua* convenient medium of exchange) into 'money'. This might be 'countable-useful' (slaves, cattle, furs) or 'countable-ornamental' (teeth, beads, shells) (Grierson 1977: 33, see also Hoover 1996).

Grierson finds it implausible that the concept of money, as accounting for value in the abstract, could emerge from subjective preferences and bilateral barter. As an alternative, he conjectures that the concept of money has its origins in a very early social institution for the settlement of disputes, later examples of which are known as *wergeld* (Grierson 1977: 19). *Wergeld* (worthpayment) was one of a range of institutions in early society that sanctioned payment of damages and compensation for injury and insult according to a fixed scale of tariffs. These were both precise and very detailed in their attempt to cover all exigencies (Grierson 1977: 20). Grierson offers a theory of the actual historical basis for the 'logical origins' of money in money of account:[19]

> The conditions under which these laws were put together would appear to satisfy, much better than the market mechanism, the prerequisites for the establishment of a monetary system. The tariffs for damages were established in public assemblies, and . . . Since what is laid down consists of evaluations of injuries, not evaluation of commodities, the conceptual difficulty of devising a common measure for appraising unrelated objects is avoided.
> (Grierson 1977: 20–1)[20]

There are, then, very good theoretical grounds for arguing that the idea of money – that is to say, its logical origins as the social practice of accounting for value – originated outside the market. Such arguments were well established by the German historical school over century ago but were expurgated from the pure theory of exchange in post-*Methodenstreit* economics. In concentrating their attention on the notion of money-stuff (money as a commodity with exchange value) the theorists were unable to see that, more fundamentally, money – as money of account – was the means by which genuinely 'market value', as opposed to individual subjective preference, could be created (see, for example, von Mises 1953 [1912]: 461–81).[21] The essential elements of multilateral exchange in the decentralised market economy – debt contracts and price-lists – are made possible by money of account and not by commodities acting as the media of exchange. Furthermore, the actual money-stuff that comprises the means of payment:

> namely that by delivery of which debts contracts and price contracts are discharged . . . *can only exist* in relation to a money of account . . . And the Age of Chartalist or State Money was reached when the State claimed the right to declare what thing should answer as money to the current money of account.
> (Keynes 1930: 3–4, emphasis added)

The social production of money as a means of payment and store of abstract value

Once the concept of abstract monetary accounting (unit of account) was available to society, the next step was the development of a standard of value based on commodities in the ancient Near Eastern empires in the period from 3000 to 1000 BC (Goldsmith 1987: ch. 2, Keynes 1982: 223–93). For example, the *shekel* in Babylon was originally fixed at 1 *gur* (1.2 hectolitres of barley) and later at a more manageable 8.3 grams of silver. However, these societies were essentially non-monetized command economies with only very small trade sectors. The overwhelming majority of payments were rents and taxes to religious and secular authorities. There was no coinage and payment was made in commodities, labour services, or silver by weight (*shekel, mina, talent*) (Goldsmith 1987). It was on the basis of their centralized bureaucratic social structures that Babylon and its neighbours were able to establish 'chartal money' (Knapp 1924): that is, the monetary practice of using a fixed standard in conjunction with money of account. It should be stressed that the authorities not only fixed the standard, but also many of the prices of taxes, rents, and so on, and these remained stable over time. In short, monetary practice has its logical origins in money of account and its historical foundation in the chartal money of early bureaucratic empires. It was not, *pace* Menger, the spontaneous product of the market.

Coinage, which integrated all the attributes (unit of account, means of exchange/payment, store of value) in the form of money-stuff, came 2,000 years later in Lydia and Greece (Davies 1994). Centralized monarchical states and developments in metallurgy made it possible to embody money

Historical and sociological origins 27

of account, standard/store of value, and means of payment/exchange in a single object. This was a critically important development in that it greatly expanded the scale and scope of impersonal market exchange. The coinage system reached its apogee in the Roman Empire and '[i]ts "sound money" was accepted over an area larger than any other before or after the nineteenth century' (Goldsmith 1987: 36).

Before the changes in social, political and economic structure that culminated in the emergence of capitalist credit-money, the developmental sequence of the social structure of monetary practice was as follows:

- The concept of money as a measure of value for representing and accounting for the (utilitarian and symbolic) worth of social positions and roles (money of account) (Grierson 1977).
- Authoritatively-fixed standards of value based upon quantitative relations between commodities expressed in money of account. For example the cattle standard and the barley standard in Egypt and Mesopotamia, 3000 BC (Keynes 1982, Goldsmith 1987).
- Authoritatively-standardized means of payment/stores of value, denominated in money of account, for payment of taxes and tithes (chartal money). An example is the silver *shekel* based on the barley standard. No coinage, payment by weight in silver. 2000 BC, in Babylon (Keynes 1982, Goldsmith 1987).
- Coinage. Uniform units of precious metal by fineness and weight: minted coins in Lydia and Ionian Greece, c. 600 BC (Davies 1994), and 'symetallic' coinage systems. Precious metal means of payment of taxes and debts (legal tender) and base metal tokens as media of exchange. For example, in Augustan Rome: the gold *aureus* and silver *denarius* supplemented by the *sestertius* of copper, zinc and tin, and the *quadrans* of copper (Goldsmith 1987: 36).

The use of specific institutionally-legitimate debts as means of payment is arguably one of the most important developments in the history of humanity's organizational or infrastructural power. As I indicated earlier, money-proper itself comes to consist in a particular form of social relation. This development freed the production of the means of payment from the physical constraints of territory and geology. Credit money brought the possibility of a controlled or managed elasticity of supply for money and made possible the financing of the capitalist enterprise. At this time, money became an *autonomous force of production* (Keynes in Smithin 1994: 2, Schumpeter 1994 [1954]: 318, Ingham 1999).[22] However, modern credit money cannot be explained simply as the direct result of the need for more efficient monetary representation in an economy whose dynamic lay elsewhere in real factors such as technology, the division of labour, or capital-labour 'social relations of production' (Ingham 1999). The credit money form was the result of particular geopolitical conditions and social structural changes in the reawakening of Europe after the collapse of the Roman Empire and its coinage system.

The disintegration of Rome produced a *dissociation* of money of account and means of payment. When coinages (*moneta reale*) resumed in the myriad political jurisdictions of a now fragmented medieval Europe, they were integrated by a *moneta immagineria* (money of account) – that is, by the 'practice of counting in pounds, shillings and pence – already sanctioned by the glory of Charlemagne' (Einaudi 1953 [1936]: 230). The Christian ecumene of the Holy Roman Empire was too weak to support a centralized minted coinage, but it was able to provide the normative basis for a common *moneta immaginaria*. This dissociation of money of account and means of payment was of critical importance in providing the conditions for the emergence of merchants' private bank money, which was based on the bill of exchange. (See the references in Ingham 1999 to the later American school of historical economics of, for example, Usher, Lane, and deRoover. See also Wray 1990 and Spufford 1988.) These bills were denominated in the *moneta immaginaria* (money of account) and existed in an unstable relationship with the myriad coinages. Eventually when the practice of drawing bills became detached from any real commodities, and rested only on the drawer's promise to pay, they became autonomous means of payment ('dry exchange'). After a long struggle, money ceased to be the monopoly prerogative of the sovereign (Boyer-Xambeu 1994).

However, it is important to note in relation to chartalism – 'the doctrine that money is peculiarly a creation of the state' (Keynes 1930: 4) – that the merchants' private bank-credit money that developed out of the bill of exchange only became money-proper when the states joined the bank giros (see Wray 1990). Moreover, as 'the state had become the largest receiver and the largest maker of payments in the society' (Weber 1978: 167), it was almost inevitable that this development would occur. This fusion of state and bank credit money developed first in the Italian city-states during the fifteenth and sixteenth centuries, then spread to Holland and, most decisively, to England with the formation of the Bank of England in 1694. The widespread use of debt as a means of payment outside the networks of traders required the state to establish the legal depersonalization and negotiability of debt by which the simple credit of the personal IOU, recorded in unit of account, could become credit *money* (Carruthers 1996, Ingham 1998b, 1999). All subsequent developments have been the extension, elaboration, and refinement of this evolutionary leap in monetary practice.

It is important that chartalism is not confused with crude monetary nominalism. Barbon's much earlier assertion, for example, that 'money is a value *made* by law' (Jackson 1995: 11, emphasis added) is, if taken literally, equally as untenable as the neoclassical dictum that it is made entirely in exchange on the basis of individual rational calculations of utility. As

Weber emphasized in his generally favourable critique of Knapp, state theory only applies to money's *formal validity*, or its status as legal tender. Money's *substantive validity*, the expectation that 'recipients estimate that they will, within the relevant time horizon, be able to utilize it in exchange to procure goods at an acceptable exchange ratio' (Weber 1978: 75), no more follows from formal validity than does the neoclassical assertion that the converse is the case.[23]

At first glance this distinction might appear to be the basis for a neat division of intellectual labour in the social sciences. Once the nominal monetary instrument has been classed as formally valid and placed at the disposal of economic agents by the state, its value and utility (substantive validity) is determined by the market; that is, by rational maximizing agents who will only hold it if its capacity as a store of value is known. An implication of the Keynesian conception of radical uncertainty is that the relationship cannot be expressed quite so neatly in this way; that is to say, as the state proposing and the market disposing (Hicks 1989). Not only is money's formal validity (as means of payment) established by fiat, its exchange value (substantive validity) is also irreducibly fiduciary, and here the 'state or community' (Keynes 1930: 4) also plays an important role in producing the 'promise of last resort'.

Willingness to hold money is influenced by rational appraisal of current estimations of its future value; but this can never be more than a guide to further *action* that itself will, in part, *determine the future value of money*. Money's capacity to store value depends on a willingness to hold money in the present. In other words, the effectiveness of money as a store of value is based, to an important degree, on a commitment to a course of action that is based on trust that others will continue to accept our money. Effective trust is more than a 'weak form of inductive knowledge'; it is rather a 'supratheoretical belief'(Simmel 1978 [1907]: 179).[24] In holding money as an abstract store of value and means of payment, we trust that our claim on future goods will be met, and in this sense, as I have already argued – following Simmel, Schumpeter, and later Hicks – all money is *credit*.[25]

At this level of generality and abstraction, however, such formulations beg the question. As Ganssman has observed, appeals to the obvious importance of 'trust' and 'confidence' in the analysis of monetary systems have 'as much explanatory value as saying that credit come from *credere*' (Ganssman 1988: 293). That is to say, the social production of trust and confidence and the conventional basis for holding money needs to be explained.[26] At present, this problem cannot be pursued beyond a comment on two aspects of the problem: the generation of impersonal trust or legitimacy; and the ideological construction of money and its relation to monetary theory.

Money as a store of abstract value consists in the social system of monetary production which entails the creation of monetary legitimacy which is form of *impersonal trust* (Schapiro 1987). However the market is not in the business of trust-building. In the face of radical uncertainty, self-fulfilling long-term trust is rooted in social and political legitimacy whereby potentially untrustworthy 'strangers' are able to participate personally in impersonal complex multilateral economic relationships.[27] In this respect, the impersonal social relation of money *is* the invisible hand. The basic chartalist argument would appear to be incontrovertible. The story has been told many times: the production of trust in money and modern credit money in particular has been inextricably bound up with the rise of the modern constitutional state (see, for example, Hicks 1969, 1989; Dickson 1967).

Social conventions based on no more than either an equilibrium of competing interests or consensual agreement are, Douglas has argued, particularly fragile (Douglas 1986, see the discussion in relation to money in Carruthers 1996). She maintains that enduring social institutions require a stronger foundation:

> There needs to be a analogy by which the formal structure of a crucial set of social relations is found in the physical world, or in the supernatural world, or in eternity, anywhere, so long as it is not seen as a socially contrived arrangement.
>
> (Douglas 1986: 48)[28]

In other words, enduring institutions are based on an *ideology* in which socially constructed arrangements are seen as *natural* (or supernatural); and, by implication, *universal* and *immutable*. If successfully enacted, ideological naturalization conceals the social production and malleability of institutions. Until the twentieth century, the ideological naturalization of money was achieved and its social construction concealed by the identification of 'real' money with its commodity form. However, with the appearance of credit money, the fiction of a universal, immutable, natural monetary standard became increasingly difficult to sustain. As Schumpeter observed, 'metallists' were either 'theoretical' and therefore mistaken in their belief that the only true form of money was precious metal; or else they were 'practical metallists' in that they understood that this form of money-stuff would be trusted more readily than a mere promise to pay. Indeed, it was on the basis of both these standpoints that the economically advanced nations spent most of the nineteenth century trying to devise monetary schemes that would make paper behave as if it were gold.[29] Naturally it behaved in this way to the extent that people believed that it would.

This ideology of money survived the commodity form to which it refers. However, monetarism, with its rhetoric of the control of actual 'quantities' of money, was probably its final incarnation. As I have suggested, a good deal of confusion has been caused by the retention of the conceptual and theoretical apparatus of the erroneous commodity-exchange theory of money in modern economics' attempt to comprehend modern credit money. But ever more transparently, the production of money now consists of the attempt to control the price of debt through interest rates and by the monitoring of the degree to which this monetary policy is deemed to be managed correctly in relation to orthodox economic theory.

Monetary authorities in the different jurisdictions are required, to repeat Keynes's apt phrase, to 'move forward in step' (Keynes 1930: 26–7). Nevertheless, it is still strongly implied that the correct steps are those which keep pace with 'outside forces' which remain couched in a naturalistic rhetoric: for example, the variables representing the *natural* rate of unemployment.[30] However, the increasing openness and reflexivity of central bank policy formulation in order to establish credibility in the dialogue with ever more powerful foreign exchange markets might only serve further to ideologically denaturalize money and weaken the very institutions it is designed to strengthen. It is perhaps ironic that the tenets of economic orthodoxy regarding transparency might have this effect.[31]

Conclusions

The concepts that comprise the theoretical apparatus of most mainstream economic approaches to money all derive from the commodity-exchange theory in which money is *essentially* a commodity (or direct symbol). In some accounts, it is seen primarily as a veil over the real exchange ratios between other commodities. It can also be seen as a 'quantity' or 'stock' that circulates or flows with some degree of short-run autonomy. This is not the place to examine the subtleties and contradictions of this general position. In any event, money is a 'thing'. However, such metaphors fail fully to capture money as socially constructed and constituted by social relations between the monetary and other economic agencies. A number of very general conclusions might be drawn.

The properties of money and *how* it is able to perform its functions are constituted by the social relations of the monetary system. First, the monetary authority possesses the legitimate power to construct and maintain both the money of account and standard of value. This is the formal validity that provides what might be seen as the socio-technical means by which the other monetary and economic agencies *account* for their economic interrelations and produce monetary value. As Knapp and other state theorists maintained, money of account and standard of value are not themselves monetary value, but they provide the footing by which such value can be determined.[32]

Second, legitimately-sanctioned agencies – mints, ministries of finance in conjunction with public and private banks – directly produce valid 'money-proper'; that is, the legal means of payment and attendant media of exchange. Technological and social changes have transformed the money-stuff of the means of payment from commodities by weight, to coins, to signifiers of debt recorded in books or electronically. These may also be media of exchange, but this is not commonly so. The latter have taken myriad forms, from base metal tokens to cheques, plastic cards and so on. The production of money is a relatively autonomous socially enacted process.

Third, the users of money – the owners, controllers, and producers of commodities and money – enact the relationship between the two. That is to say, there is no automatic tendency to an equilibrium of supply and demand of money and goods that arises from individual calculations of utility. The two sides – money and goods – are, from a sociological standpoint, distinct and relatively autonomous, as Keynes and Minsky maintained.[33] On the goods production side, agents attempt to monetize their market power either by bidding up prices in money of account, or by the expansion of value through borrowing and the creation of debt denominated in money of account (Weber 1978: 108, Maier 1978). On the money side, agents attempt to preserve and store value in money form and to control its supply in order to exact interest; and/or they forge new social relations of credit (monetary innovations), which they hope will be validated by the monetary authorities as a liquid asset. According to this view, money consists in those economic interrelations that are 'monetized' in money of account and periodically settled by a legal or chartal means of payment (see also Hoover 1996). Again, it is important not to confuse the technological changes in monetary forms with fundamental monetary practice and relations. In this respect, it is commonly held that the above characterization of money applies only to the modern world. Technology, it is argued, has transformed money so that it has become 'dematerialized', 'virtual', or even 'postmodern' (see Leyshon and Thrift 1997). However, Babylon and the Champagne Fairs of the late Middle Ages, for example, operated with an 'imaginary money' (money of account) and a means of eventual settlement in exactly the way I have outlined. The difference between these eras and our own is in the technological means for making and keeping account and in the overall level of monetization, not in the essentials of monetary practice. The debate on what money is has been confused by logical and category errors, especially the conflation of the 'things' and 'social relations' of monetary practice.[34]

Money, then, is not simply an 'exogenous stock' that may be added to at will; but neither is it exclusively an 'endogenous flow' that is ultimately accommodated by the monetary authority. (See Wray 1990, Pollin 1991.) The familiar antinomy is too extreme and, arguably, tells us as much about economic theory as it does about the actual historical and social production of money. The former theory is an anachronistic adaptation of an inaccurate commodity theory, and the latter is an equally one-sided characterization of capitalist bank credit. However, the central dynamic in the creation of modern money necessarily involves both sides in the continuously-negotiated (re)construction of the rules and practices by which the monetary authority will sanction the monetization of the various claims made in price bids, new credit instruments and so on. Economic discourse plays its part, but the monetary authority 'does not simply apply the rules of a monetary system which somehow seems to it ideal, but its acts are determined by its own financial interests and those of important economic groups' (Weber 1978: 172). In other words, a complex triangular power struggle between the monetary authority, the banking system, and the agencies of production is at the centre of the process.

Moreover, this free play of conflicting interests is essential if monetary systems are to perform the functions of arriving at and storing of value in an abstract form. As Weber argued, in his elaboration of the 'Austrian' view, the possibility of 'the formal rationality of monetary calculation' is dependent on quite specific substantive conditions. Money prices are the result of power struggles and of compromises and they are 'instruments of calculation only as estimated quantifications of relative chances in this struggle'. Consequently, money 'is not a mere 'voucher' for unspecified utilities'; rather it is 'primarily a weapon in this struggle'(Weber 1978: 107).[35] Any equilibrium of price stability or interest rates is the expression of a balance of power that underlays any equation of quantities of money and goods.

Permanent monetary stability in a capitalist economy can only be considered to be theoretical possibility if we accept the assumptions of neutrality and a natural tendency towards economic equilibrium. But neither is helpful in the explanation of money's logical or historical conditions of existence. We must conclude, therefore, that all monetary systems, if they are to produce market prices and produce and store abstract value, are necessarily precarious and unstable. Consequently, they require constant intervention to both regulate and legitimize monetary practice and policy, and to control economic agents' disruptive and destabilizing pursuit of self interest (Ingham 1998b). It must be stressed that this is not a matter of intervention *in extremis*, but a permanent, ongoing social reproduction of money through the readjustment of power relations, the social construction of the norms by which we move 'in step', and an endless ideological quest for the optimally 'correct' and, therefore, 'natural', universally applicable monetary policy.[36]

Finally, money – as it is constituted by real social relations – is an autonomous and active element in economic life. The somewhat contradictory quantity/neutrality assumptions have produced distorted ideas of economic activity which impede our efforts to understand the ubiquity and normality of fluctuations in the price level and monetary crises. Consequently, they have had serious policy implications. As I have already suggested, this relative autonomy in the manufacture of money, which is an essential part of the 'struggle for economic existence' (Weber 1978), has double-edged or contradictory effects. In the classic Keynesian formulation, it is the means of creating expanded value in the form of commodities; but it is also the means of their destruction (Schumpeter 1934 [1912], Kindleberger 1984, Minsky 1986). This attribution of real force and efficacy to money does not entail a metaphysical nominalism or, more prosaically, a form of 'money illusion'. This is so only if the economy is taken to comprise nothing of importance other than commodities and their 'real' relations, as these result from individual optimizing strategies. Alternatively, as Keynes clearly saw, first in Babylon and then in the early twentieth century, money is an expression of human society's capacity for self-transformation. It is arguably the most powerful of our 'social technologies' (Stinchcombe 1965); but it is one over which we have, inevitably, a most insecure grasp.

Notes

1 I am very grateful to Geoff Harcourt for guiding me to this literature, especially Wray (1990) and also the work of John Smithin (1994, 1996).
2 By 'logical' origins is meant the general conditions of existence for money (or any other institution). This is to be distinguished from 'historical' origins in the sense of the earliest empirical evidence for the use of money. The distinction is used by Schumpeter (1994 [1954]), but is also to be found in Keynes's (1983: 56) review of Hawtrey's *Currency and Credit*, where he locates the logical origins in money of account.
3 Letter to Lydia Lopokova 18 January 1924, in Keynes (1983: 1–2).
4 A persistent example of such historical inaccuracy, in the face of considerable evidence to the contrary, is the assertion that goldsmith's receipts for bullion held for safe-keeping were the precursors of modern banknotes and credit money. See, for example, Begg, Fischer and Dornbusch (1991: 404). The conjecture accords with the commodity exchange theory of money. However, bills of exchange, promissory notes, and the like, that is, signifiers of debt, were the source of modern credit money (Ingham 1998b).
5 Keynes endorses Knapp's 'chartal' theory at the beginning of *A Treatise on Money*, and had earlier favourably reviewed a book published in German, popularizing Knapp's ideas (Keynes 1983: 400–3). The question of the applicability of orthodox economics to the primitive, ancient and classical economies was an important issue in the *Methodenstreit* between the German historical school and the economic theorists at the turn of the century. Babylon's economic system also played a part in the dispute's recrudescence in social anthropology in the 1950s and 1960s, between the Polanyian substantivists and the opposing formalists. Polanyi's *Trade and Markets in the Early Empires* (1957) argued that the economic theory of the market did not apply to the production and circulation of goods by means of reciprocity and/or redistribution. Unfortunately, the substantivist critique implicitly endorsed the orthodox theory of money. The focus remained firmly on media of exchange, which, in their ancient or primitive pre-coinage form, were seen as 'limited purpose' as opposed to the 'general purpose' media of exchange of modern markets systems. As we shall see, Keynes's emphasis on money of account transcends the question of the primitiveness of money-stuff.
6 I shall be concerned only with the basic assumptions of microeconomic analysis and have taken it for granted that mainstream macroeconomics, whether New Classical or New Keynesian, entails the orthodox microfoundations of money.
7 Such views are traceable to Hume in the essay *Of Money* (1752):

Money is not properly speaking, one of the objects of commerce, but only an instrument which men have agreed upon to facilitate the exchange of one commodity for another. It is none of the wheels of trade: It is the oil which renders the motion of the wheels smooth and easy.

(Hume, quoted in Jackson 1995: 3)

Modern neoclassicism's interest in 'trust', which is increasingly seen as important in the study of money, follows this viewpoint exactly. Trust lubricates economic exchange, but is not an essential element (Arrow 1972).

8 See for example Hecksher, in Lane and Riemersma (1953).
9 The term 'enacted' is used to indicate a fundamental difference between the orthodox economic methodology and a sociological approach. In the former money and goods are integrated and brought into equilibrium as a result of individual utility maximizing decisions. By implication, monetary policy, for example, must accommodate itself to the forces of supply and demand created by those decisions; otherwise it will make errors based on either ignorance or folly. Alternatively, the notion of social enactment assumes inherent uncertainty and the active creation of an economic regime that is the outcome of the conflict between the relatively autonomous interests of the producers and consumers of both money and goods. For example, an inflation target of (say) 2.5 per cent is a negotiated outcome, and is involved in the creation of an economic reality rather than the state of affairs derived from economic analysis.
10 In their important critique of the neoclassical theory of money, Heinsohn and Steiger (1989) follow Keynes in linking money with contract, and, then, argue that money has it origins in the institution of private property. (See also Wray 1990). However, I shall argue that the idea of money – that is money of account – is anterior to contract and price lists (Keynes 1930, Hicks 1989, Grierson 1977). See also Weber (1981 [1924]): 'From an evolutionary standpoint, money is the father of private property'.
11 Working within the orthodox framework the 'New Monetary Economics' has suggested that information technology might more closely match wants, and keep account of decentralized credit relations, and thereby render money-stuff redundant. Reference is made to 'sophisticated barter' or 'credit-barter' systems (Cowen and Kroszner 1994). Notwithstanding any practical difficulties, or the problem of trust in a totally decentralized and depersonalized trading system, it should be noted that these systems are not barter but 'cashless'. They are not 'moneyless' because they use a money of account. For an example of exchange using money of account and payment in kind, see Baxter's (1945) study of eighteenth century Boston.
12 Functionalism – the explanation of institutions by their functions – entails the risk of treating effects as causes, for example, as in money evolving to overcome the inefficiencies of barter. There is the further problem of functional alternatives. Assuming that a functional benefit can be identified, it is not logically possible to specify which particular institution might perform the role. For example, see the reference below to Samuelson's (1966 [1958]) analysis of the 'function' of money as an intertemporal store of value.
13 This is a typical example of the circular reasoning in much neoclassical economics. See the discussion of Hahn's unsuccessful, but highly revealing, attempt to establish the 'microfoundations' in Ingham (1996).
14 It would appear that it was entirely as a result of his extreme theoretical stance in the *Methodenstreit* that Menger refused to accept that money had more than a single function (see Melitz 1974: 8). The German historical school stressed the importance of money as a means of unilateral payment between states and their members, and Menger presumably thought that in admitting this as a

separate function he might implicitly endorse the state theory of money expounded first by Knies and then by Knapp.

15 Indeed this distinction had been embodied in dual currency systems that had existed from the earliest times: base metal tokens were used a media of exchange for everyday spot transactions and precious metal coinage as legally valid means of payment for the settlement of debts, especially tax debts (Goldsmith 1987). Even as late as the early nineteenth century in Britain local coinage was commonplace (Davies 1994). More recently, local exchange trading schemes (LETS) have developed their own media.

16 'Money may slip through our fingers unless its role in transactions is made esssential' (Hahn 1987: 42).

17 'If you want more wheat, you can go out and raise wheat, if you want more of any kind of manufactured goods, you can produce them; but if the people want more money they cannot bring money into existence' (William Jennings Bryan, quoted in Jackson 1995: 18).

18 The common relationship that the owner of money and the settler have to a social group – the claim of the former to a service and the trust that this claim will be honoured – provides the sociological constellation in which money transactions, as distinct from barter are accomplished.
(Simmel 1978 [1907]: 178)

See also Guttman's excellent Post Keynesian informed analysis (1994: 30–1). It is interesting to note here how easy it is to fall back into orthodoxy and its confusions: 'An economy that uses money as a commodity (e.g., precious metals), which producers can produce for themselves cannot be distinguished from barter' (ibid.: 30). However, without a money of account, the commodities are not money. Guttman does retrieve the situation with a reference to Keynes's astute remark that the rupee was a 'note printed on silver' (ibid.: 491).

19 'Behind the phenomenon of coin there is the phenomenon of money, the origins of which are not to be sought in the market but in a much earlier stage in communal development, when worth and *wergeld* were interchangeable terms' (Grierson 1977: 33). See also writers in the German historical school summarized in Einzig (1966).

20 This analysis may be construed as a Durkheimian sociology in which money of account/measure of value is seen as a collective representation of basic elements of societal structure (Ingham 1996). The punitive and compensatory tariffs expressed both the utilitarian and moral components of society. *Wergeld* symbolically represents society's two faces in prescribing recompense for *both* insult and injury. On the one hand, it accounted for the functional worth of the contribution of social roles to societal welfare by assigning a tariff to the loss or impairment of their individual incumbents; for example, young men of fighting age were worth more than old women and so on. On the other hand, such schemes of functional or utilitarian worth were embedded in moral legitimations that directly reflected the hierarchical status order of society. Compensation for the loss of a Russian nobleman's moustache, for example, was four times greater than for the loss of a finger (Grierson 1977: 20). *Wergeld* was the codification of the social values without which the assessment of functional contribution would have remained anomic and open to settlement only by constant recourse to socially and economically debilitating blood feuds. Payment of the tariff, could, of course be made in kind; that is to say, money of account is anterior to the other definitive property of money (means of payment); but it does not *logically* follow.

21 See, for example, the thorough and otherwise excellent, account, of 'primitive money' by the economist Melitz (1974). He concludes that the concept of

money of account can originate 'outside of trade', but that 'money' can only be established in exchange.
22 'the development of the law and practice of negotiable paper and of "created" deposits afford the best indication we have for the dating the rise of capitalism' (Schumpeter 1994 [1954]: 78)
23 In other words, the two sides of the coin:

> The heads of a coin underwrites the fact that money is originally a relation between persons in society; whereas 'tails' is capable of entering into a quantitative ratio independent of the persons engaged in any particular transaction . . . Conventional economic reasoning fails to enlighten us because it is so unremittingly one-dimensional. The coin has two sides for good reason – both are indispensable.
> (Hart 1986: 638).

24 See also Luhmann (1979: 26): 'In the last resort, no decisive grounds can be offered for trusting'. Although economic explanations refer increasingly to trust, rational choice/expectations theories can, strictly speaking, have no place for it. Trust would be made unnecessary by more or better information. Thus, in narrowly economic treatments, trust tends to be reduced to confidence based on empirical knowledge. However, this conflation of trust and confidence produces a logical contradiction in which it is argued that trust is based on the very thing that it is held to replace: perfect information.
25 It has been argued with some justification that Schumpeter was a reluctant and equivocal 'creditist'.
26 As soon as the highly restrictive assumptions of rationality and the calculation of probabilistic statements about future events are relaxed, or seen to be untenable, some orthodox economists look to the other social sciences to augment their explanations. However, the importation of concepts such as trust and convention is a methodologically *ad hoc* procedure in that they refer to non-rational action which has no *theoretical* status in economics. Keynes's work, for example, is replete with *ad hoc* categories, such as 'animal spirits' or conventions, which were necessary to explain the economic action that was anomalous from the point of view of (neo)classical theory. However, unless such concepts are grounded in a wider explanatory scheme they merely introduce additional tautologies into economic explanation (Ingham 1996a).
27 Hart points out that Adam Muller's *A New Theory of Money* (1816) was a systematic challenge to the view that the existence of money was governed by the laws of commodity exchange. This line of reasoning informed the theories of Simmel, Knapp, Weber, and ultimately, Keynes, in their insistence that 'money is a symbol of something intangible, *an aspect of human agency*, not a thing like a lump of coal' (Hart 1986: 646, emphasis added). In Hart's opinion, which I endorse, Schumpeter was wrong to dismiss this as metaphysical nonsense (Schumpeter 1994 (1954): 421–2).
28 Note the similarity between this formulation and my Durkheimian interpretation of the foundation of money in money of account.
29 The debate between the Currency and Banking schools in the early nineteenth century most clearly shows the intellectual foundations of the 'natural' and 'social' conceptions of monetary production that informed the intense debates over monetary policy in the nineteenth century and beyond. See also Carruthers and Batt (1996) on the 'Greenback' era after the American Civil War. As I discovered to my naive surprise some time ago, the ideology of the gold standard during this period bore very little relation to the actual operation of the domestic and international credit money system operated by the

Bank of England and the City of London (De Cecco 1974, Bloomfield 1963, Ingham 1984, 1994).

30 It should be noted that the accountancy practices that form part of 'moving in step' in the construction of acceptable levels of credit money are not only rational techniques, but also rhetorical and ideological in their construction of legitimate and credible promises to pay. For example, double-entry bookkeeping is regarded as 'an essential condition for the existence of money-accounting' (Weber 1978: 97); but I would also argue that it is also the means by which a legitimate 'credible' credit money is actually created. See Carruthers (1991) on the rhetorical import of accountancy techniques.

31 Some of the criticism of the newly independent Bank of England's new Monetary Policy Committee (1997–) that has begun to appear in the orthodox financial press might be interpreted this way. It has been suggested that the lack of unanimity by the committee of 'experts' cannot provide the decisiveness and appearance of certainty that the markets desire. The open disagreement in the published minutes is transparent, as orthodox economic analysis would prescribe, but exposes the fact that the economic numbers, even if they are considered to represent 'outside forces', none the less are subject to different and equally valid interpretations. There is even discussion of the social psychology of committee decision-making and how this might contribute to systematic policy errors; for example, an expert might not wish to concede the superiority of a competing argument. In short, the new arrangements are, in Douglas's (1986) terms, exposing the fragility of an equilibrium or group consensus and the social construction of money. Furthermore, it will be interesting to see how the European Central Bank will be able to maintain resistance to this fashion for demonstrating that they can be seen to be marching in step.

32 Again, it is important to note that these authorities need not be states as such, but simply the agreed regulatory agency or 'community', as Keynes expressed it.

33 In Keynes's rather obscure phrase: 'the marginal efficiency of money is determined by forces partly appropriate to itself'. See also Smithin (1996).

34 The development of electronic money has caused a great deal of intellectual confusion, and, in this respect, there are frequent references to the 'end of money' (see Ingham 1998a on Angell 1997).

35 These arguments were, of course, at the centre of the 'socialist calculation' debate in the 1920s and 1930s.

36 As Mirowski, for example, has pointed out, the balance between the expansion of value through the creation of debt and inflation, in modern capitalism, is:

> socially constructed and therefore non-mechanical, [thus] . . . further institutions are required to intervene continually to offset one trend or the other [and] [t]he overriding problem of all market-orientated societies is to find some means to maintain the working fiction of a monetary invariant.
>
> (Mirowski 1991: 579)

It would be interesting to consider the fragility of social order and the need for its constant enacted reproduction as stressed in the sociological work of Goffman and the 'ethnomethodologists'. For an accessible exegesis and discussion of social agency, see Giddens (1984).

A fundamental dispute about how best to manufacture money in implied in the debate over the best way to repair the 1997–8 financial crisis. Notwithstanding all the other important aspects of the situation, it would seem that there are important social differences in the way credit money is created in the

East Asian and Anglo–US systems. With more interdependent and longer-term debt relations, the former can produce 'more' money; but the Washington consensus considers this 'unsound' and believes that the world should conform to its norms.

References

Baxter, W. T. (1945) *The House of Hancock: Business in Boston 1724–1775*, Cambridge, Mass.: Harvard University Press.
Begg, D., Fischer, S., and Dornbusch, R. (1991) *Economics*, 3rd edn, Maidenhead: McGraw Hill
Bloomfield, A. I. (1963) 'Short Term Capital Movements under the pre-1914 Gold Standard', *Princeton Studies in International Finance* 11: 1–48
Boyer-Xambeu, M. T., Deleplace, G. and Gillard, L. (1994) *Private Money and Public Currencies: The Sixteenth Century Challenge*, London: M. E. Sharpe.
Carruthers, B. G. (1991) 'Accounting for Rationality: Double-Entry Bookkeeping and the Rhetoric of Economic Rationality', *American Journal of Sociology* 97, 1: 31–69.
—— (1996) *City of Capital: Politics and Markets in the English Financial Revolution*, Princeton: Princeton University Press.
Carruthers, B. G. and Babb, S. (1996) 'The Color of Money and the Nature of Value: Greenbacks and Gold in Post–Bellum America', *American Journal of Sociology* 101, 6: 1556–91.
De Cecco, M. (1974) *Money and Empire*, Oxford: Oxford University Press
Clower, R. W. (1984) 'A Reconsideration of the Microfoundations of Money', in D. A. Walker (ed.), *Money and Markets: Essays by Robert W. Clower*, Cambridge: Cambridge University Press.
Cowen, T. and Kroszner, R. (1994) *Explorations in the New Monetary Economics*, Oxford: Blackwell.
Davies, G. (1994) *A History of Money from Ancient Times to the Present Day*, Cardiff: University of Wales Press.
Dickson, P. G. M. (1967) *The Financial Revolution in England: A Study in the Development of Public Credit, 1688–1756*, New York: St Martins Press.
Dodd, N. (1994) *The Sociology of Money*, Cambridge: Polity Press.
Douglas, M. (1986) *How Institutions Think*, London: Routledge
Einzig, P. (1966) *Primitive Money in its Ethnological, Historical and Economic Aspects*, London: Pergamon Press.
Einaudi, L. (1953 [1936]) 'The Theory of Imaginary Money from Charlemagne to the French Revolution', in F. C. Lane and J. C. Riemersma (eds), *Enterprise and Secular Change*, London: Allen and Unwin.
Ganssman, H. (1988) 'Money – A Symbolically Generalized Medium of Communication? On the Concept of Money in Recent Sociology', *Economy and Society* 17, 4: 285–315.
Giddens, A. (1984) *The Constitution of Society*, Cambridge: Polity Press.
Goldsmith, R. W. (1987) *Premodern Financial Systems*, Cambridge: Cambridge University Press.
Grierson, P. (1977) *The Origins of Money*, London: Athlone Press.
Guttman, R. (1994) *How Credit-Money Shapes the Economy*, London: M. E. Sharpe.
Hahn, F. H. (1982) *Money and Inflation*, Oxford: Blackwell.
—— (1987) 'The Foundations of Monetary Theory', in M. DeCecco and J. Fitoussi

(eds), *Monetary Theory and Economic Institutions*, London: Macmillan.
Hart, K. (1986) 'Heads or Tails: Two Sides of the Coin', *Man* (n.s.) 21: 637–52.
Hecksher, E. (1953) 'Natural and Money Economy', in F. C. Lane and J. G. Riemersma (eds) *Enterprise and Secular Change*, London: Allen and Unwin.
Heinsohn, G. and Steiger, O. (1989) 'The Veil of Barter: the Solution to the "Task of Obtaining Representations of an Economy in which Money is Essential"', in J. A. Kregel (ed.), *Inflation, Income Distribution and Capitalist Crisis*, London: Macmillan.
Hicks, J. R. (1989) *A Market Theory of Money*, Oxford: Clarendon Press.
Hoover, K. (1996) 'Some Suggestions for Complicating the Theory of Money', in S. Pressman (ed.), *Interactions in Political Economy: Malvern After Ten Years*, London: Routledge.
Ingham, G. (1984) *Capitalism Divided? The City and Industry in British Social Development*, London: Macmillan.
—— (1994) 'States and Markets in the Production of World Money: Sterling and the Dollar' in Corbridge, S. *et al.* (eds), *Money, Power and Space*, Oxford: Blackwell.
—— (1996a) 'Some Recent Changes in the Relationship between Economics and Sociology', *Cambridge Journal of Economics* 20: 243–75.
—— (1996b) 'Money is a Social Relation', *Review of Social Economy* 64, 4: 507–29.
—— 1998a) 'Still a Lot of Value Left in Money', *Financial Times*, 6 January 1998, London.
—— (1998b) 'On the Underdevelopment of the "Sociology of Money"', *Acta Sociologica* 41, 1: 3–18.
—— (1999) 'Capitalism and Money and Banking: A Critique of Recent Historical Sociology', *British Journal of Sociology* 50, 1: forthcoming.
Jackson, K. (1995) *The Oxford Book of Money*, Oxford: Oxford University Press.
Jones, R. A. (1976) 'The Origin and Development of Media of Exchange', *Journal of Political Economy* 84, 4: 757–75.
Keynes, J. M. (1930) *A Treatise on Money* (2 vols), London: Macmillan.
—— (1982) *The Collected Writings of John Maynard Keynes*, vol. XXVIII, *Social, Political and Literary Writings*, Cambridge: Cambridge University Press.
—— (1983) *The Collected Writings of John Maynard Keynes*, vol. XI, *Economic Articles and Correspondence*, Cambridge: Cambridge University Press.
Kindleberger, C. (1984) *A Financial History of Western Europe*, London: Allen and Unwin.
Knapp, G. F. (1973 {1924}) *The Starter Theory of Money*, New York: Augustus M. Kelley.
Leijonhufvud, A. (1973) 'Life Among the Econ', *Western Economic Journal* 11, 3: 327–37.
Leyshon, A. and Thrift, N. (1997) *Money/Space*, London: Routledge.
Luhmann, N. (1979) *Trust and Power*, Chichester: Wiley and Son.
Maier, C. (1978) 'The Politics of Inflation in the Twentieth Century', in J. H. Goldthorpe and F. Hirsch (eds), *The Political Economy of Inflation*, London: Martin Robertson.
Melitz, J. (1974) *Primitive and Modern Money*, Reading, Mass.: Addison Wesley.
Menger, K. (1892) 'On the Origins of Money', *Economic Journal* 2, 6: 239–55.
Minsky, H. P. (1986) 'Money and Crisis in Schumpeter and Keynes', in H.-J. Wagener and J Drukker (eds), *The Economic Law of Motion of Modern Society*,

Cambridge: Cambridge University Press.
Mirowski, P. (1991) 'Postmodernism and the Social Theory of Value', *Journal of Post Keynesian Economics* 13, 4: 565–82.
von Mises, L. (1953 [1912]) *The Theory of Money and Credit*, London: Jonathan Cape.
Polanyi, K., Arensberg, C. and Pearson, H. (1957) *Trade and Markets in the Early Empires*, New York: Free Press.
Pollin, R. (1991) 'Two Theories of Money Supply Endogeneity: Some Empirical Evidence', *Journal of Post Keynesian Economics* 13, 3: 366–96.
Robertson, D. H. (1928) *Money*, London: Nisbet.
Rogers, C. (1989) *Money, Interest and Capital: A Study in the Foundation of Monetary Theory*, Cambridge: Cambridge University Press.
Samuelson, P. A. (1966 [1958]) 'An Exact Consumption-Loan Model of Interest With or Without The Social Contrivance of Money', in J. Stiglitz (ed.), *The Collected Scientific Papers of Paul A. Samuelson*, vol. I, Cambridge Mass.: MIT Press.
Schumpeter, J. A. (1934 [1912]) *The Theory of Economic Development: An Inquiry into Profits, Capital, Credit, Interest and the Business Cycle*, Cambridge, Mass: Harvard University Press.
—— (1994 [1954]) *A History of Economic Analysis*, London: Routledge.
Simmel, G. (1978 [1907]) *The Philosophy of Money*, London: Routledge.
Smithin, J. (1994) *Controversies in Monetary Economics: Ideas, Issues and Policy*, Aldershot: Edward Elgar.
—— (1996) *Macroeconomic Policy and the Future of Capitalism: The Revenge of the Rentiers and the Threat to Prosperity*, Aldershot: Edward Elgar.
Spufford, P. (1988) *Money and its Uses in Medieval Europe*, Cambridge: Cambridge University Press.
Swedberg, R. (1987) 'Economic Sociology: Past and Present', *Current Sociology* 35, 1: 1–216.
Weber, M. (1978) *Economy and Society*, vol. 1, Berkeley: University of California Press.
—— (1981 [1987]) *General Economic History*, New Brunswick, N.J.: Transactions Publishers.
White, H. (1990) Interview in Swedberg, R. (ed.) *Economics and Sociology: Redefining their Boundaries: Conversations with Economists and Sociologists*, Princeton: Princeton University Press.
Wray, L. R. (1990) *Money and Credit in Capitalist Economies: The Endogenous Money Approach*, Aldershot: Edward Elgar.

3 Modern money

L. Randall Wray

What is money and where did it come from?

We all know the traditional answers to these questions. Our homogenous-globule-of-desire forefathers were inconvenienced by barter until they spontaneously hit upon the idea of using tobacco, furs, huge rocks, landmarks, and wives as media of exchange.[1] Over time, greater efficiency was obtained as *homo economicus* coined precious metals, and market efficiency was enhanced by free banks, which substituted paper money backed by precious metal reserves.[2] All would have been fine and dandy except that evil governments came along, monopolizing the mints, creating central banks that debased the currency, and interfering with the invisible hand of the market. This finally resulted in abandonment of commodity money, substitution of a fiat money, and central bank-induced inflation. If only we could return to that Peter Pan Never-Never Land (*laissez-faire*), free of Captain Hook and the Crocodile (central bank and government), with privately supplied free bank money greasing the mighty wheels of entrepreneurial commerce!

The problem is that the Never-Never Land imagined by the Paul Samuelsons and other textbook writers simply never, ever, existed. There is no evidence of barter-based markets (outside trivial prisoner-of-war cases), and all the evidence about the origins of money points to state involvement. This is not to say that there have never been private monies, nor is it my intention to claim too much of a role for government in the evolution of the financial system. However, what I will argue here is that from the beginning, government played an important role in determining what would function as unit of account, which, as Keynes argued, is 'what really counts'. I will be brief on the historical account of the origins of money, not because this is uninteresting, but rather because it is tangential to the main concern, modern money. Even if the Samuelsonian story about the origins of money were true (which it is not), all modern states operate with a fiat money, rather than with Samuelson's 'tobacco, furs, and wives' as money. However, some knowledge of history does provide illumination on the nature of what could be called modern, or state, money.

A brief history of money

Anthropological evidence is often used in an attempt to support the conventional story. For example, exchange among tribes, or 'purchase' of wives through exchange of primitive valuables within tribes, is offered in support of the story of barter-based market exchange, while use of cowry shells or huge stone wheels (as in the case of the Uap islanders) as 'media of exchange' is supposed to demonstrate the ancient origins of money.[3] However, on closer inspection, it becomes obvious that these examples do not support the Samuelsonian hypothesis about the origins of markets and money.

Exchanges in tribal society were ceremonial in nature, an outgrowth of the practice of reciprocity, and were designed to bring tribal members closer together rather than to maximize the advantage of the transactors. Indeed, the parties to the transaction usually had no choice as to the items to be exchanged, and the purpose of many such exchanges was to equalize wealth (Polanyi 1971, Dalton 1982, Malinowski 1921). Relative prices were never subject to the 'higgling and haggling' of market forces but were set by custom (Polanyi 1971). Similarly, one finds on close examination that there was no universal equivalent or *numéraire* in which prices could be quoted. The 'primitive monies' turn out to be at most 'single purpose money', or better, 'primitive valuables', rather than generalized media of exchange (Neale 1976, Dalton 1982, Malinowski 1921). It appears quite unlikely that markets developed out of tribal ceremonial exchange, and improbable that general purpose money could have evolved from primitive valuables.

It is more likely that the practice of measuring value came from the elaborate compensation schedules developed to prevent blood feuds. These required measuring the debt one owed for injuries, actual and imagined, inflicted on others. The *wergeld, bridewealth, cumhal,* and so on, were specific, and were established in public assemblies. They were not the result of individual higgling and haggling.[4] However, there was not much reason to standardize *wergeld* payments, since the compensation schedules fixed payment in items commonly available. It is far more likely that standardization occurred with the development of upper classes and the temple communities, and later, the palace communities. All the evidence points to the common origins of money, debts and writing, in the tax levies of the palaces.

In the beginning, the temples might have simply demanded that each village provide 10 per cent of everything produced, but with the development of the palace and the expansion of its domain, tax payments became standardized in terms of quantities of wheat or barley grain. These grain standards formed the basis for all the early money of account units, such as the *mina, shekel, lira,* and pound. Money, then, originated not as a cost minimizing medium of exchange, but as the unit of account in which debts to the palace (tax liabilities) were measured. As the area over which taxes were imposed increased, palaces found it useful to farm out tax collections to private tax farmers. The first evidence of lending at interest comes from the practice of payment of taxes by the tax farmers, who then took bond servants and charged interest on the village tax debts. With interest rates normally running at 33 per cent, interest was capitalized and the wealth and power of the tax farmers grew until the debts were cancelled by the emperor in a periodic 'redemption' or 'year of jubilation'. This normally occurred in the thirtieth year of his reign, or upon his death when a new emperor began with a clean slate. Of course, much of the terminology (redemption, forgiveness, hallelujah) as well as the attitudes toward interest (labelling it usury) carried through to religious beliefs and civil practice.[5]

The clay *shubati* (received) tablets record these and other debts (Innes 1913). Each tablet indicated a quantity of grain, the word *shubati*, the name of the person from whom received, the name of the person by whom received, the date, and the seal of the receiver. The tablets were either stored in temples where they would be safe from tampering, or sealed in cases which would have to be broken to get to the tablet. Unlike the tablets stored in temples, the case tablets could and did circulate. A debt could be cancelled and taxes paid by delivering a tablet recording another's debt, whereupon the case which recorded the cancelled debt could be broken to verify the debt terms.

This was general practice for several thousand years before King Pheidon of Argos issued the first coin in the seventh century BC.[6] In other words, taxes, debts, and price lists existed for thousands of years, with 'fiat money' clay tablets circulating before anyone had the bright idea of reducing transactions costs by creating money through stamping precious metals as coins. Were coins the first money? Were they created to reduce transactions costs in markets? Did they reduce transactions costs? Were coins important in market exchanges? The answer to all these questions is no! Markets got along just fine without coins both before and after their invention. From the earliest times, markets operated on the basis of credits and debits, and even the smallest sales to consumers took place on credit, which could be carried on the books of the merchant for years before being cleared.[7] Furthermore, if anything, coins increased market transaction costs, as we shall see in a moment.

Let us skip forward a couple of thousand years to medieval Europe, where coins were certainly well known, but little used. As Mitchell Innes said: 'For many centuries, how many we do not know, the principal instrument of commerce was the tally' (Innes 1913: 394). This was a stick of hazelwood, notched to indicate the amount of the purchase or debt, created when the buyer became a debtor by accepting a good or service from the seller who automatically became the creditor. The date and the debtor's name were written on two opposite sides of the stick, which was then split so that the notches were cut in half with the name and date on both pieces of the tally. The split was stopped about an inch from the base of the stick so that one piece, the 'stock', was longer than the other, called the 'stub'. The creditor would retain the stock (from which our terms capital and corporate stock derive) while the debtor would take the stub (a term still used as in 'ticket stub') to ensure that the stock was not altered. When the debtor retired his or her debt, the two pieces of the tally would be matched to verify the amount of the debt. Wooden tallies were not the only records as there was nothing unique about hazelwood. There appear to have been copper tallies in Italy from 1000 to 2000 years BC, purposely broken at the time of manufacture to provide a stock and stub. And really, the encased *shubati* tablets were nothing more than tallies, with the case resolving the tampering problem so that no stub was required.

A merchant holding a number of tally stocks against customers could get together with another merchant holding tally stocks against him and clear his own tally stub debts. In this way, great medieval 'fairs' were developed to act as clearing houses allowing merchants to settle their mutual debts and credits without the use of a single coin. While textbooks say that these fairs were early, markets, the retail trade probably originated as a sideline to the clearing-house trade.[8]

There are, then, several problems with the textbook, market-place story. First, the tally debts (in the form of clay tablets) are at least 2,000 years older than the oldest known coins. Second, the denominations of all the early precious metal coins (even the least valuable) were far too high to have been used in everyday exchanges. For example, the most common denomination of the earliest electrum coins would have had a purchasing power of about ten sheep.[9] They might have sufficed for wholesale trade of large merchants, but they could not have been used in day-to-day retail trade. It is also quite unlikely that coins would have been invented to facilitate trade, as the Phoenicians, and other peoples with sophisticated trade, managed without coins for many centuries.

Indeed, in most cases the introduction of coins would have been a less efficient alternative. While we are accustomed to a small number of types of coins (always issued by government, with perhaps one coin for each denomination) the typical case until recently was a large variety of coins, sometimes including many with the same face value but different exchange value, issued by a wide variety of merchants, kings, feudal lords, barons and others. In Gaul at one point there were 1,200 different coinages.[10]

The textbook story relies on choice of a particular precious metal precisely to reduce the transaction costs of barter. However, in reality the consumer was faced with a tremendous number of coins of varying weight, denomination, alloy, and fineness. It is difficult to believe that the typical member of these societies would have been more able to assess the value of a coin than the value of, say, a cow. Rather than reducing transaction costs by using precious metals, it would likely have reduced transactions costs to use cows! It is not a real counter-argument that cows are less divisible, because the coins were far too valuable to have been used in daily transactions in any event.

In other words, lower-cost alternatives to coin were already in use. Hazelwood tallies or clay tablets had lower non-monetary value than precious metals. Thus, it is unlikely that metal coins would be issued to circulate competitively (for example, against hazelwood tallies) unless their nominal value was well above the value of the embodied precious metal. It is not surprising that for early coins this was almost always the case.

What then are coins, what are their origins, and why are they accepted? Coins appear to have originated as government 'pay tokens' (in Knapp's colourful phrase), as nothing more than evidence of debt.[11] Given the large denomination of the early coins and their uniform weight (their purity probably could not have been tested at the time, so it would not have been uniform), coins were most likely invented by kings to make a large number of uniform payments in the form of precious metal to reduce counterfeiting (Cook 1958, Redish 1987). According to Cook (1958), coins were probably invented to pay mercenaries. It was probably recognized from the very beginning that the purpose of the coin was to give the population a convenient means for paying taxes. Use of these early coins as a medium of exchange was probably an 'accidental consequence of the coinage', and not the reason for it.[12] So from the very beginning, coins were intentionally minted to provide state finance. This explains the relatively large value of the coins, which were evidence of the state's debt to 'soldiers and sailors' (Innes 1913: 399).

Coins, then, were mere tokens of the crown's debt, like the tally. But why would the crown's subjects accept hazelwood tallies or token coins? Innes supplies the answer:

> The government by law obliges certain selected persons to become its debtors. This procedure is called levying a tax, and the persons thus forced into the position of debtors to the government must in theory seek out the holders of the tallies and acquire from them the tallies by selling to them some commodity in exchange for which they may be induced to part with their tallies. When these are returned to the government treasury, the taxes are paid.
>
> (Innes 1913: 398)

Until recent times, the vast majority of government spending and the revenues collected by inland tax collectors in England were in the form of the tallies. Each taxpayer did not have to individually seek out a crown tally, because matching the crown's creditors and debtors was accomplished 'through the bankers, who from the earliest days of history were always the financial agents of government' (Innes 1913: 399).

Use of the hazelwood tallies continued in England until 1826 when they literally went out in a blaze of glory. After 1826, when tallies were returned to the Exchequer, they were stored in the Star Chamber and other parts of the House of Commons. In 1834, in order to save space and economize on fuel it was decided that they should be thrown into the heating stoves of the House of Commons: 'So excessive was the zeal of the stokers that the historic parliament buildings were set on fire and razed to the ground' (Davies 1994: 663).

The inordinate focus of economists on precious metal coins and market exchange then appears to be misplaced. The key concept is debt, and specifically, the ability of the state to impose a tax debt on its subjects. Once it has done this, it can choose the form in which subjects can pay the tax. Certainly the government's tokens can also be used as a medium of exchange, but this *derives from* its ability to impose taxes, and is necessitated by imposition of the tax (if one has a tax liability but is not a creditor of the crown, one must offer things for sale to obtain the crown's tokens). Private coins (such as those of Gaul), like the government coins, are tokens of private indebtedness. These coins could be issued for example by feudal lords or ecclesiastics, as their debt which they then accepted as payment of feudal rent or tithes (Innes 1913, MacDonald 1916). Clearly, acceptability of these private coins in 'private pay communities' was not contingent on the non-money value of the coins, for example by the precious metal contained in them, or even by the promise of redeemability for precious metal or royal coins. See the discussion below.

There are other matters which we could examine, such as the widespread belief that evil kings purposely debased their coins by reducing gold content to obtain seigniorage. However, the value of the coins was not generally determined by the gold content.[13] The coins were nothing but evidence of the crown's debt, hence, it would make no sense to debase them. Instead, kings periodically 'cried-down' the nominal value of their token coins as a well-recognized method of taxation; rather than delivering one coin to pay a tax, one had to deliver two. I could also go into the eighteenth and nineteenth century development of the gold standard, which occurred in response partly to the crying-down and partly to the considerable confusion and mystification over the image of gold as the guardian of the value of the currency. This is quite interesting because it is only after the purposeful and visible hand of government imposed the gold standard (in the nineteenth century) that we finally achieved anything like the sort of monetary system that the orthodox economists imagine to have sprung from the minds of atomistic globules of desire. However, let us turn to the nature of modern money in the next section.

The chartalist or state money approach

The chartalist or state money approach can be traced from Adam Smith through to John Maynard Keynes. In this approach, money is a creature of the state. The state *defines* money as that which it accepts at public pay offices, mainly in payment of taxes. I shall briefly examine the views of Smith, Knapp and Keynes, and some related arguments (primarily of Minsky and Lerner) before turning to the policy implications of this approach.

According to Smith, as long as paper money is redeemed on demand for gold (or silver), it circulates at par with the gold coin. 'Whatever is either bought or sold for such paper, must necessarily be bought or sold as cheap as it could have been for gold and silver' (Smith 1937: 308). If paper money is not redeemable on demand, then it may circulate at a discount. He discussed the case where redeemability might be uncertain, or might require a wait:

> Such a paper money would, no doubt, fall more or less below the value of gold and silver, according as the difficulty or uncertainty of obtaining immediate payment was supposed to be greater or less; or according to the greater or less distance of time at which payment was exigible.[14]
>
> (Smith 1937: 309)

As an example, Smith gave the case of the American colonies, which typically offered conversion only after a wait of several years and did not pay interest on the paper for the waiting period. Still, these colonies passed legal tender laws:

> to render their paper of equal value with gold and silver, by enacting penalties against all those who made any difference in the price of their goods when they sold them for a colony paper, and when they sold them for gold and silver.
>
> (Smith 1937: 311)

Smith decried such regulations as 'tyrannical' and ineffectual, for the colony currency would fall relative to the English pound. However, he also noted that Pennsylvania:

> was always more moderate in its emissions of paper money than any other of our colonies. Its paper currency accordingly is said to never to have sunk below the value of the gold and silver which was current in the colony before the first emission of paper money.
>
> (Smith 1937: 311)

Here there is some ambiguity, for he had not previously argued that the depreciation of a non-convertible currency was a function of the *quantity* of the currency issued, but now he seemed to argue that the more moderate emission of Pennsylvania forestalled depreciation.

In the following paragraph he seems to have solved the puzzle. If a paper money whose redeemability is uncertain (or is subject to conditions such as a waiting period) is *accepted in payment of taxes*, and if it is not excessively issued *relative to the tax liability*, then it need not depreciate relative to coinage:

> The paper of each colony being received in the payment of the provincial taxes, for the full value for which it had been issued, it necessarily derived from this use some additional value, over and above what it would have had, from the real or supposed distance of the term of its final discharge and redemption. This additional value was greater or less, according as the quantity of paper issued was more or less above *what could be employed in the payment of the taxes* of the particular colony which issued it. It was in all the colonies very much above what could be employed in this manner.
> (Smith 1937: 312, emphasis added)

Thus, the depreciation noticed in the colonies occurred precisely because the note issue was well above what was required in payment of taxes. A wiser government could not only prevent depreciation, it might even cause paper money to carry a premium over coins:

> A prince, who should enact that a certain proportion of his taxes should be paid in a paper money of a certain kind, might thereby give a certain value to this paper money; even though the term of its final discharge and redemption should depend altogether upon the will of the prince. If the bank which issued this paper was careful to keep the quantity of it always somewhat below what could easily be employed in this manner, the demand for it might be such as to make it even bear a premium, or sell for somewhat more in the market than the quantity of gold or silver currency for which it was issued.
> (Smith 1937: 312)

In summary, an essentially *non-redeemable* paper money could actually circulate *above par* even under a gold standard if it were legally required by the state in payment of taxes, and if the quantity issued were kept 'somewhat below what could easily be employed in this manner'. According to Smith, the key is not really redeemability, nor is it legal tender laws that attempt to 'render their paper of equal value with gold and silver'. It is the acceptance of the paper money in payment of taxes and the restriction of the issue in relation to the total tax liability that gives value to the paper money. Importantly, Smith recognized that this paper money need not be government fiat currency, for his argument was predicated upon the recognition that the paper money is the liability of the banking system. All that mattered was that the state accepted these banknotes in payment of taxes, in which case they could circulate at par, or even at a premium, relative to coinage.

Georg Friedrich Knapp put forward a *state* theory of money, similar to, but more general than, what is known as the chartalist approach. This approach is opposed to the metallist view, according to which the value of money *derives from* the value of the metal standard (e.g gold or silver) adopted. More generally, according to Knapp, metallists try to 'deduce' the monetary system 'without the idea of a State'. This, he believes, is 'absurd' because 'the money of a state' is that which is 'accepted at the public pay offices' (Knapp 1924: vii–viii; see also Goodhart 1989). It is thus impossible to separate the theory of money from the theory of the state.

According to Knapp, debts are expressed in a unit of value, 'the unit in which the amount of the payment is expressed' (Knapp 1924: 8) and discharged with means of payment, 'a movable thing which has the legal property of being the bearer of units of value' (ibid.: 7). What then determines which things will act as means of payment to discharge debts? Knapp noticed that means of payment are occasionally changed, so that sometimes one type of material (say, weighed or coined gold) will cease to be accepted and another (say, weighed or coined silver) suddenly take its place. Therefore, while the means of payment may be a definite material, it is not bound to any particular material (ibid.: 8–25). 'Validity by proclamation is not bound to any material. It can occur with the most precious or the basest metals' (ibid.: 30). The fundamental insight was his recognition that these transitions always require that the state announce a *conversion rate* (say, so many ounces of gold for so many ounces of silver). The debts were always nominal and were never actually metallic. All debts are converted to the new metal, which proves that all units of account *must be* nominal. Hence, the names chartalist, and more specifically state, theory of money, since the proclamation is made by the state. In Knapp's view, a chartal money is a 'pay-token':

> When we give up our coats in the cloak-room of a theatre, we receive a tin disc of a given size bearing a sign, perhaps a number. There is nothing more on it, but this ticket or mark has legal significance; it is a proof that I am entitled to demand the return of my coat. When we send letters, we affix a stamp or a ticket which proves that we have by payment of postage obtained the right to get the letter carried. The 'ticket' is then a good expression . . . for a movable, shaped object bearing signs, to which legal ordinance gives a use independent of its material. Our means of payment, then, whether coins or warrants, possess the above-named qualities: they are pay-tokens, or tickets used as means of payment . . . Perhaps the Latin word 'Charta' can bear the sense of ticket or token, and we can form a new but intelligible adjective – 'Chartal.' Our means of payment have this token, or Chartal, form. Among civilized peoples in our day, payments can only be made with pay-tickets or Chartal pieces.
>
> (Knapp 1924: 31–2)

Note that like the tin disc issued by the cloakroom, the material used to manufacture the chartal pieces is wholly irrelevant: it can be gold, silver, or common metal; it can be paper. In any case, 'Money always signifies a Chartal means of payment. Every means of payment we call money. The definition of money is therefore a Chartal means of payment' (Knapp 1924: 38). Chartalism is often identified with the proposition that legal tender laws determine that which must be accepted as means of payment. However, Knapp's analysis went further:

> If we have already declared in the beginning that money is a creation of law, this is not to be interpreted in the narrower sense that it is a creation of jurisprudence, but in the larger sense that it is a creation of the legislative activity of the State, a creation of legislative policy.
> (Knapp 1924: 40)

What is the nature of this legislative activity that determines what will be the chartalist money accepted within the jurisdiction of the state?

> What forms part of the monetary system of the State and what does not? We must not make our definition too narrow. The criterion cannot be that the money is issued by the State, for that would exclude kinds of money which are of the highest importance; I refer to bank-notes: they are not issued by the State, but they form a part of its monetary system. Nor can legal tender be taken as the test, for in monetary systems there are very frequently kinds of money which are not legal tender . . . We keep most closely to the facts if we take as our test, that the money is accepted in payments made to the State's offices. Then all means by which a payment can be made to the State form part of the monetary system. On this basis it is not the issue, but the *acceptation*, as we call it, which is decisive. State acceptation delimits the monetary system. By the expression 'State-acceptation' is to be understood only the acceptance at State pay offices where the State is the recipient.
> (Knapp 1924: 95)

Thus, it is the decision of the state to accept at state pay offices, and not legal tender laws, that creates a chartal money.

Knapp extended his analysis to include bank money:

> The bank makes notes and offers them in payment to its customers. Issuing notes is not a special business . . . but a special way in which the bank endeavours to make its payments . . . It tries to pay in its own notes instead of in money issued by the State, because then with a comparatively small capital it can make greater profits than it otherwise could.
> (Knapp 1924: 131)

Acceptability of banknotes in private transactions is not (as was commonly believed) due to the bank promise to convert these to coinage In other words, bank money did not derive its value from the gold reserves or specie coin into which it promised redemption. 'A bank-note is a chartal document . . . and the bank issuing it is pledged by law to accept it for a payment of that amount' (Knapp 1924: 134). Whether banknotes are convertible is irrelevant. 'An inconvertible bank-note, then, is not a nullity, but has this in common with the convertible bank-note, that it is a till-warrant of the bank' (ibid.: 134). What is important is that the note:

> is a private till-warrant available for payments to the bank . . . but clearly the customers of the bank can use it for payments between themselves, as they are sure it will be taken at the bank. These customers and the bank form, so to speak, a private pay community; the public pay community is the State.
>
> (Knapp 1924: 134)

Knapp goes further than Smith in his recognition that banknotes do not derive their value from the reserves (whether gold or government fiat money) held for conversion, but rather from their use in the 'private pay community' and 'public pay community'; this, in turn, is a function of 'acceptation' at the bank and public pay offices. Within the private pay community (or 'giro'), bank money is the primary money used in payments; however, payments in the public pay community require state money.[15] This can include bank money, but note that generally delivery of bank money to the state is not final or definitive, because the state will present it to banks for redemption (for reserves). Bank money when used in the public pay community is not 'definitive' unless the state also uses it in its own purchases.

What makes banknotes state money? 'Bank-notes are not automatically money of the state, but they become so as soon as the State announces that it will receive them in epicentric payments [payments to the state]' (Knapp 1924: 135). If the state accepts notes in payment to the state, then the banknotes become 'accessory' and the business of the bank is enhanced 'for now everybody is glad to take its bank-notes since all inhabitants of the State have occasion to make epicentric payments (e.g. for taxes)' (ibid.: 137). States often required that banks make their notes convertible to state-issued money 'one of the measures by means of which the State assures a superior position to the money which it issues itself' (ibid.: 140), because if the state accepts banknotes in payment, but does not make payments in these banknotes, then the notes will be redeemed, leading to a drain of reserves. (Indeed, governments and central banks used redemption or the threat of redemption to discipline banks.)

In times of distress, however (frequently during wars that required finance provided by banks), governments would pass laws ending convertibility, announce that the state would henceforth make payments in terms of the banknotes, and thereby declare that the banknotes were '*valuta*' money (that is, the money accepted by the state and in which the state makes its payments, in which case it becomes the definitive or ultimate means of payment used even in the private pay community) (Knapp 1924: 143). Usually this was for one bank only, the bank which became the central bank. Through action of the state, then, paper money can become *valuta* money.

> At first bank-notes and Treasury notes are employed only as accessory money... The mournful hour arrives when the State has to announce that it can no longer pay in the money that was till then *valuta* [say, coined gold] and that those warrants themselves are now *valuta*.
> (Knapp 1924: 196)

At this point we have a chartalist, inconvertible, paper money, as do all modern developed countries.

Keynes's account was quite similar. According to Keynes, the ' money of account' is the 'primary concept' of a theory of money. It 'comes into existence along with Debts, which are contracts for deferred payment, and Price-Lists, which are offers of contracts for sale or purchase' (Keynes 1930: 3). In turn:

> Money itself, namely that by delivery of which debt-contracts and price-contracts are discharged, and in the shape of which a store of General Purchasing Power is held, derives its character from its relationship to the Money-of-Account, since the debts and prices must first have been expressed in terms of the latter.
> (Keynes 1930: 3)

He further clarified the distinction between money and the money of account: 'the money-of-account is the *description* or *title* and the money is the thing which answers to the description' (Keynes 1930: 3–4).

Following Knapp, Keynes argued that the state determines what serves as the money of account as well as dictates what 'thing' will be accepted as money:

> The State, therefore, comes in first of all as the authority of law which enforces the payment of the thing which corresponds to the name or description in the contracts. But it comes in doubly when, in addition, it claims the right to determine and declare what thing corresponds to the name, and to vary its declaration from time to time – when, that is to say, it claims the right to re-edit the dictionary. This right is claimed by all modern states and has been so claimed for some four thousand years at least.
> (Keynes 1930: 4)

The 'Age of Chartalist or State Money' had been reached, when the state 'claimed the right not only to enforce the dictionary but also to write the dictionary' (Keynes 1930: 5). Let me emphasize that Keynes believed the age of State money to have begun 'at least' four thousand years ago, so that the state theory of money would certainly apply to all the 'modern' economies including those living under the gold standard in the nineteenth century. Even a gold-based commodity money is state money.

Privately issued debt – such as that issued by banks – might be accepted in settlement of transactions even if it is not declared by the government to be money; it can circulate 'side by side' with 'State Money' (Keynes 1930: 6). However, the state might 'use its chartalist prerogative to declare that the [bank] debt itself is an acceptable discharge of a liability' (ibid.). Bank money then becomes a 'Representative Money' (ibid.):

> At the cost of not conforming entirely with current usage, I propose to include as State-Money not only money which is itself compulsory legal-tender but also money which the State or the Central Bank undertakes to accept in payments to itself or to exchange for compulsory legal-tender money.
>
> (Keynes 1930: 6)

In a footnote to this passage, he goes on: 'Knapp accepts as "Money" – rightly I think – anything which the State undertakes to accept at its pay-offices, whether or not it is declared legal-tender between citizens' (ibid.: 6–7). Therefore, like Knapp, Keynes's analysis goes beyond legal tender laws to identify state acceptance as the key to determining what will serve as money.

According to Keynes, 'State money may take any of three forms: *Commodity Money, Fiat Money* and *Managed Money*, the last two being subspecies of *Representative Money*' (Keynes 1930: 7). Commodity money is defined as 'actual units of a particular freely-obtainable, non-monopolized commodity which happens to have been chosen for the familiar purposes of money', or 'warehouse warrants for actually existing units of the commodity' (ibid.). Fiat money is representative money 'which is created and issued by the State, but is not convertible by law into anything other than itself, and has no fixed value in terms of an objective standard' (ibid.). This is distinguished from managed money, which 'is similar to Fiat Money, except that the State undertakes to manage the conditions of its issue in such a way that, by convertibility or otherwise, it shall have a determinant value in terms of an objective standard' (ibid.: 8).

Managed money is according to Keynes the most generalized form of money, which can:

> degenerate into Commodity Money on the one side when the managing authority holds against it a hundred per cent of the objective

standard, so that it is in effect a warehouse warrant, and into Fiat Money on the other side when it loses its objective standard.

(Keynes 1930: 8)

In other words, a full-bodied (say, one ounce) gold coin valued at one currency unit would qualify as commodity money, while a paper note which is convertible to gold against which a fractional gold reserve is held would qualify as managed money, even if the conversion rate is one currency unit per ounce of gold. Thus, a gold standard system can be operated as either a commodity money or as a managed money. On the other hand, a representative money can take the form of either a managed money (a paper note convertible on demand to gold, or even to a foreign currency as in a currency board system) or a fiat money (no promise to convert at a fixed exchange rate to precious metals or foreign exchange). Keynes argued that even a gold standard, whether a commodity or a managed money system, operates as a state money system. In either case, the state can always 'rewrite the dictionary', for example, by adopting a silver standard and a conversion rate (say, one ounce of gold for twelve ounces of silver). State money can be held by banks, by the central bank, and by the public:

> The State-Money held by the Central Bank constitutes its "reserve" against its deposits. These deposits we may term *Central Bank-Money*. It is convenient to assume that all the Central Bank-Money is held by the Member Banks – in so far as it may be held by the public, it may be on the same footing as State-Money or as Member Bank-Money, according to circumstances. This Central Bank-Money *plus* the State Money held by the Member Banks makes up the Reserves of the Member Banks, which they, in turn, hold against their Deposits. These Deposits constitute the *Member Bank-Money* in the hands of the Public, and make up, together with the State-Money (and Central Bank-Money, if any) held by the Public, the aggregate of *Current Money*.
>
> (Keynes 1930: 9–10)

Any payments to the state using 'Member Bank-Money' will cause member banks to lose 'Central Bank-Money' or 'State Money held by the Member Banks': that is, reserves.

As Keynes and Knapp recognized, member bank-money is the primary 'thing' answering to the 'description' – money – used in private transactions (or within the private pay community). When accepted in payment of taxes, it is also used in the public pay community, but it is not 'definitive' from the perspective of member banks because they must deliver reserves (mainly central bank-money) whenever taxes are paid using member bank-money.

In summary, with the rise of the modern state, the money of account (the description) is chosen by the state, which is free to choose that which will qualify as money (the thing that answers to the description). This goes beyond legal tender laws, which establish what can legally discharge contracts, to include that which the state accepts in payment at its pay-offices. The state is free to choose a system based on commodity money, fiat money, or managed money. Even if it chooses a strict commodity system, the *value* of the money does not derive from the commodity accepted as money, '[f]or Chartalism begins when the State *designates* the objective standard which shall correspond to the money-of-account' (Keynes 1930: 11).

> [M]oney is the measure of value, but to regard it as having value itself is a relic of the view that the value of money is regulated by the value of the substance of which it is made, and is like confusing a theatre ticket with the performance.
>
> (Keynes 1983: 402)

Once it is recognized that the state can 'write the dictionary', it becomes obvious that the nominal value of a commodity (or managed) money cannot be derived from the value of the objective standard. It is then a small step to a fiat money with no objective standard, because in all three cases the state determines the nominal value of money. This is done when the state establishes what it will accept at public pay offices, as well as the nominal value of the thing accepted.

Hyman Minsky presented a view of money that was based on the state money approach. He emphasized the endogeneity of money, that is, the view that money is created during the normal, and important, processes of a capitalist economy, and is not created and dropped by helicopters (as in Milton Friedman's famous exogenous money story). For the most part, bank money is created as banks make loans.

> Money is unique in that it is created in the act of financing by a bank and is destroyed as the commitments on debt instruments owned by banks are fulfilled. Because money is created and destroyed in the normal course of business, the amount outstanding is responsive to the demand for financing.
>
> (Minsky 1986: 249)

A loan is nothing more than an agreement by a bank to make payments now on the basis of a promise of the borrower to pay later. 'Loans represent payments the bank made for business, households, and governments in exchange for their promises to make payments to the bank at some future date' (Minsky 1986: 230).[16]

All of this occurs on the balance sheets of banks; the 'money' that is created by a bank is nothing more than a credit to another bank's balance sheet.[17] According to Minsky, there is a pyramid of liabilities with the liabilities of the central bank at the top. Bank liabilities are convertible on demand into central bank liabilities, which are used for interbank clearing (as well as for conversion of bank liabilities to 'cash' held by the public, resulting in a net reserve drain).

> The payments banks make are to other banks, although they simultaneously charge the account of the customer. In the receiving bank, the payments are credited to a depositor's account . . . For member banks of the Federal Reserve System, the interbank payments lead to deposits shifting from the account of one bank to the account of another at Federal Reserve banks. For nonmember banks, another bank – called a correspondent – intervenes, so that the transfers at the Federal Reserve banks are for the accounts of correspondents.
> (Minsky 1986: 230–1)

Thus, payments among banks occur on the balance sheet of the Fed as banks use 'Fed money' (reserves) to settle net debits from their accounts. 'Whereas the public uses bank deposits as money, banks use Federal Reserve deposits as money. This is the fundamental hierarchical property of our money and banking system' (Minsky 1986: 231). This is, of course, the same hierarchical arrangement noted by Knapp (in his public and private pay communities) and by Keynes.

In an argument very similar to Knapp's, Minsky explained that people accept bank money in part because they can use it to meet their own commitments to banks. 'Demand deposits have exchange value because a multitude of debtors to banks have outstanding debts that call for the payment of demand deposits to banks. These debtors will work and sell goods or financial instruments to get demand deposits' (Minsky 1986: 231). In other words, according to Minsky, bank money has (nominal) value precisely because it can be used to retire debts to banks, and is accepted at 'bank pay offices'. The borrower retires his/her promise to the bank by delivering bank liabilities at the future date, and the need for bank liabilities to retire one's own liabilities to banks leads one to accept bank liabilities in payment for goods and services delivered. Rather than focusing on money as a medium of exchange, this focus is on money as means of payment, to retire liabilities.

This led Minsky back to the Smith/Knapp recognition that taxes give value to the money issued by the government:[18]

> In an economy where government debt is a major asset on the books of the deposit-issuing banks, the fact that taxes need to be paid gives value to the money of the economy . . . [T]he need to pay taxes means that people work and produce in order to get that in which taxes can be paid.
> (Minsky 1986: 231)

Even though most taxes are actually paid using bank money, because of the hierarchical arrangement, banks can make these payments to government only by using central bank money, that is, by losing reserves.

Another economist writing after Keynes, Abba Lerner, also wrote on the state money theme, and insisted that:

> [W]hatever may have been the history of gold, at the present time, in a normally well-working economy, money is a creature of the state. Its general acceptability, which is its all-important attribute, stands or falls by its acceptability by the state.
>
> (Lerner 1947: 313)

Just how does the state demonstrate acceptability?

> The modern state can make anything it chooses generally acceptable as money.... It is true that a simple declaration that such and such is money will not do, even if backed by the most convincing constitutional evidence of the state's absolute sovereignty. But if the state is willing to accept the proposed money in payment of taxes and other obligations to itself the trick is done. Everyone who has obligations to the state will be willing to accept the pieces of paper with which he can settle the obligations, and all other people will be willing to accept these pieces of paper because they know that the taxpayers, etc., will accept them in turn.
>
> (Lerner 1947: 313)

This seems to be about as clear a statement as one can find. Even if it has not always been the case, it surely is now true and obvious that the state writes the 'description' of money when it denominates the tax liability in a money of account, and defines the 'thing' that 'answers to the description' when it decides what will be accepted at public pay-offices. The thing which answers to the description is widely accepted *not* because of sovereignty alone, *not* because of legal tender laws and *not* because it might have (or have had) gold backing, but because the state has the power to impose and enforce tax liabilities and because it has the right to choose 'that which is necessary to pay taxes'. Keynes emphasized that this right 'has been so claimed for some four thousand years at least'. Although Keynes was not a historian and one might quibble over the exact number of years since states first claimed these rights, there can be no doubt that all modern states do have these rights.

As Lerner said 'Cigarette money and foreign money can come into wide use only when the normal money and the economy in general is in a state of chaos' (Lerner 1947: 313). One might only add that when the state is in crisis and loses legitimacy, and in particular loses its power to impose and enforce tax liabilities, normal money will be in a state of chaos. This can lead, for example, to use of foreign currencies in private domestic transactions. In all other cases, it is state money which is used as the ultimate means of settlement, and state money is that which the state accepts in payment of taxes. All other monies used domestically are denominated in the state money, with their liquidity and acceptability related to (although not strictly determined by) the ease with which they can be converted to state money. In the chartalist approach, the public demands the government's money because that is the form in which taxes are paid. The state uses taxes as a means of inducing the population to supply goods and services to the state, supplying in return the money that will be used to retire the tax liability. In the modern economy, it *appears* that taxes are paid using bank money, but analysis of reserve accounting shows that tax payments always lead to a reserve drain (that is, a reduction in central bank liabilities), so that in reality only the government's money is definitive and finally discharges the tax liability.

Policy implications deriving from this view of money

The chartalist or state money view has important policy implications. Once the state imposes a tax on its citizens, payable in a money it creates, it does not need the public's money in order to spend; rather, the public needs the government's money in order to pay taxes. This means that the government can buy whatever is for sale in terms of its money merely by providing its money. Because the public will normally wish to hold some extra money, the government will normally have to spend more than it taxes. In other words, the normal requirement is for a government deficit. Deficits are not to be feared. As Lerner argued, the implication is that all the conventional wisdom about government finance is confused and must be replaced with a 'functional finance' approach. According to him:

> The central idea is that government fiscal policy, its spending and taxing, its borrowing and repayment of loans, its issue of new money, and its withdrawal of money, shall all be underaken with an eye only to the results of these actions on the economy and not to any established traditional doctrine about what is sound or unsound.
>
> (Lerner 1943: 39)

He went on to list two 'laws' of functional finance:

> The first financial responsibility of the government (since nobody else can undertake that responsibility) is to keep the total rate of spending in the country on goods and services neither greater nor less than that rate which at the current prices would buy all the goods that it is possible to produce.
>
> (Lerner 1943: 39)

When spending is too high, the government should reduce spending and raise taxes; when spending is too low, the government should increase spending and lower taxes.

> An interesting corollary is that taxing is *never* to be undertaken merely because the government needs to make money payments.... Taxation should therefore be imposed only when it is desirable that the taxpayers shall have less money to spend.
> (Lerner 1943: 40)

If the government is not to use taxes to make money payments, then how are these to be made? According to Lerner, the government should not turn to borrowing for the purposes of spending, because 'The second law of Functional Finance is that the government should borrow money only if it is desirable that the public should have less money and more government bonds' (Lerner 1943: 40). In other words, the purpose of taxes and bonds is not really to finance spending as each serves a different purpose. Taxes remove excessive private income while bonds offer an interest-earning alternative to money. The government should meet its needs by 'printing new money' whenever the first and second principles of functional finance dictate that neither taxes nor bond sales are required. Government deficits do not require borrowing by the government (bond sales), rather, the government provides bonds to allow the public to hold interest-bearing alternatives to non interest-bearing government money. In summary, Lerner argued:

> Functional Finance rejects completely the traditional doctrines of 'sound finance' and the principle of trying to balance the budget over a solar year or any other arbitrary period. In their place it prescribes: first, the adjustment of total spending (by everybody in the economy, including the government) in order to eliminate both unemployment and inflation, using government spending when total spending is too low and taxation when total spending is too high; second, the adjustment of public holdings of money and of government bonds, by government borrowing or debt repayment, in order to achieve the rate of interest which results in the most desirable level of investment; and third, the printing, hoarding or destruction of money as needed for carrying out the first two parts of the programme.
> (Lerner 1943: 41)

According to this view, the supply of government money (or base money) is determined by government purchases, including goods, services, and assets purchased by the treasury and the central bank. Much of this currency will be removed from circulation as taxes are paid. The rest ends up in desired hoards, or flows to banks to be accumulated as bank reserves. Thus, *fiscal policy* determines the quantity of base money supplied. *Monetary* policy drains excess reserves (mainly as a result of government bond sales by the treasury, but also through open market sales by the central bank), removing them from member bank accounts, and replacing them with bonds voluntarily purchased.

As Boulding (1950) had argued, fiscal policy has more to do with the quantity of money issued by the government, while monetary policy has to do with regulation of financial markets, and most importantly, with determination of short-term interest rates. Once monetary policy has set an overnight interest rate target (Fed funds rate in the US), it has no choice but to supply reserves when banks are short, or to drain reserves when banks have excess reserve positions. Otherwise deficient reserves would drive the overnight rate up and excess reserves would drive it down, which in either case would force the central bank to miss its targets. In other words, reserves are not discretionary from the point of view of monetary policy, as the central bank must always accommodate, and nor is the supply of privately-issued money discretionary. The only policy instrument available to the central bank is the short-term interest rate.

Keynes said that the two outstanding features of the monetary economy are its tendency to generate an arbitrary and inequitable distribution of income and its failure to provide for full employment.[19] In large part, the arbitrary and inequitable distribution of income result from an interest rate that tends to be too high. Keynes argued that interest rewards no genuine sacrifice, and compounding ensures that the distribution will go to the *rentier*. He linked unemployment to the desire for liquidity; only monetary economies have unemployment. By definition, whatever is technically feasible in a non-monetary economy can get done. If the pharaoh observes there are some idle men about, he puts them to work to build a pyramid. Financing can never get in the way of pyramid-building, although insufficient quantities of real resources or lack of technical know-how can act as real barriers. It is only the modern economy that appears to be financially unable to do what is technically possible. The US, Japan and Germany are supposed to have to suffer unemployment because they all are too poor to put the unemployed to work because their governments are 'broke'. They are supposed simply not have the money to employ those without jobs.

As the state or chartalist approach to money demonstrates, this is nonsense. Governments issue money to buy what they need; they tax to generate a demand for that money; and then they accept the money in payment of the tax. If a deficit results, that simply indicates that the population wishes to hoard some of the money. The deficit is of no consequence to the government; it merely allows the population to save in the form of government money. If the government wants to, it can let the population trade the money for interest-earning government bonds, but the government never *needs* to borrow its own money from the public. Taxes and bonds, therefore, have nothing to do with financing a government's spending. They necessarily *follow* spending rather than precede it.[20]

This does not mean that the deficit cannot be too big, that is, inflationary. It can also be too small, that is deflationary. At the end of the twentieth century, most of the developed capitalist countries have deficits which are so small that there is real danger of a massive, world-wide deflationary spiral. There are tens of millions of people who need jobs. By some accounts, there are more idle workers now than there were at the depths of the Great Depression. In a monetary economy, unemployment is *de facto* evidence that the deficit is too small. Any modern economy can hire all those unemployed at some announced fixed wage, and let the deficit float as high as necessary without worrying about inflation, since by setting the wage the government sets the price. In a very real sense, those employed in such a programme become a labour 'buffer stock' which will serve as a price-stabilizing 'reserve army' of the *employed*. I have called this the employer of last resort programme, and it is very similar to what Wendell Gordon, Bill Mitchell, Hyman Minsky, and Philip Harvey have all (independently) advocated in recent years.[21]

Sweden used to have something like this, and interestingly, justified its full employment programme on the argument that Sweden was too small and too poor to afford unemployment; it needed to have everyone working in order to compete. This, it seems to me, is the right way around. No economy that operates on the basis of a chartal money needs to accept unemployment either because it cannot 'afford' to give jobs to the unemployed, or because inflation would be 'too inflationary'. Full employment can always be afforded, and indeed, any rational analysis would argue that unemployment cannot be afforded. If it is achieved through something like an employer of last resort programme, it will actually be less inflationary than the current system, which relies on unemployment and waste of resources to reduce inflationary pressures. As Keynes argued three-quarters of a century ago, on the precipice of the Great Depression:

> The Conservative belief that there is some law of nature which prevents men from being employed, that it is 'rash' to employ men, and that it is financially 'sound' to maintain a tenth of the population in idleness for an indefinite period, is crazily improbable – the sort of thing which no man could believe who had not had his head fuddled with nonsense for years and years. . . . .. Our main task, therefore, will be to confirm the reader's instinct that what *seems* sensible *is* sensible, and what *seems* nonsense *is* nonsense. We shall try to show him that the conclusion, that if new forms of employment are offered more men will be employed, is as obvious as it sounds and contains no hidden snags; that to set unemployed men to work on useful tasks does what it appears to do, namely, increases the national wealth; and that the

notion, that we shall, for intricate reasons, ruin ourselves financially if we use this means to increase our well-being, is what it looks like – a bogy.

(Keynes 1972: 90–2)

One can only hope that before the next great depression, the policy implications of modern money are understood.

Notes

1 The terminology 'homogenous globule of desire' comes from one of the most famous statements in the history of economic thought:

> The hedonistic conception of man is that of a lightning calculator of pleasure and pains, who oscillates like a homogenous globule of desire of happiness under the impulse of stimuli that shift him about the area but leave him intact . . . Self-imposed in elemental space, he spins symmetrically about his own spiritual axis until the parallelogram of forces bears down upon him, whereupon he follows the line of the resultant. When the force of the impact is spent, he comes to rest, a self-contained globule of desire as before.
>
> (Veblen 1919: 73–4)

According to Paul Samuelson:

> Inconvenient as barter obviously is, it represents a great step forward from a state of self-sufficiency in which every man had to be a jack-of-all-trades and master of none. . . . If we were to construct history along hypothetical, logical lines, we should naturally follow the age of barter by the age of commodity money. Historically, a great variety of commodities has served at one time or another as a medium of exchange: . . . tobacco, leather and hides, furs, olive oil, beer or spirits, slaves or wives . . . huge rocks and landmarks, and cigarette butts. The age of commodity money gives way to the age of paper money. . . . Finally, along with the age of paper money, there is the age of bank money, or bank checking deposits.
>
> (Samuelson 1973: 274–6)

2 See, for example, Selgin and White (1987) for an account of free banking.
3 See Furness (1910).

4   The general object of these laws was simple, that of the provision of a tariff of compensations which in any circumstances their compilers liked to envisage would prevent resort to the bloodfeud and all the inconvenient social consequences that might flow therefrom. . . . The tariffs for damages were established in public assemblies, and the common standards were based on objects of some value which a householder might be expected to possess or which he could obtain from his kinsfolk. Since what is laid down consists of evaluations of injuries, not evaluations of commodities, the conceptual difficulty of devising a common measure for appraising unrelated objects is avoided.

(Grierson 1977: 19–21)

5 M. Hudson, 'How the Debt Overhead led to Fiscal Crises in Antiquity: from Babylonia to Leviticus, Financial Tensions Between Tax Collectors and Creditors', lecture given at the Jerome Levy Economics Institute, March 1998.

6 See Innes (1913) and Heinsohn and Steiger (1983).
7 See McIntosh (1988: 557).
8 The clearing houses of old were the great periodical fairs, whither went merchants great and small, bringing with them their tallies, to settle their mutual debts and credits. . . . At some fairs no other business was done except the settlement of debts and credits. . . . Little by little as governments developed their postal systems and powerful banking corporations grew up, the value of fairs as clearing houses dwindled.

(Innes 1913: 396–7)

9 See, for example, Cook (1958: 257–62).
10 See MacDonald (1916: 29–35).
11 See Knapp (1924).
12 See Crawford (1970: 46) and Cook (1958).
13 '[T]he general idea that the kings wilfully debased their coinage in the sense of reducing their weight and fineness is without foundation' (Innes1913: 386).
14 Smith goes on to give the example of banks in Scotland which adopted an 'optional clause' which allowed them the option of withholding redemption for six months after presentation (in which case they paid interest for the period). These notes typically suffered a discount of 4 per cent relative to coins in trade.
15 Note, again, that this is also why private coinages (for example, in Gaul) were accepted in private pay communities.
16 In 1913, Mitchell Innes presented a view quite similar to Minsky's:

Debts and credits are perpetually trying to get into touch with one another, so that they may be written off against each other, and it is the business of the banker to bring them together. . . . There is thus a constant circulation of debts and credits through the medium of the banker who brings them together and clears them as the debts fall due. This is the whole business of banking as it was three thousand years before Christ, and as it is today.

(Innes 1913: 402–3)

17 As the borrower spends the created money, a cheque drawn on the first bank is deposited with another.
18 This has been recently recognized by Goodhart, who argued, 'The use of such state-issued fiat currency was supported by several factors. First the state levies taxes and can insist that these be paid in state-issued money. This ensures that such fiat currency will have some value' (Goodhart 1989: 36). Similarly, James Tobin argues, 'By its willingness to accept a designated asset in settlement of taxes and other obligations, the government makes that asset acceptable to any who have such obligations, and in turn to others who have obligations to them, and so on' (Tobin 1998: 27).
19 See Chapter 24 of Keynes's *General Theory* (1936).
20 See Wray (1998a, 1998b).
21 See especially Gordon (1997) and Wray (1997).

References

Boulding, K. (1950) *A Reconstruction of Economics*, New York: Wiley.
Cook, R. M. (1958) 'Speculation on the Origins of Coinage', *Historia* 7: 257–62.
Crawford, M. (1970) 'Money and Exchange in the Roman World', *Journal of Roman Studies* 60: 40–8.

Dalton, G. B. (1982) 'Barter', *Journal of Economic Issues* 16, 1: 181–90.
Davies, G. (1994) *A History of Money from Ancient Times to the Present Day*, Cardiff: University of Wales Press.
Furness, W. H. (1910) *The Island of Stone Money: Uap of the Carolines*, Philadelphia and London: J. B. Lippincott.
Goodhart, C. A. E. (1989) *Money, Information and Uncertainty*, Cambridge, Mass.: MIT Press.
Gordon, W. (1997) 'Job Assurance – the Job Guarantee Revisited', *Journal of Economic Issues* 31: 826–34.
Grierson, P. (1977) *The Origins of Money*, London: Athlone Press.
Harvey, P. (1989) *Securing the Right to Employment*, Princeton: Princeton University Press.
Heinsohn, G. and Steiger, O. (1983) 'Private Property, Debts and Interest, or: The Origin of Money and the Rise and Fall of Monetary Economies', *Studi Economici* 21: 3–56.
Hudson, M. (1998) 'How the Debt Overhead Led to Fiscal Crises in Antiquity: From Babylonia to Leviticus, Financial Tensions Between Tax Collectors and Creditors', lecture given at the Jerome Levy Economics Institute, March.
Innes, A. M. (1913) 'What is Money?' *Banking Law Journal* May: 377–408.
Keynes, J. M. (1964 [1936]) *The General Theory of Employment Interest and Money*, New York: Harcourt-Brace-Jovanovich.
—— (1972) *The Collected Writings of John Maynard Keynes*, vol. IX, *Essays in Persuasion*, ed. D. E. Moggridge, London: Macmillan.
—— (1976 [1930]) *A Treatise on Money*, vol. I, *The Pure Theory of Money*, New York: Harcourt-Brace-Jovanovich.
—— (1983) *The Collected Writings of John Maynard Keynes*, vol. XI, *Economic Articles and Correspondence, Academic*, ed. D. E. Moggridge, London: Macmillan.
Knapp, G. F. (1973 [1924]) *The State Theory of Money*, Clifton: Augustus M. Kelley.
Lerner, A. P. (1943) 'Functional Finance and the Federal Debt', *Social Research* 10: 38–51.
—— (1947) 'Money as a Creature of the State', *American Economic Review* 37, 2: 312–17.
Malinowski, B. (1921) 'The Primitive Economics of the Trobriand Islanders', *Economic Journal* 31: 1–16.
MacDonald, G. (1916) *The Evolution of Coinage*, New York: Putnam.
McIntosh, M. K. (1988) 'Money Lending on the Periphery of London, 1300–1600', *Albion* 20, 4: 557.
Minsky, H. P. (1986) *Stabilizing an Unstable Economy*, New Haven: Yale University Press.
Neale, W. C. (1976) *Monies in Societies*, San Francisco: Chandler and Sharp.
Polanyi, K. (1971) 'Aristotle Discovers the Economy', in K. Polanyi, C. Arensberg and H. Pearson (eds), *Trade and Market in the Early Empires*, Chicago: Regenery.
Redish, A. (1987) 'Coinage, Development of', in J. Eatwell, M. Milgate and P. Newman (eds) *The New Palgrave: Money*, New York: Norton.
Samuelson, P. (1973) *Economics*, ninth edition, New York: McGraw-Hill.
Selgin, G. and White, L. H (1987) 'The Evolution of a Free Banking System' *Economic Inquiry* 25: 439–58.
Smith, A. (1937 [1776]) *An Inquiry into the Nature and Causes of the Wealth of Nations*, New York: Modern Library.
Tobin, J. (1998) *Money, Credit, and Capital*, Boston: Irwin McGraw-Hill.

Veblen, T. (1919) *The Place of Science in Modern Civilization*, New York: B.W. Huebsch.

Wray, L. R. (1990) *Money and Credit in Capitalist Economies: The Endogenous Money Approach*, Aldershot, Edward Elgar.

—— (1997) 'Government as Employer of Last Resort: Full Employment without Inflation', Jerome Levy Economics Institute, Working Paper no. 213, December.

—— (1998a) 'Money and Taxes: The Chartalist Approach', Jerome Levy Economics Institute, Working Paper no. 222, January.

—— (1998b) *Understanding Modern Money: The Key to Full Employment and Price Stability*, Cheltenham: Edward Elgar.

4 The property theory of interest and money

Gunnar Heinsohn and Otto Steiger

> Money is a paradoxical entity. Its origin is, like that of language, an enigma in the human history.
>
> (Iwai 1981: 113)

> There is such a chaos in the theories of the rate of interest that one has to lump them into several groups to come close to the main theories. . . . It is a characteristic of the theory of the rate of interest that the question why there is a rate of interest at all already occupies a large space.
>
> (Lutz 1967: 9, 1980: 541)

Possession and property: physical use of resources in mere production systems versus the business operations of an economy

Our property theory of interest and money intends to answer what we regard as economic theory's core question: what is the loss which has to be compensated by interest? We completely differ from the answers given so far. We accept neither a temporary loss of goods nor a temporary loss of money as the cause of interest. When money – as an anonymized title to property – is created in a credit contract, the interest causing loss is the loss of an immaterial yield which we have called the *property premium* (Heinsohn and Steiger 1996). In the money-creating and the money-forwarding credit contract, property has to be encumbered. Through this collateralization, the freedom of property is temporarily blocked, that is, the property premium is given up.

A property premium arises automatically whenever property titles are added to possessional titles to resources and goods. This is usually done after revolutions against feudal types of society or by simply applying the laws of property to newly-won or conquered territories which up to then had known only possessional rights as tribal or feudal societies. It is a legal act, not previous savings or accumulation of goods, which allows a high level of *per capita* consumption which makes the difference between mere possessional systems of production and a genuine economy which is always property driven, or directed by business operations. Correspondingly, an economy, not production as such, disappears when property is abolished.

An economic theory deserving the name is still lacking because economists have never caught up with scholars of law who, since the times of Ancient Rome, have made great efforts to differentiate between possession and property. Economists do not bother about this distinction because they focus on an eternal *homo oeconomicus,* and therefore, assume that business operations are inherent in all types of human society.

Mankind, however, knows three distinctive systems of material reproduction of which only one is occupied with business operations. Reproduction means the production, distribution, consumption and occasionally the accumulation of goods necessary for survival. These three types are:

- The *customary* or *tribal* society. It regulates production, distribution and consumption for its unfree members collectively by reciprocity, that is, by transactions which are putatively altruistic. There are no independent institutions of law where the collective's member can file a suit to enforce the rules of reciprocity.
- The *command* or *feudal* society. It is regulated by coercive redistribution. Production, distribution, consumption and accumulation are organized by ruling castes or aristocracies. They extract planned levies from a class of unfree serfs. In case of need, these classes are entitled to rations, portions from central storages which they have to fill in advance. The rations, though belonging to an intertemporal set of activity, must not be confused with credit in kind. They do not generate interest, money, or collateral. In state socialism, the nobility is replaced by a proletarian *avant-garde* which maintains the loyalty of unfree 'peasants and workers' by guaranteeing them a permanent share of the planned production. It goes without saying that there are no independent institutions of law where members of a command society can file a suit to execute their shares.
- The *property*-based society as a system of free individuals abolishes most of the traditional rules of reciprocity and command. It directs production, distribution, consumption and accumulation by interest and money and special contracts. Independent courts of law enforce the fulfilment of these contracts.

The difference between customary and command societies on the one hand, and the property-based society on the other, is a principal and not a gradual one. Tribal or aboriginal, feudal and socialist, societies may run undisturbed for very long periods of time. In any event, they do not entail property but only *possession*.[1] Possessional rights are restricted to the physical use of resources. The possession-based societies, therefore, are condemned to a mere control of resources. This control is executed through orders that cover the transformation of resources into goods – including storage and, sometimes, accumulation – and their distribution.

In the possession-based societies the phenomena of money, collateral and interest are notoriously absent. Malinowski summarized centuries of research on tribal societies as follows: 'There is no regular market, hence no prices, hence no mechanism of exchange, hence no room for currency – still less for money' (Malinowski 1935: 45). The reflux of loaned goods is neither guaranteed nor secured by collateral. Nothing akin to interest is offered to generate the type of reciprocal assistance common within tribes. Therefore, even cattle-herding nomads do not focus on the offspring of the animals lent to fellow tribesmen 'but were concerned with the loaned [cattle-] capital only' (Laum 1965: 60). Barter exchange as the commonly assumed precondition of money could never be verified:

> Barter, in the strict sense of moneyless exchange, has never been a quantitatively important or dominant model of transaction in any past or present economic system about which we had hard information. . . . Moneyless market exchange was not an evolutionary stage . . . preceding the arrival of monetary means of market exchange.
> (Dalton 1982: 185–8)

Therefore in 1984 it was proposed to replace the barter paradigm of money by a private property paradigm of money (Heinsohn 1984: 120).

Feudal societies were no less intensively explored for money, interest and credit arrangements than tribal ones, but with the same disappointing results. Mycenaean feudalism, which was famous for its frequent use of precious metals, had no idea of the monetary operations which became so 'mighty a machine' in the succeeding property-based Greek city states:

> What we see of the economic system is the activity of the palace, which exacts produce and no doubt much else from the king's subjects, and doles out rations and materials when something has to be done, with exact notes of what has been received or issued and what should have been . . . *There is no suggestion of money, or of any standard by which values might be compared, items just being counted, weighed, or measured as they stand.*
> (Andrewes 1967: 29, emphasis added)

In the most developed command society – that of late state socialism – economic researchers nursed some hope because terms like money and interest, credit and debt were used. However, these notions merely applied to instruments of the commanding authority. They had nothing to do with corresponding notions in a property-based economy. At the best, they were poorly-understood imitations. What were called the 'state bank' and 'commercial banks' formed a monobank system where the latter were branches of the former. The state bank did not hold assets by which it could regulate or even manage the issuing of its banknotes. Its assets were untradeable liabilities of public households, and of administrative and production units. These 'titles' did not represent claims to anything. The state bank's 'credit' only gave access to those real goods whose production was intended in the plan of the central authority. Parallel to the production of goods, state means of payment were printed and distributed according to the plan in the form of notes of the monobank as well as demand deposits at its branches. These notes and deposits were called money, but they were simply anonymized ration cards and interest and collateral played no essential role in their credit assignment. These cards did not give an absolute command over resources but functioned as an entitlement to obtain the centrally-planned and produced goods. Thus, these cards had nothing whatsoever to do with anonymized titles to property that are the money of property-based societies.

Collateral was an alien concept. All forms of property, but not individual or collective possessions, were prohibited. The socialist 'firm', therefore, could be neither bought nor sold, nor could it obtain credit by pledging its possessions. Inter-enterprise credit was prohibited, and neither a money nor a capital market could emerge. The credit system was used by the central authority for the redistribution of cash surpluses showing up at the producers. The role of what was called 'interest' was as an instrument of control or incentive to amortize credit and, therefore, negligible. Naturally in such a system the 'debtor' did not face the danger of bankruptcy if he or she was unable to meet dues. At the worst, a penal 'interest' had to be paid, thereby reducing the amount reserved as extra pay to directors and workers.

It goes without saying that possession does not disappear in the property-based society. Property titles are only added to possessional rights. Every property title has a possessional side, but not every possessional title has a property side. The possessional right determines who may *physically* use which resource or good in what manner, at what time and place, to what extent and by exclusion of whom. The property title has nothing to do with these rights of physical use. Its right is the right to burden with a legal claim. This claim encompasses the *non-physical* uses of encumbering the property for backing money and collateralizing credit, enforcing and selling.

Land is a good example to illustrate the difference between the use of a possession title and the activation of a property title. In all three societal types – customary, command and property-based – fields are possessionally tilled to yield a physical return. Business operations, however, are not performed with the soil, but with the fence around the field. The fence, of course, does not stand for the posts and wiring of the enclosure, which may be utilized in all three types of society to demarcate the rights to possessional uses. In our picture the fence stands for the property title to the field. Thus, a field can be possessionally or physically harvested and non-physically encumbered at the same time. Only the latter operation belongs to a truly economic realm of business.

However, possessional use within a property-based society differs dramatically from merely possession-based societies because it may have to serve the claims burdenable on the property titles. Whereas in mere possession-based societies, possessed resources are only controlled, in property-based societies they are put to an *economic* use. 'Economic' means more than efficiency or optimality. In each societal structure human beings and many animal species, may try to handle resources with as little waste as possible or, to use mainstream's definition of economics, to create an optimal relation between ends and scarce means of alternative uses. To translate such universal propensities of living creatures into axioms of an eternal *homo oeconomicus* is the unsolvable task of economic theory. A genuine economy does not show the advantage-oriented behaviour of an unfettered *homo oeconomicus,* but is the offspring of the institution of property which forces every human being – altruistic or selfish – to obey its laws.

The failure of economists to comprehend the institution of property

There is no economic theory deserving the name because economists have never come to terms with property. This judgement may sound exaggerated but has recently been supported by one of the most eminent scholars of the theory of property rights or the new institutional economics, Harold Demsetz: 'Although our theoretical ideas about capitalism have improved as mainstream economics developed, they have never matured into a theory of capitalism' (Demsetz 1998: 146).

Whereas we blame a complete negligence of the institution of property, institutional economics complains that property rights have received too little attention from both classical and neoclassical economists:

> What has mainstream economics been doing for 200 years if it has not been studying capitalism? From Adam Smith and David Ricardo to Alfred Marshall and Léon Walras, economists directed their efforts toward understanding micro and macro operations of the price system. The property rights system, however, is only implicitly involved in the theory that emerged. This theory . . . takes the property rights foundation of capitalism for granted. It does not investigate the role of property rights arrangements.
> (Demsetz 1998: 144)

Let us take a closer look at Demsetz's question about what economists have done with capitalism in the last two centuries. We can divide them into three major schools of economic thought: classical economics, neoclassical economics and Keynesianism.[2] Our approach and the three major schools of economics have to analyse one and the same economic system. They all explicitly concede the existence of money and interest, and the necessity to explain these fundamentals. Moreover, they all make use of the term 'property'. Our analysis will show, however, that the three schools have failed really to comprehend the formative economic role of property. They resemble a fish which does not know of water before it is pulled out of it. None of them can grasp property's unique capacity to be *encumbered* and to serve as *collateral*, yet it is this very capacity that alone creates interest and money.

Classical economics

The focus of classical economics is private property. There is hardly any notion in classical texts that is stressed more powerfully than this blessing or curse of capitalism. Adam Smith could not imagine a society even in its 'early and rude state', like a tribal 'nation of hunters' (Smith 1776: 47), without the existence of property. In an advanced state of society property, according to Smith, only shifts from 'common property' to individual or 'private property', with profit and rent as its specific characteristics and added as new sources of income to wages:

> As soon as stock has accumulated in the hands of particular persons, some of them will naturally employ it in setting to work industrious people, whom they will supply with materials and subsistence, in order to make a profit by the sale of their work. . . . As soon as the land of any country has all become *private property*, the landlords, like all other men, love to reap where they never sowed and demand a rent even for its natural produce.
>
> (Smith 1776: 48–9, emphasis added)

Classical economists were convinced that property is defined as the physical use of goods which has existed throughout history: goods, however, which are mere possessions. Classical economics does not deliver an economic theory but a sociological concept of power over goods and resources. Economic categories certainly present in the real world – especially private property, profit and rent – are grafted on to this concept. In the early and rude state, all members of the society rule the resources. In the advanced state, it is only the class of private proprietors, Karl Marx's capitalists, that has power over resources. This exclusivity enables capitalists and landlords to employ labourers and tenants for the extraction of profit and rent as well as the continuation of their position. Therefore, capitalism as a system of power becomes the label of the economic system of the classical school.

Classical economists analyse the economy of the real world as a *barter* or *real exchange* economy. They see it at work in the state of 'common property'. The barter economy originates in a supposed inherent tendency of human beings to gain mutual advantages by exchanging their goods and resources. It brings about the division of labour as a tremendous productive force only limited by the extent of the market. The market, however, plays only a subordinate role in the reproduction of capital, that is the capitalists' power over resources.

Money is identified with coins minted out of an existing stock of bullion, that is, of already produced commodities. Thus, money is neither created in a credit contract nor extinguished after repayment. Though some classical economists (most prominently Ricardo) know that money is loaned only against good securities and interest, the credit creation of banknotes or paper money is not regarded as having any impact on the economic process. The latter is solely determined by the existing stock of capital goods. Furthermore, it is not demanded that the quantity of paper money has to be redeemable in bullion: the only requirement is that it is regulated in accordance with the value of the bullion so that neither inflation nor deflation can arise. Paper money is regarded as a tool to mobilize more easily the existing quantity of bullion – seen as a part of circulating capital – and to reduce the transaction costs of carrying bullion around. Money is seen as a mere facilitator of barter, a special good to solve the problem of double coincidence of wants. As unit of account, it is perceived as a universal instrument and measure of commerce.

Moreover, the rate of interest is not seen as an independent force driving the economy. It only appears in the advanced stage of private property with profit and rent as its new sources of income and is, therefore, disconnected from money as a means of exchange which already exists at the stage of common property. Interest, therefore, is regarded as a derivative revenue from profit, which is an offspring of the power to use capital in private exclusivity. Capitalist lords who must borrow money for the use of capital, which gives them the opportunity of making profit, have to compensate the lenders – the 'moneyed class' (Ricardo 1817: 89) – by paying interest because the latter suffer the loss of making profit themselves.

Classical economics knew that this borrowing was done in their time by discounting real bills. These bills, however, are not analysed as titles to the property of their endorsers but as possessional titles to the already-produced goods on the exchange of which the bills are issued. This idea brought about the *real bills doctrine* according to which the quantity of banknotes could never exceed the value of produced goods. Collateral is not recognized as a title to non-physical property which could be employed for obtaining credit, while at the same time its possessional, or physical, side continues to be used by the debtor.

Neoclassical economics

Neoclassical theory does not look any deeper into the distinction of property from possession than its predecessor. It is convinced that a property title must be analysed as a possessional right which is the empowerment to the physical use of resources and goods. This is exemplified by one of the leading early neoclassical economists, Irving Fisher:

> But what is meant by *owning* wealth? We answer: to have the *right to use it*. To have a right is called *property* or, more explicitly, a *property right*. . . . The right of a person to the uses of an article of wealth may be defined as his liberty, under the sanction of law and society, to enjoy the *services* of that article.
>
> (Fisher 1906: 18–20, emphasis added)

Modern general equilibrium theory does not differ from Fisher's view. This may be exemplified by Gérard Debreu who defines 'private ownership economies' as 'economies where the consumers *own the resources* and control the producers' (Debreu 1959: 78). In his phrase 'consumers own the resources' the term 'own' simply means 'possess', since in Debreu's model the consumers' selling of resources to the producers entitles the latter to enjoy the use of the resources.

The identification of property with a right physically to use a good also characterizes the neoclassical school of new institutional economics, most prominently represented – besides Demsetz – by Armen Alchian: 'A *property* right to a good is a right to select among its, and only its, feasible *physical uses* or conditions' (Alchian 1992: 223, emphasis added). Like the classical economists, Alchian and Demsetz draw a dividing line between communal or state property rights on the one hand and individual or private property rights on the other. In distinction from the former, the latter 'right has the consequent income and wealth assigned to a specified person, who can alienate the right to others in exchange for at least similar *rights* to other *goods*' (Alchian 1992: 223, emphasis added, see also Demsetz 1998: 154).

Demsetz runs the same course in defining property rights by focusing on the 'rights of use' of resources (Demsetz 1998: 151). Yet, he openly admits the difficulty of identifying the very core of property rights: 'They designate the owner as that person or group, as compared to others, that exercises the most important subset of exclusive, alienable, and presumptive rights. There is no easy way to generalize "important subset"' (Demsetz 1998: 146). Stuck on the track of possession, what he desperately looks for as the general quality of property is constituted by the right of the proprietor to encumber it for backing the issue of money and to collateralize it for obtaining credit. To the best of our knowledge, neither Demsetz nor any other member of the new institutional school ever comes close to encumbrance and collateral as the all-important facets of property that make the difference between a mere system of production and a genuine economy. They have not so far correctly baptized their approach as the possessional rights school.

One would expect that, by explicitly looking at the topic of possession, a scholar would finally understand its difference from property, and would no longer lump possessional rights under the term property. The *New Palgrave Dictionary of Economics and the Law* (Epstein 1998) excels in devoting an entire entry to possession, to our knowledge for the first time in an economics text. Where does it get us? Is it understood that a mere possessional right excludes encumbrance and collateralization? This possibility is not even mentioned. On the contrary, possession is defined 'as the source of all property rights' (ibid.: 62). This statement confirms our view that the new institutional school merely deals with the aspect of possession when it uses the term property: 'People own property so that they may possess it, just as they possess it, so that they may use it' (ibid.: 68). The possibility of a separation between property and possession is seen only when the protection of possession is analysed in the transfer of possession from one owner to another. However, the fundamental economic difference between a title to property that can be encumbered and a possessional right to physical use never comes to mind.

Consequently, the institutional school never makes the distinction between societies which only have individual and collective possession and societies that have individual and collective property titles in addition to individual and collective possession. Property, therefore, is also seen at work in tribal, feudal and socialist societies where only the relations between private and common rights to use resources, that is, only possessional rights, are really analysed though constantly called property rights (Bailey 1998, Libecap 1998, Pistor 1998).

The confusion of property with possession, the physical use of goods, also dominates neoclassical economic historians who try to identify the causes of growth. Using the ideas of the new institutional economics, they believe that economic growth 'will occur if property rights make it worthwhile to undertake socially productive activity' (North and Thomas 1973: 8). Again, a difference is made between common and private property but not between possession and property. The authors blame a 'common-property *resource*' for stagnation as well as decline because:

> each *user* has an incentive to exploit the *resource* without regard to *other users*, which results in continual deterioration of the resource. . . . Since no one owns the resource there is no incentive to conserve the resource or to improve efficiency in its *use*.
> (North and Thomas 1973: 19, emphasis added)

This, they assume, can only be achieved by changing property rights from common use to individual or private use.

Such a view does injustice to both possession-based societies and property-based societies. The connection between a lack of efficiency and 'no one owns' is without foundation because there is always a possessor – individual or collective – in possession-based societies. Efficiency, therefore, cannot be due to the superiority of individual over common activity. The confusion of property with possession in neoclassical theory is most visible in the economic concept of an individual who optimizes given and, therefore, scarce initial endowments of goods and resources. This individual however is not a proprietor but only a possessor. Nevertheless, via the concept of optimizing the physical use of goods, neoclassical theory advances beyond the classical non-economic concept of power over resources and tries to live up to the demands of a genuine economic theory. However, the confusion of property with possession does not allow an explanation of what forces an individual to economize his resources other than by the *ad hoc* hypothesis of given endowments. Since the scarcity of goods is a characteristic of every society without enabling every society to develop an economic system, it cannot be an endowment *per se* by which an individual advances from an efficient use of his power over resources to their economizing. The latter must be due to something entirely different from the possessional use of goods.

Like their classical predecessors, neoclassical economists analyse the economic system as a barter or real-exchange economy. Unlike classical economists, however, they focus on the market as the strategic centre where all individual optimization decisions are realized. Therefore, they are not interested in the different stages of power over resources but in the *market system*, and they label the economy a *market economy*.

Neoclassical money – like classical money – is simply a special good. Today it is no longer seen as a bullion commodity, a produced stock, but as intrinsically worthless 'outside' money. It forms a stock of fiat money, exogenous to the economic process and controlled by the open market operations of the monetary authority. It is assumed that these operations mainly consist in buying and selling state debt titles, which are also seen as something exogenous to the economy.

As in classical economics, money is not supposed to play an independent active role, although it may disturb the economy by causing inflation or deflation when not kept from increasing and decreasing appreciably. Therefore, the central bank has to guarantee the postulated neutrality of money by controlling the money supply in accordance with the needs in the market for goods. Thus, money is seen merely as an instrument to reduce the transaction costs of the underlying barter exchanges. As an intrinsically worthless standard good or *numéraire*, it merely facilitates the determination of the relative prices of all other goods. In the 'best developed model' of the neoclassical real-exchange economy, 'the Arrow-Debreu version of an Walrasian general equilibrium . . . in which all conceivable contingent future contracts are possible'(Hahn 1982: 1), an 'intrinsically worthless money' is neither needed nor wanted. Since, however, the existence of such money cannot be doubted by anyone, it poses the 'most serious challenge' (ibid.) to neoclassical theorists. Milton Friedman, the most prominent neoclassical monetary theorist, explicitly fears this money as 'unexplored terrain' (Friedman 1992: 262).

What is the loss to be compensated by interest in neoclassical theory? As with classical theory, interest is not acknowledged as a monetary phenomenon. Yet, it is not seen as a compensation for the loss of profit of the 'moneyed class'. In neoclassical time preference theory, interest is the compensation for the loss a consumer suffers by sacrificing consumption of his income goods today which he values higher than their future consumption. The consumer demands a premium for this saving which allows the enjoyment of a larger consumption tomorrow. To realize the premium the consumer has to find a producer, who in a credit contract lends the saved present goods – merely carrying a money envelope – against the pledge of a rate of interest. Interest can only be paid when the producer diverts the savers' goods to the production of future consumable goods, that is, when he or she adds new real capital to existing resources with a resultant net gain in the ability to produce future consumables. The ratio of this net gain to the new capital that generated it, is regarded as the yield on, or the marginal product of, capital. In equilibrium, this neoclassical profit is just equal to the rate at which the saver abstains. Therefore, thrift and productivity are the forces which determine the neoclassical rate of interest. In neoclassical economics, however, these forces are axiomatic preconditions without which its theory of the rate of interest is unhinged. A genuine economic theory cannot simply postulate these forces but has to lay open their cause.

In open contradiction to existing credit contracts in which creditors retain their goods, lending current resources in neoclassical theory literally means a temporary transfer of their physical use and entails, therefore, a material loss. Such a loss of goods, however, is never part of debt contracts in property-based societies. As we have seen, it would rather be typical in custom and command systems where, however, nobody is entitled to interest.

Collateral, which obviously plays a decisive role in existing debt contracts, has only recently been recognized by neoclassical authors (Kanatas 1992). With few exceptions, until the 1980s the credit market was analysed as a market for goods. In other words the price on the credit market, the rate of interest, was determined solely by the demand for and supply of credit. In the market for goods, an excess demand was met in the short term by an increase of prices, and in the long term by a rise of supply induced by the short-term rise in prices, leading to a reduction in prices. In the credit market, however, an increase in demand met by a rise in its price – the rate of interest – would lead to the problem that interest is only a *promised* price. The creditor other than the supplier of goods has to take into account that the ability of the debtor is directly correlated to the levels of the rate of interest promised. In the worst case, the level of interest settled upon may push the debtor to bankruptcy and pull the creditor in the same direction.

To avoid this risk, it is assumed that the lender circumvents market rules which would require an increase of the rate of interest. The doctrine postulates that this circumvention is carried out by the application of the peculiar technique of 'credit rationing' (Jaffee and Stiglitz 1990). It requires a ranking of debtors according to their creditworthiness. The criterion for this worthiness is provided by information on the assets potential debtors can pledge as collateral. Since such a procedure is alien to market principles, it leaves neoclassical economists uneasy. There is no systematic place for it in their theory of exchange, because the physical use of collateral is not exchanged but stays with the debtor. Instead of reconsidering their entire theory in face of such a scandalous violation of its main exchange principle, neoclassical economists sheepishly occupy themselves with what the debtor could do with his collateral. It is, therefore, only seen as being 'subject to borrower manipulation' or diminishing the borrower's incentive to maintain the value of his pledged assets which forces lenders to 'costly monitoring' (Kanatas 1992: 382). Similarly, a secured credit is explained 'as a salutary instrument' of the creditor to enforce a 'debtor's bond against waste' (Adler 1998: 405).

All that can be seen from neoclassical studies concerning collateral is that they are unclear, and that they result in conflicting signals about the creditworthiness of borrowers. Some 'predict a positive association between observable risk (of opportunistic behaviour by borrowers) and the amount of collateral required', while others predict 'a negative relation between the necessary collateral and the borrower's unobservable risk of default'. In view of these ambiguous results of neoclassical collateral models, there is 'little definitive evidence on the relative economic importance of the ... explanations regarding collateral' (Kanatas 1992: 382). Thus, neoclassical authors at best can see that the possession of the collateral remains with the debtor and is therefore prone to manipulation. They have no idea, however, that the debtor suffers a peculiar – though immaterial – loss by temporarily activating his right to encumbrance when he collateralizes his property title.

Keynesianism

Of the different schools of Keynesianism, only the German school of Monetary Keynesianism has seriously tried to overcome the barter-exchange foundations of both classical and neoclassical theory. It postulates that a command over goods and resources presupposes the command over *money*. Therefore, it focuses on the *money system* and labels the economic system not a market but a *monetary economy* (Riese 1995). Monetary Keynesians blame neoclassical theory's inability to advance beyond a theory of possession on the latter's adherence to barter-exchange. They make great efforts to separate possession from property. By identifying every creditor with a proprietor and every debtor with a possessor, however, they fail to see that in a credit contract both creditor and debtor are proprietors as well as possessors. In the credit contract, they only activate their property titles whereas their possesional titles are not touched.

Monetary Keynesianism's strength lies in the insight of money as not being a good which facilitates exchanges or which can be employed as a store of value but as something that can do what goods can never do, ultimately settle creditor–debtor contracts. Money, therefore, is merely seen as a means of payment, and the central bank as the sole producer of money in its role as lender of last resort has to guarantee commercial banks' ability to make payments

Though Monetary Keynesianism also sees money as something provided exogenously to the economy, it makes a point that it is always created in an interest-bearing credit contract which has to be carefully distinguished from a contract between a commercial bank and a non-bank. While the latter is characterized by the creditor's risk to lose the money loaned, the former does not entail this risk because the central bank itself produces the money it loans. Therefore, other than the commercial bank, the central bank does not require collateral from its debtors to secure its loan.

On the question of the loss for which interest is paid, monetary Keynesianism answers in the negative for the central bank's rate of interest. There is no loss. Central bank money is created 'out of nothing' (Riese 1995: 60). Central bank credit contracts, thus, differ from commercial bank contracts not only in the sphere of collateral but also in the realm of interest. It is postulated that the central bank rate of interest serves as a clever tool to keep the money created *ex nihilo* scarce in relation to existing resources, so that it makes money attractive enough for economic individuals to give goods in return for it. The second type of interest arises in the loan contract of a commercial bank or any other holder of money because money's *liquidity premium* – the ability finally to settle contracts – is lost. This theory of the rate of interest presupposes the existence of money kept scarce by another rate of interest. Monetary Keynesians, therefore, stagger between two rates of interest of which the explanation of one presupposes the unexplained existence of another.

As a title secured by property , and with all due right without intrinsical value, money can appear to be created *ex nihilo* only from the viewpoint of possession, because no use of goods is transferred from a creditor to a debtor. However, money is *never* created *ex nihilo* from the viewpoint of property, which must always exist *before* money can come into existence. Starting with property, one can eventually complete Joseph Schumpeter's unfinished critique of the real bills doctrine. As early as 1926, he had observed that money wanted by an entrepreneur in a credit contract:

> is not based upon goods already produced ... [and, therefore] the creation of *new* purchasing power [is] created *out of nothing* – out of nothing even if the credit contract by which the new purchasing power is created is supported by [real] securities.
> (Schumpeter 1926: 109–73, original emphasis)

The observation that the creation of money is not limited by the value of already-produced goods is correct. Schumpeter fails, however, because he identifies 'real securities' with the possessional, not the property side of pledged collateral. Therefore, he has to downplay its role as only supportive.

While Schumpeter at least takes notice of securities in the creation of money, Monetary Keynesians never mention them at all except to stress that money is exogenous to the economic process. However, one prominent Keynesian has noticed – albeit in a footnote – that not only the rate of interest but also collateral must be taken into account when analysing credit operations:

> We now know that it is not enough to think of the rate of interest as a single link between the financial and industrial sectors of the economy; for that really implies that a borrower can borrow as much as he likes at the rate of interest charged, no attention being paid to the security offered.
>
> (Hicks 1980–1: 153)

Monetary Keynesians' axiom that money is created out of nothing leads to a strange reading of the asset side of the central bank's balance sheet. They suppose that it does not contain securities but only the information that all central bank money is created in a credit contract. In other words, the asset side is merely a list of outstanding claims against commercial banks who have pledged nothing but to refund and pay interest.

This analysis, however, can barely disguise the fact that their money is simply a given, in very much the same way as the endowment of goods is a given in neoclassical theory. A difference in method exists only insofar as the latter audaciously presupposes the scarcity of the endowments, thereby making them valuable, while the former links scarcity and, thereby, value on money by desperately invoking a special rate of interest. How does the scarce money turn the economy into a monetary one?

In neoclassical economics, the consumer owns the resources and controls the producers, a process in which money is not essential. In monetary Keynesianism, the commercial banks – as the typical asset holders – possess assets and control the producers who need money to acquire resources. Neoclassical entrepreneurs need savers for investment while monetary Keynesian entrepreneurs can start without any saving whatsoever as long as banks are willing to loan them money.

How do the banks acquire assets? First, the banks receive scarce money from the central bank, which they then loan to producers in exchange for claims – the assets – to refund the money and pay interest. The commercial bank's credit contract is seen as something fundamentally different from the credit contract between the central bank and a commercial bank. While in the latter, only scarce money is produced to guarantee the commercial banks' ability to make payments, in the former, contract money is lost to a producer. This debtor needs this money because it provides the only means to obtain resources. By investing this money in production the debtor creates income, but only does so if it is possible to earn a rate of profit at least equal to the rate of interest demanded by the bank. Thus, it is the rate of interest which forces a rate of profit into the world by keeping investment in capital goods scarce. Since nobody can guarantee the fulfilment of the debtors' obligations, there is always the creditors' risk. Therefore, the creditors permanently have to choose between increasing their assets with the risk of losing wealth, and securing their assets, thereby abstaining from increasing their wealth. This means that asset holders decide the employment of resources.

Both neoclassical economists and Monetary Keynesians assume a dichotomy between the monetary sector and the real sector. In the former, consumers make the decision how much producers can invest on the market for goods, with money only playing a supportive role. In the latter, asset holders make the decision how much producers can invest: the goods' market is dominated by the asset market. Since the asset market presupposes the existence of scarce money, the latter rules the roost. What Monetary Keynesians cannot see, however, is that nobody can become a producer in a monetary economy without having collateralizable property titles, and no money can be created without these titles.

All three schools are hampered by the failure to comprehend the institution of property. They only know of possessional titles. Classical economics focuses on who possesses these titles. Neoclassical economics focuses on the scarcity of these titles. Monetary Keynesians focus on scarce money that keeps these titles scarce. The latter's merit lies in the concept of money as a non-good. They can, however, only identify a non-good with a 'nothing' by reducing the economic realm to just two entities: the existence of goods and the non-existence of goods. There is, however, a third entity, the property title, which exists in addition to the possessional title to goods.

The distinctive characteristics of the property-based economy

A title to property never comes naturally. It can only be brought about by a legal act, which by definition is intangible and does not alter the possessional state of resources. As soon as property is created – *ex nihilo* – it carries the unearned property premium. It must be stressed that this premium does not derive from the physical use of resources. Nor does it accrue from some pre-existing money stock.

Property titles do not replace possessional titles but are added to them. Possessional titles are also abstract, in the sense that they are records to be kept in verbal or written form. They always specify only the rights to the physical use of resources, whereas property titles contain different, non-physical uses, at the core of which are the rights to encumber and to sell.

Though the property titles are immaterial legal constructs, they bring about relations which dramatically alter the blood and command relations of the tribal or feudal societies which are transferred by the development of property ownership. In this process the obligations between fellow tribesmen are softened, and obedience to a class of lords is abolished. Property titles inhibit the traditional extra-economical covenants supplied by everybody's possessions, because the latter have to be ready to service the obligations incurred by activating the property titles: that is, they have to earn interest. Thus, property titles *definitively* transform the way in which the possessional titles to resources are exercised.

Property premium and the rate of interest

In property-based societies, as opposed to mere possession-based societies, there are two types of returns: first, the return of the physical use of the possessed goods and resources or, in other words, a material yield, and second, the return of the title to the property of the goods and resources which is an immaterial yield. The starting point for understanding an economic system is the latter return, which we have labelled the *property premium*.

What is the meaning of property premium? It is a non-physical yield of security which accrues from property as long as it is unencumbered and not economically activated. The premium allows proprietors to enter credit contracts, and is a measure of the potential of individuals to become creditors and debtors. It entails the capacity of a creditor to issue anonymized claims against his property, which we will call *money*. By creating such titles the creditor encumbers his property, or blocks his or her freedom over it for the time of the loan contract. The property premium also entails the capacity of a debtor to borrow these titles by pledging other claims – titles to his property – as *collateral*, thereby also encumbering property. In both cases, goods and resources are neither transferred nor touched. Creditors and debtors continue to acquire the returns of the material yield due to the possessional rights to their resources. Credit operations, thus, never interfere with the physical use of resources, but only deal with titles to property.

Property titles are always transferred in creditor–debtor contracts in which both creditor and debtor are proprietors. These contracts are divided into mere *credit contracts* and *sales contracts*. In the former, claims to property are transferred but not claims to possession, rights to the physical use of goods or resources. In the latter, claims to property are transferred *uno actu* with claims to possession. Sales contracts are always subordinated to the credit contracts whose fulfilment they serve.

The activation of property titles decisive for an economy arises out of their *temporary* transfer in credit contracts. In such a contract a creditor, who blocks his property but retains its possessional side and continues to use it, faces a debtor, who receives anonymized claims backed by creditor property. In turn, the debtor has to accept a specified claim of the creditor as liability to refund what has been received for a fixed term. To secure the specified claim, the debtor has to block the property as collateral and to accept the creditor's privilege to execute it in the case of default on his obligation. Even if no specified collateral is named, in the case of a so-called secure debtor, this does not mean that credit is given without good security. The very definition of a secure debtor is that the quality of assets belonging to him or her is beyond doubt: 'It is not ordinarily possible to examine in detail the entire assets of an applicant for a loan. . . . But the furnishing of security makes scrutiny of the general solvency of the borrower unnecessary' (Hawtrey 1932: 126). The more secure the debtor, the easier it is for the creditor to execute his claim in case of default. It goes without saying that in a contract with a secure debtor, the creditor never abstains from his right to enforce. The less secure a debtor, the more precisely the collateral has to be specified.

The debtor, like the creditor, retains the possessional side of the property and continues to use it. This underlines once more that backing and collaterizing never means a transfer of property, but only its temporary blocking on the side of both contract partners.

In activating property to back anonymized claims against it, the creditor forgoes the property premium accruing only from property that is unencumbered and free. This loss gives rise to an additional title, the claim to offset the creditor's loss of property premium. This claim comes in addition to the claim for refunding. In the credit contract, not only the creditor but also the debtor loses the property premium when the property is collateralized. In the explanation of the rate of interest, it has to be understood that losing the creditor's property premium does not give the creditor the debtor's property premium. Both property premiums are lost entirely during the credit contract.

The main question about the loss which has to be compensated by interest, therefore, has to be answered by the *loss of the creditor's property premium*. Interest, therefore, is not a compensation for a loss of goods of the creditor as in neoclassical theory. Furthermore, interest is not a compensation for the fact that the creditor is not allowed to touch the rights of the debtor to continue with the use of the possessional side of the collateral. The debtor, after all, puts up not goods as collateral, but property. In the ancient institution of *antichresis* in which the creditor is permitted to use the possessional side of the debtor's collateralized property, the yield going to the creditor only means that it is cleared with the demand for interest, not that the creditor abstains from interest. Finally, the rate of interest does not compensate the loss of liquidity premium, because the creditor only abstains from money which already has been created against a rate of interest and, therefore, cannot explain the rate of interest.

Collateral covers not only the debtor's inability to refund, but also the debtor's inability to pay interest. This does not mean, however, that the demand for collateral derives from the demand for interest. By putting up collateral the debtor cannot entice the creditor to abstain from interest.

Securities used as collateral in a credit contract are not riskless. There always exists a hierarchy of risk of property titles, with land carrying the least risk, through real capital goods and tradeable assets up to contracted income, which carries the most risk. Rank plays a role in the determination only of the *rate* of interest. Therefore, the *pure* rate of interest determined by the level of the property premium can be raised by a *risk premium*, which reflects the rank of the securities furnished. This premium must not be confused with the property premium.

Money of account and money proper

The creditor cannot help but establish his own standard at the very moment he issues the claims to property we call money in a credit contract. These claims must not be confused with the title which is the contract itself. The standard chosen must reckon the issued claims in abstract terms, that is, it must be a standard of measurement which Keynes (1930: 3) has termed '*money of account*'.[3] Money of account, therefore, means a standard reckoning money. It must not be confused with a standard of measurement which is derived from a standard physical good as *unit of account* or *numéraire* as in neoclassical theory.

In the neoclassical barter economy, the commodity chosen as unit of account is assigned the price 1 (one) and serves as the *nominal* anchor for the prices of all other goods. However, this anchor can only determine their *relative* prices The exchange ratios which express the relative prices, the quantities of the goods which are exchanged according to their marginal utility, are measured in the price 1. Thus, they are relative prices expressed only in a *numéraire* money.

In the property-based economy, however, a creditor does not need a commodity selected as a nominal anchor. Instead he issues anonymized claims to his property, but never to his possessional goods, denominated in his money of account. Credit contracts are not expressed in terms of setting a money of account, nor are they expressed in property titles receiving prices in this standard and thereby being nominal or *money* prices.

Because the debtor's collateral must have the same value as the claims to the creditor's property, the former's property titles together with the creditor's are the first to be denominated in the money of account. The *pricing* takes place in the market for these titles, the credit or asset market. The degree to which the creditor's titles are demanded for redemption and the debtor's titles are capable of fulfilling the obligations to refund and to pay interest, determine the levels of their money prices in a first round.

We have seen that credit contracts are not expressed in an existing standard good. Neither are they expressed in a standard arbitrarily set by an authority. The money of account stands for property titles which exist beyond and in addition to goods. Their encumbrance or non-encumbrance stimulates or limits economic activity. A money of account cannot arise independently of these titles. This has been sensed in Ralph Hawtrey's famous phrase that debt contracts are not defined in terms of money, but that 'money must be defined in terms of debt' (Hawtrey 1930: 545). In the same vein, Keynes has seen that 'a money of account comes into existence along with debts' (Keynes 1930: 3).

This insight is a blow to the real bills doctrine. An excessive supply of banknotes, according to this doctrine, can never occur as long as banks restrict themselves to lending totally secured by real bills, that is, goods already produced. The famous fallacy of this doctrine does not lie in its search for a limitation of the issue of banknotes. The true fallacy lies in the fact that the proponents of the doctrine do not understand that a limit set by existing goods stands in obvious contradiction to the money forwarded against the real bills of exchange which are used to produce these real goods. Thus, they do not understand what the banks really rely upon when they accept the real bills. They rely upon the property titles of the endorsers of the bills, against every one of which they can execute when the bill must be protested for want of payment. These property titles alone allow for credit contracts in which money can be issued before the production of goods, which therefore can never be the limit for money.

The trivial fact that property titles permanently undergo market valuations in no way disqualifies them as collateral. The undoubted problems which these oscillations create for the stability of the value of money cannot be abolished simply by eliminating collateral in the money creation process. There is no alternative to collateralized property. Rather, the possible devaluation of property titles is taken into account by the money-creating creditor by a careful selection of low-risk securities, and by securing riskier ones with appropriate 'capital' or reserves, the margin of assets over liabilities.

Keynes has been well aware that the money of account 'is the primary concept in the theory of money'. What we have termed an anonymized claim to property, Keynes calls 'money itself' or 'money proper' without, however, seeing the property titles behind it. Yet, he clearly recognizes that money proper 'derives its character from its relation to a money of account, since the debts and prices must first have been expressed in terms of the latter' (Keynes 1930: 3). This means that money proper cannot help but be emitted *uno actu* with the establishment of a loan contract.

In principle, every proprietor can as a creditor issue anonymized claims against his property. All these types of money proper take the form of transferable documents which are titles or claims redeemable on the issuer's property. As this money is only created in a collateralized loan contract, it is necessarily a means to discharge all forms of debt contracts, credit and sales contracts alike.

The credit creation of money results in two different documents, both denominated in terms of the money of account: first, the interest-bearing document secured by debtor's collateral, and second, the non-interest-bearing document backed by property of the creditor. The first document is the credit contract by which the second document is *uno actu* issued and loaned as money proper. Therefore, *money is created in a credit contract but is not itself a credit*. The banking schools' identification of money with credit could only arise because its adherents never distinguished between the essence of a credit title, which always is enforceable in terms of something other than itself, money proper, and the essence of money proper which, though created in a credit contract, is not enforceable in terms of something other than itself. In other words, credit is only a title to money, and money is not what is today erroneously termed 'credit money'. It goes without saying that such titles to money – most prominently demand deposits – can serve as substitutes for money proper in the clearing of mutual claims. However, they cannot serve finally to discharge a debt.

The interest-bearing document, or credit, is a specified title: it is a contract between a specified creditor and a specified debtor. It binds the named debtor to refund to the named creditor the money proper loaned, to pay interest, and to collateralize property for the creditor. As a tradeable asset, the identity of the creditor can change, while the bond and the name of the debtor is always the same.

The non-interest-bearing document – the money proper – is an anonymized title in so far as only the issuer of this document is named, but no debtor. This means that everybody who holds this claim does so without interest, because it is paid by the debtor named in the credit contract. The issuer of the money wants the named debtor to refund it, but is not interested in having the contract presented against the debtor otherwise. Though this document binds the creditor to redeem it in property, whether this possibility occurs depends on the quality of the property, as well as the quality of the collateral of the debtors. Therefore, the anonymized title – the money proper – represents only an *option* for the current holder to present it to the creditor-issuer and have it redeemed. The obligations fixed in the specified title – the credit – are not optional in character, but definite.

Although we use Keynes's concept of money proper, it must be kept in mind, that Keynes – in clear contradiction to our view – identifies money proper with 'state money'. In his analysis of the credit contract, he stresses that mere acknowledgements of debt can serve as substitutes for money proper in the settlement of transactions. When used in this way he calls them 'bank money' in the sense of credit money. Keynes is well aware that this money must not be confused with money proper. However, when bank money no longer represents a private but a public debt:

> The State may then use its chartalist prerogative to declare that the debt itself is an acceptable discharge of a liability. A particular kind of bank

money is then transformed into money proper – a species of money proper which we may call representative money. When, however, what was merely a debt has become money proper, it has changed its character and should no longer be reckoned as a debt, since it is the essence of a debt to be enforceable in terms of something other than itself.

(Keynes 1930: 6; see Stadermann and Steiger 1999b)

The concept of state money has led Keynes (1936, 200) to recommend 'government printing money' to finance public expenditure against unemployment (Stadermann and Steiger 1999b). The concept has also survived in mainstream monetary economics where money is defined as a public debt (Tobin 1963: 8). This view reflects periods in the history of monetary systems in which governments frequently circumvented the labourious process of pledging good securities for the issue of money, by allowing non-marketable state debt to be transformed into money proper. However, such an issue of money has more often than not disturbed, and sometimes even destroyed, money systems.

In the property-based economy of antiquity, private pre-bank issuers of money competed with each other, leaving the strongest as the first *credit* banks:

> The credit contract as a legal document, collateral and charging of a rate of interest most probably had been practised before the emergence of [state] temple banks. The private contracts are much older than the clerical ones. We assume that private individuals, merchants or proprietors have invented the debt contract.
>
> (Bogaert 1966: 66).

The credit banks founded by private individuals became *uno actu* banks of issue. In collateral-secured credit contracts, they issued money proper in the form of precious metal documents, coins, which were redeemable in their property. Once coin existed, governments of ancient city states tried to make a gain – seigniorage – by monopolizing the mints and paying their debts with state coins:

> The coin most probably was invented by private individuals for business operations. However, images like the Lydian lion, the bee of Ephesus, etc., indicate that the state soon took over the issue.
>
> (Chantraine 1979: 1448)

This decision of the state indeed brought a transformation of state debt into a species of money proper which was fundamentally different from the credit creation of money backed by private property. It became the earliest form of state money. The survival of this praxis even in the property-based economy of modern times may explain to some extent why monetary economists have not seen the fundamental difference between state money and money proper as a claim to property.

Furthermore, the use of precious metals in minting coins since antiquity has blurred the view of money as an anonymized claim to property and nurtured the idea of a *commodity money* as distinct from intrinsically worthless paper money. It was – and still is – believed that up to the abolishment of the gold standard, only gold or other precious material was genuine money, while banknotes only represented money because they could be redeemed in gold. Gold, however, was just part of the *property* against which banknotes were issued. To redeem the notes in gold, banks were even forced to transform other property into gold to satisfy the redeemer. The dominance and popularity of precious metal coins (contributing to the misunderstanding of money) was only owing to their being less prone to manipulation and forgery.

In modern times, as in antiquity, the credit bank also becomes the bank of issue and not the *deposit* bank The popular view that paper money was invented by goldsmiths who as primitive versions of the deposit bank, issued receipts on gold deposited with them, blurs the fact that money cannot deposited with a bank before it is created in a credit process.

Therefore we are not surprised to find that the first banks in modern times who issued money consisted of mergers of proprietors in the role of both creditors and debtors. In the beginning, the money created by these banks – their banknotes – was loaned only in interest-bearing contracts to shareholders of these banks:

> A number of men of property join together in a contract of banking. . . . For this purpose, they form a stock which may consist indifferently of any species of property. This fund is engaged to all the creditors of the company as a security for the notes they propose to issue. So soon as confidence is established with the public they grant credits or cash accounts, upon good security [to the non-bank public also].
>
> (Steuart 1767 II: 150)

The solvency of a bank is based on the property of its creditors or shareholders. The creditworthiness of a bank, however, grows with the soundness of its non-shareholder debtors. The evolution from a mere shareholder bank to a developed bank of issue has also been elaborated by Steuart:

> When paper is issued for no value received the security of such paper stands alone upon the original capital of the bank, whereas when it is issued for value received that value is a security on which it immediately stands, and the bank stock is, properly speaking, only subsidiary.
>
> (Steuart 1767 II: 151)

In Steuart's one-tiered system of private banks of issue, which create redeemable banknotes, it is clearly evident that both the property premia of creditor and debtor are lost and must therefore be compensated by a rate of interest. The non-bank – normally an entrepreneur-debtor – loses the property premium by collateralizing encumberable property to the bank of issue. The latter loses property premium by providing 'original capital', that is, reserves.

Why does one proprietor become a creditor who issues money to gain interest while another proprietor encumbers property and pays interest? Would it not be smarter for the latter to issue money against securities and thereby avoid the payment of interest? The proprietor who obtains money through a loan from someone else has the advantage that he or she cannot be forced to redeem money notes with property. Of course, it is necessary to collateralize the property, but the proprietor continues with the use of its possessional side as long as obligations to the creditor are fulfilled. Again, this advantage has been discovered by Steuart in his discussion of the issue of paper money:

> And for what does he [the debtor] pay that interest? Not that he has gratuitously received any value from the bank; because in his obligation he has given a full equivalent of the notes; but the obligation carries interest, and the notes carry none. Why? Because the one circulates like money, the other does not. For this *advantage*, therefore, of *circulation*, not for any additional value, does the landed man pay interest to the bank.
> (Steuart 1767 II: 131, emphasis added).

Irredeemable fiat money without security?

In today's two-tiered banking system, unlike the one-tiered system of private banks of issue with redeemable banknotes of Steuart's time, the commercial bank cannot produce the money proper for which the non-bank has to put up collateral. The commercial bank can, however, create documents or notes in which demands against the non-banks, their clients, are notified, and which it can make marketable as *good* securities like bonds. The central bank, as the only institution which is allowed to produce money, accepts these documents only if they are low risk: that is, secure assets. To get commercial bank paper acknowledged by the central bank it is, therefore, necessary – but in no way sufficient – for it to embody a collateralized demand of a commercial bank against a non-bank client. It is the latter who gives the document value by securing it with encumbered property.

To make an asset really acceptable for issuing money, the commercial bank which offers it to the central bank has to stand bail for its debtor by providing reserves. This means that the money proper issued by the central bank is secured twofold: by property of the non-bank client and by property of the commercial bank. In this collaterizing procedure, the commercial bank as debtor to the central bank loses property premium, which is not transferred to the latter but lost for the contract period. The commercial bank, of course, retains the possessional rights of its reserves, their yield. Like its non-bank debtor, therefore, the commercial bank does not lose any material returns. The property premia of both the commercial bank and the non-bank are lost, and therefore must be compensated by interest. This obligation falls on the commercial bank which pays it to its creditor, the central bank.

What happens in the central bank? It issues central banknotes against the market value of the assets which the commercial bank has offered. The central bank can realize this offer by buying these titles or accepting them as collateral. Other than the banknotes of private banks of issue and those of central banks under the gold standard, today's central banknotes are *non-redeemable*. The irredeemability creates the impression, not only for laymen and Monetary Keynesians but for most economists, that central banknotes are unsecured and therefore created 'out of nothing'.

The false impression of unsecured central bank money is partly owing to the essential role of the central bank to guarantee – as a lender of last resort – the commercial banks' ability to make payments. In other words, it guarantees always to provide them with the liquidity they demand. For this lender of last resort function, however, two rules must always be obeyed, as stated by the actual inventor of this function, Walter Bagehot:

> There are two rules. First. That these loans should only be made at a very high rate of interest. . . . Secondly. That at this rate these advances should be made on all good banking securities and as largely as the public ask for them.
>
> (Bagehot 1873: 187)

Bagehot was always aware that the function of lender of last resort must never be misunderstood in such a way that, at the counter of the central bank, commercial banks can unload their last and worst titles and obtain money without paying well for it. As Hawtrey observed:

> The essential duty of the central bank as a lender of last resort . . . cannot mean that it should lend to any bank that needs cash, regardless of the borrowing bank's behaviour or circumstances. Neither a commercial concern nor a public institution could undertake to supply cash to insolvent borrowers.
>
> (Hawtrey 1932: 126)

For this view Bagehot develops two reasons: first, the protection of the reserves of the central bank 'as far as possible', and second, the protection of the 'sound' people, the people 'who have good security to offer' (Bagehot 1873: 188). What is the aim of this double protection? By accepting 'bad bills or bad securities . . . the Bank will ultimately lose' (Bagehot 1873: 188), or as Hawtrey (1932: 126) put it: 'A commercial concern in particular cannot afford to take risks out of proportion to its own capital'. Furthermore, Bagehot emphasized that in this case the 'sound' people will restrict their offer of good securities if 'unsound' people can get money for bad securities (ibid.). Monetary economists have always overlooked that the readiness of the public to come forward with good securities to get money is not a given, and is prone to change (Stadermann 1994: 200).[4]

The twofold securing of the assets entering the balance sheet of the central bank is still not sufficient for the issue of genuine money proper. A third condition must first be fulfilled, as Bagehot's analysis shows. The central bank too has to secure the issue of its notes by providing reserves, thereby securing its notes threefold. The reserves are especially necessary when the central bank buys the assets offered outright or when it buys foreign currencies and gold. The elimination of the risk of falling values of these titles must be further supported by using the technique of repurchase agreements when buying assets, and by the valuation of foreign currencies and gold not at their actual market, but at their purchase price.

The provision of reserves by the central bank means only that their property side is employed, while the possessional rights to their yields remain untouched. Holding the reserves ready, that is, blocking them, brings about the loss of property premium, which has to be compensated by the rate of interest. This rate has to be paid by the commercial banks which receive central bank money. The banks and, as it circulates, all other receivers of this newly-created money in the form of central banknotes and deposits at the central bank, gain what Keynes and his followers have identified erroneously as the cause of the rate of interest: a liquidity premium. We can see now that the latter is a result and not the cause of the rate of interest. We can also see that an invoked central bank rate of interest is not necessary to understand why the central bank has to charge interest because of the loss of property premium it suffers when holding reserves. Of course, the non-bank public which demands the money already created does not fare any better than the commercial bank which has to pay interest to get it created in the first place.

Bagehot's good securities presented at the discount window of the central bank, are now considered secondary, because the bulk of central bank money is created against debt titles of the state. Since the former are analysed as a 'borrowed base' of the creation of central bank money and, therefore, as coming from inside the economy, while state debt apparently forms a 'non-borrowed base', the latter are 'viewed as being created from outside the economy' (Axilrod and Wallich 1992: 77). Accordingly, Bagehot's 'open discount window' has been replaced by an 'open open-market window'. Therefore, it can be argued, any public lack of readiness to offer good private securities can always be offset by the state's issue of debt titles.

It is true that a government bond can be the most secure and liquid title. This, however, is not due to a separation from property titles inside the economy. On the contrary, a state which issues debt titles issues property titles. They are underlaid with the entire property of its citizens. One could say that the state's most powerful property title lies in its right to enforce all property within the society by executing its tax sovereignty. However, state debt titles are only less risky than private ones as long as the base of propertied citizens inside the economy is reasonably capable of serving the debt incurred in their name by their government. If this capacity is in doubt, neither the non-bank public nor commercial banks will continue to buy these titles, and this will quickly expose how closely they must remain tied to the inside of the economy. Thus, state debt titles can turn into bad securities as much as the titles of the 'unsound' people Bagehot had in mind. Such titles have to be refused by a genuine central bank.

The holder of central banknotes needs as much protection as the 'sound' people who hold titles denominated in the same money of account as these notes. Thus, a stable value of money has to be guaranteed no less than a stable exchange value when it is transformed into titles on the money proper of another central bank: foreign currency. The central bank can achieve this not only by demanding hefty interest for its notes, but also by good, riskless titles so it always can buy back its notes without loss. (In other words, it must control their quantity sufficiently). If a central bank is not capable of drawing its notes out of circulation, a rise in the general price level at home and/or devaluation of the currency abroad may occur. These losses will entice prospective holders of domestic currency to look for another currency that is better secured. At this point extra economic pressure is frequently applied to prevent such a flight. This force is always the direct result of measures in the issue of money originating outside the economy.

Since money proper can be created only *uno actu* with a credit contract, there is no basis for the idea of hoarding money. The popular view of hoarding in form of a money chest, the contents of which are stored to be loaned against interest whenever appropriate, derives from the lack of understanding money and interest. Hoarding only occurs when the material used to produce money proper has a rising commodity price. Banknotes printed on gold or silver, therefore, can be hoarded for their commodity value. Intrinsically worthless materials used for money proper usually do not share such a fate, the exception being a deflationary crisis.

We have shown that a money-creating process results in two types of titles: the credit contract as a claim to money proper against the debtor, and money proper as a claim to property of the creditor. When the contract is fulfilled, not only the former but also the latter title is destroyed. This may be done by the central bank actually burning its refunded notes. If the central bank uses its notes again in new loan contracts – as banks

Property theory of interest and money 93

always did in the past with their precious metal money proper (coins) – the impression of a fund or pool of money may arise again. Yet, the issuers of money never hold the money they have issued, and the money they issue does not come from a money vault. Before the refunded money-proper documents, which indeed are stored in a vault, can be used again as money in a *new* credit contract, they are *not* money but only blanks. As such they have to be guarded very carefully in their vaults, because in their material quality and appearance they cannot be distinguished at all from properly-issued money.

The peculiar characteristics of a property-based economy

Our theory tries to show that interest and money cannot be understood without the institution of property and the concept of the property premium. It is this institution, but not an intentional set of rules, which gives rise what can justifiably be called an economy. How does property bring about the peculiar characteristics of a property-based economy, such as the production of commodities and the market, profit and accumulation, free wage labour and technical progress, as well as business cycles with boom and crisis?

We start with the entrepreneur as the typical debtor. In an interest-bearing and collateralized contract denominated in a money of account, he has received money proper. With this money he has *uno actu* obtained its liquidity premium, which empowers him, by disbursing money proper, finally to settle debt contracts in the form of credit contracts *and* sales contracts. As soon as money proper is created, the liquidity premium can be transferred to all forms of assets, from demand deposits to tradeable assets and real capital, which are not money proper and which therefore cannot finally discharge contracts. The ease of the re-transformability of the different forms of assets into money proper determines the level of their liquidity premium or the degree of their liquidity.

Since means of production can only be bought with an advance of money proper for which interest has to be paid, these means are not the *capital* itself. They acquire the character of capital goods or real capital only by going through the money proper advanced. Capital itself, therefore, is always advanced money proper. Therefore it is not necessary for anyone to abstain from consuming pre-existing goods or to save them in order that real capital can emerge. The advanced money proper never represents existing goods possessed by someone, it represents immaterial property titles. *They are encumbered but never transferred.* Thus, the formation of capital is not limited by goods or resources but by the readiness with which proprietors collateralize property, or abstain from the property premium.

As soon as the entrepreneur has bought the means of production with money proper, they exist for that entrepreneur unavoidably and always as moneyed quantities. This means that their real quantities must be *valued* with *prices* which are expressed in the same money of account as the credit contract, that is, in nominal *money* prices. The same holds true for the goods produced with the means of production, because the value of these goods must at least be equal to the capital plus interest. It is this typical monetary production which distinguishes a *commodity* from a mere good. Therefore, the entrepreneur is not interested in production of goods *per se*, or mere quantities, but in production values measured in money prices, or sums of money proper.

The demand for a rate of interest forces upon the entrepreneur a value of production, expressed in terms of quantity, time, money or price, which must be greater than the money proper advanced as capital. This demand thus necessitates a value surplus in the production of commodities, the rate of *profit*. The interest-generated profit brings about the accumulation so characteristic of a property-based economy. Thus, unlike in mere possession-based societies, this mechanism does not depend on a previous accumulation of saved goods. The dynamics so typical for property-based societies are disconnected from an endowment of resources. They wholly depend on immaterial titles to property created *ex nihilo* but encumberable for the credit issue of money proper and its loan as capital.

The money-priced production of commodities necessarily leads to the commodity *market*. This market is an institution to obtain money proper because it is the only means with which the obligations of the debt contract to refund and to pay interest can be fulfilled. Therefore, the market is not an institution where goods are exchanged to the mutual benefits of their possessors, either according to the preference of consumers determined by marginal utility (neoclassical theory) or according to the cost of production (classical theory).

In the property-based economy, loan contracts are primary, and sales contracts have to follow suit. Commodities enter the picture only in sales contracts. Thus, it is the loan contract that constitutes the ultimate *business operation*. While in the credit contract the entrepreneur is a debtor of a demand for money proper, in a sales contract he becomes a creditor of a demand for money proper, as a proprietor of a commodity. In an analogy to the credit contract, the seller as creditor faces a buyer as debtor. The buyer becomes the proprietor of the commodity only after fulfilling the obligation to pay the demanded price. Before the fulfilment of this obligation, the buyer is only a possessor of the commodity, and as such must pay interest like a debtor in a credit contract.

A typical characteristic of modern property-based economies is the institution of *free wage labour*. The essence of this institution is that an individual has a possession and a property side as a *free* person. This means that the individual cannot lose his or her own property, unlike a slave collateralizable or saleable by his or her proprietor. Therefore, the individual can only use the possessional aspect by selling labour time in a wage contract to an entrepreneur. This contract, again, is denominated in the money of account of the credit contract, and the labourer's demand is for a *money wage*. Since the entrepreneur can obtain the money proper advanced as a wage only against interest, it is the labourer who has to bring about the value required to cover the interest owed. Marx's famous surplus value does not derive from a power relation in the process of production, but is the compensation for acquiring money – the wage – without paying interest.

The wage contract, like the credit contract, must always be fulfilled without any guarantee of entering a sales contract, without which the entrepreneur cannot fulfill his obligations. To increase the chances of finding potential buyers on the commodity market, the entrepreneur competes with other indebted entrepreneurs. In its purest form the competition is price competition, which however, is limited by the sums owed in the credit contract and the wage contract. Therefore, entrepreneurs are always forced to reduce the number of labourers, and their obligation to pay wages, through technical progress. Why do they not start with substituting capital goods? Money paid as wages is always irredeemably lost, while money paid for capital goods can to some extent be redeemed because, unlike the labourers, they are the entrepreneur's property.

To explain business cycles in a property-based economy, one has to focus on collateral as a measure of a debtor's *creditworthiness*. The good securities which debtors have to pledge to get access to credit have no material or eternal value. As an asset, collateral is always subject to *market valuation*, which is determined by the expected rate of profit and the existing rate of interest. The value of an asset increases or decreases when its expected rate of profit rises or falls and the rate of interest falls or rises. In equilibrium both the expected rate of profit and the existing rate of interest are equal to the existing property premium.

A *boom* starts when the expected rate of profit is high in relation to the rate of interest, or in other words, the creditworthiness of debtors rises. Creditors become more ready to encumber property for the creation of money to be advanced as capital to entrepreneurs. Property premia and the rate of interest are both lowered in a boom. Moreover, the creditworthiness of debtors rises, because the lower rate of interest increases the value of their collateral. This process is supported by asset markets. It can best be observed in markets for securities – the typical good securities pledged as collateral – where the value of these titles has to rise when interest falls. There is, however, no straightforward relationship between a low rate of interest and high collateral values. The combined boosting of creditworthiness, the rise in collateral value, lures ever more proprietors into debt.

Because the limit for credit is not set by a physical frontier, creditors always fear inflation, a reduction in the value of the money returned by the debtors, and especially so in a boom. Inflation fears result in a rise of the real rate of interest in the credit market, and force the central bank to a more restrictive monetary policy. With rising interest, collateral values fall. A *recession* may occur, and eventually lead to a crisis.

A *crisis* is always characterized by a devaluation of property pledged as collateral. The creditworthiness of debtors is reduced. The sums owed are fixed, while the value of securing collateral may fall below them. The property premium soars, and so does the liquidity premium on money. *Panics* may occur. The rise of liquidity premium does not cause the crisis, it only reflects it. Banks as creditors are left with insufficiently-secured demands, while banks as debtors cannot take flight from the fixed contracts with their depositors.

Attempts to refinance at the central bank are hampered because in the crisis good securities are more scarce than ever. Interventions to turn the tide are mostly helpless because there is no institution in the property-based economy which can supply good securities. Since no one can reduce the property premia of creditors by showering collateral over debtors, the crisis has its way.

Summary

Economic theory's most intractable enigma pertains to the loss for which interest is charged. This riddle is inseparable from the enigma of the creation of money. Our chapter demonstrates that the neoclassical theory of the rate of interest – determined by real factors, productivity and thrift or investment and savings – falls short, because in a loan contract it is not real income goods that are transferred, but money which precedes goods. This was seen by Keynes when he observed that investment requires money and not savings, or in other words that money but not savings must precede investment.

However Keynes's alternative explanation, that interest is a payment for a creditor's loss of liquidity premium, an immaterial yield of security, also falls short, because it simply presupposes the existence of money and the latter's command over it.

By relating money's liquidity premium to the property premium, another immaterial yield of security, it can be shown that the former is only a measure of money's capacity to fulfil money-denominated contracts. This additional immaterial yield is a premium that flows from property titles as long as they are unencumbered and free. Property premium, thus, accrues from property's capacity to become blocked. In blocking property by encumbering it, the property premium is lost. This loss becomes the basis for interest and money.

Property titles exist in addition to possessional titles. The former are rights to encumber property in order to back money, or to pledge it as collateral in order to obtain credit, while the latter are rights to the physical use of goods and resources. Possessional titles have existed throughout history, but property titles are only found in property-based societies. Property titles are absent in pure tribal and feudal societies, which explains why interest and money, the business operations of an economy in its true sense, are wanting there.

Thus, money as an anonymized title to property can be created only in property-based societies. It is issued in a credit contract in which the creditor establishes a money of account as standard of measurement and valuation. Money proper owes its very existence to the money of account. It has to be kept in mind that this contractual money of account has nothing to do with the neoclassical unit of account or *numéraire,* which refers to a good as the standard.

For the issue of money proper, property has to be blocked temporarily. This also holds true in the case of non-redeemable central bank money. Blocking property means that both the issuer-creditor of money and his debtor have to encumber property. The former has to encumber the property for backing the money issued, while the latter has to encumber the property by pledging it as collateral for securing the debt. Thereby, both contract partners lose property premia: the creditor loses his or her property premium without gaining the debtor's. To compensate for this loss the creditor demands interest, while the debtor gains the liquidity premium on money.

The immaterial premium on property thus gives rise to both the material yield of interest in the process of the creation of money, and the immaterial yield that is money's liquidity premium. Both yields are at work in addition to the existing material yields of the physical use which the creditor and debtor make of their possessional rights. Both sides continue with their goods' possessional capacity to earn a material yield which exists beyond their property titles. Therefore the physical use of goods is never transferred in a loan contract, as mainstream theory of the rate of interest suggests. The permanent transformation of immaterial property premia into material rates of interest drives the economic juggernaut of the property-based society.

Postscript to Professor Nikolaus Läufer and other critics

In Summer 1998, we received a fierce critique of our property theory of interest and money from Professor Läufer (Läufer 1998). He believes that money based on anonymized claims to property is the same as a commodity money. Furthermore, he identifies our key concept of the property premium as a risk premium. He also maintains, without reference, that the distinction between possession and property is well known to economists. The substance of all his points is explicitly dealt with in this paper without, however, referring to Läufer or similar positions by name. (See also the debate in Betz and Roy 1999.)

Notes

1 We speak of property, not of *ownership*, because the latter term is ambiguous, and means *both* property and possession.
2 We do not discuss mercantilism, which antedates these schools of thought and whose ultimate formulation was provided by James Steuart (1767). Some of Steuart's ideas are used in our presentation. For a detailed discussion see Stadermann and Steiger (1999a).
3 Keynes has borrowed the term from R. G. Hawtrey (1919: 2). It was, however, invented by Steuart (1767 I: 526). It has to be established that neither of these authors has understood that it is the creditor who establishes the standard.
4 With the exception of Hawtrey and Stadermann, Bagehot's second rule has not received the prominence it deserves in the literature on central banking. See, e.g., Smith (1936), Sayers (1957), Goodhart (1988, 1992), and, most recently, Genovese (1997), Humphrey (1997) and Schwartz (1997).

References

Adler, B. E. (1998) 'Secured Credit Contracts', in *The New Palgrave Dictionary of Economics and the Law*, London: Macmillan, 405–10.
Alchian, A. A. (1992) 'Property Rights', in *The New Palgrave Dictionary of Money and Finance*, London: Macmillan, 223–6.
Andrewes, A. (1967) *Greek Society*, Harmondsworth: Penguin.
Axilrod, S. H. and Wallich, H. C. (1992) 'Open-Market Operations', in *New Palgrave Dictionary of Money and Finance*, London: Macmillan, 74–7.
Bagehot, W. (1914 [1873]) *Lombard Street: A Description of the Money Market*, London: Smith, Elder.
Bailey, M. J. (1998) 'Property in Aboriginal Societies', in *The New Palgrave Dictionary of Economics and The Law*, London: Macmillan, 155–7.
Betz, K. and Roy, T. (eds) (1999) *Geld, Zins und Eigentum in der Geldwirtschaft: Beiträge zum Symposion über Heinsohns und Steigers 'Eigentum, Zins und Geld'*, Marburg: Metropolis, forthcoming.
Bogaert, R. (1966) *Les origines antiques de la banque de dépôt: une mise au point Accompagnée d'une esquisse des opérations de banque en Mésopotamie*, Leiden: A. W. Sijthoff.
Chantraine, H. (1979) 'Münzwesen', in *Der Kleine Pauly*, Munich: Deutscher Taschenbuch Verlag, 1447–52.
Dalton, G. B. (1982) 'Barter', *Journal of Economic Issues* 16: 181–90.
Debreu, G. (1959) *Theory of Value: An Axiomatic Analysis of Economic Equilibrium*, New Haven and London: Yale University Press.
Demsetz, H. (1998) 'Property Rights', in *The New Palgrave Dictionary of Economics and the Law*, London: Macmillan, 144–55.
Epstein, R. A. (1998), 'Possession', in *The New Palgrave Dictionary of Economics and the Law*, London: Macmillan, 62–8.
Fisher, I. (1906) *The Nature of Capital and Income*, New York: Macmillan.
Friedman, M. (1992) 'Quantity Theory of Money', in *The New Palgrave Dictionary of Money and Finance*, London: Macmillan, 245–64.
Genovese, F. C. (1997) 'Bagehot, Walter (1826–1877)', in *Business Cycles and Depressions: An Encyclopaedia*, New York: Garland, 29–31.
Goodhart, C. A. E. (1988) *The Evolution of Central Banks*, Cambridge, Mass.: MIT Press.

—— (1992) 'Central Banking', in *The New Palgrave Dictionary of Money and Finance*, London: Macmillan, 321–5.
Hahn, F.H. (1982) *Money and Inflation*, Oxford: Blackwell.
Hawtrey, R. G. (1923 [1919]) *Currency and Credit*, London: Longman.
—— (1930) 'Credit', in *Encyclopaedia of the Social Sciences*, New York: Macmillan, 545–50.
—— (1932) *The Art of Central Banking*, London: Longman.
Heinsohn, G. (1984), *Privateigentum, Patriarchat, Geldwirtschaft: Eine sozialtheoretische Rekonstruktion zur Antike*, Frankfurt am Main: Suhrkamp.
Heinsohn, G. and Steiger, O. (1996) *Eigentum, Zins und Geld: Ungelöste Rätsel der Wirtschaftswissenschaft*, Reinbek: Rowohlt.
Hicks, J. R. (1980–1) 'IS–LM: An Explanation', *Journal of Post Keynesian Economics* 3: 139–54.
Humphrey, T.M. (1997) 'Lender of Last Resort', in *Business Cycles and Depressions: An Encyclopaedia*, New York: Garland, 391–2.
Iwai, K. (1981) *Disequilibrium Dynamics: A Theoretical Analysis of Inflation and Unemployment*, New Haven and London: Yale University Press.
Jaffee, D. and Stiglitz, J. (1990) 'Credit Rationing', in B. M. Friedman and F. H. Hahn (eds.), *Handbook of Monetary Economics*, Amsterdam: North-Holland.
Kanatas, G. (1992) 'Collateral', in *The New Palgrave Dictionary of Money and Finance*, London: Macmillan, 381–3.
Keynes, J. M. (1930) *A Treatise on Money*, vol. 1, *The Pure Theory of Money*, London: Macmillan.
—— (1936) *The General Theory of Employment, Interest and Money*, London: Macmillan.
Läufer, N. K. A. (1998) 'The Heinsohn-Steiger Confusion on Interest, Money and Property', mimeo, University of Konstanz, June.
Laum, B. (1965) *Viehleihe und Viehkapital in den asiatisch–afrikanischen Hirtenkulturen*, Tübingen: J. C. B. Mohr.
Libecap, G. D. (1998) 'Common Property', in *The New Palgrave Dictionary of Economics and the Law*, London: Macmillan, 317–24.
Lutz, F. A. (1967 [1956]) *Zinstheorie*, Tübingen: J. C. B. Mohr.
—— (1980) 'Entwicklung der Zinstheorie', in *Handwörterbuch der Wirtschaftswissenschaft*, Stuttgart: G. Fischer, 541–7.
Malinowski, B. (1966 [1935]) *Coral Gardens and Their Magic*, vol. I, *Soil-Tilling and Agriculture Rights in the Trobriand Islands*, London: Allen and Unwin.
North, D. C. and Thomas, R. P. (1973) *The Rise of the Western World: A New Economic History*, Cambridge: Cambridge University Press.
Pistor, K. (1998) 'Transfer of Property Rights in Eastern Europe', in *The New Palgrave Dictionary of Economics and the Law*, London: Macmillan, 697–712.
Ricardo, D. (1951 [1817]) *On the Principles of Political Economy and Taxation*, in P. Sraffa, (ed.) *The Works and Correspondence of David Ricardo*, Cambridge: Cambridge University Press.
Riese, H. (1995) 'Geld: Das letzte Rätsel der Nationalökonomie', in W. Schelkle and M. Nitsch (eds) *Rätsel Geld: Annäherungen aus ökonomischer, soziologischer und historischer Sicht*, Marburg: Metropolis.
Sayers, R. S. (1957) *Central Banking after Bagehot*, Oxford: Clarendon Press.
Schumpeter, J. A. (1934 [1926]) *The Theory of Economic Development: An Inquiry into Profits, Capital, Credit, Interest, and the Business Cycle*, Cambridge, Mass.: Harvard

University Press.

Schwartz, A. J. (1997) 'Central Banking', in *Business Cycles and Depressions: An Encyclopaedia*, New York: Garland, 88–91.

Smith, A. (1937 [1776]) *An Inquiry into the Nature and Causes of the Wealth of Nations*, New York: Modern Library.

Smith, V. C. (1990 [1936]) *The Rationale of Central Banking and the Free Banking Alternative*, Indianapolis: Liberty Press.

Stadermann, H.-J. (1994) *Die Fesselung des Midas: Eine Untersuchung über den Aufstieg und Verfall der Zentralbankkunst*, Tübingen: J. C. B. Mohr.

Stadermann, H.-J. and Steiger, O. (1999a) 'James Steuart und die Theorie der Geldwirtschaft', in H.-J. Stadermann and O. Steiger (eds) *Herausforderungen der Geldwirtschaft*, Marburg: Metropolis, forthcoming.

—— (1999b) *Allgemeine Theorie der Wirtschaft*, forthcoming.

Steuart, J. (1767) *An Inquiry into the Principles of Political Oeconomy: Being an Essay on the Science of Domestic Policy in Free Nations*, 2 vols., London: A. Millar and T. Cadell.

Tobin, J. (1967 [1963]) 'Commercial Banks as Creators of Money', in D. D. Hester and J. Tobin (eds) *Financial Markets and Economic Activity*, New York: Wiley.

5 The credit theory of money: the monetary circuit approach

Alain Parguez and Mario Seccareccia

Introduction

The starting proposition of what is commonly described as the theory of the monetary circuit (TMC) is that, in a monetary economy in which buyers and sellers engage in economic transactions, 'money' is the by-product of a balance sheet operation of a third agent who, in modern parlance, can be dubbed a 'bank'. In particular, money *always* emerges as a debt (or liability) issued by this third agent on itself, which has as counterpart a credit simultaneously granted to buyers of goods and services within an economy. In this three-way balance sheet relation, every transaction entails the simultaneous creation or destruction of debt, and every seller of goods and services accepts payment of this bank liability on the basis of its general purchasing power or value. The value of this bank liability (or money), however, is not the consequence of some intrinsic characteristic, be it utility or liquidity. It stems, rather, from the certainty that accepting bank debt as payment is to acquire a right on the existing as well as future output that will be created by the agents who have been granted bank credit. Furthermore, these debts would not be legal titles to acquiring present and future real wealth were it not for the direct or indirect role played by the state in endorsing them.

In this regard, the TMC sheds light, among other things, on the historical origin of money. In accordance with Innes (1913) and Heinsohn and Steiger (1984), there can be private debt and credit contracts before the existence of money. This is because money emerges both causally and historically as a result of prior debt and credit relations. Money appears when a community (usually through the legal apparatus of the state) bestows the characteristic of being a legal title to a share of present and future wealth on debts issued by a specific agent. Money has, therefore, a pure 'extrinsic' value (Wray, 1998) that is generated by money's role in the industrial circulation.[1] In the 'efflux' phase (to use Tooke's original expression) of monetary circulation, debts are issued to allow private firms (as well as the state) to start the production process via the credits granted to them by the issuing banks. These debts are then extinguished or cancelled when firms (and the state)

102 *Alain Parguez and Mario Seccareccia*

reimburse the creditor banks by acquiring enough of the bank debt in circulation. In the case of firms, this occurs through the sale of commodities in the product market and/or securities in the financial market, and, in the case of the state, taxes and/or government securities. This is what could be described as the 'reflux' phase of the monetary circuit. Credit money, as a rule, is thus created only to be destroyed in the circulatory process and not to be held.

From this general conception of money, we can deduce the two major propositions of the TMC. First, money is, and has always been, a debt created *ex nihilo* by bank credit advances that are granted either to permit the generation of real wealth or to acquire existing physical assets. Second, there is no alternative between debt financing on the one hand, and the tapping of existing liquid resources (or accumulated savings) to 'finance' expenditures, on the other. At the macroeconomic level, spending in a monetary economy is always and everywhere in the nature of debt financing.

This chapter is divided into two major sections. We begin with a detailed exposition of the theory of money underlying the TMC. In this first section, we shall try to explain why many of the debates pertaining to this approach are the consequence of a fundamental misunderstanding of the dynamic process of money creation. A second section discusses why the TMC is a major advance relative to other existing approaches to money.

The nature of money in the monetary circuit

The simple model of the monetary circuit

As has been emphasized in our introduction, the economic process has always been supported by a set of debt contracts in all organized societies, including the despotic ultra-centralized systems of ancient Egypt and the former Soviet-style regimes of Eastern Europe (Wittfogel 1959). Historical records clearly suggest that, regardless of the type of pre-existing property relations in ancient societies, there can be debt contracts while currency does not yet exist. For instance, Babylonian bills of exchange, regulated by the Code of Hammurabi, and book entries, such as the wheat deposits in ancient Egypt, were all in the nature of credit–debt relations even before such societies had developed coins or other well-defined circulating media of exchange (Einzig 1966: 328).

Interestingly, and in conflict with the views of Heinsohn and Steiger (1984, 1994), even in societies in which communal property was the norm, forms of credit/debt relations existed as long as individuals held informal personal possessions rather than titles based on codified private property rights. To substantiate this, we shall take the example of the aboriginal people living in the Hudson's Bay area of present-day Canada during the pre- and early post-contact era. Given the rugged climate of the region, it is well known that the original nomadic people living around the Hudson's

Bay had developed primitive debt/credit relations based on gift exchange prior to European contact (Ray 1996: 88, Davies 1994: 11–12). When the Europeans did attempt to establish commercial fur trading relations with them, these people of the sub-Arctic fur trading area had no difficulty in establishing formal credit/debt relations *vis-à-vis* the European traders. The Amerindians had no concept of European currency, but they understood credit/debt relations perfectly well. Indeed, a cashless credit economy evolved with respect to the European fur trading enterprises, such as the Hudson's Bay Company. As in the modern TMC, the fur trading companies were to advance credit in the form of European traded goods and, through formal double-entry book-keeping based on an abstract unit of account called the *Made Beaver*, aboriginal trappers would then seek to extinguish their debts by harvesting beaver and other highly valued fur bearing animal pelts (Ray and Freeman 1978: ch. .9). These credit/debt relations emerging in semi-nomadic societies, such as those of the Indians of the sub-Arctic region of Canada (where land remained collective property, even after European contact), would suggest that private property rights are not a necessary prerequisite to the appearance of such relations in primitive economies. We agree with Heinsohn and Steiger (1984), however, that private credit/debt relations predate more advanced monetary systems based on state coins or private bank liabilities as circulating medium.

Indeed, in more modern monetary capitalist economies with entrenched private property rights, money appears when there exists a set of agents, which we shall call 'banks' (including the central bank), whose debts are accepted by all other agents in an economy as a means of payment to settle their own debt commitments. Banks are deemed to be so creditworthy that no holder of their debts would ever ask for reimbursement either in kind or in the debt of another agent. Banking institutions enjoy, therefore, the capacity of freely issuing debt without it being subject to an exogenous resource constraint. This means that banks can create these debts *ex nihilo* when they grant credit to non-bank agents who must spend them to acquire real resources. Bank credit entails the advancing of loans of newly-created bank debt to economic agents who cannot depend on some pre-existing stock of bank liability, which itself would be the result of previously-incurred outstanding bank credit in the economy.

Once credit has been advanced, however, non-bank agents become committed to paying back their loans at some future date by collecting the required quantity of bank debt out of their cash receipts, either from the sale of newly-produced commodities, or from the sale of titles to existing wealth. When initial borrowers reimburse their loans, there is an instantaneous cancellation of both the individual agent's debt towards the banks and the debts that the latter had issued on themselves to finance the loans. In the TMC, these conventional loans are what is regarded as credit money. This money is endogenously created *ex nihilo* when banks grant credit and it is extinguished or cancelled when the outstanding credit is reimbursed.

This dynamic flux and reflux process is the essence of the monetary circuit. Its different phases are directly mirrored in banks' balance sheets. In the initial phase when banks grant credit, they issue new debts upon themselves which they lend to non-bank agents. Since these debts are money, the latter appears as an increase in banks' liabilities which is equivalent to the newly-held deposits of the non-bank public. Logically accounted for as an equivalent increase in bank assets, the counterpart of this newly-created money is the forward debt of non-bank agents in the form of loans to be paid back at some definite date in the future.

The second phase of the monetary circuit is the period during which non-bank agents spend the money that they have borrowed to acquire real resources, which are generally labour and produced commodities. Sellers of labour services or commodities acquire the quantity of money which was created in the first phase. In the balance sheets of banks, there appears a mere transfer of deposits or liabilities from one group of individual holders to another: the sellers of commodities and labour services. These new holders of money owe nothing to banks. On the contrary, one may infer that it is the banks that owe something to these holders of money. Some Post Keynesian writers (e.g. Moore 1988) have interpreted this sellers' holding of bank debts as 'convenience lending' to banks. This interpretation has also been more recently advocated by heterodox French economists such as Gnos (1998). Sellers of labour services and produced commodities are indeed the new holders of bank liabilities but, we believe, they cannot also be considered as bank creditors. This is because money is merely debt that the banks have issued on themselves *ex nihilo*. The amount of this credit money that was initially advanced was not based on what this subsequent group of convenience 'lenders' wished to hold but on the amount that the initial borrowers wished to spend.

In the third and last stage of the monetary circuit, the initial holders of bank debts seek to recover them in the reflux process out of their receipts generated by their initial expenditures. They can now replenish their deposits and pay back their loans. At the same time banks can recoup the debts that they had issued on themselves to finance those loans and thereby extinguish their own implicit debts. The counterpart of this process is the cancellation of the initial borrowers' forward debt to banks. In the balance-sheet operation of the banks, this third stage of the monetary circuit is accounted for as an equivalent reduction in bank assets and liabilities.

The definition of money

From this simple model of circulation of bank debts, we can draw a first definition of money. Money cannot be, and never has been, a commodity whose value stems from its scarcity. Some circuitist writers have deemed it to be a pure token (Graziani 1998). While not disagreeing with this, one may more correctly argue that it is an abstract or virtual token, since it is merely a debt that banks have issued on themselves. The value of this money (or its purchasing power) cannot be inferred on the basis of some neoclassical scarcity principle, since the quantity of new debts issued by banks is constrained only by the expressed demand for money of non-bank agents. The latter need this money in order to spend it on the acquisition of real resources. In the productive sphere, money exists therefore as the means of payment that gives rise to a sequential chain of transactions leading to the creation of new wealth. Money cannot be defined, as is traditionally done by economists, in terms of its presumed functions of unit of account or store of value. A monetary economy does require a unit of account but, in such an economy, accounts are settled in the prevailing monetary unit. The debts banks issue on themselves are denominated in the unit of account because it is the means of acquisition that ensures a viable circulation process upon which the creation of real wealth is based.

As previously mentioned, economies have existed without the use of money, such as ancient Egypt, or in which money played an insignificant role, but which had a state-imposed unit of account, such as the former Soviet Union. This would suggest that money's existence cannot be understood on the basis of this function. In much the same way, since we have argued that money is created *ex nihilo* to finance loans, and is destroyed only when these loans are repaid, its existence cannot depend on its store of value function. Such a function is inconsistent with the notion of money. Money exists and has a value only as long as it is spent by non-bank agents for the purpose of creating future wealth. The hoarding of money in the form of bank deposits merely obstructs the process of wealth creation upon which the value of money depends. Indeed, it is this inconsistency which explains why the traditional demand for money as a component of wealth has a potentially destabilizing role within the monetary circuit.

Money is credit-driven

This definition of money requires that there are agents capable of issuing debts upon themselves that are generally accepted by all other agents as a means of payment. Certain conditions must be fulfilled for the emergence of these banking agents in an economy. First, the state must either implicitly or explicitly come to endorse fully bank debts. This endorsement has two major consequences.

Amid the class of debtors, banks are now deemed as so creditworthy that no one would consider asking them to reimburse their debts either in commodities or in debts of other agents. Banks are therefore able to issue liabilities at will, which are implicit debts on themselves. Because of the state endorsement of these debts as the ultimate guarantor of their liquidity, it would be wrong to conceive holders of bank liability as bank creditors. In a sense, given its endorsement by the state, one can legitimately argue that money is always fiat money, even when the state is not issuing it and the role of the state is marginal. The state's power to create money at will is the logical consequence of its role in the endorsement of bank activity. Having the legal authority to bestow on bank debt the characteristic feature of money, the state has also the power to issue debt on itself that will be money, freely convertible into bank liability. Regardless of the material support of these conventional debts in the form of gold, silver, copper coins or paper notes such as bank money, these coins or paper notes have an essentially extrinsic value because each holder is certain to possess a legal claim on real resources, and because it can serve ultimately as a means of settling one's debts. The very notion of a commodity money is an illusion which confuses the material support of money with money itself.

The historical process has been to shed the commodity guise of money and to integrate further state money within the activities of commercial banking, with the last phase of this integration being the creation of the state's own banking department: the central bank. In this latter case, the state's endorsement of the monetary activity of banks is now operated through the central bank which, as the ultimate purveyor of liquidity, further empowers commercial banks to lend their own debt to creditworthy borrowers without constraint. At the same time, the state is now entitled to finance its desired expenditures by credits granted by the central bank. In the accounts of the central bank, money is now created as debts issued by the latter on itself and appears as an increase in liabilities. This money is advanced to the state and accounted for as an equivalent increase in the central bank's assets. However, a small share of these central bank debts may still necessitate some material support in the form of legal tender banknotes, and these would also be accounted as central bank liabilities.

It follows, therefore, that money, whatever its material support, is always a debt created *ex nihilo* to finance loans. We believe that this analysis is consistent with the historical record. As was mentioned at the beginning of this section, credit money and banks pre-date pure state money which was directly issued by the state authority as coins and later notes and central bank liabilities (Innes 1913, Heinsohn and Steiger 1984, 1994). In many societies, such as Mesopotamia as early as the seventh century BC, and Greece after Solon's Reform in the fifth century BC (Davies 1994), the state's monetary requirements were financed by private bank credits. However, regardless of whether these requirements are financed by private banks or a central bank, loans can never be financed by some pre-existing deposits. Moreover, since credit money is created to finance loans to private agents and/or the state, it is by its very nature an endogenous variable. The neoclassical scarcity principle can never be applied to the creation of money.

We have argued that credit money could not exist without the state, and that all credit-driven money is by its very nature a fiat money, irrespective of whether it takes the form of a commercial bank or central bank liability. On the other hand, state power alone cannot guarantee the existence and survival of a viable monetary system. History records many examples of the complete collapse of monetary systems, such as in Russia before the First World War, immediately after the Revolution, and in the late 1990s, as well as in Germany after both World Wars. In each of these historical episodes, the state failed in its effort to maintain the stability of the existing monetary systems and was faced with an untenable situation of hyperinflation. But how can one explain it? Mainstream economists point to the excessive creation of money, but one must also explain it in reference to what it is excessive.

Contrary to the traditional quantity theory based on the excessive creation arising from the careless use of the government's printing press, our analysis points to a slightly different explanation and suggests why another condition must be met for the existence of money. Rules of creditworthiness must ensure that banks issue debts on themselves to finance loans that ultimately lead to a creation of new real wealth. If banks were to issue liabilities to finance loans that could never support the generation of future real wealth, these debts would be deprived of value and no one would accept them. We may, therefore, put forth the following more general definition of money:

> Money is at all times the liabilities issued by banking institutions which have been endorsed by the state primarily for the purpose of financing the formation of future real wealth. This money has a real extrinsic value because every holder of these liabilities has acquired a claim on the future physical wealth that results from the initial bank credit advances.

The role of firms

Such a definition explains why business enterprises and the state have special access to bank credit. Firms must borrow credit money to finance their desired acquisitions of real resources needed to carry out their production plans. They have first to spend money to acquire the labour services required for the production of the planned output of consumption and capital goods out of their existing capital stock. It is firms' spending (including that of public sector enterprises) on labour services which therefore determines labour income. According to our general principle of circulation, firms (and banks) no longer owe anything to wage earners as soon as income is paid.

Firms have also to spend in order to maintain or increase their stock of capital goods by acquiring the newly-available equipment goods produced by the capital goods sector. Abstracting from any specific assumptions regarding the degree of integration of business enterprises, we see no logical reason why investment, the acquisition of the newly-produced capital goods, should not be financed by bank loans. Some heterodox economists (see Bailly 1992) have argued that, if that were so, one would be espousing some new version of the old loanable funds theory. They assume that if firms also borrow money to finance investment, it would mean that they are borrowing pre-existing deposits generated by the payment of wages. However, this latter interpretation succumbs to the general criticism that we made previously against the mainstream theory of money. Regardless of whether it goes towards the financing of the wage bill or the purchase of capital goods, the TMC suggests that when banks grant loans they issue new debts that generate new deposits *ex nihilo*. They cannot, as a group, lend pre-existing deposits. Moreover, to the extent that the purpose of these loans is the creation of real wealth, money emerges to generate new production either for direct consumption (consumer goods proper) or for indirect consumption, by replenishing or increasing the stock of real capital, including inventories.

Consumption goods are usually acquired when income earners spend their income which is initially financed by money creation. This credit money created to finance income should permit the generation of the new output and the realization of the value of a share pertaining to articles of direct consumption. Conversely, the value of the share devoted to future consumption or investment must also be realized by loans entailing creation of money that would finance the acquisition of newly-produced equipment goods (Seccareccia 1996, 1998).

As has been shown in previous articles on the TMC (Parguez 1996, Seccareccia 1996), such an extensive conception of the role of credit advances is the necessary requirement for the validity of money. All debts issued by banks are claims on real wealth. If credit were restricted to the financing of wages, the value of equipment goods would not be realized in accordance with the initial expectations of firms (and banks). The newly-created money would lead to the creation and monetary validation only of articles of current consumption, and not of the capital goods that would also be needed to sustain production and consumption in the long term.

As argued above, banks must apply a set of financial criteria to their borrowers that allow the former to assess the creditworthiness of the borrowing firms so as to measure the latter's ability to generate real wealth, as well as to establish norms for banks themselves, in their capacity to lend their debts to the requisite borrowers. The creditworthiness of firms is usually measured by the profits that they individually target. On the other hand, the creditworthiness of the banks themselves (which sustains the conventional nature of the debts that they issue on themselves) is positively related to their own bank-specific capital values as determined by the monetary value of their equity that forms the collateral of their loans (Parguez 1998). In the case of firms, this ability to generate profits out of current expenditure is measured by the targeted ratio of profits to income expenditure, which has been described elsewhere as the monetary *mark-up* (Parguez 1998). The more banks want to ensure that the commitments of their borrowers will generate wealth, the greater would be the monetary mark-up that they impose on business enterprises. Firms' capacity to earn the targeted profit (via their mark-up policy) is thus the prerequisite for continued access to bank credit, and is a critical factor in establishing the viability of the overall credit money system.

Some circuitist writers have raised doubts about the ability of firms to earn profits within the framework of the monetary circuit (Renaud 1998). Others have postulated that only producers in the consumer goods sector could extract monetary profits (Gnos 1998, Vallageas 1998). In our opinion, both interpretations seem to thrive on a misunderstanding of the circulation process. As shown above, profits are not the pecuniary difference between the reflux and the initial injection of money. Rather, they are generated by the excess of receipts from the sales of commodities over the initial income expenditure paid to the workers. While the nature of circulation establishes an ultimate equality between the efflux and the reflux of money, this is not contradicted by the fact that the initial flux of money is always superior to the income expenditure by firms.

Firms in the capital goods sector must also be able to earn profits from the sale of their output. These money profits are equal to the difference between the selling price of the new equipment goods and their income costs, with the market value of these new capital goods reflecting long-term expectations of profits by firms wishing to acquire these commodities.

This is merely a restatement of the theory of profits in the investment goods sector put forth by Keynes in the *Treatise on Money*. Firms wishing to acquire more capital goods in order to meet a forecasted future increase in consumption borrow an amount of money equivalent to the value of the additional capital goods by placing their orders for new equipment from the capital goods sector. In this process, the sellers of both sectors realize their money profits and the monetary circuit is now completed with the flux matching the reflux of credit money. All profits are now used to repay the loans which had been the prior source of investment finance and, at the same time, the credit money originally created is extinguished. It is, in part, for this reason that we reject the view put forth by Nell (1998) who has argued that, in order to minimize transaction and borrowing costs, and thereby the number of transactions in a production economy, the optimal quantity of credit money ought to be just equal to the wages paid in the equipment goods sector. Nell's view, which is based on the principle of cost minimization as well as on a peculiar notion of money, would perhaps also succumb to further criticism (which we discuss in a separate section) of the neoclassical conception of money.

Since loans are granted to firms by commercial banks chartered by the state, their own creditworthiness will ultimately depend on their ability to earn profits out of their credit-creating activity. In the long run, the existence of money requires that bank profits generate enough equity value to match the value of assets sustained by banks' own desired monetary mark-up. Consequently, we can spell out this stability condition for the monetary system:

> The rate of interest charged on credit advances, which is the primary source of bank profits, must be high enough to support an amount of bank equity equal to that generated by bank assets resulting from the monetary mark-up imposed on firms.

From this, there ensues the concept of exogeneity of the rate of interest. By its nature, the rate is imposed by banks on firms and it can be included as part of the creditworthiness rules to which firms have to comply. There has been some discussion in the heterodox literature on the capacity of firms to pay interest to banks (Léonard 1987). With the existence of interest, firms would not be able to meet their obligations to the banks since the reflux would now exceed the initial efflux. This, however, arises because of a misunderstanding of the requirements of monetary circulation.

The problem is not the incapacity of firms to pay interest but the ability of banks to realize profits consistent with an equality between the flux and the reflux of credit money. We have argued that banks issue debts on themselves, and these ought to allow firms to pay all their production costs: wages, the share of profits advanced to *rentiers* and interest payments. When banks credit firms with an amount equal to the interest requirements, they increase both their liabilities and their assets. Firms have to pay back the debts issued to finance interest expenditure by running down their deposits to pay interest to banks. In the process, bank liabilities decrease while bank assets increase by an equivalent amount, thereby generating an increase in banks' net worth. Banks recycle a portion of the increased assets to pay wages to their employees and dividends to their shareholders. These expenditures further build up demand for the commodities and services of the non-bank sector. However, while banks may even acquire assets of business enterprises, usually by default, their ability to create money for their own purposes is strictly bounded by the expenditure which is required to sustain their own credit-creating activity.

The role of the state

The nature of monetary circulation also affects the role of the state as producer of public goods in modern economies. To provide society with its desired amount of public goods, the state has to spend money to acquire both a share of the labour force and a share of the available supply of capital goods. However, the state cannot spend the proceeds of taxes to obtain such goods, because taxes cannot be raised unless there is already a pre-existing money in circulation. Logically speaking, taxes could only be levied in the *future* as the final outcome of the initial expenditures of firms and the state, when all private agents will have received their gross income and/or spent it. Hence, taxes could be levied on gross employment income (primarily wages and salaries) paid by the state and by business enterprises (income taxes), on expenditures arising from household income (value added and sales taxes), or on firms' gross profits generated by their sales to households, banks and the state (corporate profit taxes).

Taxes must therefore be conceived as a component of the reflux phase of the monetary circuit, while state expenditures are a necessary component of the flux phase. The latter expenditures must normally be financed by credits granted to the state by the central bank, unless such a bank does not exist (as in nineteenth century USA) or, if it exists, it is prohibited from engaging in such financing (as in the European Monetary Union). In these latter cases, state expenditures would be financed via the holding of government securities by commercial banks. However, in the more common case in which a central bank does exist, the bank would behave much as private commercial banks *vis-à-vis* other non-bank agents. By crediting the spending branch of the state (the treasury), the central bank grants loans by issuing debts on itself. The counterpart of these loans is a forward debt specifying the amount of these debts that the state has to collect through taxes to extinguish its debt obligations to the central bank. The collection of taxes simultaneously cancels a share of central bank debt issued in the first phase of the monetary circuit as well as an equivalent debt of the treasury.

The remaining quantity of central bank liability arising from government spending is normally referred to as the government deficit: a purely *ex post* notion which can be accounted for only in the reflux phase of the monetary circuit. Since it is an *ex post* value, the deficit is by its very nature already financed. When mainstream economists speak of 'deficit financing' or the 'monetization of the deficit', they display a profound misunderstanding of the nature of monetary circulation. Contrary to firms' indebtedness to commercial banks, the state has the power to determine the amount of its debt to the central bank, since it is a pure conventional debt, a debt of the state to itself. The state can *plan* the amount of its future deficit, which is the ultimate consequence of its power of endorsing bank debts as money. Since commercial bank debts are entirely convertible into state money, a significant portion of the state money that is injected into the economy will be transformed into commercial bank debts. Such a conversion allows commercial banks to acquire central bank liabilities which appear in their assets as reserves. Conversely, a share of commercial bank money will, at the same time, also be converted into state money by private agents wishing to hold cash or legal tender. In this process, commercial banks would be losing reserves, and drawing down their deposits at the central bank. In a modern economy, this commercial bank absorption of reserves from state expenditures will normally exceed their losses of reserves determined by the public's demand for cash. As a consequence of their legal convertibility, the private sector can pay taxes in the form of commercial bank debts in the final stage of the monetary circuit. Since the state will require the conversion of bank deposits into its own money through its banking branch, commercial banks will lose reserves in the reflux phase of the monetary circuit. Assuming a given and low preference for cash on the part of the public, we therefore reach the conclusion that the higher the state deficit, the greater is the net increase in commercial bank reserves.

From this analysis of the role of the state within the monetary circuit, we may draw some crucial propositions regarding the endogenous nature of money:

- First, the quantity of newly-created money is always determined by the effective or expressed demand for credit from firms or the state.
- Commercial banks only meet creditworthy demand for loans which comply with the required monetary mark-up or profitability criteria that is reflected in the rate of interest that they impose on firms. Effective demand for loans is the result of firms having already adjusted their planned expenditures to the commercial banks' creditworthiness norms. Consequently, the effective demand for loans is always equal to the quantity of newly-created bank money. In part, however, these criteria of creditworthiness also depend on commercial banks' own credit worthiness as reflected in their capacity to convert freely their own liabilities to those of the central bank.
- The central bank must ultimately play an accommodating role. Even if it wishes to act otherwise, it will fail because of the existence of state expenditures. For instance, let us assume that the central bank tries to impose some required ratio of cash reserves to bank liabilities. As has been shown, banks' net increase in reserves merely mirrors the state deficit. On the other hand, the net increase in commercial bank liabilities reflects the amount of the initial debts incurred by firms *vis-à-vis* the banks which the former cannot reimburse after their sales of commodities and financial securities. In an economy in which the state deficit is significant, the net increase in reserves would usually be greater than the increase in bank liabilities. The *ex post* ratio of reserves to bank liabilities would be higher than the required ratio, thereby preventing any coercive action by the central bank. If anything, the latter would be engaged in a futile action of trying to mop up excess reserves within the banking system to prevent the interbank funds rate from falling below some targeted level (Mosler 1997–8).

Competing approaches to the theory of money and the TMC

We wish now to compare the TMC, which we believe to be a dynamic theory of money, with three other major approaches that have dominated the literature in monetary economics: the neoclassical theory of money, the Post Keynesian theory and the neo-chartalist approach.

An assessment of neoclassical theory

To discuss the neoclassical approach to the theory of money, we have to try first to encapsulate this approach into a set of major propositions. In drawing up this list, we seek to emphasize only the propositions shared by most neoclassical economists. In each case, we shall inquire about the relevance of the proposition in relation to the theory of the monetary circuit.

Barter and monetary exchange

The starting proposition of the neoclassical approach going back to Jevons (1875) and Menger (1892) is that money is to be *introduced* within an otherwise pre-existing pure barter economy. All neoclassical economists accept the barter economy analogy as the reference system within which money appears (Clower 1969). The introduction of money as a simple intermediary or means of exchange to facilitate the two-way barter system, however, merely increases the number of transactions in such an economy. For instance, before the introduction of money, barter entailed a two-way direct exchange between firms and sellers of productive services, as in Walras's original production model. The introduction of money merely breaks up such barter transactions into three indirect exchanges. Assuming that there exists a financial capitalist who possesses money as a third agent, firms must now exchange their output for money held by this third agent so as to be able to purchase productive services. Sellers of productive services must then exchange that money for the goods previously acquired by the financial capitalist. This same type of multiplicative effect on the number of transactions is to be found, for instance, in Hayek's analysis of a production equilibrium (Hayek 1941). All monetary transactions are *de facto* of the same nature as barter exchange with a *numéraire* money having been introduced to it. They are simply exchanges of commodities of equal pre-existing value with *numéraire* money having a specific intrinsic value like any other commodity. This value is not created by the exchange but rather exists prior to it. In effect, it is an existence condition for the exchange itself.

Since monetary transactions pertain to two commodities of equal pre-existing value, they cannot be debt relations. Because of their theory of exchange, neoclassical economists have never been able to deal properly with debt–credit relations. Historically two solutions have been offered to this question.

The first explanation implied that banks are pure intermediaries allocating a pre-existing stock of commodity money among agents needing capital. Within the context of this, deposits make loans or, perhaps more correctly, savings make loans. This tradition was followed by Hayek (1931, 1941), Gurley and Shaw (1960), Koopmans (1933) and many others, including those referred to by Realfonzo (1998). If, however, banks were to lend more money than the amount that they had obtained as original deposit liabilities, the law of exchange of equivalent values would have been broken and, as a consequence, a cumulative neo-Wicksellian process of inflation would be the outcome of this excess of credit (Seccareccia 1990).

A second solution offered by neoclassical theorists interprets the role of banks as the supplier of pure accounting services. When all trading is closed, there may still remain some transactors who, because of imperfect information or indivisibility in the barter process, find themselves indebted to other transactors, and therefore require money to settle their debts. Banks emerge in the clearing process with holdings of an exogenous stock of money which is then provided to all those transactors facing a financing constraint. This view is found in some of the early works of Clower (1967), Starr (1972) and Ostroy (1973) and is reviewed in Parguez (1975).

For either of these two solutions, the TMC invalidates their starting proposition. As we have argued previously, banks issuing debts on themselves for the financing of loans can never be intermediaries between savers and borrowers. Even when banks are forced into a position of advancing new loans in order to compensate for the high liquidity preference of the public, they do not in fact lend savings (Graziani 1996) since savers do not 'lend' their deposits to banks. Banks have to issue new loans in order to refinance any outstanding debts by firms. Consequently, they can never be pure intermediaries nor suppliers of accounting services that do not create money.

Money and utility

A second major proposition of the neoclassical conception of money as a pure medium of exchange is based on the presupposition that money exists because it has a specific intrinsic value. As put forth by Koopmans (1933) and later by Patinkin (1965), the value of money must be explained in the same way as the value of any other commodity, by the principle of marginal utility. This proposition has two major consequences.

First, money has a specific utility if, by using it as an intermediary in exchange, it increases the real wealth of transactors. Unfortunately, neoclassical economists have never provided a substantive proof for this proposition. As implied by the first proposition, money is introduced in an already perfect system of exchanges leading to a general equilibrium consistent with utility maximization for every transactor (Hahn 1982).

Second, even if a proof for the utility of money were to be found, it would merely explain the existence of a specific demand for money.

However, this Patinkinesque demand for money is not an indirect demand for commodities and services, but a reflection of the share of the aggregate stock of wealth which is held in money form instead of being exchanged for physical commodities and services. Herein lies the well-known paradox that money would derive its specific value from its role as intermediary in transactions, but its utility can only be derived if it is *held* by economic agents. In equilibrium, therefore, the whole stock of commodity money would be hoarded, and money would not play any role in circulation! For such reasons, this second proposition of neoclassical monetary theory contradicts what we have described as the dynamic nature of money analysed within the TMC, in which money is never a commodity possessing any intrinsic value. It is a pure conventional debt issued to generate a sequence of transactions leading to the formation of real wealth.

Money exogeneity

In neoclassical economics, money must also be scarce to have a specific value. The scarcity principle implies that the available quantity of money must be independent of the set of demand schedules for both money and other commodities. As emphasized by the neoclassical school from Walras onwards, the requirement of exogeneity became a logical necessity for the application of the scarcity principle. In this way, as an exogenous variable, money can never be credit-driven and hinge on the loan-granting actions of commercial banks. To achieve this result, banks are assumed not to create money because they are considered as pure financial intermediaries, with the supply of money being determined by the exogenous actions of the central bank, as in the standard monetarist model. However, the error of the monetarist school was to confuse logical necessity with empirical reality which invalidates this third proposition of neoclassical economics. Within the TMC, the quantity of money is strictly endogenous since it is loan-determined and cannot be set by the exogenous actions of the central bank.

The Post Keynesians and the TMC

Unlike the situation in neoclassical economics, it is more difficult to compare the Post Keynesian theory of money *vis-à-vis* the TMC because there exists no unified Post Keynesian conception of money. We shall try, therefore, first to address what the broad Post Keynesian approach and the TMC have in common, then to discuss what is deemed to be unclear, or perhaps missing, within the Post Keynesian tradition.

Points of convergence

All Post Keynesian economists agree with the theory of the monetary circuit on the rejection of the first proposition of the neoclassical theory of money. They have accepted the credit/debt theory of money whereby money is always a debt issued by banks on themselves to finance loans. For this reason, they also reject the third proposition of neoclassical economics. Money is always endogenous because its quantity is demand-determined. Numerous Post Keynesians have thus broken away from Keynes's conception of money as it was spelled out originally in Chapter 17 of the *General Theory*. Money cannot be conceived as a commodity having a scarcity value amid other existing commodities in the system to which the equimarginal condition is applied.

However, within the Post Keynesian literature, the so-called 'horizontalist' view is perhaps the closest to the circuit theory of money (Rochon 1999). Within the Kaldor-Moore horizontalist model, banks always issue debts on themselves to finance loans granted to firms that are seeking to acquire real resources. In our opinion, the famous interest/money space horizontal diagram of the money supply rightly spells out that, for a given level of interest rates, banks accommodate all creditworthy demand for loans. Furthermore, horizontalists endorse the circuitist view that the central bank cannot directly control the quantity of credit money. What the central bank can control is the level of interest rates charged by the banks on their loans, with the latter setting their loan rates by merely fixing a mark-up on the base rate established by the central bank. Interest rates are, therefore, exogenous since they are not determined by a market mechanism that adjusts the demand for money to a fixed supply. Given bank mark-ups, the level of interest rates is determined by the behaviour of the central bank in targeting a specific inflation rate.

Indeed, horizontalists reject two crucial aspects of the *General Theory* conception of money. First, like the theory of the monetary circuit, they question the link between money and uncertainty. Keynesian uncertainty cannot *in esse* explain the existence of money, since firms would need bank loans to finance expenditures even within a stationary or ergodic environment. Money is a right to acquire real wealth generated by previous loans, and if sellers of real resources were absolutely uncertain about the outcome of the loan process, they would never accept payments in bank liabilities. Uncertainty can only have an impact on the creditworthiness rules imposed by banks, thereby altering the effective demand for loans. Second, horizontalists have emphasized the distinction between the demand for loans and the Keynesian demand for money, the latter of which is merely the demand for liquid balances emerging *ex post* out of the credit money previously issued to finance loans. Much like the TMC, therefore, they conclude that there can never be an excess supply of money (Lavoie 1992).

Diverging opinions

Some Post Keynesian economists, who have remained too strongly connected with the monetary economics of the *General Theory*, have been unable to grasp fully the consequences of the TMC and do not dissociate themselves completely from the second proposition of neoclassical economics. The latter proposition pertaining to the stock demand for money was of crucial importance for the *General Theory* explanation of the non-neutrality of money. As is well known, the Keynes of the *General Theory* emphasized the demand for money as a component of aggregate wealth along Marshallian lines. Portfolio holders choose to hold money instead of other commodities because of its intrinsic liquidity characteristic. On the other hand, he assumed an exogenous quantity of money in accordance with the neoclassical scarcity principle. From his hybrid analytical framework, in Chapter 17 of the *General Theory* Keynes could then explain why the endogenous rate of interest, determined on the basis of the scarcity principle, could be the source of the average expected rate of profit in the economy. A strong rejection by Keynes of the second proposition of neoclassical monetary economics would certainly have jeopardized and, perhaps, could have led to an unravelling of the whole *General Theory* analytics.

These difficulties notwithstanding, many Post Keynesians, for instance, Dalziel (1995) and Howells (1995, 1997), have explicitly maintained the Keynesian demand for money as a crucial analytical device in explaining the dynamics of a monetary economy even in an endogenous money context. Moreover, some such as Chick (1992) and Howells (1995, 1997) do not accept the principle of an absolute credit-driven money. There would always be the possibility that money could be created through pure portfolio operations by the central bank. Others refuse to recognize that the central bank cannot have power over bank money creation via quantity constraints. That would supposedly depend upon the willingness of the central bank to be accommodating in satisfying the liquidity needs of commercial banks. Even horizontalists display some reluctance on this question. Moore (1996), for instance, accepts that there had been times when the central bank was not accommodating. However, much of this debate arises because Post Keynesians postulate a central bank without the state and ignore the impact of state expenditure on bank reserves. In contrast with what we have tried to do, they do not apply the endogeneity principle to the state itself (Moore 1988).

Even when they address the role of credit, many Post Keynesians, including some horizontalists, impose constraints on what can be financed by credit money. For instance, in Moore (1988) bank loans only go towards the financing of firms' circulating capital requirements. Like Wray (1990), Moore himself conceives of loan financing as a means of bridging the gap between firms' expenditure and revenue. Hence, banks issue debts for the sole purpose of financing deficits. This view is completely at odds with the TMC which shows that firms' or governments' deficits can only be accounted in the reflux phase of monetary circulation. Such a misunderstanding of the financing process is perhaps best revealed by the way in which profits are conceived in investment financing. Post Keynesians, especially of Kaleckian pedigree, make the distinction between internal financing of investment out of business-retained earnings and external or debt financing. As has been discussed elsewhere (Seccareccia 1998), this distinction is somewhat misleading since in the TMC the internal generation of finance via business profits is merely the macroeconomic outcome of the new indebtedness of other agents in a monetary economy.

This inability on the part of some Post Keynesians to sever links with the second proposition of neoclassical monetary theory may perhaps also explain why some, such as Chick (1992), have endorsed an evolutionist conception of money. Accordingly, there would have been at least three stages of monetary evolution. In the first stage, banks are pure intermediaries which recycle previous savings since they cannot freely issue debts on themselves. In a second stage of this historical evolution, banks can issue debts on themselves because of the accommodating role of a central bank. There is apparently also a third stage, the disintermediation one, in which banks are presumed to go to the financial markets actively to raise funds via liability management. Funding out of these markets to acquire necessary cash reserves would be substituted for pure bank credit, thereby further eroding the reserve constraint on the ability of banks to provide credit. As our earlier discussion of the history of money has shown, however, such an evolutionist view of monetary developments is somewhat equivocal since banks have never been pure intermediaries.

The neo-chartalist approach and the TMC

While neoclassical economists point to the efficiency gains of introducing money in the context of barter exchange, and while Keynes had emphasized its liquidity role in the context of fundamental uncertainty, there is a third view on the existence of money. We may describe this third approach, as it has been put forth by Mosler (1997–8), Bell (1998b) and Wray (1998), as the neo-chartalist approach.[2]

The starting proposition of the neo-chartalist approach is that money is always a creation of the state and that the state can ultimately impose any token as money simply by requiring that tax liabilities be paid in such a unit. In this regard, taxes appear as the fundamental prerequisite to the existence of money. By varying the public's tax liability, it is assumed that the state can even determine the value of money, its purchasing power. From these propositions, neo-chartalists derive a conception of monetary circulation that is closer to the TMC than, say, that put forth by Keynes in the *General Theory*.

Taxes are required to impose state money by inducing private agents to sell real resources to the state in order to obtain sufficient money to settle their accounts with the latter. Taxes cannot, therefore, be used to finance state expenditures. The state must first inject money into the economy by issuing at will the token in which it has decreed taxes must be paid.

According to the neo-chartalist approach, in modern economies the state token is essentially created when the central bank issues debt on itself at the request of the treasury. When taxes are paid *a posteriori* in the reflux process, they extinguish an equivalent quantity of the state-created money. From this circuitist analysis of the financing process of the state, neo-chartalist writers are brought to reject the conventional analysis of budget deficits.

The orthodox notion of government deficit financing and the so-called 'monetization' of deficits is highly misleading and, indeed, a misnomer. Since deficits are merely *ex post* accounting values measuring the net flux/reflux process pertaining to the state sector, they have already been financed. As was shown earlier in our discussion of the TMC, the counterpart of the state budget deficit is both an increase in the private sector holdings of money and an increase in bank reserves. However, as soon as bank reserves become excessive, the banks will stop borrowing reserves in the funds market and thereby deprive the central bank of any power of intervention. Indeed, if reserves are excessive, banks will actually try to purchase new bonds, whose effect would be to push up bond prices and thus bring about a collapse in interest rates. We can also assume that other private sector holders will attempt to do the same, thereby further accelerating the fall in the level of interest rates in the economy. From this, we can infer that the state must issue new bonds just to keep interest rates at some target level defined by the monetary authorities. Neo-chartalists would generally agree with what is essentially a Post Keynesian horizontalist position, that the central bank sets the base level of interest rates (see Wray 1998). However, any uneasiness with the horizontalist position by neo-chartalists may be due to the fact that Post Keynesians tend to have a theory of the central bank without the state. A careful understanding of this link, and the role of the treasury, along the lines that we have spelled out previously, would probably bring these two views closer to the circuitist position.

However, an important difference between the TMC and the neo-chartalist view relates to the emphasis that the latter places on taxes. As we have defended in our historical discussion, viable monetary systems existed during periods of economic history when taxes were quite insignificant. What matters, therefore, was not whether tax liabilities were of any significance but rather whether, largely through the legal system, the state endorsed existing banks by allowing them to issue debts on themselves. For very long historical periods, state money had been quite negligible in relation to the circulation of bank liabilities. By linking the existence of money exclusively to that of taxes, neo-chartalists are led to find money in societies where there are heavy taxes levied *in natura*. Taxes can more easily be levied if there is a state-imposed unit of account which would serve as money (Wray 1998). Ironically, such a definition of money as a pure unit of account is very close to the Walrasian conception of *numéraire* money in which it is the (state) auctioneer that chooses a *numéraire* before efficient trading takes place!

The state can endorse central and/or private bank liabilities, but it cannot impose the value of money. While the neo-chartalists seem to identify a positive relation between the value of money and the amount of tax liabilities in an economy, what actually matters is rather the nature or composition of state expenditure. In other words, what is consequential to the value of money is primarily the ability of state expenditure to increase the real wealth of society either directly, through the production of public goods, or indirectly, through their capacity to foster private investment expenditures. If state money is issued merely to finance wasteful expenditures that have no serious positive consequences on the private or collective wealth of a community, the effect in the long run would be to depreciate the value of money, regardless of the power of taxation of the state.

Finally, the neo-chartalist theory of money logically implies that state money precedes private bank money. In other words, the creation of state money upon which taxes can be collected is followed by the emergence of commercial bank money when the state accepts private bank liability in payment of taxes. As emphasized by Bell (1998a), bank money is hierarchically inferior or subordinate to state money. Banks' credit activity is a leverage on the existing stock of state money (Wray 1998). This presupposition signifies that state money is endogenous but bank money is not since, in the final analysis, it is constrained by the variation of the former. This conception of the monetary system which, as it stands, hovers closely to a textbook analysis of how bank money is created, needs to be better articulated. As we have sought to show in our discussion of the relations among banks, firms and the state, the TMC can provide neo-chartalists with a more comprehensive framework of analysis.

Conclusion

In this chapter, we have discussed the main outlines of the TMC approach to money and contrasted this with alternative approaches, including neoclassical theories and contemporary heterodox views. As far as the latter are concerned, we have tried to argue from the beginning that both Post Keynesians and neo-chartalists will find a more cogent and coherent integration of money and commercial banking within the general framework of circulation as enunciated within the TMC. With its broad analytical framework, the TMC is able both to accommodate and to offer meaningful solutions to many of the enigmas presently confronting competing heterodox theories of money.

Notes

The authors wish to thank Marc Lavoie for his helpful comments.

1 As defined by Keynes (1930) in the *Treatise on Money*.
2 The approach is originally anchored in the work of Knapp (1924).

References

Bailly, J.-L. (1992) 'Nouvelles considérations sur le motif de "finance" de John Maynard Keynes', *Économie Appliquée* 45, 1: 105–27.
Bell, S. (1998a) 'The Hierarchy of Money', Working Paper No. 231, Jerome Levy Economics Institute, April.
—— (1998b) 'Can Taxes and Bonds Finance Government Spending?', Working Paper No. 245, Jerome Levy Economics Institute, July.
Chick, V. (1992) *On Money, Method and Keynes: Selected Essays*, ed. P. Arestis and S. C. Dow, London: Macmillan.
Clower, R. (1967) 'A Reconsideration of the Microfoundations of Monetary Theory', *Western Economic Journal* 6, 1: 1–8.
—— (1969) 'Introduction', in R. W. Clower (ed.), *Monetary Theory*, Harmondsworth: Penguin.
Dalziel, P. (1995) 'The Keynesian Multiplier, Liquidity Preference and Endogenous Money', *Journal of Post Keynesian Economics* 18, 3: 311–31.
Davies, G. (1994) *A History of Money: From Ancient Times to the Present Day*, Cardiff: University of Wales Press.
Einzig, P. (1966) *Primitive Money in its Ethnological, Historical and Economic Aspects*, Oxford: Pergamon Press.
Gnos, C. (1998) 'La thése de l'endogénéité de la monnaie: la contribution de la théorie du circuit', mimeo, University of Bourgogne, September.
Graziani, A. (1990) 'The Theory of the Monetary Circuit', *Économies et Sociétés* 24, 6: 7–36.
—— (1996) 'Money as Purchasing Power and Money as a Stock of Wealth in Keynesian Thought', in G. Deleplace and E. J. Nell (eds), *Money in Motion: The Post Keynesian and Circulation Approaches*, London: Macmillan.
—— (1998) 'The Monetary Theory of Production' mimeo, University of Rome, March.
Gurley, J. G. and Shaw, E. S. (1960) *Money in a Theory of Finance*, Washington: Brookings Institution.
Hahn, F. H. (1982) *Money and Inflation*, Oxford: Blackwell.
von Hayek, F. A. (1931) *Prices and Production*, London: Routledge.
—— (1941) *The Pure Theory of Capital*, Chicago: University of Chicago Press.
Heinsohn, G. and Steiger, O. (1984) 'Marx and Keynes – Private Property and Money', *Économies et Sociétés* 18, 4: 37–71.
—— (1994) 'A Private Property Theory of Debts, Interest and Money', *Économies et Sociétés* 28, 1–2: 9–24.
Howells, P. G. A. (1995) 'The Demand for Endogenous Money', *Journal of Post Keynesian Economics* 18, 1: 89–106.
—— (1997) 'The Demand for Money: A Rejoinder', *Journal of Post Keynesian Economics* 19, 3: 429–35.
Innes, A. M. (1913) 'What is Money?', *Banking Law Journal* May: 377–408.
Jevons, W. S. (1875) *Money and the Mechanism of Exchange*, London: D. Appleton.
Knapp, G. F. (1924) *The State Theory of Money*, London: Macmillan.
Koopmans, J. G. (1933) 'Zum Problem des Neutrales Geldes', in F. A. von Hayek (ed.) *Beiträge zus Geldtheorie*, Vienna: J. Springer.
Lavoie, M. (1992) *Foundations of Post-Keynesian Economic Analysis*, Aldershot: Edward Elgar.

Léonard, J. (1987) 'Le paradoxe de l'intérêt et la crise de l'économie monétaire de production', *Économies et Sociétés* 21, 9: 149–68.

Menger, K. (1892) 'On the Origin of Money', *Economic Journal* 2, 6: 239–55.

Moore, B. J. (1988) *Horizontalists and Verticalists: The Macroeconomics of Credit Money*, Cambridge: Cambridge University Press.

—— (1996) 'The Money Supply Process: A Historical Interpretation', in G. Deleplace and E. J. Nell (eds) *Money in Motion: The Post Keynesian and Circulation Approaches*, London: Macmillan.

Mosler, W. (1997–8) 'Full Employment and Price Stability', *Journal of Post Keynesian Economics* 20, 2: 167–82.

Nell, E. J. (1998) *The General Theory of Transformational Growth*, Cambridge: Cambridge University Press.

Ostroy, J. M. (1973) 'The Informational Efficiency of Monetary Exchange', *American Economic Review* 63, 4: 597–610.

Parguez, A. (1975) *Monnaie et macroéconomie: théorie de la monnaie en déséquilibre*, Paris: Economica.

—— 1996) 'Beyond Scarcity: A Reappraisal of the Theory of the Monetary Circuit', in G. Deleplace and E. J. Nell (eds), *Money in Motion: The Post Keynesian and Circulation Approaches*, London: Macmillan.

—— (1998) 'Government Deficits within the Monetary Production Economy: The Tragedy of the Race to Balanced Budgets', mimeo, University of Besançon, March.

Patinkin, D. (1965) *Money, Interest and Prices: An Integration of Monetary and Value Theory*, 2nd edn, New York: Harper and Row.

Ray, A. J. (1996) *I Have Lived Here Since the World Began: An Illustrated History of Canada's Native People*, Toronto: Lester.

Ray, A. J. and Freeman, D. B. (1978) *Give Us Good Measure: An Economic Analysis of Relations Between the Indians and the Hudson's Bay Company Before 1763*, Toronto: University of Toronto Press.

Realfonzo, R. (1998), *Money and Banking: Theory and Debate (1900–1940)*, Cheltenham: Edward Elgar.

Renaud, J.-F. (1998) 'The Problem of the Monetary Realization of Profits in a Post–Keynesian Sequential Financing Model: The Two Solutions of the Kaleckian Option', mimeo, University of Lyon II, May.

Rochon, L.-P. (1997) 'Keynes's Finance Motive: A Re-Assessment', *Review of Political Economy* 9, 3: 277–93.

—— (1999) *Credit, Money and Production: An Alternative Keynesian Approach*, Cheltenham: Edward Elgar, forthcoming.

Seccareccia, M. (1990) 'The Two Faces of Neo-Wicksellianism during the 1930s: The Austrians and the Swedes', in D. E. Moggridge (ed.) *Perspectives on the History of Economic Thought*, vol. 4, Aldershot: Edward Elgar.

—— (1996) 'Post Keynesian Fundism and Monetary Circulation', in G. Deleplace and E. J. Nell (eds), *Money in Motion: The Post Keynesian and Circulation Approaches*, London: Macmillan.

—— (1998) 'Pricing, Investment and the Financing of Production within the Framework of the Monetary Circuit: Some Empirical Evidence', mimeo, University of Ottawa, May.

Smithin, J. (1997) 'An Alternative Monetary Model of Inflation and Growth', *Review of Political Economy* 9, 4: 395–409.

Starr, R. M. (1972) 'Exchange in Barter and Monetary Economies', *Quarterly Journal of Economics* 86, 2: 290–302.

Vallageas, B. (1998) 'The Circuit Analysis, the Monetary Economy of Production and the Multisectoral Analysis', mimeo, University of Paris-Sud, June.

Wittfogel, K. (1959) *Oriental Despotism: A Comparative Study in Total Power*, Princeton: Princeton University Press.

Wray, L. R. (1990) *Money and Credit in Capitalist Economies: The Endogenous Money Approach*, Aldershot: Edward Elgar.

—— (1998), *Understanding Modern Money: The Key to Full Employment and Price Stability*, Cheltenham: Edward Elgar.

6 Money and effective demand

Victoria Chick

Introduction

In Post Keynesian theory we are accustomed to drawing an aggregate demand curve which slopes upward in a space defined by the value of output (PQ, price times quantity of output) and the amount of employment (N). It is plausible enough: a rise in employment should surely imply a rise in total expenditure. However if we compare the aggregate demand curve of the neoclassical synthesis, we find it is downward sloping in P, Q space. Since N and Q are positively related, prices must fall as employment increases. By contrast, in Post Keynesian theory we either assume that costs and prices are constant as output and employment rise or that prices rise as output rises to cover rising costs. There is a simple explanation of the difference, contained in the basic message derived from the work on the finance motive and endogenous money: that a rise in effective demand is accompanied, in Post Keynesian theory, by a rise in the money supply. By contrast, aggregate demand in the neoclassical synthesis is based on the assumption that the money supply is fixed. Unless there is some compensating variation in velocity, then a rise in Q entails a fall in P.

Readers will have noticed a slippage between 'aggregate' and 'effective' demand in the previous paragraph. In Post Keynesian theory, cost conditions combine with demand to determine both output and prices, while in the neoclassical synthesis, prices are a monetary phenomenon only and output is determined by the labour market and technology. What needs to be argued is that to some extent prices (and output) in Post Keynesian theory are also a monetary phenomenon, though money only plays an enabling or an accommodating role, not a causal one. Money also has implications for the multiplier, which is only the dynamic path of effective demand following an autonomous change in expenditure. This role for money is only the mirror image of elements already present in Post Keynesian theory, but it is one which needs some attention.

The theory of endogenous money states that support of some expenditures and productive processes by bank credit creates new money. This new money in turn provides the extra purchasing power needed to raise prices as output expands. In the Post Keynesian vision of endogenous money, not only is the money supply flexible, but the money supply process is *connected* to the same processes which result in a rise in effective demand. In the neoclassical vision, the level of the money supply is determined by the monetary authorities who 'fix' it wherever they wish, for reasons which are not explained but are entirely separate from the determination of effective demand.

The essential neoclassical vision is of a zero-sum game, while for Post Keynesians both the existence of slack resources and – most importantly – an endogenous money supply create the possibility of positive-sum outcomes. This conflict of understanding as to how the economic system works has probably come up many times before, but I offer one example: crowding out. It is easy to imagine that the neoclassical view that government expenditure and investment are substitutes is due to their assumption of full employment, but this answer is too easy: full employment is a sufficient but not a necessary condition for crowding out. Crowding out may occur at less than full employment if the money supply is fixed, because a rise in government expenditure financed by borrowing raises the rate of interest and crowds out other interest-sensitive expenditure, in other words, investment. Keynes (1936: 200) explained that this is exactly why the maximum effect from public works is only obtained by financing the expenditure by new money, which will keep interest rates stable, not by borrowing, which will cause rates to rise. If the money supply rises in financing investment, there need be no crowding out.

If only one could stop there! But the relationship between money and effective demand is far from simple, and certainly not one-to-one. Not only have many causes of changes in bank credit been mooted in endogenous money theory, but there have also been other versions of the relation between effective demand and the money supply, particularly in the work of the circuit theorists and of the school of Bernard Schmitt. I cannot possibly review these different theories exhaustively, but it does seem to me that the issues raised by these different approaches to the connection between money and effective demand should have at least an airing, with a view to discovering where some of the unresolved problems lie. I shall start with the finance motive and the development of endogenous money theory. This should put us in a better position to see, in subsequent sections, how the alternative approaches fit in.

The finance motive

Keynes's approach to money in the *General Theory* was to analyse the effects of the money supply after it had come into existence and, famously, to treat the money supply as given. The only hints of a role for bank borrowing come in the discussion of the maximum effect of government expenditure, the offhand remark that the significance of the rate of interest to the determination of investment was its role as the cost of borrowing (Keynes 1936: 165) and the discussion of borrower's and lender's risk (Keynes 1936: 144–5). From the didactic point of view, this procedure had some desirable effects: it redefined the rate of interest as a monetary variable, and separated the rate of interest from the rate of profit. But while Keynes broke the classical dichotomy between the monetary and real aspects of the economy, this device simultaneously created a new dichotomy between flows (the analysis of income) and stocks (portfolio analysis). This dichotomy is all too easily translated back to the classical form. The portfolio already consists of purely monetary assets, and to restore the dichotomy the first step was to reinterpret income as 'real', but this left the concept of interest as a monetary phenomenon unaffected. Restoring the classical dichotomy in full required the further step of redefining the portfolio, and the money supply itself, in 'real terms', so that money was once again the chief determinant of prices. These changes were in due course made.

From the modelling point of view, Keynes's technique usefully avoids many of the dimension problems entailed in mixing stocks and flows (Bushaw and Clower 1957, Lloyd 1960). Stock-flow problems remain in Keynes's liquidity preference theory because of the inclusion of transactions demand with portfolio elements (Chick 1981), but at the same time it entails ignoring the monetary counterpart of each flow transaction. We say that consumption is behaviourally related to income (the aspect that Keynes considered), but it is also financed by income (which he did not discuss). The counterpart of income as finance may be the use of bank credit or the transfer of deposits in the payment of wages, and the counterpart of consumption is the use of these deposits to pay for goods. Keynes's single-entry bookkeeping does no harm when the system is in a steady state, as the circular flow of income can be stated either in money or in terms of goods and labour time. But when the level of income changes, we need to know more.

Keynes was pushed into acknowledging the need to say more about the monetary side of expenditure by the debate which followed the publication of the *General Theory*. In articles in 1937, 1938 and 1939, Keynes developed the idea of the *finance motive*. When this material was taken up again in the 1970s and early 1980s it was more or less decided that Keynes had tried to make the valid point that investment needed a source of finance, which he assimilated to the demand for money. Keynes called this additional source of demand for money the finance motive, to be considered along with the transactions, precautionary and speculative motives for holding money. As an additional demand for money the finance motive would raise the rate of interest, a conclusion which, it is believed, he had earlier tried to avoid as it was reminiscent of loanable funds theory. Portraying the finance of investment as an additional money demand also avoids the obvious conflict with his assumption that the money supply is given.

If any debate in economics may be said to have a conclusion, the point taken from the finance motive debate was that it was useful to have the role of bank credit in the finance of investment acknowledged, but that Keynes had been wrong to try to assimilate this demand for bank credit to money demand as an additional motive. Rather it should be seen as part of the process of the supply of money (Graziani 1987). This message was then transformed into part of the theory of endogenous money.

Endogenous money

The concept of endogenous money has taken many forms in Post Keynesian theory, but as Howells (1998) has recently concluded, the point on which all agree is that money comes into the system as a result of a rise in some element(s) of expenditure being financed by bank credit, which creates deposits. Investment has more usually been identified as the important element, though shortly after a period of strong 'trade union pushfulness' Moore (1985) proposed a rise in the wage bill as the main instigating source. Howells (1998) emphasizes consumer spending, and both he and Dow (1993) analyse the use of bank credit to purchase assets. Let us follow some of these suggestions through.

The most familiar story is based on bank finance of investment, so we shall start there. The investment represents an increase over an existing equilibrium situation. It will be seen that in contrast to the 'bastard Keynesian' understanding of the multiplier as referring only to expenditure, here we are reflecting Keynes's emphasis (1936: ch. 10) on production as well as expenditure, on effective rather than aggregate demand.

Case I

An entrepreneur wishes to buy a piece of equipment and arranges an overdraft limit to finance its purchase. Suppose first that the equipment is available 'off the peg'. The equipment is bought and the supplier banks the entrepreneur's cheque. For simplicity assume there is only one bank, whose advances and deposits rise. At the macro level, investment demand, profits, advances and the money supply have risen, and inventories have fallen. Output and employment are not affected in this period. What happens next depends on how the capital-goods producer reacts to the unexpected sale and the unexpected additional deposit. He is in a position to expand output, using his increased deposit to pay for additional workers, if he believes this demand will be repeated in future. He can add to reserves, held in the form of financial assets; or he can repay some outstanding debt.

Case II

Now suppose the entrepreneur decides to build a piece of capital equipment, in his own factory, or to extend the plant. The investment is to be produced within the period. Let the producer of capital equipment arrange an overdraft to pay the additional wage bill which expansion of production entails. When the wage bill is paid, the deposits of workers rise, which is the monetary manifestation of the increase in income. Workers then spend their income, partly on consumption by transferring deposits to retailers, who place increased orders with producers, and partly on financial assets, by transferring deposits to the former owners or to current issuers of these assets. Production of consumer goods rises to meet the demand, employment increases and deposits are transferred to workers, and so on. This is the multiplier. In second and subsequent rounds, increased cashflow from sales (transfer of deposits from consumers) may be used to finance the additional wage bills in the consumer goods industries. The overdraft may be paid off either from increased sales, if the investment pays off promptly, or from the proceeds of one or other form of funding, such as floating long-term debt or equity (Chick 1984, 1997, Studart 1995).

Case III

The last example was made simple by the assumption that the investment was produced in-house. Somewhere between this example and the purchase of equipment out of stocks (Case I) is a more complex case, in which equipment is to be produced for a client. Once again let us suppose that the increase in the wage bill is paid by bank borrowing, which sets off the multiplier as before. When the equipment is delivered and payment is required, either (Case IIIa) the entrepreneur also borrows, or (Case IIIb) he pays by transferring a claim to a deposit, which may entail his first realizing assets. In Case IIIa, where both production and expenditure are supported by bank lending, the expenditure loan pays off the producer's overdraft, so that the amount of monetary increase and its effects are the same as for producing in-house. Both the initial shift in demand and the subsequent movement 'along the curve' represented by induced consumption have their monetary counterparts, but only the shift is accompanied by new money. The induced expenditure and output are financed by transfers of deposits. If the entrepreneur pays out of his positive bank balance (Case IIIb), the producer's debt is cancelled and the money supply, taking account of both the payments to workers and the cancellation of an equivalent debt, is unchanged. Thus there is no automatic provision in this case for new money to circulate in support of induced consumption, or, indeed, for the new level of investment to be sustained. If there is to be a multiplier, new credit limits will have to be negotiated to support increased employment in the consumer goods industries.

Case IV

For completeness, and for a useful comparison with other approaches, let us make a rather unKeynesian assumption that, rather than the producer making equipment for an unknown but expected market sale, the entrepreneur not only places an order but also pays at least part of the price up front, with subsequent instalments. This permits the producer to pay the workers out of these payments. The only issue is whether the entrepreneur borrowed the money or transfers a deposit, as in Case III. The first alternative (Case IVa) will of course result in new money; the second will not (Case IVb).

So we reach a first conclusion, that although effective demand and the money supply are related, the relationship is far from simple and depends on the fine detail of the source of payments and their timing. The extent of a multiplier reaction also depends on these matters, and this point was disguised in Keynes's treatment. There are further assumptions lurking under these examples which need to be delved into, because they divide the protagonists mentioned in the introduction. Let us introduce the basic idea put forward both by the circuit theorists and the Schmitt school, that the fundamental lending activity of banks, and the basic role of what they call money, is the support of working capital for production of both consumer goods and investment goods.

Money as a means of financing working capital

The circuit school is associated with the names of Parguez, Graziani and M. Lavoie, and the Schmitt school includes Cencini, Gnos and Rossi. While they have their differences, some of them profound, there is an important element in common. This element is a story which goes as follows: at the start of the economic circuit or opening of a 'quantum period' (Schmitt 1982), firms secure from banks the right to facilities which allow them to pay their wage bill.[1] Graziani would call this right 'credit', and once exercised, 'money'. This facility permits production to take place, generating income. To the Schmitt school, Graziani and his followers misidentify money as credit (Cencini 1985: 144); among the former school, money is described variously as the 'numbers' emitted by banks in making payments or the action which results in credit and/or deposits. Whichever it is, it exists only for the duration of the payment process. Deposits for this school are not money but a form of wealth (Graziani 1996: 139).

Both schools seems to agree that when workers use their income (received in the form of deposits) to consume, the act of consumption destroys the 'money', as payments to firms are used to repay the debt incurred. With consumption, not only the initial credit but also (explicitly in the Schmitt school) income is destroyed. The destruction of credit closes the 'circuit'.

The Schmitt school emphasize the generative power of labour to create income and the role of this activity to give value (purchasing power) to 'money': they argue that income, which they equate to the wages paid to labour, is the basis of 'money', and that money's nature is that of a 'vehicle' for the circulation of income (Cencini 1995: 17–21), thus deriving a kind of 'production theory of money' in contrast with Keynes's 'monetary theory of production.'

The conundrum which remains is why the value of something (or some action) which is, by their description, evanescent, or destroyed almost as soon as it is created, should be of interest. Graziani admits to a similar puzzle, when he points out that in a world of perfect certainty, this 'money, while still being a necessary element in a monetary economy, would no longer be an observable variable' (Graziani 1996: 143).

In these approaches, investment is not singled out for special treatment: it does not matter whether production takes place in the consumption goods industries or the capital goods industries. And whereas my Post Keynesian cases involve bank credit both for working capital and for expenditure on final product, Graziani regards the finance of working capital (whether devoted to the production of consumption or investment goods) as the *only* legitimate use of bank credit. At least I think legitimacy is at issue when he says 'can' and 'cannot', for whether banks ought to lend for the purchase of commodities as opposed to their production: 'A bank cannot buy commodities by means of its own credit . . . bank credit can only be used in order to bridge the gap between production and resale of commodities' (Graziani 1990: 15).

Graziani (1990) refers to the finance of working capital as 'initial finance' because it starts off the circuit. In contrast, the finance of investment is called 'final finance', as, he states, this comes at the end of the economic circuit.

> Final finance is liquidity that firms get back as proceeds from sales of commodities or from new issues on the financial market. . . . What matters to firms is that final finance be sufficient to cover total initial finance. If this happens, firms will be able to repay their debt to the banks.
> (Graziani 1990: 15–16, commas and italics suppressed)

Starting with this proposition, he argues that to finance investment amounts to banks buying commodities with credit and thus acquiring these commodities without giving anything in return. Stretching a point, the most a bank could do is to finance the 'temporary holding of a capital good which has subsequently found a buyer who has financed the purchase by means of his own income. . . . [T]he final outcome should be that the bank gets back its money' (Graziani 1990: 15).

A comparison with the Post Keynesian approach

There are several points of disparity between a Post Keynesian description of the role of bank credit, such as those in the above cases, and circuit theory. First there is a question of definitions. To Post Keynesians, money is bank liabilities, that is, deposits (cash is irrelevant here). This, it should be emphasized, conforms to the definition used by central banks and international statistical agencies. The hallmark of this money is its liquidity or general acceptability, as a means of payment, or as the unit of account for debt contracts. Bank liabilities are to be sharply distinguished from bank credit, the advances which count as bank assets, even though bank credit is used to effect payments and is responsible for the creation of bank deposits. By contrast, these two schools refer to bank credit as money, Schmitt does so explicitly, to emphasize the role of this credit in effecting payments. (There is an echo here of the debates on what aspect of money is its prime or unique function.) Parguez (1996) distinguishes between 'credit-money' (by which he means bank credit used to effect payments) and 'asset money' (deposits). Although credit and money are often confused in the Post Keynesian literature and elsewhere, for those who are careful to distinguish the two sides of the balance sheet, 'credit-money' usually refers to the fact that money takes the form of loans to banks (deposits), rather than full-bodied coin.[2]

These differences of language reflect differences in the concept of money. The circuit school argues against the evolutionist view that money has changed its form through the centuries and that there are theoretical implications of this. They argue that it is the credit base which *defines* money, and that it has always been so: for them, exchange with full-bodied coin is barter.

> An economy using as money a commodity coming out of a regular process of production, cannot be distinguished from a *barter economy*. A true monetary economy must therefore be using a *token money*, which is nowadays a paper currency . . . Even a metallic coin is credit money: as Keynes once said, a rupee is a 'note printed on silver'.
> (Graziani 1990: 10, original emphasis)[3]

There are some similarities with the emphasis that Hicks in his last book (1989) placed on the early development of credit and the role of the market in creating money, though his account is evolutionary and more inclusive.

I may not speak for all Post Keynesians, but in my view, the feature which distinguishes money from credit is the general acceptability of deposits, as against the personal quality of credit. The central mystery of modern banking is that expenditure against a bank credit agreement gives rise to deposits, which transforms a bilateral contract into a liquid, multilaterally accepted, asset. In Post Keynesian thinking, the status of money is given to banks' liabilities, not their assets. This does not diminish the importance of credit, but while the circuit and Schmitt schools aver that credit *is* money, the Post Keynesian school argues that it is the proximate *cause* of money.

Second, the circuit story assumes that wage earners have positive deposits and make payments by transferring them, while all firms use overdrafts to finance their working capital needs (Hicks's 'overdraft economy'). The opposite assumption, that all firms finance production out of current cashflow (Hicks's 'autoeconomy'), may be suitable in the steady state but does not allow for expansion except through efficiency, or the zero-sum game. It will be seen that in the Post Keynesian cases above, the consumer goods industries were portrayed as financing working capital out of cashflow. Which is the more realistic assumption should be a matter of fact. The facts are only partly helpful, since one cannot tell what an overdraft is used for, or how large are weekly sales in comparison to the wage bill, but they at least make it clear that the truth is somewhere in between. Some firms have positive deposits, usually with 'sweep' arrangements timed to the payment of wages, some have overdrafts, and still others (they must bank with more than one institution) have both.

The idea that all agents, or at least all firms, have overdrafts and therefore there is no 'demand for money' (that is, a demand to hold deposits as more than a suspense account) is a familiar one from Kaldor and Trevithick (1981) and from Moore (1988), and its implications are well known. The circuit school takes the same extreme position, in the interest of having clear-cut macroeconomic aggregates, in which firms are borrowers from banks and households are deposit-takers.

The third disparity concerns the finance of expenditure on final product, as opposed to labour. The first puzzle is Graziani's statement that this constitutes the purchase of commodities by the banks. I would describe the same event as follows. The buyer purchases the commodity (capital goods, in the case at hand), and the bank purchases (accepts) the buyer's promise to pay, just as it accepts the firm's promise when it lends to pay a firm's wage bill. To say that this type of transaction takes place does not imply that the bank holds the capital permanently (indeed the bank never holds it at all), or even finances it permanently. The latter is the job of *funding*. Funding need not – indeed almost never does – take place 'out of the buyer's own income', as in Graziani's description, but rather is provided by capturing someone else's saving through the issue of securities or equity. Investment may be funded at the outset, or the proceeds of funding may used to pay back bank loans (see Studart 1995, and Chick 1984, 1996). The investment is not expected to pay for itself out of sales (in other words, its own income) until the end of its life, but this seems the only stage of the process allowed by Graziani's analysis. The definition of finance as final payment was at the heart of Asimakopulos's argument (1983) that final payment is completely different from Post Keynesian conceptions of either finance or funding because it refers to the repayment of debt, while finance and funding are processes of incurring debt.

The point from the circuit theory which survives the differences outlined above is that in every period, much more money is created than survives to the next period, owing to the widespread use of overdrafts. These authors have performed the service of showing that every element of effective demand is connected with banking activity, but their definition of money (Post Keynesian credit) coupled with the assumption that overdrafts are universally the source of working capital and are destroyed by workers' expenditure, leads Schmitt's school to deny the existence of a multiplier, in the same way that Kaldor and Trevithick (1981) and Moore (1988) deny the possibility of an excess supply of money. The circumstances conform to the Post Keynesian cases IIIb and IVb, where new overdrafts have to be negotiated if there is to be a multiplier as it is not automatically financed.[4] The widespread but not universal overdraft status of firms results in a qualification of the multiplier which may need some attention from Post Keynesians.

Other sources of finance of investment

Perhaps the reason that investment was singled out by Keynes as the engine of growth was that this type of expenditure was, at least in the time Keynes was writing, the main user of all types of credit. Of the other candidates for the role of autonomous expenditure, the public sector was comparatively small, and exports had been hammered by protectionism. Aggregate household income had risen above subsistence, so the household sector was the chief saving sector and companies were the main borrowers. This established the important point that saving and investment were activities carried out by different groups with no market to set a 'price' to equilibrate these activities. By and large, Keynes left the matter there, and went on to establish that the rate of interest was set by another set of concerns altogether, the supply of money and liquidity preference.

Then the interpreters and the textbooks took over. In their interpretation, the criterion which decides whether investment alters the level of income is the comparison with saving: if investment exceeds saving, income will rise. This looks at the issue from the 'real' side. But from the macroeconomic point of view, saving has no independent meaning (Keynes 1973: 210). How then can we maintain simultaneously that (monetary) investment precedes (monetary) saving, and evaluate the income-creating potential of investment? We can only argue *ex post*: when investment and money income have increased by the same amount, we can infer that the increase has been financed by bank lending and that the resulting increase in money balances constitutes *ex post* saving. We can also infer that the amount of saving represented by new money is, in that period, not derived by portfolio decisions but is the acceptance of deposits as the counterpart of income (generated by investment) before there is any realization that income and the money supply have increased.[5]

We, like Keynes, can see government expenditure in a similar light to investment, in so far as it is matched by an increase in the money supply, and there is an immediate increase in money income (and the money supply, and *ex post* saving). Any increase in income from bond-financed expenditure depends on incomplete crowding out.

Company borrowing for investment may take many forms other than bank credit, including the issue of long-term securities or debentures and the issue of equity shares or rights. However, Keynes did not bring out well the fact that investment financed in these latter ways would have a different impact on effective demand than finance which gives rise to new money. When other sources of borrowing finance investment, they do so by the transfer of monetary wealth, the product of previous saving. This is a zero-sum game which reallocates financial resources, as we have seen earlier. The contribution to income of investment financed in these ways is through gains in efficiency or scale, whereas an investment accompanied by new money immediately causes a rise in money income. Once again it is clear that the monetary or financial side has implications for effective demand which have been fudged.

There is the further issue of the importance of internal finance, especially in the UK and USA, which is often emphasized by Post Keynesians. It is certainly true that internal funds represent a major source of funds, particularly in the financial systems often described as 'market-based', where the stock and bond markets rather than the banks provide long-term funding. However the argument is usually microeconomic. At the macroeconomic level there are two main sources of internal funds: current cashflow and holdings of financial assets. To use current cashflow for investment there must be an excess of current income over current expenditure (the wage bill and raw materials costs). Obviously this source cannot be used for projects which form a large part of any firm's budget, especially when it is remembered that interest and dividends remain to be paid out of gross profit. Therefore the bulk of internally-financed investment must come from holdings of financial assets. These represent the temporary abode of purchasing power for which the flow counterparts are Keynes's 'supplementary costs' (the maintenance fund), the sinking fund for the replacement of capital, and reserves, that is, prior saving on the part of firms. To use owned financial assets to finance the acquisition of real capital entails selling those financial assets. At the macro level, this will raise the rate of interest. The effect on investment will thus be felt through the mechanism of liquidity preference and crowding out, and the effect on aggregate income must depend, as in the case of financing by issuing bonds, only on the efficiency of the investment.

Bank credit for consumption

From a 'real' perspective, or an income-flow perspective, consumption for an economy as a whole, as opposed to the perspective of an individual, is normally well within the limits of that economy's income, even in an open economy. (It is no accident that, despite the politicians' homely rhetoric of 'living beyond our means', a balance of payments deficit is otherwise known as 'net foreign investment' rather than 'net foreign consumption'). The obvious simplifying assumption is that in a closed economy, consumption cannot exceed income except by running down stocks, first of inventories and then of capital (for example, by failing to maintain housing). This is normally only done in wartime. This fact richly justifies the simple consumption function $C = C(Y)$, and makes something of a nonsense, *at the macroeconomic level*, of 'intertemporal choice', which is an essentially microeconomic idea.

The function $C = C(Y)$ thus embodies the idea that aggregate consumption is financed by current cashflow, or transfers of deposits in payment of wages. What of consumer bank credit? Bank credit, we have agreed, increases money income and the money supply. Can it not therefore influence the level of income just as much as it can when supporting investment? In terms of $C = C(Y)$, a net bank credit to the consumer sector as a whole would raise both C and Y. It also increases the volume of deposits, and someone must hold them. This holding, it will be recalled, counts as saving. The consumer sector cannot provide the holders, since the increase in income has gone entirely to consumption (that is what the loans were for). So it must fall to the company sector to hold its unexpected profits (which are the result of the extra consumption) in the form of increased deposits, and for the government's unexpected tax receipts also to be held in this form. This mechanism can support a consumer boom. If all firms, and government, are always in overdraft, the boom would be cut short by the destruction of money at the first round. The increased importance of consumer bank credit in comparison to its level in Keynes's time may be important for long-term growth if consumer credit even partially crowds out investment in productive capacity.

The financing of stock transactions

Another aspect of the relation between aggregate demand and modes of finance, which has barely been touched in the Post Keynesian literature, is liquidity preference, in particular speculative demand. Keynes treated speculative demand as a portfolio decision. In Hicks's terms this area of activity, taken by itself, was an autoeconomy: it was assumed that transactions took place between people who possessed the means of payment, and exchange did not entail borrowing. Thus the only significance of liquidity preference (LP) for effective demand operated through its effect on the rate of interest and thence to investment. Now, not only has endogenous money made it difficult (though not impossible) to take the stock of money as given, as Keynes did, but the suggestion, made long ago, that speculators borrow to speculate has only rarely appeared in Post Keynesian economics.

Two papers which do allow speculation to enter the overdraft economy are Dow (1993) and Howells (1996). Dow takes a very broad concept of speculation, in which the decision to produce is as speculative as the decision to hold assets. This is correct of course, and this broad view sits well with Parguez's description (1996) of credit being granted to support 'bets' on the future through production for an unknown market. However I wish to restrict my meaning to the activity of trying to capture capital gains rather than earning an income from prospective yields. This definition conforms to that of Keynes (1936: 159), though he confines his attention to securities. Howells on the other hand emphasizes housing as an important element in consumer credit-financed expenditure in Britain in the last three decades, given that much of it was bank-financed after the Finance Act of 1983 and the Building Societies Act of 1986.

The basic point regarding the finance of trade in existing assets on the basis of bank credit should be clear: this activity expands the money supply without directly creating effective demand. Banks have always engaged in this activity. In Britain, a traditional division of labour between banks and discount houses dictated that banks should only buy seasoned gilts, not new issues. Seasoned securities do not provide their issuers, government or companies, with new money and so are not directly connected with expenditure. The effect on demand is through the interest rate. The extent of bank finance for purchases of existing assets has escalated with the rise of interbank lending and the development of derivatives and repurchase agreements.

Similarly, bank lending for house purchase, particularly on the expectation of a rising market, leads to a self-fulfilling rise in house prices, fuelled by new liquidity. (Had the same expansion of credit which occurred in the 1980s housing boom been channelled into current expenditure, measured inflation would have been higher than it was. The political might-have-beens are interesting to contemplate.) Higher prices may, according to Tobin's q, stimulate new house-building, but the flow is certain to be small compared with the existing stock. As we saw all too recently, the unwinding of the bull market in housing takes place chiefly through negative equity and repossessions rather than expansion of the stock. Dow (1993) points, as did Minsky (1996), to the displacement of bank credit from the support of production, and above all investment in response to the prospect of bigger gains in purely financial dealings.

These wealth effects are badly integrated into the theory of effective demand. It is standard to add a wealth variable to the consumption function. This procedure, as I have explained, is based on microeconomic reasoning and is not *generally* valid at the macro level. A capital gain to an individual may be matched by a capital loss, or a rise in the fraction saved of another person's income, or, if the source of the gain is bank finance, it may be accompanied by a rise in the money stock. Only the latter case creates new liquidity. The effect of a change on consumption in the value of wealth *not* supported by new bank credit could better be modelled by a change, if any, in the marginal propensity to consume (owing, say, to differences in the savings propensities of the buyer and the seller of the financial asset). The point is that capital gains in a zero-sum game cannot be spent by society as a whole, although they can be spent by an individual. If the gain was facilitated by a bank overdraft, resulting in new deposits when spent, this of course no longer holds. These are shades of the confused debate in the 1960s over whether money is net wealth.

The Cencini apparatus, assuming he would countenance lending for non income-creating expenditures at all, would counter that every bank deposit is matched by an equal promise to pay, and that therefore money cannot be net wealth. The first part of the sentence is of course true, but the flaw in the *sequitur* is that money counts as wealth now and the debt only has to be paid later. If that were not so, no one would ever borrow to buy anything, which is contrary to what we observe.

Conclusion

I have, I believe, shown that the financial counterpart of spending decisions, including spending to pay for labour, has an influence on the extent of expansion which can be expected. Not all expenditure is financed by bank lending, and not all bank lending is used for expenditure on current output, hence the somewhat prolix exposition of this paper. However, if this middle ground is embraced, the foundations of polar positions can be understood and at least partly reconciled.

Appeal to the facts is of limited use. When observing a change in aggregate income, we know next to nothing about the borrowing configuration which brought about that change. Yet this configuration determines whether our game is zero-sum or positive, and that, in turn, determines the extent of subsequent expansion. If in the first round new money goes immediately into an account which is overdrawn and is extinguished in its entirety, the existence of a multiplier depends on the banks being willing to negotiate further loans for expansion, which in turn will depend on the liquidity position of the banks and alternative lending opportunities available to them. If, by contrast, new deposits circulate for a time amongst those with positive balances, the Keynesian multiplier is not impeded for any lack of finance. Undoubtedly the most common position is, as usual, somewhere in between.

Notes

I am deeply indebted to Sheila Dow for her generous response to my many demands for discussion of the points in this paper. I wish to say that they have been stimulating and reassuring, without implicating her in the result. I am also indebted to her, to Christine Nisbet of the University of East London, and to John Spiers of the UCL Library for bibliographical assistance.

1 Both schools tend to argue in terms of loans, not overdrafts, but there is no difference of principle, and I shall stick to my overdraft model.
2 See Rossi (1998) for some good examples.
3 The use of Keynes's phrase to make a point about the essence of money appears again in Graziani:

> A first key point is firmly made by Keynes, namely that money is not and cannot be a commodity money. Even metal coins are token money, not different in substance from paper money. The Indian rupee, he writes, "is a note printed on silver".
>
> (Graziani 1996: 145)

What Keynes actually said was, '*in existing conditions*, the rupee, being a token coin, is virtually a note printed on silver' (Keynes 1913: 26, emphasis added). In other words, the token quality of the coin permits that description, and the token quality is being contrasted with full-bodied coin. See also Cencini (1995: 26–30).
4 The 'revolving fund', itself slightly imperfect, will at best only cater to a steady level of expenditures. See Chick (1996).
5 My 'acceptance' of money is Moore's (1988: 300) 'convenience lending', or Hicks's (1967) 'non-volitional' demand for money.

References

Asimakopulos, A. (1983) 'Kalecki and Keynes on finance, investment and saving', *Cambridge Journal of Economics*, July.
Bushaw, D. W. and Clower, R. W. (1957) *Introduction to Mathematical Economics*, Homewood, Ill.: Irwin.
Cencini, A. (1985) 'Replica al commento di Augusto Graziani', *Studi Economici* 25: 143–9.
—— (1995) *Monetary Theory, National and International*, London: Routledge.
Chick, V. (1978) 'Keynesians v. Monetarists: The End of the Debate – Or a Beginning?', *Thames Papers in Political Economy*, Spring.
—— (1981) 'On the Structure of the Theory of Monetary Policy', in D. Currie *et al.* (eds) *Macroeconomic Analysis: Current Problems and Theories in Macroeconomics and Econometrics*, London: Croom Helm.
—— (1984) 'Monetary Increases and their Consequences: Streams, Backwaters and Floods', in A. Ingham and A. M. Ulph (eds) *Demand, Equilibrium and Trade: Essays*

in Honour of Ivor F. Pearce, London: Macmillan.
—— (1992) *On Money, Method and Keynes: Selected Essays*, ed. P. Arestis and S. C. Dow, London: Macmillan.
—— (1996) 'The Multiplier and Finance', in G. C. Harcourt and P. A. Riach (eds), *A 'Second Edition' of the General Theory*, London: Routledge.
Dow, S. C.(1993) 'Speculation and the Monetary Circuit with Particular Reference to the Euro-Currency Market', in S. C. Dow, *Money and the Economic Process*, Aldershot: Edward Elgar.
Graziani, A. (1984) 'The Debate on Keynes's finance motive', *Economic Notes* 1: 5–33.
—— (1987) 'Keynes's Finance Motive', *Économies et Sociétés* 4: 23–42.
—— (1990) 'The Theory of the Monetary Circuit', *Économies et Sociétés* 6: 7–36.
—— (1996) 'Money as Purchasing Power and as a Stock of Wealth in Keynesian Economic Thought', in G. Deleplace and E. J. Nell (eds), *Money in Motion: The Post Keynesian and Circulation Approaches*, London: Macmillan.
Hicks, J. R. (1967) *Critical Essays in Monetary Theory*, Oxford: Oxford University Press.
—— (1989) *A Market Theory of Money*, Oxford: Clarendon Press.
Howells, P. G. A. (1996) 'Endogenous Money and the "State of Trade"', in P. Avestis (ed.) *Keynes, Money and the Open Economy: Essays in Honour of Paul Davidson*, Cheltenham: Edward Elgar.
Kaldor, N. and Trevithick, J. A. (1981) 'A Keynesian Perspective on Money', *Lloyds Bank Review* 139: 1–19.
Keynes, J. M. (1913) *Indian Currency and Finance*, London: Macmillan.
—— (1936) *The General Theory of Employment, Interest, and Money*, London: Macmillan.
—— (1937a) 'Alternative Theories of the Rate of Interest', *Economic Journal* 47, reprinted in Keynes (1973).
—— (1937b) 'The "Ex-Ante" Theory of the Rate of Interest', *Economic Journal* 47, reprinted in Keynes (1973).
—— (1938) 'D.H. Robertson on "Mr Keynes and Finance"; A Comment', *Economic Journal* 48, reprinted in Keynes (1973).
—— (1939) 'The Process of Capital Formation', *Economic Journal* 49, reprinted in Keynes (1973).
—— (1973) *Collected Writings of John Maynard Keynes*, vol XIV, *The General Theory and After: Part II, Defence and Development*, ed. D. E. Moggridge, London: Macmillan.
Lloyd, C. L. (1960) 'The Equivalence of the Liquidity Preference and Loanable Funds Theories and the New Stock-Flow Analysis', *Review of Economic Studies* 27: 206–9.
Minsky, H. P. (1996) 'Uncertainty and the Structure of Capitalist Economies', *Journal of Economic Issues* 30: 357–68.
Moore, B. J. (1985) 'Wages, Bank Lending and the Endogeneity of Credit Supply', in M. Jarsulic (ed.) *Money and Macro Policy*, Boston: Kluwer-Nijhoff.
—— (1988) *Horizontalists and Verticalists: The Macroeconomics of Credit Money*, Cambridge: Cambridge University Press.
Parguez, A. (1996) 'A Reappraisal of the Theory of the Monetary Circuit', in G. Deleplace and E. J. Nell (eds), *Money in Motion: The Post Keynesian and Circulation Approaches*, London: Macmillan.
Rossi, S. (1998) 'Endogenous Money and Banking Activity: Some Notes on the Workings of Modern Payments Systems', mimeo, UCL.
Schmitt, B. (1982) 'Time as Quantum', in M. Baranzini (ed.) *Advances in Economic Theory*, London: Blackwell.
Studart, R. (1995) *Investment Finance in Economic Development*, London: Routledge.

7 The invisible hand and the evolution of the monetary system

Kevin Dowd

Introduction

This paper re-examines the old question of the desirability of a monetary system devoid of any state intervention.[1] However, instead of examining monetary *laissez-faire* by means of standard neoclassical analysis, with its emphasis on formal optimization, it examines *laissez-faire* from the viewpoint of conjectural history. It investigates how the monetary system might plausibly evolve from some initial primitive state, driven primarily by the self-interested behaviour of the parties involved, and without any form of government intervention.

Why a conjectural history approach? Part of the answer is that a conjectural history provides a simple but insightful way of explaining the functions of the various institutions involved in the development of the monetary system. For example, in the story of the goldsmiths, it provides an elegant and powerful explanation for the emergence of paper currency. A conjectural history also provides an effective way of examining a relatively unfamiliar system such as monetary *laissez-faire*. Seeing the conjectural history unfold gives us a feel for how *laissez-faire* might actually work, and also helps to break the conditioning against it that most of us were given when we first learned our economics. The conjectural history helps us to counter such preconceptions and see the *laissez-faire* system for what it is. Instead of appearing odd because it has no central bank, *laissez-faire* comes across as very natural, and it is the departures from *laissez-faire* that appear out of place, or at least in need of justification.

A conjectural history provides a benchmark to help assess the world we live in, but it is important to appreciate that it is *not* meant to provide an accurate historical description of how the world actually evolved. The conjectural history is a useful myth, and it is no criticism of a conjectural history to say that the world failed to evolve in the way that it postulates. Imagine that it could be proved beyond doubt that the Doge of Venice in the sixteenth century had been shrewd enough to recognize that a bank need not maintain a hundred percent reserve ratio:

> What then of our goldsmiths' story? Does the fact that the Doge beat the invisible-hand [i.e., conjectural history] explanation to it rob the invisible-hand explanation of its explanatory import? I suggest that the answer is No, and that the argument for this answer goes beyond the mere 'feeling' that we may have that the account of how something could have arisen without anyone devising it is 'interesting' or 'illuminating' in its own right. . . . The argument . . . is that even if the invisible-hand explanation turns out not to be the correct account of how the thing *emerged*, it may still not be devoid of validity with regard to the question of how (and why) it is *maintained*. . . . The availability . . . of a cogent invisible-hand story of how the pattern in question could have arisen . . . may, I believe, contribute to our understanding of the inherently self-reinforcing nature of this pattern and hence of its being successful and lasting.
>
> (Ullman-Margalit 1978: 275, original emphasis)

Regardless of its historical accuracy, the conjectural history therefore helps to explain why certain institutions persist, and this in turn helps illustrate the functions they perform.

Apart from wishing to investigate the desirability or otherwise of monetary *laissez-faire*, it also makes sense to focus on *laissez-faire* for methodological reasons. One reason is that there is a sense in which the analysis of *laissez-faire* (or, anarchy, if one prefers) *must* logically come prior to the study of other forms of social order. We cannot assess claims for the necessity of some form of government intervention – the establishment of a central bank, say – without analysing the properties of a social order in which this intervention is absent. For example, to claim that central banking is superior to free banking is to imply the existence of a problem inherent in free banking that central banking puts right, and we cannot justify such a claim without *some* study of the properties of a free banking system. We must analyse the system without the intervention if we are to be able to assess whether the intervention itself is justified.

Dealing with a *laissez-faire* social order also has the advantage that it helps us to focus on the extent to which the solutions to social problems emerge, or fail to emerge, spontaneously from within the social order, without relying on the *deus ex machina* of state intervention to sort them out. The individuals involved then either solve those problems for themselves or else have to live with them unsolved. However, if we introduce the government into the picture, we tend to underrate the extent to which the parties involved can solve their problems, and we create a corresponding temptation to see state intervention as the solution to whatever problem we are dealing with. All too often, a writer will identify a problem, think of a way in which the government can ameliorate it, and presume that he or she has found a solution. Ignoring the government provides a mental discipline that helps us avoid the distraction of such spurious solutions and allows us to concentrate on the real issue, the extent to which individuals in society can solve their own problems.

The early evolution of the economy

Let us begin with an initial primitive, anarchic, state of society. Individuals live in groups (such as clans), have well-defined preferences, and have endowments consisting of various commodities, chattels, and natural abilities. Individuals can combine these endowments with their own time and effort to produce goods (for example, they can harvest food) and engage in other economic activity (that is, exchange and consumption) to improve their well-being. To begin with, most economic activity is organized hierarchically. There is little exchange between groups or between individuals within groups, and concepts of private property are primitive.

However, over time people gradually discover that they can better themselves by exchange, and the practice of barter spreads. Trade is initially more or less sporadic, with potential trading partners meeting each other randomly as in Jones (1976), but as it spreads, a set of social conventions develops spontaneously around it. These relate to good places to find trading partners, the rules of bargaining, and so on. These conventions reduce the costs to individuals of searching for trading partners and carrying out trades with them. The trading process therefore becomes more orderly, and trading fairs and *markets* gradually evolve at which people meet every so often to exchange their goods.

At the same time, trade also alters individuals' relationships to their groups. Individual activity is increasingly directed at people outside their group, and the old group hierarchy slowly breaks down. Individuals form new relationships with each other, and principal among these are *firms*, or organizations in which some individuals agree to take certain kinds of orders from others, in return for agreed compensation. Firms enable certain types of activities to be coordinated more efficiently than would otherwise be the case, and thereby enable individuals to reap specialization gains that would otherwise be unobtainable (Coase 1937). As time goes on, an increasing proportion of economic activity is carried on through markets and firms, people become increasingly specialized, and the older groups lose their distinctiveness and gradually merge into a unified economy.

Indirect exchange and the emergence of a dominant medium of exchange

Barter has the drawback that trade can only take place if individuals overcome the coincidence both of wants and of timing problems (Goodhart 1989: 2). A lot of search – and consequently a lot of valuable time – is therefore typically required to carry out a trade, and the outcome of a search is often very uncertain. At some point, individuals start to resort to indirect exchange, so that instead of accepting only the good they want to consume, they accept another good with the intention of exchanging that for the good they are really looking for. If the intermediate good is well-chosen, an individual who resorts to indirect exchange ought to be able to obtain the desired good with less difficulty than otherwise, and reduce the overall trading costs (Menger 1892: 247–9).

A good choice of an intermediate commodity would be a good that is heavily traded, so that the person who has the commodity one wants will be more likely to accept the commodity one has to offer. It should also have a readily recognizable exchange value, be easily portable and non-perishable. Over time, individuals gradually switch to indirect exchange and converge on these kinds of goods to carry out their trades. This convergence makes these goods even more saleable and therefore further increases their desirability as intermediate goods (Menger 1892: 250–2). In the end, this self-reinforcing process leads to a relatively small number of goods – and perhaps only one – becoming generally accepted as the dominant intermediate good(s).

Historically, the preferred intermediary goods have often been precious metals. These were well-suited to be intermediate goods because their quantity and quality were relatively easy to assess compared to most other goods, and the fact that their value was high relative to their weight meant that storage and transport costs were relatively low (Menger 1892: 252–5). For the sake of simplicity, we can assume that the process converges on one single good – gold – as the dominant intermediary commodity.

The unit of account

The use of an intermediate commodity considerably simplifies the exchange process. Individuals with goods to sell need look only for individuals with the recognised intermediary good, and trade fairs now become much simpler because of the associated reduction in the number of trading posts. If there are n goods to be traded, there would be $n(n-1)/2$ separate trading posts under pure barter, one for each pair of goods. However, with a dominant intermediary good, the number of trading posts can be cut to $(n-1)$. This is one trading post for every commodity to be exchanged for the intermediate good, and an individual with a particular good to sell need only operate (or look for) a single trading post, instead of the $(n-1)$ separate posts that previously dealt with the good under barter. Indirect exchange also means that the individual need keep account of only $(n-1)$ exchange ratios (or prices) instead of having to keep account of $n(n-1)/2$ exchange ratios as before.

Since the intermediary good, gold, is now handed over in most (if not all) trades, it is natural that prices – the exchange rates of goods – be quoted in terms of gold weights. A trader with a good to sell or buy will post prices in terms of the weight of gold he or she is willing to accept or pay:

A seller pursues self-interest by posting prices in terms of the media of exchange he or she is routinely prepared to accept. This practice economizes on time spent in negotiation over what commodities are acceptable in payment and at what rate of exchange. More importantly, it economizes on the information necessary for the buyer's and the seller's economic calculation. Posting prices in terms of a numeraire commodity not routinely accepted in payment, by contrast, would force buyer and seller to know and agree upon the numeraire price of the payment media due. This numeraire price of the payment medium would naturally be subject to fluctuation, so that updated information would be necessary. A non-exchange-medium numeraire would furthermore be subject to greater bid-ask spreads in barter against other commodities, as by hypothesis it is less saleable, than the medium of exchange. It would therefore serve less well as a tool of economic calculation.

(White 1984: 704)

The economy has now evolved to the point where gold is not only used as the dominant *medium of exchange*, but where agents also use gold units to express the prices of other goods. Gold therefore provides the *medium of account*, and the *unit of account* – the unit in terms of which prices are expressed – is a specified weight of gold. A good real-world example of this evolutionary process is the famous POW camp described by Radford:

Starting with simple direct barter, such as a non-smoker giving a smoker friend his cigarette issue in exchange for a chocolate ration, more complex exchanges soon became an accepted custom. . . . Within a week or two, as the volume of trade grew, rough scales of exchange values came into existence. . . . It was realized that a tin of jam was worth ½ lb of margarine plus something else; that a cigarette issue was worth several chocolate issues, and a tin of diced carrots was worth practically nothing. . . . By the end of a month, when we reached our permanent camp, there was a lively trade in all commodities and their relative values were well-known, and expressed not in terms of one another — one didn't quote bully in terms of sugar – but in terms of cigarettes. The cigarette became the standard of value. . . . [Everyone] including non-smokers, was willing to sell for cigarettes, using them to buy at another time and place. Cigarettes became the normal currency.

(Radford 1945: 191)

Cigarettes thus became both medium of exchange and medium (and unit) of account. In our hypothetical economy, gold is both medium of exchange and medium of account, and the unit of account is a particular unit of gold.

If we call this unit the dollar, we can then say that prices are expressed in terms of dollars, but the dollar itself is a specific amount of gold.

The evolution of coinage

Although gold might be the most convenient intermediate good to use, it still leaves individuals with the inconvenience of having to assess the weight and purity of heterogeneous lumps of gold. To avoid this inconvenience, traders begin to deal in standardized lumps of gold (such as gold rings or bars) and put their own marks on them so that they do not need to reassess their value when they next see them. A trader can then look at the marking and shape of any piece of gold offered, and if the trader recognizes them he or she can have some confidence that they are of their claimed weight, and dispense with the inconvenience of weighing them again.

We therefore arrive at the beginning of *coinage*. There is now a demand for readily authenticated pieces of gold, and *mints* arise to meet this demand by casting gold into coins and charging a fee for the service. Since the demand for each mint's service depends on the reputation of its coins, each mint has an incentive to maintain its reputation by making it as difficult as possible to tamper with its coins without being detected (for example, by making coins round, so that tampering is more apparent), and by issuing coins of full-bodied weight. Market forces will also lead mints to issue coins of standardized weight and fineness, so coins will be issued in standard dollar amounts. Any mint that issued non-standardized coins would impose additional inconvenience on its customers and have to charge a lower minting fee to compensate them. It would therefore find it difficult to survive against competitors who issued standardized coins.[2]

The development of banking and the adoption of bank currency

The development of bank currency

A natural further development is that of bank currency, and its gradual displacement of gold coinage as the dominant medium of exchange. One way to think about this process is suggested by the familiar story of the goldsmiths, and this story of course also gives us one account of how banks might evolve. The use of coins still involves considerable costs, particularly those of storing, protecting and moving coins around. To save on some of these costs, some people come to be prepared to pay others to store their gold for them. Goldsmiths and some merchants already have facilities to keep large amounts of gold, and can therefore keep additional quantities of it at a relatively low marginal cost. These people find it profitable to accept gold for safekeeping for a fee that many current holders of gold are willing to pay, and depositors are issued with receipts that give them the right to demand their gold back.

Invisible hand and evolution of money 145

As the practice of making gold deposits spreads, it increasingly happens that when two parties agree to an exchange, one goes to withdraw some gold, and then hand it over to the other who promptly deposits it again, often with the same goldsmith. Provided that the party accepting payment is satisfied that the goldsmith will still honour the commitment to pay back the gold, it is more convenient for that party simply to accept the goldsmith's receipt and save everyone the trouble of withdrawing the gold and depositing it again. The receipts of goldsmiths therefore begin to circulate as media of exchange in their own right, and the practice of using such receipts as exchange media gradually replaces the older practice of using gold coins. The receipts now become banknotes, and the goldsmiths who issue them become bankers.

The development of fractional-reserve and deposit banking

As time passes, the goldsmith-bankers notice that demands for redemption and new deposits of gold largely tend to cancel each other out over most periods, and so *net* withdrawals are generally quite low. They then realize that they could lend out much of the gold deposited with them and earn interest on it, and still face little danger of being unable to meet depositors' demands for redemption. They therefore start to lend out the gold (that is, they reduce their reserve ratios below 100 per cent) and then compete for additional gold deposits to lend out. Their competition eliminates the earlier fees charged for accepting deposits, and they are soon offering interest payments to attract deposits. As bank currency is increasingly used as an exchange media, bank borrowers increasingly accept loans of bank currency instead of loans of gold, and so the banks can make loans simply by issuing more of their own currency. The practice of making gold loans then gradually diminishes, and these effectively disappear by the time that gold itself loses its role as medium of exchange. In the end, the banks only hold gold because they need it to satisfy public demands for redemption.[3]

The convertibility of bank currency and the 'law of reflux'

While bank currency is increasingly used as a medium of exchange, competition still forces the banks to keep their currency – their notes and deposits – convertible into gold. These liabilities are legally-binding promises on the part of the bank that issued them to redeem them (buy them back) under the conditions called for in the contract, and those conditions will normally call for the bank to do so on demand. The holder of a dollar bill – which is legally only a claim to a dollar, not a dollar itself – therefore has the right to demand redemption for one dollar (that is, for gold), and a bank that fails to meet such a demand exposes itself to the penalty for defaulting on a contract.

To understand why banks should maintain the convertibility of their currency, it has to be appreciated that convertibility is a guarantee that their currency will retain its value in terms of gold. A bank cannot simply discontinue convertibility without notice, since it is bound to honour the contractual promise on outstanding currency to redeem it when required to. A bank can therefore only abandon convertibility by announcing its intention to retire its convertible currency and replace it with inconvertible currency. Any potential currency-holder will interpret such an announcement as an indication that the bank intends to allow the value of its currency to depreciate. If the bank has no such intention, why would it want to dispense with the convertibility guarantee? The potential currency-holder will therefore refuse to accept the inconvertible currency, and the bank will lose its market share to those competitors who are willing to provide the public with convertible currency. To abandon convertibility unilaterally is thus tantamount to surrendering one's market share to rivals. Indeed, even if the banks *as a whole* organized a concerted abandonment of convertibility, they would still have no way to prevent *new* banks from undercutting them by offering the public convertible currency. Any concerted abandonment of convertibility would *ipso facto* create profit opportunities for new entrants who were willing to satisfy the public demand for convertible currency, and all the banks that abandon convertibility would lose their market share. Under conditions of free entry, the threat of potential competition prevents even the banks as a whole from being able to abandon the convertibility guarantee. Competition among the banks forces them to maintain convertibility because the public demand it.

The commitment to maintain convertibility implies that banks can only keep in circulation those issues the public are willing to hold. If a bank issues more currency than the public want to hold, the excess issues will be returned and banks will be legally compelled to redeem them, as a 'law of reflux' operates by which unwanted issues are returned to the banks who must redeem them. The circulation of bank currency is then limited by the demand to hold it. Banks cannot issue currency *and* keep it in circulation, *without* the public demand to hold it. If a bank wishes to increase its currency circulation, it must therefore increase the public demand for its currency. To do so, it must fight more aggressively for market share, open more branches, improve its reputation, advertise more, and so forth.

Bank safety and soundness

Since a bank will normally find it profitable to operate on a fractional reserve, it will not have the gold on hand to redeem all its outstanding notes and deposits if they were all presented at once. The bank can therefore only continue to operate if it can persuade a major proportion of its creditors not to demand redemption. It can only do that if it maintains their confidence by persuading them that their investments are safe and that they can get their money back any time they want it. Therefore, over any given period of time, most of them will feel no need to redeem.

In order to provide this reassurance, the bank must persuade its customer that its finances are sound: that is, the bank must be seen as having a sufficiently high *net worth* (or *capitalization*) that it can not only pay off current debts, but could still pay them off even in plausible bad-case scenarios where it suffered major losses on its loan portfolio. If a bank has a sufficiently high capitalization that it can withstand any plausible losses and still pay off its creditors without too much difficulty, then those creditors can be reasonably confident that their investments are safe. A bank can also take measures to maintain its soundness by issuing subordinated debt, avoiding excessive risks in its lending, employing qualified and reliable staff, and having its books regularly audited and its creditworthiness regularly rated.

If it is to retain the confidence of its customers, the bank must also maintain its ability to meet demands for redemption when they should arise. In other words, it must protect its liquidity. At the very minimum, a bank must maintain a certain amount of gold coins, relative to its outstanding demandable liabilities, so that it can meet unforeseen demands for redemption. Given that such reserves are costly to hold, the bank will need to trade off the liquidity benefits of holding them against their holding costs, but experience over time will indicate what an appropriate reserve ratio might be. The bank will also supplement this primary liquid reserve by holding secondary reserves consisting of assets that are less expensive to hold, but that can also be sold quickly at relatively little cost should the bank need to buy more reserves. It could also take out credit lines with other institutions, giving it the right to draw credit if necessary.

Should the bank be faced with unexpected demands for redemption, it would respond in the first instance by drawing down its primary reserve. If the demands continued, it would replenish its gold reserves by drawing down the credit lines it had taken out earlier, by taking out new loans, or by selling some of its secondary reserve assets. Provided the bank maintains its soundness, it should have little difficulty obtaining the loans it needs, and it can be reasonably confident of being able to protect its liquidity and meet redemption demands without defaulting. Indeed, those redeeming a bank's liabilities would have no desire to hold gold as such, but would convert them into other assets. Much of the gold would therefore be redeposited in the banking system. Other banks would then be flush with gold and, provided they were satisfied about the soundness of the bank wanting the loan, it would be in their interests to lend to it. A sound bank should therefore have no real difficulty obtaining the gold it needs.

The irony is that a bank that protects its soundness and liquidity would be very unlikely to face large demands for redemption *precisely because* its creditors would have confidence in it. The very fact that it can persuade its creditors that they can have their funds back whenever they want them is usually enough to ensure that most of them will not want to redeem: in most cases, there is no point demanding redemption if one's investment in the bank appears to be safe. The bottom line is that, although a safe and liquid bank always faces the theoretical possibility of a run, a run will not actually occur unless something happens that shatters public confidence and gives creditors explicit reason to fear for the safety of their funds. However, if a bank fails to take appropriate measures to maintain its soundness, a point will come when creditors lose confidence and run, and the bank will have difficulty withstanding the run when it occurs. A run thus serves the socially-useful purpose of putting a bad bank out of business, and the potential threat of a run keeps the other banks healthy by forcing them to keep their houses in order.[4]

Financial instruments replace gold as redemption media

While banks need to protect themselves against demands for redemption, they also have an incentive to reduce the cost of the reserves they hold to meet such demands. These costs will fall anyway as the banking system develops, because public demands for redemption will fall as their confidence in banks gradually grows, and the lower demands for redemption imply that the banks can operate on lower reserve ratios. However, at some point the banks will reduce these costs further by offering alternative, lower-cost redemption media instead of gold. We must keep in mind that gold is still relatively costly to store and hold, and bears no explicit return, while financial instruments involve lower holding costs and often yield explicit returns for the holder. It is therefore in a bank's interest to offer to redeem its liabilities using less costly redemption media: and it is in the public's interest to prefer such redemption media to gold.

To qualify as a suitable redemption medium, an asset should have a value largely independent of the bank that uses it as a redemption medium: that is, the bank cannot redeem its own liabilities using more of the same. Obvious examples are the debt or equity of other firms, including the debt or equity of another bank. If a bank uses a financial instrument instead of gold as a redemption medium, there may be a possibility that the issuer will default, that the asset will fall in value, and so on, but if members of the public were not satisfied with a particular redemption medium they could always refuse to accept it (for example, by refusing to accept bank debt that specified that particular redemption medium). If the public accept a particular redemption medium, the very fact that they do so implies that they consider that redemption medium to be at least 'as good as gold' and that they are willing to accept any risks that its use entails.

Banks now redeem their issues, not with a particular *weight* of gold as they did before, but with financial instruments (or other redemption media) of the same *value* as that weight of gold. The earlier directly-convertible gold standard in which banks redeemed their liabilities directly with gold has thus given way to an indirectly-convertible gold standard in which they redeem their liabilities with something else.[5] The only remaining monetary purpose of gold is now to provide a definition for the dollar.

The development of a mature *laissez-faire* monetary system

The unit of account, the price level and the gold anchor

However, the unit of account, the dollar, is still legally defined as a particular weight of gold and, legally speaking, a banknote with a face value of $1 is still only a claim to a dollar. None the less, by this stage in the economy's evolution gold will have disappeared from circulation, and when a vendor posts a price of one dollar in a shop window this indicates a willingness to accept a dollar note issued by a reputable bank rather than gold as such. Indeed, since gold has disappeared from circulation the vendor might be quite unfamiliar with gold coins and even unwilling to accept them. The dollar note would be more liquid than gold itself, even though the dollar note is legally only a claim to some redemption medium of the same value as the gold dollar. What this means is that even though the dollar is still legally defined in terms of a particular weight of gold, the term 'dollar' as used in everyday trade by now refers to the units in which exchange media are denominated (what might be referred to as the 'banknote dollar') and *not* to units of gold or gold dollars as such. There is an important distinction between the term 'dollar' in everyday use, which refers to the bank-currency dollar, and the legal definition of the dollar, which refers to the value of a particular amount of gold.

Given this distinction between the bank-currency dollar and the (gold) dollar itself, we can now say that when they issue convertible currency, banks do so according to a rule by which they maintain the price of gold in terms of bank-currency dollars. The fixed bank-currency price of gold then ties down the market price of gold by unleashing arbitrage forces to return the market price of gold to its fixed par value should it ever depart from it. If the price of gold on the market rises significantly above the par value maintained by the banks, arbitragers would make a profit by redeeming currency for redemption media, selling the redemption media for bank currency and ending up with more currency than they started with. In the process, the outstanding quantity of currency would fall, and the falling quantity of currency would put downward pressure on the market price of gold in terms of bank currency. Conversely, if the market price of gold were to fall too low, arbitragers would demand more currency from the banks, and use the currency obtained in this way to buy more redemption media, and end up with more redemption media than they started with. The supply of bank currency would rise, and the market price of gold would rise back towards par. Any discrepancy of the market price of gold from the par price maintained by the banks would set in motion arbitrage forces that would return the market price to par.

The price level under this system is then determined by the forces that determine the relative price of gold against goods and services in general. Since the nominal price of gold is effectively fixed by the rules of the indirectly-convertible gold standard, the relative price of gold can therefore move if and only if there is a corresponding opposite change in the price level. The relative price of gold will rise if and only if the price level falls, and *vice versa*. Hence, any factor that causes the relative price of gold to rise will cause the price level to fall, and any factor that causes the relative price of gold to fall will cause the price level to rise. For example, an event such as unexpected discovery of gold ore will lead to a greater gold supply. Given the demand for gold, the gold market will only equilibrate if the price of gold falls relative to goods and services. Since the nominal price of gold is fixed, the relative price of gold can only fall if the price level itself rises. Hence, the gold discovery leads to a higher price level. Conversely, a factor such as a rise in the demand for gold will lead to a rise in the relative price of gold, and the relative price of gold can only rise if the price level falls. A rise in the demand for gold will therefore lead to a fall in the price level.

The replacement of the gold anchor

The price level under the gold standard thus depends on supply and demand in the gold market, but these factors are unlikely to produce the degree of price stability that the individuals living in our economy would prefer. The price instability produced by the gold standard imposes various costs on the public: they find it harder to distinguish between 'true' price signals and irrelevant price noise, and therefore make mistaken decisions they would otherwise have avoided, they would have less peace of mind about the future, and so forth. A time therefore comes when the banks decide to reduce price instability by changing the gold anchor that ties down the nominal price level. Given that the price level under the gold standard is only as stable as the relative price of gold, the banks can generate a more stable price level by replacing the gold price level anchor with an alternative anchor based on a commodity or commodities with a more stable relative price. The most likely candidate is a basket of goods and services, rather than any single alternative commodity. The banks then announce that from a certain future date onwards, they will use the term 'dollar' in new contracts to refer, not to a particular amount of gold as previously, but to a particular amount of a specified basket of goods and services (or something equivalent). This new 'basket dollar' will have the same value as the earlier gold dollar on the day it is first introduced, so as to avoid any jumps in the relative price of the anchor (and, hence, the price level) when the new dollar is brought in, and the public will accept the new basket dollar because they themselves prefer the greater price-level stability it would creates.[6]

The monetary standard has now evolved into an indirectly-convertible system based on a commodity-basket anchor chosen for its desirable price-level properties. Gold no longer has any monetary purposes whatsoever: as medium of exchange, medium of redemption or unit of account. The only vestige of gold in the monetary system is the use of the old term 'dollar' – which used to refer to a particular weight of gold – as the name of the unit of account, and even the dollar is now legally defined in terms of a basket of goods and services. Gold no longer has any substantial role to play in the monetary system.

International dimensions

Under *laissez-faire* conditions, we might expect similar monetary systems to develop more or less across the world. We would also expect the various local and regional economies, which were initially separate from each other, to coalesce into one, increasingly integrated, world economy. What kind of international monetary system will result? One possibility is that this world economy will use only one currency unit (for example the dollar), whose value is tied to a particular commodity anchor. However, it is also possible that different currency units might coexist with each other, each dominant in a particular part of the world (dollars in the North America, pounds in the British Isles, and so on). If there is more than one currency unit, one or more of these will be primary currency units tied to specific commodity anchors, and those units that are not specifically tied to commodity anchors will be tied at fixed rates of exchange to other currency units that are. All currency units will be tied – directly or indirectly – to commodity anchors.

If there was only one primary currency unit, we would have a situation reminiscent of the post-war Bretton Woods System, under which other currencies were tied to the dollar, and the dollar was tied to a 'basket' of gold. However, the dollar would now be tied to a broader commodity basket rather than gold. All exchange rates would now be fixed, since there would be only one primary currency unit and all others would be tied to it.

It is also possible that there might be more than one primary currency unit, each of which was fixed to its own commodity anchor. The exchange rates between the primary currency units would then fluctuate with changes in the relative prices of the anchor baskets. However, these baskets should have fairly stable relative prices if we assume that each anchor is chosen to stabilize a price index. Exchange rate changes should therefore be relatively small and infrequent. Any other currencies, if there are any, will then be tied to one of these primary currencies. Each of these satellite currencies will therefore have a fixed exchange rate against the primary unit to which it is tethered, and also against any other satellite currencies tied to the same primary unit, and a (slightly) floating exchange rate against all other currencies. This would engender a series of currency blocs, each of which was a fixed-exchange rate system based on a primary currency, and exchange rates between these various blocs would fluctuate slightly against each other.

However, even if there is more than one currency unit in use, there is no reason for the number of currency units under *laissez-faire* to reflect the number of nation states, as is (just about) the case under the current system. Under *laissez-faire*, there is no link between a currency unit and a nation state, and therefore no reason for currency areas to match national territories. Indeed, since there are considerable benefits when people use the same currency unit (such as lower accounting costs and zero currency-exchange costs), we might expect the *laissez-faire* currency areas to be larger on average than present currency areas, and better aligned to economic fundamentals such as trading patterns.

In sum, *laissez-faire* would give us one of three possible monetary arrangements:

- A single currency unit used throughout the world, and tied to a specified commodity anchor.
- A system of fixed exchange rates, in which all other currencies are tied to one key currency, which is itself anchored to a particular commodity anchor.
- A system of fixed-exchange-rate currency blocs fluctuating a little against each other, each of which is tethered to a particular anchor.

If there were multiple currency units, we would also expect them to cover larger areas than present-day units, and to cover areas that made more economic sense.

The evolution of the monetary system under *laissez-faire*: an overview

It perhaps useful at this point to pause and consider the main stages of development of our hypothetical monetary system under *laissez-faire*. These stages are summarized in Table 7.1. The first stage, the Age of Mints, is that in which full-bodied gold coins reign as the dominant medium of exchange (MOE), and these same coins also provide the medium of account (MOA), or the medium in units of which prices are expressed.

This first stage then gives way to the second, in which banks arise and issue currency, and this bank currency displaces coins as the dominant MOE. This second stage is a textbook gold standard, in which bank currency circulates as the main exchange medium, but this currency is denominated in units of gold and banks stand ready to redeem their currency for gold. Gold therefore functions as the MOA (or, if one prefers, unit of account, UA), as the anchor of the system, and as the banks'

Table 7.1 The stages of development of the monetary system under *laissez-faire*

Stage of development	Key features	Comments
Coinage	Gold as MOE Gold as MOA/UA	Use of gold coins as full-bodied money
Directly-convertible gold standard	Bank currency as MOE Gold as MOA/UA/anchor Gold as MOR	Textbook gold standard Bank currency displaces coins as MOE
Indirectly-convertible gold standard	Bank currency as MOE Gold as MOA/UA/anchor Financial assets as MOR	Financial assets replace gold as MOR
Indirectly-convertible commodity-basket standard	Bank currency as MOE Commodity basket as MOA/UA/anchor Financial assets as MOR	Commodity basket replaces gold as MOA/UA/anchor Gold has no monetary role

Notes:
MOE medium of exchange
MOA medium of account
UA   unit of account
MOR medium of redemption.

medium of redemption (MOR). Relative to the previous stage, gold has lost its function as the MOE but acquired a new function as the MOR.

The third stage arises as banks replace gold with less costly redemption media, financial instruments, and so on, and the gold standard becomes indirectly convertible. Instead of being convertible directly into given amounts of gold, bank currency is now convertible into redemption media of the same value as those given amounts of gold. Gold retains its function as the MOA/UA and anchor, but has now lost its function as the MOR.

The fourth and final stage is where gold is replaced as the MOA/UA/anchor by a commodity basket chosen for its more desirable price-level properties. Gold no longer has any substantive monetary role, and the gold standard has been replaced by a commodity-basket standard.

Assessing the *laissez-faire* system

So how does *laissez-faire* actually fare?

Efficiency

One approach is to assess it by its efficiency, and it turns out that the *laissez-faire* system is efficient by virtually any sensible criterion:

- All feasible and mutually beneficial trades take place because there are

no barriers to prevent them. The banks provide the public with exactly the exchange media they want, and deposit interest rates, bank charges and the like are all competitively determined. The rents from financial intermediation – from issuing currency, making loans, and so on – are therefore competed away to the public.
- Banks will select appropriate reserve and redemption assets, and optimize their reserve holdings.
- The *laissez-faire* system is also efficient in a dynamic sense: unfettered market forces encourage banks and other parties to innovate and adopt good practices that have been tried elsewhere, and generally be flexible.
- Competition ensures that banks provide the degree of financial strength their customers want and are willing to pay for. If the public want stronger (better capitalized) banks, competition for market share will lead banks to increase their capitalization, and the public will get the stronger banks they want. At the same time, since capital is costly, excessively capitalized banks will not be competitive either, so competition produces banks of optimal strength, bearing in mind the public willingness to pay for it.
- The system is tethered to an anchor chosen to minimize price-level instability, and the costs associated with it.
- The costs of maintaining price-level stability (the costs of maintaining convertibility, etc.) should be minimal.
- There will either be one currency unit used everywhere, in which case there will be no currency-exchange and other associated costs; or there will be more than one currency in use, in which case currency areas will be aligned to economic fundamentals (and be optimal, in an appropriate sense).
- Unlike modern central banking systems, this free banking system is also entirely automatic. There is no 'policy problem' as conventionally understood – no need to worry about the incentives faced by the monetary or banking authorities, the time consistency of their policies, and so on – because these authorities do not exist to worry about. Everyone pursues their own self-interest, and all interests are harmonized by the market.

Stability

We can also assess the *laissez-faire* system in terms of its stability, and the *laissez-faire* system is stable in a number of different respects:

- First, it is stable in so far as it is self-sustaining: it leaves no group willing and able to overturn some essential feature of it. The *laissez-faire* system is self-sustaining because everyone already pursues their own welfare subject to their various constraints under which they operate. No one therefore has any desire to change their behaviour, given those constraints. In particular, the system does not depend on any

'guardian' who must sacrifice his or her own welfare and assume an unwanted burden to protect the public good: the safety of the system does not depend on any underpaid night-guard. And since there is no night-guard, we do not have to worry about what the night-guard might get up to while everyone else is asleep: there is no problem of 'guarding the guardians'.
- *Laissez-faire* also leads to a strong and stable financial system. The public want safe banks, and competition ensures that they get them, by providing financial institutions with incentives to maintain their financial health and cultivate public confidence. A bank that is not regarded as sufficiently strong by the public will lose public confidence, and without public confidence it will lose its market. A bank that wishes to remain in business must satisfy its customers and maintain its financial strength. Such a bank will be able to absorb non-catastrophic loan losses relatively easily and still retain public confidence and, while it will always be subject to the threat of a run, runs will not actually occur unless some event shatters public confidence in it. Far from destabilizing banks, as is often supposed, it is the threat of a run that forces banks to maintain their strength in the first place.
- The financial system is also stable in its response to fluctuations in the public demand for bank currency. Banks accommodate changes in the public's demand for currency rapidly and automatically, in much the same way that current banking systems accommodate the public demands to change one form of bank deposit into another, and accommodating these changes does not generally require major disturbances to interest rates, credit markets or economic activity.
- Last, and definitely not least, the *laissez-faire* system is stable in that it delivers price stability, and, therefore, among other things, delivers reasonable interest rate and asset price stability as well.

Conclusion

The *laissez-faire* system thus comes out with very high marks, in terms of both its efficiency and its stability. Indeed, it is hard to see how any system could conceivably fare any better. It is also a vast improvement on our current monetary system, with its excessive proliferation of different currencies; its banking weakness; its chronic instability and often crippling uncertainty; its periodic exchange rate and other crises; and its near-permanent and, often, catastrophic, inflation. As the lawyers say, *res ipse locitur*, the record of central banking speaks for itself. Which system do you prefer?

Notes

1 This paper is based on, but develops further, the previous analyses of monetary *laissez-faire* outlined in Dowd (1996b) and Dowd (1998).

2 In practice, coins of different metals usually coexisted, with the higher value ones (for example, gold) being used for large value transactions and lower value (for example, copper) being used for small transactions. However, nuances like this provide no new insights into our main concerns here, and are therefore best ignored in the present context.
3 To make their deposits even more attractive, banks would also provide depositors with transfer banking facilities, so that they can have deposits transferred to pay their debts (for example, by writing cheques against them). Banks would also develop note and cheque clearing systems to make their currency more attractive and reduce the transactions costs of redeeming and issuing currency. For more on these developments, see Glasner (1989: ch. 1).
4 This aspect of free banking is developed further in Dowd (1996a).
5 The issues involved with indirect convertibility are developed in more detail in Yeager and Woolsey (1991) and Dowd (1995).
6 The precise mechanics of such a scheme are somewhat involved, and the text deliberately sweeps them under the rug. Any reader who wants to investigate them further is referred to Dowd (1994, 1996b: ch. 14).

References

Coase, R. H. (1937) 'The Nature of the Firm', *Economica* 4: 386–405.
Dowd, K. (1994) 'A Proposal to End Inflation', *Economic Journal* 104: 828–40.
—— (1995) 'The Mechanics of Indirect Convertibility', *Journal of Money, Credit, and Banking* 27: 67–88.
—— (1996a) 'The Case for Financial *Laissez-Faire*', *Economic Journal* 106: 679–87.
—— (1996b) *Competition and Finance: A New Interpretation of Financial and Monetary Economics*, New York: St. Martin's Press.
—— (1998) 'What is Wrong with the World Financial System?', *Critical Review*, forthcoming.
Glasner, D. (1989) *Free Banking and Monetary Reform*, Cambridge: Cambridge University Press.
Goodhart, C. A. E. (1989) *Money, Information and Uncertainty*, London: Macmillan.
Jones, R. A. (1976) 'The Origin and Development of Media of Exchange', *Journal of Political Economy* 84: 757–75.
Menger, K. (1892) 'On the Origin of Money', *Economic Journal* 2: 239–55.
Radford, R. A. (1945) 'The Economic Organization of a P.O.W. Camp', *Economica* 12: 189–201.
Ullman-Margalit, E. (1978) 'Invisible-Hand Explanations', *Synthèse* 39: 263–91.
White, L. H. (1984) 'Competitive Payments Systems and the Unit of Account', *American Economic Review* 74: 699–712.
Yeager, L. B. and Woolsey, W. W. (1991) 'Is There a Paradox of Indirect Convertibility?', mimeo, Auburn University and the Citadel.

8 Aristotle on money

Scott Meikle

Introduction

Joseph Schumpeter (1994 [1954]: 63) considered Aristotle's treatment of money in *Politics* I, 8–10, to be 'the basis of the bulk of all analytical work in the field of money'.[1] Schumpeter was among Aristotle's shrewdest economic commentators and in some ways the most critically hostile, yet he regarded the analysis as penetrating and precocious. But it is perhaps more penetrating than he thought, and more deeply and interestingly flawed. The analysis is ethical as well as economic, and these two aspects are in a tension which leads Aristotle to attribute two natures to money, that of a means and that of an end. His official position is that it has only one of these natures, that of a means of exchange, and he ignores the other without giving a reason. Modern condescension should not be precipitate, however, because the tension is not one that can be avoided easily from what might be thought of as the high vantage point of modern economic thinking about money, which is just as deeply divided and in just the same way.

I

Aristotle introduces money as a development of exchange, and he sees this as evolving through four forms. The first is barter or the exchange of commodities without money, which we can represent as C–C. Barter is inconvenient because the acts of sale and purchase are fused into a single act. Money came into existence in the first place, he says, in order to make this sort of exchange easier, by allowing the sale (C–M) and the purchase (M–C) to be separated in time and place. This gives the second form of exchange, natural *chrêmatistikê* which may be represented as C–M/M–C, or for short C–M–C. Once people have become accustomed to this, Aristotle says, the third form of exchange arises, unnatural *chrêmatistikê*, in which people can come to market, not with surplus goods they have made or grown which they want to exchange for things they need, but with money. Their aim is to get money by buying goods and selling them for a greater sum. This can be represented as M–C/C–M, or M–C–M for short. This is justly discredited, he says, because it involves 'people taking things from one another' (*Politics* I: 1258). The fourth form is usury (*obolostatikê*), the lending of money at interest, M–M, or 'the breeding of money from money', which he says is the most hated sort and with reason (*Politics* I: 1258). Aristotle presents the emergence of these forms of exchange as a single process of development, and so they might appear to be accidentally different ways of doing essentially the same thing.

But interwoven with this is an analysis, which today might be called ethical rather than economic, in which he examines the end of each form. He finds that there is no single end which all forms of exchange alike serve, but two quite different ends such that some serve one and some the other. They are, therefore, accidentally similar ways of doing things that are essentially different.

Aristotle defines actions by their ends. If two activities aim at different ends, they are different however similar they may appear. C–C is acceptable because its end is the bringing together of needs with the useful things that will satisfy them (consumption), and he judges this to be natural and necessary by his usual criterion of having 'enough' (*Politics* I: 1256).[2] C–M–C, or natural *chrêmatistikê*, is also acceptable because it shares the same end, it 'is needed for the satisfaction of men's natural wants' (*Politics* I: 1257), and exchange reaches a natural terminus once a need has been met, and so its end 'has a limit'. This use of money is 'necessary and laudable' because it is a means subordinate to a natural end, and it is part of *oikonomikê*. It is to be contrasted with unnatural *chrêmatistikê* (M–C–M) and *obolostatikê* (M–M), whose end is not need or 'having enough', but the accumulation of money, and this has no natural terminus, for 'in this art of wealth-getting there is no limit of the end' (*Politics* I: 1257). The end is money, and one sum of money differs from another only in magnitude not in quality; like the exchange value it represents, it is a quantity and so it has no limit, and as an end it is irrational for that reason. This is not a case of *pleonexia*, or the desire for too much. Aristotle's point is not that those who pursue M–C–M are incontinent in their desires. His point is that, whether they are greedy or not, this is an activity whose *end* is without a limit. So C–M–C and M–C–M are quite different sorts of activity, but because they look alike they are commonly confused:

> the source of the confusion is the near connection between the two kinds of wealth-getting; in either, the instrument is the same, although the use is different, and so they pass into one another; for each is a use of the same property, but with a difference: accumulation is the end in the one case, but there is a further end in the other.
> (*Politics* I: 1257)

The distinction he is insisting on connects with his analysis of wealth. 'True wealth (*ho alêthinos ploutos*) is the stock of things that are useful in the community of the household or the polis' (*ho ploutos ho kata phusin*). The use is what counts, rather than the form of property: 'Wealth as a whole consists in using things rather than owning them; it is really the activity – that is, the use – of the property that constitutes wealth' (*Rhetoric*: 1361).[3] C–M–C aims at getting useful things or 'true wealth', but M–C–M does not, because its aim is wealth as a quantity of money, 'wealth of the spurious kind' (*Politics* I: 1257).

Aristotle's distinction between the two kinds of wealth is aligned, in turn, with the distinction between use value and exchange value, which he was the first to draw and which is the foundation of economic thought. The term 'use value' collects things as the things they are by nature; things that are distinguished by those very qualities which make one C useful for one purpose and another for another. It is these differences between the first C and the second C in C–M–C which he identifies as its point; 'it is not two doctors that associate for exchange, but a doctor and a farmer and in general people who are different (*heterôn*)' (*Ethics* V: 1133). M–C–M is indifferent to the nature of C; since C is used merely as a means to M any C will do. 'True wealth' consists in useful things, or use values, and use value is the end aimed at in C–C and C–M–C. 'Spurious wealth' is exchange value, and that is the end aimed at in M–C–M and M–M.[4] Use value falls in the category of quality, and the objects it collects are qualitatively differentiated and heterogeneous. Exchange value falls in the category of quantity, it is homogeneous and lacks species, and its instances differ only as magnitudes. So according to the doctrine of the *Categories* there is a metaphysical gap between the two, and this is the foundation of the differences between them as ends of action and as forms of wealth.

A deep ambivalence runs through the entire analysis and it erupts in three connected problems each centring on the nature of money. They pull the basis of his ethical verdicts on the different forms of exchange away from his analysis of their evolution. The basis of his verdicts is the distinction of ends, and if it should fail Aristotle would face a very unpalatable choice between holding that all the forms of exchange are equally acceptable including the 'hated' usury, and holding that all except C–C are equally unacceptable including the 'necessary and laudable' C–M–C. And if the distinction should fail for reasons arising from his analysis of exchange and money, then he would face the choice of holding on to his analysis and facing up to the unpalatable ethical choice that would follow from it, or ditching the entire economic analysis of the three chapters which would leave him with nothing at all.

II

Aristotle complains that the Delphian knife has been made to be exchanged rather than to do a job. It appears to have been a crude tool that could serve as a knife, a file and a hammer, and its advantage was that it was cheap. The smith who makes it is 'niggardly' because he makes a 'knife for many uses' when really 'every instrument is best made when intended for one and not for many uses' (*Politics* I: 1252). Because it is made to be cheap (cheaper than the three tools separately) it is made to be exchanged, so the construction of this tool is not part of the proper process of tool making where a thing is made to do a job. Hence it is not even really a tool, *a fortiori* not really a knife, and *a fortissimo* not a good knife. Its use value has been diminished by design in a compromise with exchange value. It has been deliberately constructed to perform more functions that it can perform well in order to sell at a cheap price.

It is difficult to be sure just how this is to be understood. It might amount to no more than a complaint about one particular kind of product and those who make it, and if that is all it is, we should not read too much into it. But it might be an example of an implied general criticism of the deleterious effects that exchange can have on the quality of the things produced when they are made in order to be exchanged for money. If that is Aristotle's point then the implications are more serious. This would be a criticism of the effects of money on production.

The danger of anachronism is obvious. We are excessively familiar today with the commercially-inspired adulteration of use values: foods lacking nutrition or being poisonous, planned obsolescence in consumer durables, unnecessary surgical operations done because they pay, education being made into training, and so forth, and care must be taken not to project this sort of thing back without evidence. But things of a similar nature were not unknown in the ancient world. Lots of shoddy goods were made, coin debased, and products adulterated. The Delphian knife finds a parallel in the product of 'the coppersmith who for cheapness makes a spit and a lampholder in one' (*De Partibus Animalium* IV: 683).

Aristotle himself is concerned about the effects of exchange value or money relations on the practice of the professional arts: they are practiced in perverted ways in order to make money out of them, for people not themselves engaged in trade (*kapêlikê*) but who wish to pursue money:

> do so by some other means, employing each of the faculties in an unnatural way ... [and] make all these faculties means for the business of providing wealth [*chrêmatistikas*, that is, in the context, money-getting], in the belief that wealth [of the spurious kind] is the end and that everything must be directed to the end.
> (*Politics* I: 1258)

He instances the military and medical arts, but he clearly intends the point to apply much more widely. Even philosophy can be used in this way, and this is just what the Sophists do, for the Sophist 'is one who makes money from an apparent but unreal wisdom' , and sophistry itself 'is, as we said, a kind of money making', rather than a kind of philosophy. Using an art like medicine as a way of conducting another art, money-getting, introduces a confusion of ends from which the pursuit of health can only suffer. Aristotle must take a serious view of this, because such confusion would undermine the rational ordering of ends set out at the beginning of the *Ethics* which he thinks is essential for the proper working of the polis and the pursuit of the good life.

It is true that ancient society was not a market economy, and that fact must always be held firmly in mind in considering matters of this kind. The product of labour did not universally take the form of a commodity or exchange value, since a sizeable proportion of production was undertaken for direct consumption rather than for exchange. The culture was inhospitable to the values of commerce, and they were not admired or publicly applauded, nor was public policy constructed with them at its heart. But even making due allowance for these great differences, and for avoiding modernist exaggeration and false assimilations of ancient practices to modern ones, there was still quite enough of that kind of behaviour to make it a realistic possibility that Aristotle might have intended the example of the Delphian knife to illustrate an implied general criticism.

The conditions prevailing in fourth century Athens do not make such a criticism impossible or unlikely. But even so Aristotle might still not have intended it. He does not explicitly draw the implication himself, and the best we can do is to decide how likely or unlikely it is that he had it in mind. There are two questions to be asked. Is there better reason to think that he intended the implication than that he didn't? And whether he intended it or not, is it a thought he could easily have had, and should have had if he didn't?

As to the first question, there is little explicit indication that he wants to extend the criticism beyond the smith to the makers of things generally. He is not short of opportunities, and the single criticism of the coppersmith in *De Partibus Animalium* is not enough to suggest that he was anxious to pursue them. Against this it can be said that given all that he has to say about the dangers of money-seeking behaviour, which after all is his theme in *Politics* I, 8–10, it is not very likely that he simply meant to criticize the makers of one or two particular items rather than a tendency that they illustrate.

As to the second question, if Aristotle did not think of the idea we are entitled to ask why. It would have been an obvious application of his views of true and false wealth, of wealth as use, of his criticisms of the end aimed at in M–C–M behaviour, and of the abuse of the arts for making money. Given all that, it would be astonishing if the idea had not crossed his mind. It is an obvious extension of criticisms he already advances, and given the character of his theory it is certainly one that he should have added. It is easier to believe that he suppressed it for some reason than that it never occurred to him.

The defects of the Delphian knife are not owing to faults of the smith, his skills, 'niggardliness', or his materials, but to a social cause that operates systematically where there is money, namely, that goods tend to be produced in order to be exchanged against money. Aristotle's reason for saying that the use made of a shoe in exchange is not its 'proper or peculiar use' is that 'the shoe has not been made for the purpose of being exchanged' (*Politics* I: 1257). But where there is money, this is all too likely to be the purpose for which a thing has been made. The Delphian knife illustrates the kind of failure this typically leads to, and it is difficult to see that Aristotle could be making any other point. His allusion to the 'niggardliness' of the smith (*penikrôs*) should not draw attention away from the systematic nature of the cause of the failure. The smith is to be compared with the Sophist who sells philosophy for money, or the doctor who sells medical services. It seems that C–M–C is not as innocent as Aristotle says. Its end is not to be so simply characterized as providing use value or meeting need. The fuller story will have to incorporate the possibility of the use value of products being systematically compromised by the fact that they are also made to be exchange values. But telling this fuller story would undercut the ground on which Aristotle passes C–M–C and the function of money that goes with it as ethically acceptable.

The ground was the distinction of ends he drew between C–M–C and M–C–M, and the Delphian knife example shows that this cannot be drawn in the simple way he draws it, as being the distinction between the ends of use value and exchange value. The end of M–C–M remains the accumulation of wealth as money, but it is no longer so easy to exclude that from the definition of the end of C–M–C. If the shorthand expression C–M–C is written in full as C–M/M–C, then in the act of sale C–M, we see the smith exchanging a knife with the failings Aristotle complains of, and it has those failings just because the smith's aim is to maximize M. If the smith's aim is M, not simply C as Aristotle says, then the order of the smith's acts of sale and purchase should be reversed to give M–C/C–M. The activity he is pursuing is at least partly M–C–M and not simply C–M–C. Over time his activity has the form . . . C–M–C–M–C–M–C–M–C . . ., and now it can no longer be divided neatly into a sequence of repetitions of C–M–C as . . . C–M–C/C–M–C/C–M–C. . . There is as much reason now to divide it up as . . . C–M/M–C–M/M–C–M/M–C–M/M–C . . . Unless we are to say that he only makes money not knives, as the Sophist makes money not philosophy, it no longer seems clear how we are to distinguish making money and making knives.

Aristotle's decision to permit C–M–C and forbid M–C–M now looks shaky because the distinction of ends has become blurred. Money-getting is a distinct art because it has a distinct end, and he says himself that, when a professional art like medicine is pursued for the sake of money, the ends of the two arts of medicine and money-getting 'pass into one another; for each is a use of the same thing', and this compromises the pursuit of health (*Politics* I: 1257). But Aristotle never explicitly admits that the same also applies to the artisan arts. His ethical verdicts seem more reasonable if it is supposed, as it usually is, that the activity of the trader (*kapêlos*) is the only case of M–C–M that he sets out to criticize, and that the presence of money leaves the ends of all other activities unaffected. But this supposition is clearly wrong, and so it must be asked how far along the line of activities he thinks the presence of money exerts its influence in making the end of the activity at best ambiguous between the pursuit of C and the pursuit of M.

There is no reason to think the maker of knives is any different in this respect from the maker of anything else, or that artisans are any better than professionals like the doctor, so there is no reason to think that any sort of activity should remain immune if it involves money. It is difficult to imagine that in the one field of the artisan arts, Aristotle simply forgot about the confusion of ends which arises when an art is pursued for the sake of money. He shows the smith misusing knife-making in exactly the same way that the Sophist misuses philosophy and the doctor misuses medicine. It is puzzling that Aristotle does not explicitly connect the smith into this line of criticism. The Delphian knife is such an obvious example of the same kind of shortcoming that his failure to relate it explicitly to his criticism of the effects of money as the spurious form of wealth seems to need some more convincing explanation than that he simply went to sleep at that point. It is tempting to suppose that he had a reason for deliberately excluding such considerations in this case.

If he had been determined to approve of the use of money in C–M–C, but to disbar its use in M–C–M, it would have been necessary to keep a clear line of demarcation between them. He had strong reasons for wanting to allow C–M–C and the function of money as a means of exchange. Without them, money would have no legitimate function at all, and in holding this he would have become more unrealistic and a more extreme Laconizer than even Plato, who never went so far (*Laws* 742) in spite of the fact that money was prohibited in Sparta. This would have been an uncomfortable position for Aristotle to have to occupy. His inclination was to accommodate entrenched practices which there was little chance of changing, even if this entailed some cost to more basic positions he held. His defence of slavery, so at variance with his view that the best *politeia* is one where 'anyone at all (*hostisoun*) might do best and lead a flourishing life' (*Politics* VIII: 1324), shows that he was capable of bending over backwards to do this, and Athens was hardly the place in which to expect unrealistic proposals about the use of money to be best received. To have pressed further than he did with the implications of the Delphian knife case would have forced him to choose between, on the one hand, dropping his objections to M–C–M and M–M, together with the entire analysis of use value, exchange value, wealth and exchange from which those objections follow, and on the other hand, denying the legitimacy of money in any of its functions. The course he chooses manages to accommodate two common sentiments: the usefulness of money for getting things, and the dislike of traders and moneylenders.

III

Aristotle insists that 'money was invented to be used in exchange' (*Politics*: 1258), and mainly on the strength of this he has usually been understood to hold that money is in its nature an instrument or means for the circulation of useful things or 'use values'. But his theory equally supports attributing to money the entirely different nature of an end, and obvious as this is, he ignores it and gives no reason for choosing the first view.

Roll (1961 [1938]) rightly observes that according to Aristotle's own account of the development of exchange, 'The natural purpose of exchange, the more abundant satisfaction of wants, is lost sight of; the accumulation of money becomes an end in itself.' According to Aristotle, money becomes the universal form of wealth, because 'everything can be expressed (*tetimesthai*) in money' (*Ethics* V: 1133), and many activities, perhaps most, come to be done for the sake of it as well as for the sake of their own intrinsic ends, or instead of them. What was introduced to be a means to human ends becomes an end itself, and the human ends it was meant to serve become means to it. We might have expected Aristotle to conclude that what money finally becomes is its *telos* and nature. But he insists that it is what it was originally intended to be, a means, and that its development into an end is a perversion.

Aristotle often gives origins this kind of importance. They are a good guide in identifying the natures of things; 'he who considers things in their first growth and origin, whether a state or anything else, will obtain the clearest view of them' (*Politics* I: 1252). But it is just as typically Aristotelian to find out what something really is by looking for its mature form: 'what each thing is when fully developed we call its nature, whether we are speaking of a man, a horse or a family' (*Politics* I: 1252). This method would lead to the conclusion that it is in the nature of money to become an end. So Aristotle's theory contains what is needed to deduce, by familiar Aristotelian devices in each case, two different accounts of the nature of money. But a thing cannot ultimately be both a means and an end.

For each of the other major economic concepts, wealth and exchange (*chrêmatistikê*), Aristotle gives two definitions, a use value definition and an exchange value definition, as his theory requires because of the difference of category between use value and exchange value. So perhaps he might have concluded that money has two natures, or that there are two sorts of money. A distinction between use value money and exchange value money might seem to fit, because the end of the good use of money in C–M–C is use value, and the end of its bad use in M–C–M is exchange value. But this would have been nonsense, because money *is* exchange value. Its job is to express the exchange value of each commodity independently of that commodity's own physical body. The use value of a thing is undetachable from its physical body, but its exchange value can be represented in the physical body of the money commodity, and Aristotle knew this (Roll 1961

[1938]: 35). If gold is the money commodity then it has two use values: first as the substance of wedding rings, and second as the substance useful as a means of exchange. Aristotle knew this too.[5] So he knew that the notion of 'use value money' is incoherent, and that a distinction between use value money and exchange value money is incoherent too. Money is exchange value from the outset, and it has this character in C–M–C just as much as in M–C–M and M–M. Each of these forms depends on the exchange value of C being represented independently of the physical body of C. But if money has only the nature of exchange value, then it cannot have the use value nature he wants for C–M–C.

Moreover, each form of exchange realizes a potential in the nature of money as the representative of exchange value. They constitute a single process of development arising originally from C–C, and each transition from one form to the next is part of the evolution of exchange, and results from people pursuing the possibilities in the relations and institutions they have created. Aristotle tends to think of change as a process of generation and maturation in something, and it is natural that he should present the development of exchange in the way he does. But it is strange that in the course of such a process, an entity should change its nature and become something else altogether, and this seems to be what is supposed to happen between C–M–C and M–C–M, when money ceases to be a means and becomes an end. The idea is incoherent, because a process of development is necessarily undergone by some kind of unitary nature, and without such a unity there cannot be such a process. The identification of a unity is usually a matter of identifying an end or *telos*.[6] But in his account of the development of exchange, he identifies not one end but two, so it is hard to see what the requisite unity can consist in, and without that there cannot really be a single process of development at all. Aristotle subsequently implies that this is a single process only from C–C to C–M–C, and a perversion thereafter, but this is another way of explaining what has so far seemed unconvincing in his account.

Aristotle's ambiguity about the nature of money and its end is registered by Ross in a little-known symposium with Cannan (1922), Bonar, and Wicksteed. On the one hand, Ross says of Aristotle's view of interest that 'I don't think he means that it is by an unnatural convention that money breeds money. He appears to regard it as the normal course of things that it should'. This is surely right if we have in mind Aristotle's account of the development of exchange and money. What happens in 'the normal course of things' is the result of the operations of some nature, and the appearance of interest in the course of that development is as much a part of the process as any other. It might even be said that M–M realises a potentiality in the nature of money. On the other hand, Ross also observes that:

> money produces interest, but that this is not what it was invented to do – it was invented to be used in exchange. The yielding of interest is an

unintended by-product. And since Aristotle identifies the nature of a thing with the end it is intended to fulfil, it is a legitimate gloss to say that interest-bearing is according to Aristotle no part of the nature of money.
(Ross, in Cannan 1922)

The conclusion, though Ross does not draw it, is that the bearing of interest is part of the nature of money and that it is not.

IV

Aristotle takes sides in the current debate about whether it is a good or bad thing for a city to be located by the sea, and in opposition to Plato, he decides that on the balance of advantage it is a good thing. But he makes a distinction. It is good for a city to engage in *emporikê*, because 'it is necessary that they should import from abroad what is not to be found in their own country, and that they should export what they have in excess'. But it is not good to engage in entrepôt trade. 'Those who make themselves a market for the world only do so for the sake of revenue, and if a state ought not to desire profit of this kind it ought not to have such an emporium' (*Politics* VII: 1327–31). He recognizes a danger that unless commerce is restrained, a port may develop willy-nilly into an entrepôt emporium, and he is prepared to envisage legislation to regulate the behaviour of buyers and sellers in the port: 'any disadvantage which may threaten can easily be met by laws defining the persons who may, or may not, have dealings with one another'.

It seems odd that in Book I Aristotle never so much as raises the question of legislation to regulate M–C–M behaviour in the city itself. This may be simply a matter of proportion. Such behaviour was confined to a retail trade that was very restricted compared with what we are familiar with today, and the commercial values it represented did not penetrate deeply into the social relationships of the polis in spite of Plato's bitter complaints in the *Laws*.[7] But the big extension of commerce that would follow permitting entrepôt trade would have been a more serious affair. Perhaps Aristotle was going for a compromise. It seems consistent with most of what he says and does not say that he should be prepared to put up with a certain amount of behaviour of this kind by individuals, while being against any big extension of it.

It would be easier to believe in this compromise if Aristotle had believed that M–C–M behaviour arose from individual shortcomings rather than from the systemic effect of money, but this is doubtful. He regards such behaviour as systemic because he believes it arises from the development of money, and what is wrong with it lies in the unlimited nature of the end of M–C–M, 'wealth of the spurious kind', rather than in the *pleonexia* of individuals. The common idea that wealth is unlimited does not arise from human wickedness, but from the existence of M–C–M which is 'commonly and rightly called the art of making money, and has in fact suggested the notion that wealth and property have no limit'. The perversion of the arts is not primarily owing to individual failings but to the need for money; 'the life of money-making is one undertaken under compulsion' (*Ethics* I: 1096). Aristotle does not regard money as a technical device which we pervert by turning it to wicked ends; he argues that there is an end built into M–C–M to which people adapt themselves and their behaviour.[8] The problem is whether Aristotle's belief in the systemic character of the threat posed to the community by money is consistent with the view, implicit in the putative compromise, that money-seeking behaviour can be contained without laws.

The moral ethos of Greek life was unfavourable to the values of commerce. Nearly all lending was *eranos* or friendly lending, and Aristotle himself tells us that a temple of the Graces was put up in a prominent place in the city to remind citizens that grace required that 'we should serve in return one who has shown grace to us, and should another time take the initiative in showing it' (Ethics V: 1133).[9] *Chrêmatistikê* existed, so it was a known danger, and in spite of its systemic origin, Aristotle would have been justified in thinking that it could be contained by ethical precept, or by public intervention to prevent any excessive growth of it as in the case of entrepôt trade. He did not have a crystal ball in which to foresee the full-blooded assertion of the capacity of money to erode *koinônia* and the values in *ethikê* and *politikê* which he knew and expounded, and no serious hint of its potency showed at any time in antiquity.

V

Aristotle is in two minds about money. His official view of its nature is that of a means, but this is a stipulation rather than a conclusion, because he does not argue for it. The view that money is an end is just as integral to his analysis, and his attempt to exclude it as a perversion is inconsistent with his account of the development of exchange where both views of money are integrated. It is not his analysis of exchange which pushes him towards the stipulation; the impetus from there would be towards the view that it is in the nature of money to become an end. The impetus comes from elsewhere. His decision to identify its nature by origins rather than by its *telos* is crucial in securing the stipulation, and since he does not argue for that either, the decision looks arbitrary until it is noticed how well its consequence suits the ethical and political requirements of his wider position: money cannot be abolished so there had better be an acceptable use of it, but it causes harm so there had better be an unacceptable use of it.

Aristotle's analysis throws up a host of considerations with bearings on two still contentious and unresolved questions: the nature of money and the relation between ethics and economics. His difficulty about the nature of money is not an elementary one which can be resolved easily with the resources of modern economic thought, because the same duality is present there too. It is the chief bone of contention between the friends and foes of market economy.

Adam Smith (1987 [1776]) holds, as Aristotle does, that use value or 'consumption is the sole end and purpose of all production'. Smith recognizes that money becomes the end for those engaged in business, that their operations are of the M–C–M character, and he thinks they need to be publicly regulated for that reason (unlike some of his twentieth century *soi-disant* disciples). But he thinks that the totality of those operations produces an outcome for the society that is C–M–C in character, and he resolves the tension between money as a means and as an end in that way. The pursuit of exchange value, in spite of appearances, really serves the end of use value.

In Marx's view, the market economy is a lawlike system of exchange value, and it can be interfered with to make it serve human ends better only to a limited degree. Use value is not the end but a means, and money or exchange value is not a means but the end. The system inhibits wealth and potential wealth serving human ends, because its end is something quite different, the quantitative expansion of exchange value, M–C–M. Wealth cannot be both use value at the service of the natural ends of human living, and at the same time take the form of exchange value and serve the end of expanding exchange value. These are alternatives between which we must choose. They may be made to intersect to a limited extent, but they cannot be made to intersect enough for human flourishing (Marx: 1970 [1859]).[10]

Keynes's project was to increase the extent of the intersection. He also takes the view that money becomes an end, though he regards this as owing mainly to ethical perversion in the use people make of money, rather than, as Marx thought, to something in the nature of money which produces ethical perversion in the behaviour of people. The money motive, Keynes says, is a 'disgusting morbidity, one of those semi-criminal, semi-pathological propensities which one hands over with a shudder to the specialists in mental disease' (Keynes 1931: 369). But it is a perversion we shall be able to overcome once we have enough, or in economic parlance, when there has been sufficient accumulation, and he thinks that time will come in the lifetimes of the grandchildren of his own generation. He writes:

> The distinction between a cooperative economy and an entrepreneur economy bears some relation to a pregnant observation made by Karl Marx, – though the subsequent use to which he put this observation was highly illogical. He pointed out that the nature of production in the actual world is not, as economists seem to suppose, a case of C–M–C, i.e., of exchanging commodity (or effort) for money in order to obtain another commodity (or effort). That may be the standpoint of the private consumer. But it is not the attitude of business, which is a case of M–C–M´, i.e., of parting with money for commodity (or effort) in order to obtain more money.
>
> (Keynes 1979: 81)

In Keynes's view it is possible both to continue with money and M–C–M, and to bring the money motive under moral control, thus transforming money from an end into a means.

VI

The tension between ethics and economics, visible in Aristotle, is also reproduced in modern economic thought.

The pseudo-Aristotelian *Oeconomica*, as Finley (1985) has argued, deals simply with useful things or 'use values'. It strikes a modern reader as quite un-economic, because it lacks any discussion of investment, labour costs, profit maximization, turnover and so on; it even lacks the notions of these things. The Greeks and Romans had no system of double-entry book-keeping. The legal, literary and documentary evidence for Greek and Roman accounting shows that they lacked even the ideas of debit and credit. What we might mistake for accounts are no more than inventories of use values and checks on embezzlement (Ste. Croix 1956). Serious concern with exchange value and awareness of its categories are entirely absent. A collection of 'Greek economics' published in 1923 made only a slim volume, and all its extracts have the character of the *Oeconomica*. This is not surprising since the ancient world was not based on the market economy. It was, as Finley has argued, a world primarily of use value in which markets played only a peripheral role, and if economics is the science of exchange value, it is not surprising that the Greeks did not invent it.

Since Aristotle's time, or rather in the last few hundred years, exchange value has grown from being an end which individuals may pursue, into an end which whole societies are organized to pursue. It has become the regulator of those societies through the system of markets, and, in the form of 'the economy', it has come to be the pre-eminent source of reasons for decision-making in the public realm. These changes have had profound effects on ethics, on the very conception of what ethics is, of its place in human affairs, and on conceptions of human good and even of human identity. Their accompaniment was the rise of economics to the position of an independent science.

If economics is to be seen as the science of exchange value, its magnitudes and movements, its interaction with use value, and of the requirements of its pursuit as the primary end, then the place of use value in it is that of a means rather than an end. The growth of economic thinking and of the values implicit in it, to be found in authors like Petty, were fiercely resisted and parodied throughout by moralists like Swift. What emerged was a discrete science which contested much of the ground previously occupied by *ethikê* and *politikê* in public decision-making.

The tricky relationship between ethics and the new science was dealt with in a number of different ways. Keynes had an ethical theory independent of economics.[11] But this set him apart from the mainstream of economic writing into which an ethical theory, utilitarianism, was integrated. It fitted neatly because it had been designed for this supporting and subordinate role in the first place. The origin of utilitarianism in Bentham was associated with the ambition of providing political economy with a system of ethics, or something that looked like ethics, which could be fully integrated into political economy. This was desirable because actual morality stood outside economics and was constantly making difficulties for it, setting down conditions which economics might have difficulty meeting, or not be able to meet at all. Testimony to this origin is seen in the fact, argued by Williams (1972), that utilitarianism can do so little of what a real morality is supposed to do.

Utilitarianism, unsurprisingly, fits the requirements of economics well. There is only one end, pleasure or utility, and all actions are means to it; they are therefore to be judged only on their efficacy in promoting that end, so that only the consequences of actions are significant, not the actions themselves. Utilitarianism provides economics with a simulacrum of ethics in which it is not difficult to arrange a close association between utility maximization and the maximization of exchange value. Utilitarians might deny that they are committed to the view that the common currency of happiness is money. But, as Williams says, 'they are committed to something which in practice has those implications: that there are no ultimately incommensurable values' (Williams 1972: 96–122). He adds that it is not an accidental feature of the utilitarian outlook that the presumption is in favour of the monetarily quantifiable, and that other values are forced into an apologetic dilemma:

> It is not an accident, because (for one thing) utilitarianism is the value system for a society in which economic values are supreme; and also, at the theoretical level, because quantification in money is the only obvious form of what utilitarianism insists upon, the commensurability of value.
>
> (Williams 1972: 96–122)

A second reaction to these changes is the view that economics and ethics have little or nothing to do with one another, which Lionel Robbins defended in *The Nature and Significance of Economic Science*. 'Between the generalizations of positive and normative studies', he wrote, 'there is a logical gulf fixed which no ingenuity can disguise and no juxtaposition in space or time bridge over' (Robbins 1984 [1932]: 132). He concluded that regarding economics and ethics 'it does not seem logically possible to associate the two studies in any form but mere juxtaposition ... the two fields of enquiry are not on the same plane of discourse' (ibid.). Few economists accepted his conclusions when they were published in 1932, but today most do.

Some economists are concerned that economics should have developed in the way that it has, proceeding on unrealistic assumptions about human nature and motivation, and apparently incomprehending of the intrinsic points of non-economic activities and the values they embody. Amartya Sen finds 'something quite extraordinary in the fact that economics has in fact evolved in this way' (Sen 1987: 1–2): a way which he describes as 'the self-consciously "non-ethical" character of modern economics' (ibid.). Adam Smith was after all, he points out, a Professor of Moral Philosophy, and economics was for a long time seen as something like a branch of ethics.

Looked at from an Aristotelian perspective, however, the divorce between ethics and economics seems inevitable rather than extraordinary. The activities they study aim at different ends, use value and exchange value, whose compatibility is limited. Neoclassical economics draws a conceptual connection between use value and exchange value through the notion of utility, so that the two appear inseparable and the question of whether money is a means or an end cannot be clearly formulated. For this reason neoclassical economists would deny that economics is the science only or primarily of exchange value.[12] On Aristotelian metaphysics, however, no such conceptual connection is possible because use value and exchange value fall into the different categories of quality and quantity. Pursuing them as ends requires different courses of action in each case. So the Aristotelian view must be that economics is the science of exchange value only or primarily, not of both equally. Ethics and economics are competitors over the same ground, and one can prosper only at the expense of the other. From an Aristotelian point of view it can hardly seem surprising that ethics and economics should have come apart, or that once they had, they should have proved so hard to reconcile. What should seem surprising is that they should ever have been thought to be connected.

Notes

1 Schumpeter says that Aristotle's theory of money 'prevailed substantially until the end of the nineteenth century and even beyond', adding that three of the four functions of money traditionally listed in nineteenth century textbooks of economics can be traced back to Aristotle, namely, money as medium of exchange, as measure of value and as store of value. The absence of the fourth, money as standard of deferred payments, can hardly be held against Aristotle, since there were no deferred payments in the ancient world, though Schumpeter does not offer this excuse.

2 The point of *oikonomikê* Aristotle says is *to autarkês einai*, and what he means is best rendered as 'having enough' rather than 'being self-sufficient', because the context is a discussion of avoiding deficiency, not avoiding dependence on others. Apart from considerations of context, Aristotle's definition of *autarkês* in the *Ethics* is 'that which on its own makes life worthy of choice and lacking in nothing'.

3 See also *Ethics* (VI: 1139): 'Everyone who makes something makes it for some end or purpose. What is made is not itself the final end, only what is done is that'.

172 *Scott Meikle*

4   Aristotle's position, sketched here, is dealt with in greater detail in Meikle (1991).
5   Aristotle says that 'men agreed to employ in their dealings with each other something intrinsically useful and easily applicable to the purposes of life, for example, iron, silver and the like'. Also:

> in the satisfaction of wants money became the medium of exchange by agreement. And for that reason it bears the name *nomisma*, because it owes its existence, not to nature, but to law (*nomô*), and it is in our power to change it and make it void.

6   See the discussion of wholes and ends in Clark (1975).
7   Plato criticizes the moral qualities of those engaged in commerce and the effects their activities have on relationships in the polis: commerce 'fills the land with wholesaling and retailing, breeds shifty and deceitful habits in a man's soul and makes the citizens distrustful and hostile' (*Laws*: 705).
8   Throughout the discussion in *Politics* I, Aristotle shows little interest in individual behaviour except in so far as it is affected by the presence of money, as we might expect since the work is concerned with *politikê* rather than *ethikê*. The social arrangements of money are not of the individual's making, and as individuals they have no choice but to accommodate to them if they are to live; hence 'the life of money-making is one undertaken under compulsion' (*Ethics* I: 1096). Aristotle is concerned with the nature of those arrangements before he is concerned with individual behaviour.
9   See Millet (1991).
10 Marx's strategic dispositions in laying out the relation between economics and life are obviously very close to Aristotle's, and the reason for this is that Marx got them from Aristotle. He parades the debt and cites many passages from Aristotle to support distinctions he wants to make, some of them crucial, in his discussion of the nature of money in *A Contribution to the Critique of Political Economy*. The debt is equally manifest in volume one of *Capital* where Marx gives what is the first interpretation, since the rise of political economy as an independent science, of Aristotle's discussion of the commensurability and value of commodities.
11 See Fitzgibbons (1988), especially chapter 3.
12 Mill (1987 [1842]), though not neoclassical, defines wealth as 'all useful or agreeable things, which possess exchangeable value'. Alfred Marshall (1961 [1890]) deals entirely with exchange value, dismissing use value out of hand.

References

Cannan, E. (1922) 'Who said "Barren Metal"?', *Economica* 5: 107.
Clark, S. R. L. (1975) *Aristotle's Man*, Oxford: Clarendon Press.
Finley, M. L. (1985) *The Ancient Economy*, 2nd edn, London: Chatto and Windus
Fitzgibbons, A. (1988) *Keynes's Vision: A New Political Economy*, Oxford: Clarendon Press.
Keynes, J. M. (1931) *Essays in Persuasion*, London: Macmillan.
—— (1979) *Collected Writings*, vol. 29, ed. D.E. Moggridge, London: Macmillan.
Marshall, A. (1961 [1890]) *Principles of Economics* 9th variorum edn, ed. C. W. Guillebaud, London: Macmillan.
Marx, K. (1970 [1859]) *A Contribution to the Critique of Political Economy*, Moscow: Progress Publishers.
Meikle, S. (1991) 'Aristotle and Exchange Value', in D. Keyt and F. D. Miller (eds) *A Companion to Aristotle's Politics*, Oxford: Blackwell.
Mill (1987 [1848]) *Principles of Political Economy* ed. W. Ashley, New York: Augustus

M. Kelley.
Millet, P. (1991) *Lending and Borrowing in Ancient Athens,* Cambridge.
Robbins, L. (1984 [1932]) *An Essay on the Nature and Significance of Economic Science,* New York: New York University Press.
Roll, E. (1961 [1938]) *A History of Economic Thought,* London: Faber and Faber.
Schumpeter, J. A. (1994 [1954]) *A History of Economic Analysis,* London: Routledge.
Sen, A. (1987) *On Ethics and Economics,* Oxford: Blackwell.
Ste. Croix, G. E. M. de (1956) 'Greek and Roman Accounting', in A. C. Littleton and B. S. Yamey (eds) *Studies in the History of Accounting,* Homeward, Illinois: R. D. Irwin.
Smith, A. (1981 [1776]) *An Inquiry into the Nature and Causes of The Wealth of Nations,* ed. R. H. Campbell and A. S. Skinner, Indianoplis: Liberty Fund.
Williams, B. (1972) *Morality,* New York: Harper and Row.

9 A Marxist theory of *commodity* money revisited

Steve Fleetwood

Introduction

This chapter argues that money, in its developed form, emerges at the end of a process wherein a contradiction in the activity of labouring is converted into a contradiction in the products of this activity (that is, commodities). The contradiction is eventually resolved when one of these commodities becomes money. Understanding the nature of money, then, involves tracing the contradiction from labouring activity, through the commodity, to the particular money commodity: gold or whatever.

I revisit Marx's theory of commodity money in full knowledge of the commonly-held notion that because the contemporary capitalist system is dominated by credit, *fiat*, electronic, and various other forms of non-commodity money, Marx's theory is anachronistic. As will become clear in the conclusion, however, rather than abandon Marx's theory of commodity money, an argument can be made for retaining it as a powerful explanation of money, and re-evaluating our notions of contemporary money.

The chapter consists of four parts. It starts with brief note on method and is followed, in the second part, by an explanation of how labouring activity is co-coordinated in a system of commodity production and exchange. The peculiarities of this system generate a contradiction in labouring activity, that is, between the individual, concrete and particular ways in which labouring activity is actually performed, and the social, abstract and universal form which it (strives to) adopt. The third part shows how this contradiction is converted into a contradiction in the commodity, that is, between the commodity's particular (use value) and universal (value) forms. This involves a little re-thinking of the nature of use value. The fourth part shows how the contradiction contained in the commodity is resolved when one particular commodity becomes simultaneously a commodity and money. A *résumé* then loops back to the second part and the co-ordination of labouring activity.

A note on method

I follow Reuten and William's (1988) rejection of the *analytical* method of dealing with socio-economic categories in favour of the method of systematic presentation. The analytical method proceeds by deploying the fully formed categories at the outset, then subsequently combining them (usually via the deductive method) to form a body of theoretical statements.[1] The problem with this method is that it merely states, rather than derives, the categories with which it works. The method of systematic presentation, by contrast, grounds the categories by first positing them, and subsequently deriving them via the transcendence of contradiction from the more abstract categories that pre-stage them. The presentation, therefore, unfolds from abstract to more concrete categories by successfully grounding them.[2]

In the specific context of money, the method of systematic presentation means one cannot begin by deploying money at the outset. Rather, money must be grounded as by first positioning it, then deriving it from the more abstract categories of labour, value, and commodities. Money eventually emerges, as a result, only at the very end of the presentation.

It is necessary, however, to be aware of a potential problem in using this method. Since the only form in which (say) labour can manifest itself is money, and since labour is one of the categories in which money must be grounded, one must start with labour. But starting with labour necessarily means making claims about labour that cannot, strictly speaking, be made until the introduction of money. And so a vicious circle is encountered; claims must be made at a particular stage in the presentation that cannot, strictly speaking, be made at that stage. This is a problem afflicting all attempts to explain an internally-related system, where the categories evolve dialectically and what emerges at the end was present *in nuce* at the start.[3]

Overcoming this problem requires a little patience by the reader, because it means that any claim can only be evaluated upon completion of the entire presentation: and this is why money, which was posited at the outset, emerges only at the very end of the presentation. I will, therefore, remind the reader of this point in those places where it might appear I am making a mistaken claim.

The contradiction in labouring activity

One of the most fundamental activities occurring in any human socio-economic system is that of labouring, that is, transforming the material world (which includes human knowledge) from one state to another more useful state. The many different acts of labouring must be co-ordinated with one another whenever some overall (societal) goal is successfully realized, such as building a pyramid, sowing and reaping a crop, building a car or caring for the sick. Since this co-ordination occurs in different ways in (spatio-temporally) different socio-economic systems, how, one might ask, does it occur in a capitalist system?[4]

A capitalist system is, essentially, one where labouring activity is carried out by atomized, isolated, individual producers or collectivities of producers such as firms.[5] These producers never meet to discuss the co-ordination of their activities, nor are their activities co-ordinated via a central agency. Yet, clearly, their labouring activities are co-ordinated (however badly) or the socio-economic system would grind to a halt. Labouring activity is *indirectly* co-ordinated via the systematic exchange of the products of these very activities, commodities. And the systematic exchange of commodities involves the systematic evaluation of these commodities, that is, the assignment of appropriate value magnitudes or exchange values.[6]

The systematic (as opposed to the accidental) evaluation of commodities implies that the very different objects that are produced and exchanged are commensurable, and of course, commensurate. To write, for example, two guns equals twenty coats is, quite literally, nonsense (Carling 1986: 60). Guns and coats are, by their natures, incommensurable entities, and so one needs to look elsewhere to find the nature of their commensurability. In Marxist economics, incommensurable entities are rendered commensurable, because they are products of human labour.[7] But what kind of human labour is involved here?

Labouring activity is actually performed by isolated individuals, and is concrete and particular in the sense that gunsmithing is a completely different activity from tailoring. As such, the various labouring acts necessary to make guns and coats are as incommensurable as the products themselves. Being the products of individual, concrete and particular labour, then, is not sufficient to render incommensurable entities commensurable.

However, as well as being individual, concrete and particular labouring activity also adopts social, abstract, and universal forms. Let us consider these forms in a little more depth:

> *Labour is social* in the sense that the labouring activity of an isolated individual is related to the labouring activity of many others via the commodities they each produce. Whenever an individual tailor makes a coat there are, simultaneously, thousands of other tailors doing exactly the same thing in thousands of different spatio-temporal locations. This labouring activity is social, despite the fact that the individual tailor has no *direct* relations with any of the other tailors, because his or her labouring activity is *indirectly* co-ordinated via the systematic exchange of their commodities. Notice that concrete labour does not disappear here; rather, individual labour doubles into a unity of itself and social labour.
>
> *Labour is abstract* in the sense that the concreteness of the various natural labours undertaken to produce coats and guns are abstracted from. This process of abstraction is not an epistemic matter (not something economists do in theory), rather, it is an ontic matter

Marxist theory of commodity money 177

(something that occurs in reality). And it happens, ultimately, via the market. Notice that concrete labour does not disappear here; rather, individual labour doubles into a unity of itself and social labour.

Labour is universal because it is social and abstract. Concrete and individual labour is particular in the way lions and tigers are particulars. Social and abstract labour is universal in the way animal is a universal, although unlike animal, social and abstract labour have a material existence.[8] Notice that particular labour does not disappear here; rather, particular labour doubles into a unity of itself and universal labour.

Social abstract and universal (henceforth SAU) labour is the *social form* adopted by individual, concrete and particular (henceforth ICP) labour. Because SAU labour relates the labours of individual producers and abstracts from the concrete particularity of their labouring activities, it has the potential to render incommensurable entities commensurate.[9] For this potential to become actualized, however, SAU labour must adopt an appropriate form. This is best understood by considering the forms in which, ICP labour and SAU labour strive to manifest themselves:

- First, the material distinctiveness of each act of ICP labouring manifests itself both as itself (in the sense that one can actually observe these acts), and in the form of the particular commodity it produces. When one observes the material distinctiveness of a commodity, one is indirectly observing the ICP labour that produced it.[10] But, as noted above, ICP labour cannot render incommensurable entities commensurate, in which case the systematic evaluation of commodities cannot occur; the systematic exchange of commodities cannot occur; and hence labouring activity cannot be co-ordinated.
- SAU labour, while having the potential to render incommensurable commodities commensurable, has no material distinctiveness. It can neither manifest itself as itself, nor can it manifest itself in the form of a particular commodity. SAU labour cannot manifest itself as measurable amounts of labour embodied in a commodity because only hours of ICP labour are observable, and hence measurable.[11] Simply put, one cannot walk into a shop and purchase a commodity in terms of its SAU labour content. Without an appropriate form, however, the potential cannot become actualized and SAU labour cannot render incommensurable entities commensurate. Without this, once again, the systematic evaluation of commodities cannot occur; the systematic exchange of commodities cannot occur; and hence labouring activity cannot be co-ordinated. One ends up in the same position as with ICP labouring, although in this case for different reasons.

Herein lies the fundamental contradiction of the capitalist system. Labouring activity cannot be co-ordinated in the form in which it is actually performed (ICP) and in which it manifests itself. Labouring activity can be co-ordinated if it adopts the form of SAU labour, but SAU labour cannot manifest itself as itself. At the same moment that ICP labour adopts the SAU form, the latter is itself striving to adopt another form. SAU is, as it were, struggling to find an appropriate manifestation. To run ahead of the argument a little, SAU labour needs to adopt the value form of commodities, and to adopt the price form of commodities, and this of course requires money.

This ontic contradiction motivates the epistemic shift to the next stage of the presentation. It is time to consider how the fundamental contradiction in labouring activity becomes converted into a contradiction in the commodity, that is, between the commodity's particular (use value) and universal (value) forms.

The contradiction in the commodity

Marx once remarked that the commodity, while 'at first sight an extremely obvious, trivial thing', abounds in 'metaphysical subtleties' (1990: 163). This section attempts to unravel some of these metaphysical subtleties. It begins by introducing three key sets of ideas, before proceeding to develop them a little more.

First, while it is commonplace to refer to a commodity as a *unity* of use value and value, it is not always clear precisely what this means. The idea that a commodity is a unity means that use value and value are *internally related*.[12] This means that use value is what *it* is by virtue of value being what *it* is, and *vice versa*. Put another way, a use value can only be a use value when a value is a value, and *vice versa*.

Second, most discussions imply, or even state, that the commodity is a *material* category because it refers to the useful, physical properties or bodily shape of a commodity, whereas value is a *social* category because it refers to the social form in which the bodily shape manifests itself. Despite Marx's own conflicting and confusing comments on this issue, I think this is incorrect.[13] I suggest, therefore, that use value is best conceived of triadically as first, a material entity with two social forms, which are second, use value, and third, value. In other words, use value is a social category; it is the social form in which the bodily shape of a commodity manifests itself. Rather than write 'a commodity *is* a use value', one should write 'a commodity *has* a use value form.'

Third, whilst the notion of 'becoming' is not prevalent in *Capital* volume 1, it is, by contrast, extremely prevalent in *A Contribution to the Critique of Political Economy*. Unless one is prepared to accept a metaphysics of fixed, ready-made, non-evolving entities, one has to accept that entities never are themselves; rather, they become themselves. Commodities, the use value and value forms never *are* themselves, they *become* themselves. To differentiate between an entity that has not yet become itself, and an entity that has, I differentiate between *potential entities* and (actual) *entities*. Hence I differentiate between a potential commodity and a commodity; potential use value and use value; and potential value and value.

With these three sets of ideas (partially) clarified, it is possible to uncover the metaphysical subtleties surrounding the commodity. It is, perhaps, easiest to begin with a schematic overview, then gradually enrich the scheme. What makes these metaphysical subtleties difficult to grasp, is that for a potential commodity to become a commodity, four other (different yet internally-related) moments of becoming must also occur:

- A commodity's potential use value form must become an (actual) use value form.
- A commodity's potential value form must become an (actual) value form.
- For the first moment to occur, the use value form must double into a unity of use value and value forms.
- For the second moment to occur, the value form must double into a unity of value and use value forms.

It is this reciprocal process whereby the use value form of a commodity doubles into a unity of use value and value forms (and *vice versa*) that makes the commodity a genuine *unity* of use value and value, and not just an entity with two aspects to it. Let us consider these points from the perspective of use value and value respectively.

Use value

Immediately after the production stage, the producer of a material entity has produced just that, a material entity.[14] This entity might have been produced to be a commodity with use value and value forms, but as yet it is none of these things. All one can say is that this material entity has the potential to adopt the use value form. It adopts the form of a use value, however, only when it is placed on the market and finds a buyer, because this act signals that members of society have recognized the usefulness of that entity.[15] It should be noted that in order to be placed on the market, the material entity must adopt, as well as the use value form, the value form and an exchange value form.

I noted above that use value is best conceived of triadically. Let me flesh this out a little using the example of a coat, before going on to expand upon the value form.

- When one refers to a coat *qua* coat, one refers solely to its *material dimension*; that is, to its material, physical, natural, or (as I will call it for brevity) *bodily shape*.
- When one refers to a coat *qua* use value, one is referring to *both* its material and social dimensions. A coat is a material entity with a particular bodily shape, and this shape has been *socially* registered as useful.

- When one refers to a coat *qua* value, one is referring solely to its *social* dimension.

It is important to note that the coat's bodily shape never disappears, irrespective of the form in which it adopts. Rather the coat doubles into a unity of ever-present bodily shape and social forms. Henceforth when I refer to the use value form of a commodity, I will be referring to a commodity's *socially recognized bodily shape*. A commodity is social because it is socially recognized, and material because the bodily shape is ever present.

Value

Immediately after the production stage, the producer of a material entity has produced just that, a material entity. This entity might have been produced to be a commodity, with use value and value forms, but as yet it is none of these things. All one can say is that this material entity has the potential to adopt the value form. The producer probably has a particular exchange value magnitude in mind. It becomes a value, however, only when the entity is placed on the market and finds a buyer, because this act registers the fact of the exchange value magnitude.[16] Updating Marxist terminology, one could say the entity *reflects* (not embodies) socially-necessary SAU labour. This means that the value of the socially-recognized bodily shape (use value) of commodity X is similar to the value of the socially- recognized bodily shape (use value) of commodities Y and Z. Note once again, that in order to be placed on the market, the entity must adopt a use value form as well as the value form. 'Use value as an active carrier of the exchange value becomes a means of exchange' (Marx 1976: 42).

Taking both use value and value categories together, one can draw the following conclusion. An entity (a potential commodity) becomes a commodity when it is placed on the market, when the potential value form adopts the value form, and when the potential use value form adopts the use value form. This requires that the use value form doubles into a unity of value and use value forms. Only then does the commodity become a unity of use value and value.

There is, however, still a little more work to be done on the way a commodity adopts the value form. To adopt the value form, a commodity must become an equivalent. A commodity becomes an equivalent when it can 'freely take the place of a definite quantity of another commodity' (Marx 1976: 44). And a commodity can do this only when it is *qualitatively* and *quantitatively* identical to another commodity:

> To be *qualitatively* identical means a commodity must subordinate the bodily shape that makes it different from any other commodity. The bodily shape is subordinated when a commodity adopts the value

form. As *values*, commodities are qualitatively identical. This is what makes commodities commensurable.

To be *quantitatively* identical means a commodity reflects a certain magnitude of SAU labour, that is, a socially-necessary magnitude. This is what makes commodities not only commensurable, but also commensurate. As *exchange values*, commodities are quantitatively equal.

When commodity X becomes an equivalent (to commodity Y), the owner of commodity Y perceives X as value *per se*, as the 'shape of value' (Marx 1994: 15). One sees the equivalent commodity X, not as an entity with a bodily shape, but as an entity with a bodily shape that is immediately recognized *by the owner of commodity Y (alone)* as the shape of value. This is why an equivalent can 'freely take the place of a definite quantity of another commodity'.

At this point, however, the contradiction contained in labouring activity makes its presence felt in the commodity. An 'ordinary' commodity like commodity X is a *particular* commodity. Commodity X might be an equivalent to commodity Y, but it can only be a *particular equivalent*, not a *universal equivalent*. Put another way, commodity X might be the shape of value to commodity Y, but it can only be a particular shape of value, it cannot be the universal shape of value. The owner of commodity Y might be prepared to recognize commodity X as an equivalent, but this says nothing about the owners of all other commodities who do not see commodity X as an equivalent, as the shape of value.

As has been noted, while an ordinary commodity is the product of ICP labour, it cannot render incommensurable entities commensurate. SAU labour, while having the potential to render incommensurable entities commensurable, is itself struggling to find an appropriate form, that is, it is struggling to adopt the value form of commodities. It now transpires, however, that while a commodity needs to adopt the value form, it cannot do so, because an ordinary commodity cannot become a *universal* equivalent. In other words, an ordinary commodity cannot double into a unity of particular and universal.

The contradiction contained in labouring activity and, subsequently, converted to the commodity has now reached an impasse. Marx put matters in the form of a question:

> How is it possible to present a particular commodity directly as materialised universal labour-time (or which amounts to the same thing) how can the individual labour-time materialised in a particular commodity directly assume a universal character?
>
> (Marx 1976: 46)

Using the terminology developed in this chapter, the question can be restated thus: how can ICP labour time reflected in a particular commodity represent SAU labour time?

The short answer to this question is, when one particular commodity ceases to be an ordinary commodity (that is, a commodity that is not money) and becomes money. The in-depth answer forms the subject matter of the following section.

Before this, however, it can be seen that yet again an ontic contradiction has motivated the epistemic shift to another stage of the presentation. The contradiction contained in the commodity, that is, between its particular (use value) and universal (value) forms, eventually reached an impasse which can only be resolved through one commodity becoming money.

From the commodity to the money commodity

In the example used above, commodity X became the (particular) equivalent of commodity Y. If commodity X is described as a commodity in the equivalent form, then a term is needed to describe commodity Y. Marx refers to commodity Y as a commodity in the *relative form*. These two commodities do not, however, play the same roles. The difference between equivalent and relative forms becomes clear by analysing the statement '20 m of linen is worth one coat'.

Here the value of the linen is expressed relative to the coat. What is 20 m of linen worth? It is worth one coat. The commodity in the relative form of linen is having its value expressed or reflected, while the commodity in the equivalent form of the coat is doing the expressing or reflecting. The bodily shape of the coat is immediately recognized as the (particular) shape of value, as the (particular) materialization of SAU labour.

It is worth reflecting on the bodily shape of the (particular) equivalent commodity. It is, understandably, commonplace for Marxist economists to play down the role of the bodily shape of commodities when discussing value, because the real interest is in social categories, and bodily shape is clearly a material category. While it is completely true that social categories are the real issue, bodily shape still matters for a very simple, but important reason: the bodily shape becomes the basic unit of account. The bodily shape of the coat becomes the 'natural measure' (Carling 1986: 60) of the value of the linen. Without the bodily shape, the worth of a commodity could not be expressed quantitatively. When, therefore, one asks, what is 20 m of linen worth, one can reply by attaching a magnitude. Hence, 20 m of linen is worth one coat.[17] Irrespective of the commodity that acts as the equivalent (coats, linen, cigarettes, silver, gold and so on) a magnitude is always attached to it; and it is the bodily shape that provides this unit. This bodily shape has, of course, to become the socially-approved shape of value.

At this point, with the various categories of labour, commodities, and value forms explained, the investigation can demonstrate how one ordinary commodity is singled out to become the money commodity. Marx proceeds via four stages, characterized by the following forms of value:

first, the simple, isolated or accidental form; second, the total or expanded form; third, the general form; and fourth, the money form of value.

While the method Marx employed is extremely interesting, it would be tangential to the chapter, to go into detail, so a brief explanation will have to suffice.[18] Each stage introduces a specific type of exchange with the aid of certain theoretical categories. Each specific type of exchange will be elaborated upon until certain limitations (Marx calls them 'defects') are encountered. At this point, the categories of that stage will have become insufficient to sustain any further elaboration, and the analysis shifts to the next stage with a new type of exchange and a new, richer set of categories. The four stages/forms can be visualized in Figure 9.1.

Simple, isolated or accidental forms of value

Marx starts with the simplest form of value relation, namely where two commodities are exchanged, for example, 20 m of linen equals one coat.[19] Immediately, however, one encounters the limitations of this form. The coat is the equivalent of the linen, but it is only a particular and not a universal equivalent. The coat officiates as the equivalent of the value, and that is all. The equivalent cannot, at this stage, actually be the universal shape of value. Methodologically speaking, the presence of these limitations signal the need to move on to the next stage.

(i) Simple, isolated or accidental form of value		(ii) Total or expanded form of value	
RELATIVE	EQUIVALENT	RELATIVE	EQUIVALENT
A	B	A	B C D E
(iii) General form of value		(iv) Money form of value	
RELATIVE	UNIVERSAL EQUIVALENT	RELATIVE	SOCIAL-UNIVERSAL EQUIVALENT
B C D E	A	B C D. E	M

Figure 9.1 Types of exchange
Source: Adapted from Carling (1986).

Total or expanded form of value

It is quite arbitrary which commodity appears as the relative and which as the equivalent form. Indeed the value of any one commodity (such as linen) is capable of being expressed in an indefinite number of other commodities (such as coats, tea, coffee, corn, gold or iron). The simple form of value, 20 m of linen equals one coat, could, then, be indefinitely expanded as follows:

> 20 m of linen equals one coat, or 10 kg tea, or 20 kg coffee, or 50 kg corn . . .

The linen no longer stands in relation only to the coat, but also to a chain of other commodities. 'As a commodity, it is a citizen of the world' (Marx, 1990: 154). There are, however, three limitations to the total or expanded form:

- Not only is the expression of value incomplete, it can never be completed because another commodity can always be added to the chain.
- Only one commodity at a time can have its relative value expressed in this expanded chain of commodities:

> value of linen can be expressed in coats or tea of coffee
> value of coats can be expressed in tea or coffee or linen
> value of tea can be expressed in coffee or linen or coats.

- When considering a commodity in the equivalent form, it is the material dimension that is brought into focus, or to be more precise, it is the socially-recognized bodily shape that is brought into focus. In the expression '20 m of linen is worth one coat' it is the bodily shape of one countable coat that is brought into focus. This means each equivalent commodity is materially different from all others. There is no basis for commensurability between coats, tea, or coffee. This makes each equivalent commodity unique amongst an indefinite set of others. There is no single equivalent commodity in which to express relative value. The value of the linen is expressed now in the particular equivalent 'coat', now in the particular equivalent ' tea', now in the particular equivalent 'coffee.' There is no single, unique, equivalent.[20]

Methodologically speaking, the presence of these limitations signals the need to move on to the next stage.

General form of value

The (previous) total or expanded form is no more than the sum of all the simple forms of value. It can be re-written thus:

20 m of linen equals one coat
20 m of linen equals 10 kg tea
20 m of linen equals 20 kg coffee

Here the value of linen is expressed in a series of differentiated commodities. Consider these exchanges a little more closely.

Person O exchanges 20 m of linen:

now with person P for one coat
now with person Q for 10 kg tea
now with person R for 20 kg coffee.

While person O is exchanging linen for a series of commodities, people P, Q and R are exchanging coats, tea, and coffee for *one particular* commodity, namely linen. A curious reversal takes place. The relative and equivalent forms exchange places. Instead of linen as relative, and coats, tea and coffee as equivalents, one finds coats, tea and coffee as relative and linen as equivalent. The expanded relative form is thereby reversed, so that :

One coat equals 20 m of linen
10 kg tea equals 20 m of linen
20 kg coffee equals 20 m of linen.

It is important to understand that this reversal is not undertaken by Marx for analytical convenience. He claims it has a counterpart in reality, writing:

> This expanded form of value comes into actual existence for the first time when a particular product of labour, such as cattle, is no longer exceptionally, but habitually exchanged for various other commodities. . . . The general relative form of value imposes the character of universal equivalent on the linen, which is the commodity excluded, as equivalent, from the whole world of commodities.
> (Marx 1990: 158).

This reversal has the effect of overcoming the insufficiencies of the (previous) total or expanded form:

- The expression of value is complete because one commodity is now *the* equivalent, a position it does not share with any other commodity.
- All commodities can simultaneously have their relative value expressed via *the* equivalent.
- When considering a commodity in the equivalent form, it is the

material dimension that is brought into focus. To be more precise, it is the socially-recognized bodily shape that is brought into focus. There is now only one equivalent commodity in which to express the relative value of an endless chain of different commodities.

Because an endless chain of commodities are now expressed in the physical body of one equivalent (linen), the differences constituted by the different commodities in this chain are subordinated to the value form. In the use value form, all commodities are different. In the value form, all commodities are identical; they are magnitudes of the universal equivalent. But why stop with coats, tea and coffee? The list can be expanded indefinitely:

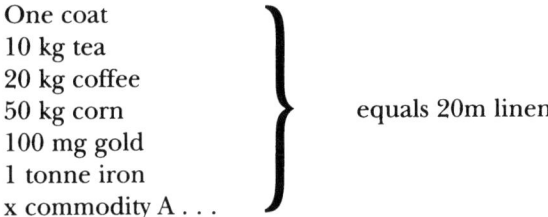

One coat
10 kg tea
20 kg coffee
50 kg corn   equals 20m linen
100 mg gold
1 tonne iron
x commodity A . . .

One commodity now stands outside the series of other commodities. This one commodity (linen), is no longer a *particular* equivalent, it is now a *universal* equivalent.

Unlike the previous stages, there are no limitations in the general form that requires the methodological shift to a different set of categories. The shift to the money form is made on the basis of social and historical reality.

Money form of value

The universal equivalent form is a form of value *per se*, the universal shape of value. Whilst it is obvious that linen is not the actual money commodity, the utility of using it as the universal equivalent is that it demonstrates that, whatever else money might be, it is actually a commodity. The final step to the actual money form is a straightforward swap between linen and gold. This is not merely an analytical convenience, a suitable choice of *numéraire*. Gold historically became the money commodity via social custom, thus:

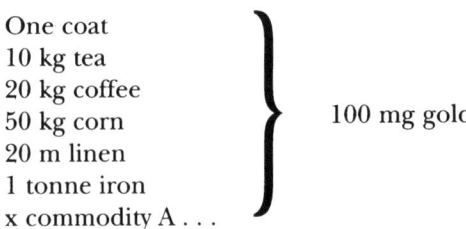

One coat
10 kg tea
20 kg coffee
50 kg corn   100 mg gold
20 m linen
1 tonne iron
x commodity A . . .

The peculiar property of the money commodity

At the end of the third section I noted whilst a commodity needs to adopt the value form, it cannot do so because an ordinary commodity cannot become a universal equivalent. In other words, an ordinary commodity cannot double into a unity of particular and universal. I then restated Marx's question: how can ICP labour time reflected in a particular commodity represent SAU labour time? While the short answer was: 'when one particular commodity ceases to be an ordinary commodity and becomes money', the more in-depth answer turns on one peculiar property of the commodity that becomes the universal equivalent.

The commodity that becomes the universal equivalent has a peculiar property that no ordinary commodity possesses: its *bodily shape* is immediately recognized as the *value shape*, or *shape of value*. By counting as the shape of value in which the relative value of all other commodities are expressed, the bodily shape of the universal equivalent is immediately its perfect form. Unlike the series of other commodities, the universal equivalent commodity does not need to dispose of its bodily shape, because it expresses value 'just as it is in everyday life' (Marx 1990: 149).

At this point, however, one encounters a problem. On the one hand, Marx writes things like 'the natural form [or bodily shape in my terminology] of the commodity becomes the form of appearance of its opposite, value'. On the other hand, he also writes things like '*use value* becomes the form of appearance of its opposite, namely value' (Marx 1990: 148, emphasis added). This ambiguity generates the absurdity that one use value of gold is that it fills teeth. To claim that the use value of a commodity is that it becomes the form of appearance of value, appears to translate into the claim that filling teeth is the form of appearance of value.[21]

This absurdity comes, in general, from not thinking thoroughly about the metaphysical subtleties of the commodity, and more specifically, from not thinking through the relation between material and social categories that in part constitute the use value form. Here my triadic conception of the commodity is helpful, although nothing need be said here about the value form. This triadic conception revealed that a commodity doubles into a unity of bodily shape and social forms, allowing it to be referred to as adopting a socially-recognized bodily shape. Consider this carefully using the example of gold.

> Because the uses of gold are, at least in part, socially constructed, gold has many uses. It might, for example, be used as a fashion item, as a work of art or, significantly, as money.
> Gold might adopt multiple roles simultaneously. It might, for example, be used to fill teeth *and* be used as a fashion item, *and* be used as money. In each of these roles, certain aspects of its bodily shape are brought into focus, whilst others are abstracted from, and one needs to be clear exactly which aspects are in focus in a specific context.

The absurdity can now be sidestepped. A commodity does not have one unique use because it is, in part, socially constructed. To claim that the use value of a commodity is that it becomes the form of appearance of value need not, therefore, translate into the claim that filling teeth is the form of appearance of value. As tooth-filling material, the role played by gold involves those aspects of its bodily shape useful for dentistry. As universal equivalent, in complete contrast, the role played by gold does not involve those aspects of its bodily shape relevant for dentistry. Rather, these aspects are abstracted from, and other aspects are brought into focus. As universal equivalent, the role played by gold involves those aspects of its bodily shape relevant for expressing or reflecting value. The usefulness of gold is that its immediate bodily shape becomes the mirror in which the value of all other commodities is expressed or reflected. And it possesses this same use value for everybody.[22] Marx puts it as follows:

> The universal equivalent . . . has the same use value for everybody – that of being the carrier of exchange value. Thus the contradiction inherent in the commodity, namely that of being a particular use value and simultaneously universal equivalent, and hence a use value for everybody . . . has been solved in the case of this one commodity.
> (Marx 1976: 48)

Unlike an ordinary commodity, the universal equivalent is both universal and particular. It is universal because it is an equivalent and it can, therefore, take the place of any commodity. It is particular since it is a commodity itself and therefore has use value, value and exchange value forms. Its particular role as use value enables it to perform its general role as universal equivalent. The ICP labour time reflected in a particular commodity can, therefore, represent SAU labour time, when one particular commodity ceases to be an ordinary commodity and becomes money.

Résumé

The second part of this chapter explained how the labouring activity of atomized, isolated, individual producers is *indirectly* co-ordinated via the systematic exchange of their commodities. This requires the systematic evaluation of very different commodities, that is, the assignment of appropriate value magnitudes or exchange values, which in turn requires commensurability. While SAU labour has the potential to render incommensurable commodities commensurable, SAU cannot manifest itself as itself. This has the following consequences: the systematic evaluation of commodities cannot occur; the systematic exchange of commodities cannot occur; and labouring activity cannot be co-ordinated.

Herein lies the fundamental contradiction of the capitalist system. Labouring activity *cannot* be co-ordinated in the form in which it is actually

Marxist theory of commodity money 189

performed (ICP). Labouring activity *can* be co-ordinated if it adopts the form of SAU, but it cannot adopt this form. The third part of the chapter shows how the contradiction contained in labouring activity becomes converted into a contradiction in the commodity, that is, between the commodity's particular (use value) and universal (value) forms. While an ordinary commodity can become a particular equivalent, it cannot become a universal equivalent. The final part of the chapter shows how the contradiction contained in the commodity is resolved when one particular commodity becomes simultaneously a commodity and money. With money we return to the start, but with the contradictions resolved.[23] Labouring activity now has a form in which to manifest itself: the universal equivalent.[24] With this, the systematic evaluation of commodities can now occur; the systematic exchange of commodities can now occur; and labouring activity can be co-ordinated. The fundamental contradiction of the capitalist system is resolved via money.[25]

Conclusion

Arguing that money is not only a commodity, but that for social and historic reasons money is gold, invites two interpretations. The first interpretation accepts the observation that the contemporary capitalist system is dominated by credit, *fiat*, electronic, and various other forms of non-commodity money, and, therefore rejects the argument that money is a commodity, on the grounds that this argument flies in the face of reality.

The second interpretation appears paradoxical. It accepts the observation about the domination of non-commodity money while at the same time it accepts the argument that money is a commodity. The paradox is resolved through the following (highly disturbing) allegation. If the analysis set out here is correct and money is a commodity, and if, furthermore, the contemporary capitalist system has abandoned commodity money, then one must at least consider the possibility that the system no longer has a universal equivalent. In other words, whilst the system still uses something called money, something that appears to be money, this something might not really be money at all. Appearances might be deceptive.

This second interpretation invites one not to treat Marx's theory of (commodity) money as a remnant of the nineteenth century, but to use it for an interrogation of the nature of contemporary capitalism. It invites questions such as the following. What forces have encouraged nation states to abandon commodity money (the gold standard and convertibility) when the result meant abandoning the universal equivalent? If abandoning the universal equivalent means abandoning the value form, what kind of capitalist system are we now experiencing? Does the abandonment of money require a more conscious administration of labouring activity and its products? Does the abandonment of money explain the emergence of artificial money such as the euro? And so on.

190 *Steve Fleetwood*

Interesting as these questions are, it was not the intention of this chapter to answer them. The intention was to allow them to be asked by revisiting the Marxist theory of (commodity) money. Some of these questions will, however, be taken up in the following chapter.

Notes

I wish to thank Peter Kennedy and Mike Williams for comments on various drafts of this chapter. While Mike and I are representatives of two (Marxist) schools of thought debating the nature of money, I hope this chapter goes some way to clarifying the argument of one of the schools.

1 On the deductive method see Lawson (1997)
2 While the distinction between the analytical method and the method of systematic presentation arguably used by Marx, is not always put in these terms, the point may be grasped by recalling Marx's criticism of the classical economists. Marx, for example, criticizes Ricardo for deploying the general category of labour, and then proceeding deductively, to derive various logical conclusions. Marx, by contrast, unpacks the term labour into a variety of forms and subsequently deriving them, arrives at socially necessary abstract labour. He does not merely deploy it at the outset. See Ilyenkov (1982), Moseley and Campbell (1997), Murray (1988), Pilling (1980), Sayer (1983), Wilson (1991) and Zeleny (1980).
3 On the relation between the logic and history of a dialectically evolving system, such as that presented here on money (that is, the relation between epistemology and ontology) see Carling (1986: 55–8) and Smith (1990: especially 94–7).
4 The following argument is elaborated upon at length in Rubin's (1990) classic book, especially the first four chapters.
5 Note that it is a specifically capitalist systems that I presuppose from here on. Note also that there is far more to commodity exchange than can be elaborated at this high level of abstraction. I am abstracting here from the myriad of social structures and institutions such as rules governing property rights, without which commodity exchange could not occur. Commodity exchange is not, in other words, a disembodied 'economic' phenomenon.

For ease of exposition, I take the unit of production to be the individual producer. Nothing is altered at this level of abstraction when these individuals are combined in a firm.
6 Strictly speaking one should write of the assignment of appropriate money prices, but since money has not yet been introduced, only posited, this cannot be done.
7 While the nature of value in economic theory is a complex issue, it cannot be discussed here. In what follows I hope to clarify, if only a little, some of the issues involved. Let me, however, dismiss one claim about commensurability. It is often supposed that because commodities are evaluated in terms of money, it is money itself that renders commodities commensurable. This is a mistake. A measure does not create the property which it measures. A measure of length, for instance, does not create the property of spatial extension. (This examle is due to Scott Meikle; see also Fleetwood (1997: 731–8).
8 In commodity exchange these individual labours are not mere fractions at the start; they become fractions of the total labour of society only insofar as their universal character achieves practical truth in the value

relations of the products entering commodity exchange.... They become universal labours of society only through equating themselves to each other through the exchange of products as values.

(Arthur 1979: 99)

9 This is in many ways analogous to the way in which extension in space abstracts from the concrete particularity of diverse extended objects. Extension in space renders incommensurable objects like bricks and paving stones commensurable, and because of this, they can be measured in metres. The measure does not create the commensurability, the property of being extended in space does.
10 While one is not usually conscious of this, one becomes conscious of it the moment the commodity fails to perform as it should, and one questions the workmanship, the quality of the individual concrete and particular labour.
11 Even though ICP labour is measurable it is incommensurable and hence cannot be the substance of value.
12 An internal relation is one where each of the things related is what it is in virtue of the others. An internal relation exists, for example, between a worker and a capitalist, or a husband and wife, but not between a postman and a barking dog.
13 Marx writes about the commodity's 'plain, homely, natural form', and differentiates between its 'natural form and value form'. That said, he also notes how commodities 'only have the form of commodities in so far as they possess a double form' (Marx 1990: 138). In a highly insightful article, Carling takes up a position I think is incorrect arguing that use values 'belong to Marx's material as opposed to social vocabulary'. A few sentences later, however, he writes that 'use values entering these relations (i.e., exchange) become commodities' (Carling 1986: 59). This is more in keeping with the position I develop here.
14 This material entity could be a service such as a clean floor. I stick with material entities and eventually commodities instead of services for ease of exposition.
15 If I spend a day nailing rough lumps of wood together in a totally inchoate manner, and, then claim I have made a coffee table, what can be made of my claim? Actually it is not for me to judge the usefulness of any entity I produce, but for the buyer. And if judgement about the value in use of an entity must be conferred by society, then this value in use must be a social category, or, more accurately, it must be a material category with social forms.
16 Lest this be taken to imply that commodities are exchanged in terms of value, let me be clear. Commodities only exchange for money prices. My position is summed up by Mohun who writes:

> Within this framework, the analysis of value as it exists in the price-form as a sum of money, and the relation between the two cannot be accomplished without a modern Marxist account of money (and its derivative form of credit) wherein *money* represents *labour-time*. In this respect, the value debate has barely begun.
>
> (Mohun 1994: 226–7)

For the reasons I discussed in the note on method above, money is always posited, but because it is not yet derived I cannot actually discuss it, and so remain with the more abstract category value.
17 As Marx (1990: 144) puts it: 'The natural form of commodity B becomes the value form of commodity A, in other words, the physical body of commodity B becomes the mirror for the value of commodity A.' It is true as Mike Williams has pointed out to me, the terms natural measure, value form, and the (metaphoric) mirror are not always clearly differentiated. My own interpre-

tation is this. A commodity adopts a value form. If this commodity comes to the equivalent commodity, then as well as retaining the value form, its bodily shape becomes the natural measure in which the relative value of all other commodities is expressed. Metaphorically speaking, the bodily shape of the equivalent commodity is like the bodily shape of a mirror and the value of the relative commodity is like the reflected image.

18 For an excellent elaboration of the method employed by Marx, see Smith (1990: ch. 5).

19 Note that it is illegitimate to place an = (equals) sign between two *different* entities, and use it to means 'equals' in a mathematical sense, because the entities are incommensurable. The sign ought to be read as meaning 'is worth'. Even here problems emerge, as this implies barter, which as an earlier note made clear, Marx thinks already presupposes money. The problem might be the recurrent methodological difficulty already identified. To avoid the implication that Marx is using a two-stage analytical approach, I suggest the following interpretation: 20 m linen is worth one coat because they both sell (systematically) at similar money prices. Marx then asks a transcendental question: what properties must money possess that allow it to facilitate this transaction? Marx, therefore posits money at the outset.

20 With the total or expanded form of value, the idea that exchange value is established via the subjective preferences of the parties in each transaction is exposed as a fiction. It could be accidental if 20 m linen exchange for one coat, or for 10 kg tea, or for 20 kg coffee and so on. If, however, 20m linen exchange for one coat, one coat exchanges for 10 kg tea, 10 kg tea exchanges for 20 kg coffee, and one coat exchanges for 20 kg coffee, and so on, can one really expect this to be mere accident? It would be quite remarkable if all these diverse exchanges between unconnected agents with their own subjective preferences resulted in a consistent series of exchange values. As Marx puts it:

> The accidental relation between the two individual commodity owners disappears. It becomes plain that it is not the exchange of commodities which regulates the magnitude of their values, but rather the reverse, the magnitude of the values which regulates the proportion in which they exchange.
>
> (Marx: 1990: 156)

This observation has significance for money's role as a *measure* of value. It is only because money is a commodity, and thereby, evaluated in the same way as all other commodities that the exchange ratios between commodities *mediated by money* can systematically be established. If 20 kg of tea and 10 kg of coffee are equal in value, and both are expressed (say) as x mg gold, then the socially-necessary (i.e., market mediated) abstract labour expended in the production of 20 kg tea, 10 kg of coffee and x mg of gold are similar. Mohun puts the matter simply: 'The only way in which units of labour time can be commensurated as sums of money is if a unit of money itself represents labour-time' (Mohun 1994: 215). It is, I feel, incumbent on those who argue money is not a commodity but a signifier, sign or symbol, to explain why both 20 kg of tea and 10 kg of coffee are systematically (that is, non-accidentally) worth x units of symbolic money, and not y units.

21 Many thanks to my colleague Mike Williams and his ubiquitous red pen for pointing out this absurdity.

22 This might seem an odd thing to say about use value, given that use value is idiosyncratic and particular. The point, however, is that the universal equivalent allows everyone to ascertain the value of commodities, just as a hammer allows everyone to knock in nails.

23 The contradictions have been resolved only in terms of this chapter. Strictly speaking, the contradictions are converted into a contradiction between the deployment of labouring activity for the purpose of increasing money capital (M–C–M´) and for the purpose of satisfying human need.
24 Hence Ingham (1998: 105) in a detailed study of money as a social relation, is not quite correct to say that Marx 'was primarily concerned with showing that money is a "mask" or "veil" over the underlying "real" social relations.' Ingham comes closer to Marx where he writes of the 'social relations that . . . appear as monetary relations' (Ingham 1998: 118). Money does mask real social relations (i.e., relations between isolated producers), it makes these relations possible.
25 Diane Elson once renamed Marx's labour theory of value as the value theory of labour. I would go one step further and rename it the monetary theory of labour co-ordination.

References

Arthur, C. (1979) 'Dialectics and Labour' in J. Mepham and D.-H. Ruben (eds) *Issues in Marxist Philosophy*, Brighton: Harvester.
Carling, A. (1986) 'Forms of Value and the Logic of Capital', *Science and Society* 50, 1: 52–80.
Elson, D. (1979) 'The Value Theory of Labour' in D. Elson (ed.) *Value: The Representation of Labour in Capitalism*, Brighton: CSE Books.
Fleetwood, S. (1997) 'Aristotle's Political Economy in the 21st Century', *Cambridge Journal of Economics* 21.
Ilyenkov, E. (1982) *The Dialectics of the Abstract and the Concrete in Marx's Capital*, Moscow: Progress Publishers.
Ingham, G. (1998) 'Money is a Social Relation' in S. Fleetwood (ed.) *Critical Realism in Economics*, London: Routledge.
Lawson, T. (1997) *Economics and Reality*, London: Routledge.
Marx, K. (1976) *A Contribution To The Critique of Political Economy*, New York: International Publishers.
—— (1990) *Capital*, vol. I, Harmondsworth: Penguin.
—— (1994) 'The Value Form', in S. Mohun (ed.) *Debates in Value Theory*, London: St. Martin's Press.
Mohun, S. (1994) 'Value, Value-Form and Money', in S. Mohun (ed.) *Debates in Value Theory*, London: St. Martin's Press.
Moseley, F. and Campbell, M. (1997) *New Investigations of Marx's Method*, New Jersey: Humanities Press International.
Murray, P. (1988) *Marx's Theory of Scientific Knowledge*, New Jersey: Humanities Press International.
Pilling, G. (1980) *Marx's Capital and Political Economy*, London: Routledge and Kegan Paul.
Reuten, G. and Williams, M. (1988) *Value-Form and the State*, London: Routledge.
Rubin, I. I. (1990) *Essays on Marx's Theory of Value*, Montreal: Black Rose.
Sayer, D. (1983) *Marx's Method: Ideology, Science and Critique in Capital*, Brighton: Harvester Press.
Smith, T. (1990) *The Logic of Marx's Capital: Replies to Some Hegelian Criticisms*, New York: State University of New York Press.
Wilson, H. (1991) *Marx's Critical Dialectical Procedure*, London: Routledge.
Zeleny, J. (1980) *The Logic of Marx*, Oxford: Blackwell.

10 A Marxist account of the relationship between commodity money and symbolic money in the context of contemporary capitalist development

Peter Kennedy

Introduction

In the previous chapter Marx's conceptualizations of the dialectical relationship between labour, exchange value and abstract labour in the derivation of money were clarified. In this chapter I wish to elaborate on these foundations to present a slightly different approach to an old problem within Marxian-inspired theories of money: namely, how one should interpret Marx's understanding of the relationship between commodity money and symbolic money.[1]

There are currently two broad interpretations. One interpretation is to argue that, despite the dramatic rise in modern forms of symbolic money, one should remain faithful to Marx's prognosis that commodity money is the basis of money in capitalist society. The problem with this interpretation is that it appears to be increasingly anachronistic when one takes into account that gold no longer plays any role in the formation of money.[2] The prime motive for holding such a theory is obvious: to relinquish the commodity basis of money would be tantamount to either outright rejection or at least becoming sceptical about the relationship between money and the law of value, and so a materialist critique of modern capitalism. Such a view seems to be confirmed by those Marxian-influenced theorists who, after careful consideration of the contemporary evidence, and with due consideration to Marx's own writings, consider symbolic money, despite its past derivation from commodity money, to be the only basis of money, past or present.

Two positions on a Marxian-inspired theory of symbolic money are definable. First, Marx's work is seen as ambiguous enough in its analysis of the relationship between commodity money and symbolic money that it appears as inessential to his wider theory of value as the regulator of economic activity (Williams 1997). Second, Marx's theoretical approach to money is seen as so contradictory that his theory of value *per se* becomes questionable (Ganssmann 1998). What we do know empirically is that the most famous commodity form of money, gold, no longer acts as an international standard of exchange and now accounts for a mere 7 per cent of central bank holdings in the top ten gold-holding economies.[3] In addition, over recent decades, in what might be seen as the inverse relationship to the fate of gold, we have experienced a plethora of new forms of symbolic values. For example, there is electronic money, futures and swaps. These have now joined symbols with a longer history such as bills of exchange, paper money, credit, stocks and shares, which have become increasingly distinct from their relation with production.[4]

In what follows I wish to affirm the contemporary viability of Marx's theory of value, while also acknowledging what appears to be a contra-indicating premise for doing so: that money no longer has a commodity basis and is in fact merely symbolic in character. I will explain that the contradistinction here is only apparent if one conceptualizes the evolving relation between commodity and symbolic money within the context of an ontological shift in the empowerment and disempowerment of the value relation between agents. The main thrust of the argument is that, while symbolic money is a necessary derivative of commodity money during the period in which the value relation is in ascendancy, once the value relation enters a process of decline, the commodity basis of money gradually diminishes and reverts to money as mere symbol.[5] In order to argue this, I need to show first that money as mere symbol does not have and has never had the ontological depth to regulate capitalism, and that capitalism necessarily requires commodity-based money if it is to remain in ascendancy. It is only on this basis that I can put forward my main argument that, despite the *necessity* of commodity money, there has been a major evolving ontological shift within capitalist relation which has signified its eclipse by symbolic forms of money.

The first section of the chapter commences with a critique of the view that capitalist relations can be constituted on the basis of mere symbolic money. On the basis of this critique, the second section sets out why, for Marx, money has of necessity to maintain its antagonistic internal relation with commodities. This claim becomes clear, it is suggested, when one pays particular attention, not just to money as the *form of value*, but also to money as the *content of value*, and, not only to money as the *content and form of value*, but to the *value relation* as the determining process in the development of the social power of money. The third section then explores contradictory processes within capitalism which lead to changes within the value relation which eventually lead to the disempowerment of the value relation. The disempowerment of the value relation, it is argued, manifests as an increasing inability to express the content and form of value through the medium of the commodity gold. Making use of Marx's observation that if you 'rob a thing of its social power . . . you must give it to persons to exercise over persons . . . as . . . [r]elations of personal dependence' (Marx 1973: 158), a number of consequences are suggested for further evaluation.

In the third section it is argued first that in as much as the content and form of value spontaneously and indirectly express abstract socially-necessary labour, their disempowerment necessarily implies an attempt to consciously/directly regulate the content of social labour, and regulate and manage at first commodity money then, increasingly, symbolic money. In other words, both the labour process and the institutions surrounding the control and distribution of money become characterized increasingly by relations of direct social dependence and political powerbroking, and less by 'spontaneous market forces'. Second, as a correlate of the above, it is argued that the conscious regulation of social labour and money takes the immediate form of an increase in the provision of social needs outside the market. However, because the value relation is based on the antagonism between capital and labour, the control over the scope and distribution of social needs remains largely in the hands of professional/administrative bureaucracies, which operate at corporate, quasi-state and state levels. The chapter takes up these issues by examining, in the context of the disempowerment of value relations, two major institutions which evolved in the latter half of the twentieth century: the Bretton Woods system and the social welfare state. The argument in the third section is that, in relation to the money problematic espoused thus far, both institutions should be seen fundamentally as institutions which arose in response to two social processes: the disempowerment of value relations and so commodity money; and the need to regulate forms of social labour and the increasingly speculative movements in symbolic money. The conclusion then reflects on the connection between the breakdown of Bretton Woods and the current dismantling of social welfarism, and what this means for our understanding of new forms of symbolic money and, therefore, contemporary capitalist social relations.

Marxism and money as a mere symbol of social relations

For Marx, the capacity of money to express value has nothing essentially to do with the natural properties of the object which comes to be recognized as money.[6] As Marx (1954: 87) argued in opposition to economic orthodoxy: 'So far no chemist has ever discovered exchange value in either a pearl or a diamond' (and neither, one should add, in gold).

Nor has the capacity of money to express value much to do with it being a mere symbol of social relations. This view, opposite to the natural view, which derived the value aspect of money from symbolic social relations rather than natural properties, acquired full expression in Simmel's monumental sociological study of money (Simmel: 1990). According to Simmel, money becomes the symbol of aesthetic indifference to the subject's demand for particular objects, and as such is able to perform the universal role of medium for the attainment and circulation of all particular objects of demand (ultimately of desire) (Simmel 1990: 74).[7]

The idea that money is merely a symbolic of value relations has become acceptable within some quarters of contemporary Marxism. For example, drawing on Marx's observation of 'the latent possibility of replacing metallic coins by tokens of some other material, by symbols serving the same purpose as coins' (Marx 1954: 126), Williams can conclude that 'it only remains to note that the social category of money is completely determined by its functions and purposes, to reach the conclusion that the commodity basis for money is systemically contingent' (Williams 1997). While this may be an ontologically accurate in *contemporary* capitalist society, it is inaccurate to perceive the result of an ontological shift as an epistemological error in Marx's logical derivation of money, as Williams tends to do.

Characterizing a Marxist theory of money *tout a fait* as essentially symbolic leads to a number of consequences wholly at variance with the general thrust of Marx's life work. For example, when money is conceived as a mere symbol of social production relations, the specific object singled out as money must then be perceived as more a matter of state contingency than ontological necessity. One can then come to the opinion that, within political limits, whatever the state gives legal sanction to as money can become the expression of the form of value and, as such, the monetary expression of the universal equivalent form of exchange. The legal sanction might be given to bullion or it might be foisted upon a paper currency. The point is, viewed as mere symbol, it does not really matter. In fact the flexibility of choice appears to be all the better, because it facilitates the logic of capitalist expansion and the efficient circulation of commodities. The logical outcome is to see the state as an enabler of a symbolic form of value, which, through an approximate stabilization of monetary supply and demand, somehow shadows the content of value (abstract labour) generated in economic exchange.[8]

Such a view, however, is only tenable if one accepts the possibility of an external relationship between the content of value (abstract labour) and the form of value (money), such that the form can be in some way separated from the content and then related contingently. To accept this possibility, however, also means accepting the possibility that the form and content of value have two separate ontologies: one economic, one political. In point of fact this is the conclusion, if not the premise, of orthodox economics, whose foundation rests on an autonomous economic sphere separate from the state: a point of view which Marx clearly rejects. For Marx, *pace* his critique of Hegel's theory of 'law', the economy and the state are internally related to value relations.[9] To conceive otherwise, however, is to move away not only from Marx's approach to money, but also from Marx's predecessors in classical political economy.

Within contemporary Marxism, the line of argument which leads to the externalization of the state and economy rests upon the prior conceptualization of an outright opposition between the form and content of value

This opposition pervades contemporary Marxism to such an extent that it becomes the implicit norm that money is all about *value form* and not *value content*. Emphasis on the value form then facilitates the conception that money expresses not so much the social power of value relations, but the social power of the state, in which the latter is increasingly seen as an external agent directing monetary policy and hence reimposing the 'symbolization' of value relations.[10]

A possible explanation for this type of approach to a Marxian theory of money is that two distinct complex social functions performed by money – measurement of value and standard of price – although recognized initially, may then be all too easily reduced to the sole function of *standard of value*. As Marx warned, '[t]he confusion between measure of value and standard of price (standard of value) is indescribable. Their functions, as well as their names, are constantly interchanged ... [yet] ... they have two entirely different functions to perform' (Marx 1954: 101). As a standard of value, the role of money is to act as a unit of measurement. Initially the units are defined by the weight of various bullion, then derivatively by public convention, as pounds, shillings, pence, farthings, and so on. The point is that, when focusing on money's function as the standard of value, the capacity to fulfil the function does not rest (directly) on the capacity to express abstract labour, but on the action of the state in deciding upon the recognized unit of measurement for price/value.

Thus, if one remains solely within this problematic, it appears a matter of state convention precisely which material object becomes the expression of money. If, however, one keeps the focus on the (primary) function of money as *measure of value*, there is a certain line of necessity involved in the choice of money. The decision which object will perform the task of money is greatly restricted, and an outcome of wider social processes, for the reason that money 'is the measure of value ... [only] ... inasmuch as it is the *socially recognized incarnation of human labour*' (Marx, 1954: 101). Likewise, although the state authorities may wish to choose any paper symbol they desire, it is '[o]nly in so far as paper money represents gold, which like all other commodities has value, is it a symbol of value' (Marx 1954: 129). To put matters as simply as possible, while the state can choose the symbol, it cannot choose the quantity of this symbol that is to express the value of a particular commodity. Why, for example, is a shirt worth ten money tokens and not a hundred?

Thus, despite referring here and there to the 'possibility of money becoming replaced by symbols', Marx is always wary of the fact that there is much more ontological depth to money than can adequately be plumbed by money's function as mere symbol. This is why neither a natural nor a symbolic concept of money will suffice. As Rubin observes in this respect:

> [b]y uncovering the naivete of the monetary system which assigned the characteristics of money to its material or natural properties, Marx at

Commodity and symbolic money in capitalism 199

the same time threw out the opposite view of money as a 'symbol' of social relations which exist alongside of money.

(Rubin 1990: 11)

Rubin then explains why:

according to Marx, the conception which assigns social relations to things *per se* is as incorrect as the conception which sees things as a 'symbol', a 'sign' of social production relations . . . [because] . . . social production relations are not only 'symbolized' by things, but are *realised through things*.

(Rubin 1990: 11, emphasis added)

We need to be clear what is being said here. It is that if it were just a matter of 'things' (for example money) symbolizing social relations, then a token backed by the legal authority of the state would perhaps suffice. I argue below that, rather than things (commodities and money) acting solely as vehicles for the expression of value, these things are also *generative of value relations*.

A Marxist theory of money as form *and* content of value

The above exposition becomes clearer when we consider that the 'things' in question (commodities, money) are *social categories* which originate from the value *relation: the* basis of value itself.[11] Value relations, in other words, the historically-specific form of social relations of production within capitalism, must necessarily generate content *and* form just like social relations of production in general. Every society, by its very definition, if it is not to be characterized by anarchy (hence its non-existence as a society), implies a definite social content and social form. In more specific terms, all societies have their social content, for example, individuals engaged in social intercourse with each other and with nature to secure the reproduction of human life. And every content has a social form, a specific mode of producing, distributing and consuming the product of labour in accordance with specific rules, laws and customs. Thus in all societies, by definition, the content must acquire form if society is to develop a social order and hence sustain itself.[12]

The crucial point is that in all societies other than capitalism, content and form are *internally* related by *direct* social bonds between agents. In capitalism this is not the case. Here social content and form are only realizable in and through *indirect* social bonds, only in and through things. These things do not merely symbolize social relations, but, rather, they facilitate the development of the *social categories* 'commodity', 'abstract labour', 'value', 'capital' and, the social category *par excellence*, 'money'. Hence, for Marx, the fact that money can be expressed by a natural object which symbolizes social production relations is entirely owing to the fact that money has a deeper ontological existence, as a social category derived from value relations which must of necessity take/realize content and form. The latter facilitate the development of the social categories and these in turn are the basis for the social power of money. Thus the social power of money as a social category rests on its ability to bring together the content and form of value, and both rest on value relations remaining in the ascendancy. From this it becomes clear that gold is not money itself, but, rather, it expresses the categorical power of value relations to establish as clearly a defined content and form as possible, given the indirect nature of this social bond.

This is why money cannot be a mere symbol, because it has to be the social embodiment of both the form and the content of value; the peculiar, categorical expression of indirect social bonds between agents. Such an ontological condition implies that, while the state may create symbols of money, it must ultimately resort back to commodity money in order to express the form and content of value relations. If history reveals to us that the state has in fact gone beyond this, then, following the logic of Marx's position regarding money, one must conclude that the capitalist system has lost its capacity to harness the content and form of the value relation to a specific money based on a specific object, (for example gold), thus allowing the state the scope to create and multiply symbolic forms of money. Money must then be seen to have lost its social power as the incarnation of value relations and be seen to have become instead an increasingly 'symbolic' and fetishist form of itself.[13] The implications of this will be considered in the final section. The immediate objective is to draw out the logic of the foregoing conclusion that, for Marx, money must be approached as the necessary expression of the form *and* the content of value.

The two qualitative functions of money

The conclusion reached above is brought into sharper focus if one turns to the two essential *qualitative* functions that money performs in capitalist society: money as the development of commodity fetishism, and money as the social co-ordinator of control over labour and surplus extraction. By recognizing the importance of these qualitative social functions of money, it becomes much clearer why the particular object expressing money must express both the content and form of value and why money can only be derived from a very limited number of commodities.

When one says that money is the expression of social relations premised on the process of commodity fetishism, one is referring to money as being the necessary outcome of relations peculiar to capitalism, where, given the discrete, private and atomized nature of labour and productive activity engendered by market relations, labour and productive activity can only become social, and products can only attain social valuation, through commodity exchange and the development of commodity-based money. In other words, in the money (value) relation, concrete purposive labour must become transformed into a new fetishized content, abstract *universal* social labour, in order that it can become purposive social labour which is able to satisfy particular social needs.

As well as establishing the specific content of value relations, money must also adopt a specific form if it is to co-ordinate the abstraction of labour which is expressed in and through commodities as exchange values. The value form maintains the internal link between production, circulation and distribution of exchange value. Take away or weaken the social capacity of the value form, and this smooth linkage breaks down; the production of use values, for example, may outstrip the primary motive of production for profit. Likewise, without the value form as automatic arbiter, wages increasingly systematically rise above the value of variable capital.[14]

Why the social power of money rests upon its expression as the form and content of value

The underlying reason why the social power of money must rest upon both the form and content of value is to contain and control the social power of labour for the purpose of increasing surplus value. Through money, the surplus is extracted in a form most adequate to those who own and control production. The control that money as the form and the content of value offers is twofold: first, control within the production process and second, control from the market place to production.[15] In the first case, for example, money must express the content of value (socially-necessary abstract labour) if it is to co-ordinate and control the private labour of agents in the process of production. It is also while under the imperative of the content of value (in conjunction of course with the form of value) that the real, as opposed to the formal, subsumption of labour to capital is realized. In this respect the development of 'time and motion' management discourse (Taylorism), alongside the increasing subordination of labour to the machine (Fordism), became the manifestations of this imperative.[16]

Simultaneously the value form of money develops its capacity to control labour from the direction of the market. By expressing itself in and through, first a limited number of objects (gold and silver), then one object (gold), the value form harnesses the power of the market over labour.[17] The development of a competitive atomized capital and labour market, and so the imperative of the profit motive, is given greater depth with the development of this supreme value form. In other words, under the directive of a value form expressed in gold, social needs are comprehensively subordinated to the profit motive in two senses. First, the very definition and scope of social needs become impregnated with their primary social function as receptacles of exchange value and potential profit. Second, when production is not considered profitable enough, then social needs will not be met.

For Marx, if money were a mere symbol (and thus had no internal connection with the content of value), then capitalism's subordination of labour could never have been achieved, and capitalist society could not have developed as it has. Capitalism is a social system requiring by its nature a social category, or medium, which must not only co-ordinate private and social labour, but also restrict the use of that labour to the requirements of accumulation. In this respect, money requires the ontological depth to express both form and content of value. In effect money has to be both labour and capital: the alienated content of labour and a form of capital conducive to surplus extraction. For these reasons, money had to be derived from its commodity basis and symbolic money could not suffice.

As illustrated by Fleetwood in chapter 9 of this volume, the commodity develops out of the need to socially validate labour. Money develops as a refinement of this process, hence it cannot lose its connection with its commodity basis, although it may be required to become ever more indirectly related. As Marx argued, to abolish the antagonism between money and commodities within capitalism would be akin to 'retaining Catholicism without the Pope' (Marx 1954: 91). The antagonism Marx refers to is essentially that between use and exchange value, which constitutes the commodity and forces it to develop a 'separate form of existence as money'. The ultimate basis of the antagonism within these social categories is the development of the value relation between agents, which amounts to the development of class relations based on the one hand on the capitalist subjection of social needs to the creation of surplus value, and on the other on counteracting resistance to this subjection.

Leaving aside the needs of the system to develop credit money and other symbolic forms of money, it is the latent antagonism inherent in the subjection and resistance to the value relation which accounts for the complex movement between commodity-based money and symbolic money. Thus the gradual debasement of coinage, the evolution of bank credit and a fractionally-backed banking system, the issue of bank token money, the suspension of convertibility, the slow demise of the gold standard, the development of the IMF and the post-Second World War dollar hegemony, the development of a reserve currency as a defence to stabilize the relative values of competing currencies, and so on are all premised on the antagonism between commodities and money, which expresses the antagonism within the value relation between production for value and production for social need. The crucial issue is that most of the above pre-suppose a more fundamental form of money by implying the questions: convertibility into what? bank tokens as opposed to what?

A distinct historical trajectory of capitalism can be discerned regarding the movement of symbolic forms of money around gold. The ascendant phase of capitalism, between 1800 and 1914, witnessed the development of the antagonism between commodity and money, which was marked by continuous fluctuations around gold of various symbolic forms of money indirectly related to gold. The 'managed' phase of capitalist decline, from roughly 1914 to 1972, witnessed a distinct, but not decisive, movement from gold under the Bretton Woods system, marked by the development of new forms of symbolic money which weakened the antagonism between commodity and money. From 1972, in the context of the breakdown of Bretton Woods system and social welfare, capitalism entered an 'unmanaged' phase of decline, where the antagonism between commodity and money all but diminished.

From the point of view of the categories of capitalism, the qualitative breakdown in the antagonism fundamentally signifies the breakdown between the content and form of value. On the one hand, this means the content of value – abstract socially necessary labour – no longer has a form adequate for its development, which is to say that concrete labour must look to other ways (alongside abstract labour) to become social labour. On the other hand, it means that money, by weakening its ontological base in the content of value, can gain an increasingly formal existence as a mere symbol of value. In this role, money (whether in the guise of currencies, paper credit or shares, and so on) begins to develop an increasingly remote relationship to the production process. From the point of view of the value relation, the movement away from gold signifies a growing incapacity of the value relation between agents to manifest a content and form adequate to the containment of the antagonism between value expansion and social needs, within bounds favourable to the former. What, however, one might ask, were the conditions which for Marx brought about the decline of the value relation and so the movement away from money as the content and form of value?

Marx suggests the beginnings of an answer. There was, he suggested, a twofold development within capitalism – what he referred to as a rising organic composition of capital and an increase in the social integration of labour – which would shake it to its foundations.[18] The very expansion of capital, Marx argued, brought about the relative displacement of labour with capital and, due to the extension and deepening of the division of world labour and the fact that labour was increasingly carried out according to the administrative plan internal to the large corporations which govern most industries, the development of social labour.

This has a number of consequences. First, the obvious one is that, given the derivation of profits from labour and profit rates from the sequence $S/C + V$, the tendency for the rate of profit to decline, which is inherent in this relationship, takes on greater actuality as the relative displacement of labour by capital develops. Counteracting tendencies such as growth in the absolute mass of surplus value, extension of the market, intensification of the use of labour power and resistance to real wage increases, make their impact felt, but ultimately have no sustained impact on long term trends in the rate of profit.

Second, as the social integration of labour develops amidst extensive and intensive developments in the social division of labour, so too does the tendency for labour to become better placed to collectivize its interests.[19] While the interests of labour are complex and contradictory, they operate within the general parameters of the antagonism between value and social need. The antagonism resides in a contradiction between two qualitatively different objectives for the use of labour and production. The result is that labour movements develop struggles within production (around control of the labour process), within the labour market (over issues of higher wages), and increasingly, struggles which spill over into the economy and society in general (around the issue of the state management of industrial relations and the employment relationship). The development of state intervention on the side of the labour movement, to match that on the side of capital, also brings to the forefront larger questions concerning the society-wide regulation of key social needs outside the profit motive and the orbit of the value relation.

One crucial result of this process is that concrete social labour, as an ontological social category, becomes more and more important as it develops as an inverse relationship to socially-necessary abstract labour. What this means is that a new social content of labour begins to challenge and supersede abstract social labour: the content of labour specific to capitalism in its ascendant phase.

Third, as a result of the above processes, a greater antagonism develops between capital's fixed and circulating functions.[20] Given the developing antagonisms within the system, capitalists are increasingly sensitive to the need to remain flexible. To a certain degree, the development of the joint stock company and secondary share issues facilitate this need. However, in the face of tendencies for profit rates to fall and for the social integration of labour to rise, the need to keep capital mobile increases beyond the capacity of joint stock company status. The result is that the developing antagonism between fixed and circulating capital functions no longer solely in the interest of expanding and developing surplus value, but also in the interests of creating institutional forms which facilitate their separation, such as the development of currency trading, secondary share issues, and, latterly, futures and swaps. This in turn exacerbates the existing tendency to generate more complex and varied symbolic forms of money, and the tendency to seek profits outside of the circuit of capital, M–C–M, and increasingly within the confines of M–M. This is already existing value mixed with increasing amounts of fictitious capital, defined as capital which has no claim on past and present labour and only a very tenuous and uncertain claim on future labour.[21]

Of course the rising organic composition of capital, social integration of labour, and the developing antagonism between fixed and circulating capital, are three social processes which develop at different rates and have different reciprocating effects upon each other. These are owing mainly to differences in the socio-economic and political traditions operative in the specific regions where the capitalist relation develops. Nevertheless, for Marx, they were conditions which of *necessity* would exert a general impact on capitalist development, in as much as they would force a decline in the value relation and thereby disempower the social power of money as the adequate expression of the form and content of value. Marx makes the observation that, with money, 'each individual possesses social power in the form of a thing. . . . [Rob] the thing of this social power and you must give it to persons to exercise' (Marx 1973: 705). A large part of the macro history of the twentieth century can be understood as the attempt to establish relations of direct social dependency in the context of the declining social power of money to regulate social relations indirectly.

I next briefly assess the practical manifestations of this theory, by outlining two instances of the direct social dependency to which capitalism has been forced to concede as a response to the disempowerment of money and, thus, the value relation: the emergence of social welfare (which ameliorates the effects of the decline in the social power of the content of value) and the Bretton Woods system (which ameliorates the decline in the social power of the value form).

The practical manifestations of the disempowerment of value relations and the rise of symbolic money

Bretton Woods: the background

When the major Western economies came off the gold standard in the interwar period, although this was not their conscious intention, they effectively eliminated the material expression of the content and form of value. By so doing they facilitated the disempowerment of value relations, which was in any case already long under way due to the inherent developments within capitalism I have already mentioned. Through the force of competition the gold standard had committed each economy continually to probe below, above and beyond world social averages in the use of technological innovation and management practices. The gold standard thus committed each economy and each specific industry within it to the accumulation of surplus value on the basis of socially-necessary abstract labour. Those economies that systematically fell behind this objective faced balance of payment difficulties, which could only be relieved by tight monetary policy and the resultant market disciplines this imposed on capital and labour. Those industries which systematically fell behind experienced falling sales, bankruptcies relieved only by rationalizations, unemployment and the further concentration and centralization of capital.

While it can be said that the recurrence of business cycles not only brought these movements to a head, but also laid the conditions for renewal, the more fundamental long-run effect of the recurrence of business cycles was to intensify the rise in the organic composition of capital, the social integration of labour, and the contradiction between fixed and circulating capital, until a point was reached where the economy moved into structural crisis.

The structural crisis brought about by these developments remained latent for a decade or more, before eventually manifesting itself during the late 1920s and early 1930s as the 'Great Depression'. During the structural crisis, economies and industries were no longer willing to commit themselves to the discipline imposed on accumulation by the gold standard. In other words, the capitalist system was no longer either able or willing to maintain commitment to surplus-value extraction based on abstract socially-necessary labour. The gold standard, as the material expression of the developed content and form of value relations, thus had to be dismantled. However, this process seriously weakened the disciplining effect on the economy of the content of value (socially-necessary abstract labour) and form of value (commodity-based money). Put another way, the decline in the value relation led to the decline in the *social* capacity of the capitalist system to subordinate social needs to the accumulation of surplus value. This was one major reason why the first reaction to the structural crisis was mass economic depression.

The second reaction to the Great Depression, which emerged more gradually, was the attempt to reconstitute capitalist social relations to take account of the new social conditions, especially the social integration of labour. The organizing power of the labour movement in the West had to be politically and socially acknowledged *and* subverted. Acknowledgement took the form of the development of social welfare, which should be seen as the development of key social needs outside the direct control of value relations and the profit motive. Subversion took two forms: first, the development of state institutions which could administer and in effect police the provision and design of social needs; second, the development of a new world money which could reconstitute the content and form of value relations, while also acknowledging the concessions to producing social needs outside the market. The new world money had to express the *disempowerment* of the value relation. In this respect the Bretton Woods system, which operated from 1944 to 1972, instituted what was ostensibly a surrogate value form around a dollar hegemony .

Bretton Woods and the disempowerment of the form of value relations

The devaluations which occurred when abandoning the gold standard during the 1930s became the basis around which currencies realigned indirectly to gold in 1944, through being fixed to the dollar as a result of the Bretton Woods agreement.[22] Thus the dollar, having devalued 70 per cent against gold, from $20.67 to $35 per ounce of gold, in 1934, became a surrogate value form for all other currencies. It was 'surrogate' because this value form originated more from political *fiat* than the laws of commodity fetishism. For example, currencies, already devalued from gold, were 'pegged' rather than 'fixed' to the dollar, while the dollar could act as symbol of world money only as long as the US economy maintained its world dominance. The surrogate nature of this re-establishment of money was further confirmed in that each economy could re-peg the relative value of its currency if IMF-backed central bank interventions in the currency markets failed, and/or the political risks inherent in deflation/reflation were thought to be too great.

This surrogate form of value gave institutional form to the disempowerment of value relations, while providing the political space to develop new relations of direct dependency between agents. These new relations were based primarily on the state's administration of social needs, either directly through welfare, or indirectly through such institutions as nationalization, fiscal intervention, state subsidy of industry, increased regulation of labour markets, wage settlements (strengthened greatly by the development of internal labour markets and the labour movement's 'voice' in the organization of the labour process) and restrictions on the flow of capital to meet preordained social needs within the domestic economy.

Social welfare and the disempowerment of the content of value relations: the British experience

Social welfare developed after 1945 in the political space provided by the Bretton Woods system. As a form of direct social dependence, it has its origin in the disempowerment of the value relation as manifested in the diminishing control and discipline of the content of value (abstract socially-necessary labour) on labouring activity and the management of labour. Labourism had three interrelated aspects operative at a national level: the management of money, the partial decommodification of labour power, and the management of the labour process.[23] Each of these social trends clearly pre-existed the welfare state. However, each social trend became more than the sum of its parts once it was consolidated on the basis of a re-commitment by capital and the state to a renewed accumulation of capital based on the dollar hegemony of surrogate form of money. The essence of Labourism is thus the management of labour and the management of money in response to the disempowerment of value relations.

By 1945 the management of money became institutionalized, after a series of long confrontations within the Treasury, Bank of England and the City of London. A new Keynesian orthodoxy was established, designed to manage money in co-ordination with production, via a combination of fiscal and physical planning mechanisms.[24] As a result, deficit budgeting, demand management, state administration of industry and the regulation of capital flows became the new watchphrases of Government and industry. The following passage from the *White Paper on Employment Policy* (1944) indicates the sea-change in economic and social policy set in motion:

> The Government accepts as one of their primary aims and responsibilities the maintenance of a high and stable level of employment after the war. . . Total expenditure on goods and services must be prevented from falling to a level where general unemployment appears.
> (Pilling 1986: 48)

For Beveridge in *Full Employment in a Free Society* (1944), nothing short of 'three rules of national finance' were to be recognized and inscribed in the new settlement:

> The first rule is that total outlay at all times must be sufficient for full employment. *This is a categorical imperative taking precedence over all other rules, and overriding them if they are in conflict with it.* The second rule is that . . . outlay should be directed by regard to *social* priorities. The third rule is that, subject to the first and second rule, it is better to provide the means of outlay by taxing not borrowing.
> (Beveridge 1944: 147)

The two quotes above indicate one fundamental change: instead of labour flowing to the requirements of capital accumulation, capital flows would be determined in the interests of regulating labour through the policing of social needs. This was, arguably, the unspoken and unwritten set of assumptions underpinning the 'universal' provision of social welfare.

The turn towards national agreement on the partial decommodification of labour was equally as sudden as the conversion to managed money. History bears out the radical shift in policy. Despite the various reforms of the 1834 Poor Law Act, and measures such as the 1905 Unemployed Workman's Act, the 1911 Social Security reforms, and the 1934 Unemployment Act, the partial and means-tested nature of such policies before 1943 ensured they never transgressed labour's status as a commodity. However, the Social Insurance Act of 1943 changed all this, effectively sanctioning the partial decommodification of labour by introducing the principle of a universal social wage, and thus breaking labour from its reliance on capital for its continued reproduction.

The turn towards a greater strategic resolve to manage the labour process also became abruptly evident from the mid 1940s onwards. Prior to this, the overwhelming historical evidence in the field of business history and labour process history suggests that *ad-hocery* ruled, where neither Taylorist practices nor welfarist principles dominated.[25] There was certainly hardly any input by the state into strategic training in preparation for the industrial management of labour prior to the decline of the gold standard. By 1941 personnel officers became compulsory in all but the smallest of factories. Membership of the Institute of Industrial Administration rose almost 500 per cent between 1939 and 1945 (517 to 2,508). Likewise, membership of the Institute of Personnel Management rose from 760 in 1939 to 5,730 by 1960 (Nivens 1967).

The post-1945 Labour government also created the British Institute of Management (BIM). Stafford Cripps and Hugh Dalton were evidently worried about the quality of British management and committed the state to providing public money to finance the creation of the BIM. Thus, direct social dependency, in the form of administrated control of labour, developed in response to the disempowerment of value relations as co-ordinator and controller of labour.

The state developed and encouraged many other management quangos, for example, the Production Efficiency Board (PES) was created in an attempt to introduce Taylorist controls over labour into British valorization processes. In the rather Orwellian domain of government departments, 'scientific efficiency' was to be the key. A Board of Trade was established to this end: 'In the long term it aims at making industry aware of the possibility of increasing efficiency by the study and application of up-to-date methods' (Tomlinson 1993: 1).

However, it was the welfare and human relations approaches, so complementary to the TUC and Labour Party's paternalistic control over labour (and so to the whole bureaucratic nexus of social welfare), which gained precedence as perhaps *the* management strategy once Labourism came into being. As Tomlinson makes clear:

> The central role of human relations in Labour's attitudes to the enterprise is evident in the focal position given to 'human factors' in the setting up of the Committee on Industrial Productivity.[26] It is also evident in the campaign by the Labour government to revive workplace Joint Production Committees on the model of those widespread during the war. The JPC campaign . . . was not a drive for industrial democracy . . . but . . . part of a programme to encourage worker co-operation and involvement without infringing on managerial prerogative.
>
> (Tomlinson 1993: 5)

The three central aspects of Labourism had become quickly and dramatically constructed by the late 1940s. Labourism underpinned the disempowerment of the value relation, especially that pertaining to the content of value. In this respect the policy of full employment, deficit budgeting, commitment to demand management, a national system of collective bargaining and a commitment to a general ethos of bureaucratic planning and moral repulsion from notions of 'free markets' epitomized the development of direct social relations of dependency in which the major objective was capitalism's control over the planning and distribution of social needs.[27]

Conclusion

This chapter has raised a number of issues regarding our understanding of the nature of money. It has suggested that the ontological depth Marx assigned to money originated from his analysis of money as both form and content of value and 'value' as founded on value relations. It has argued that money as an expression of value relations between agents is both medium and generator of social relations based on commodity fetishism. As form of value, money has to be a special commodity because it has to be the universal equivalent value of the exchange values of all other commodities. As content of value, money has to express the embodiment of abstract socially-necessary labour. Thus the social power of money rests on its ability to express social relations that embrace social production relations (including production and exchange). On this reasoning it was suggested that money has to have the ontological depth to express adequately the content and form of value, and that this can only be achieved if money itself is and remains in antagonistic relation with its commodity form.

It was then suggested that focusing on the content and form of value as expressions of value relations leads one to consider the historical specificity of both. In this respect it becomes possible to incorporate aspects of Marx's work on developments in the value relation, and relate these to the development of money. Specifically, it was suggested that a disempowerment of the value relation has occurred which now manifests as the disempowerment of the content and form of value and so of money. The argument was that as capitalism develops, money begins to lose its social power as mediator of relations of production and exchange, and as a result, social agents are forced to acquire new relations of direct social dependency. The chapter has provided brief historical examples of direct social dependency; first, as direct dependency affected money as form of value, in the establishment of managed money and the Bretton Woods system, and second, as it affected money as content of value, with the development of managed labour, social welfare and Labourism.

The crucial dimension of the two examples, and of the period of history to which they generally refer, is that two interrelated contents and forms of social organization were in existence. Specifically, the disempowerment of one (the value relation) served as the empowerment of the other (relations of direct social dependency). While the value relation requires money as universal equivalent (no matter how attenuated this is by the necessary development of credit and symbols), the relation of direct social dependency, by definition, requires commodity money to a far less extent and so adjusts to money as mere token or symbolic money. In this respect, the relations of direct social dependency use, abuse and extend the existing forms of symbolic money. Of perhaps more crucial contemporary importance, it follows that the impetus is decisively away from commodity money and towards money as mere 'symbol', although neither social relation is fully established, and indeed Labourism emerges as part of the disempowerment of capitalism, as the era of Bretton Woods revealed. This is to say that, while there can be no movement back to commodity money, there has been equally little movement to establish any deep ontological commitments to direct social relations on anything more than a dependency basis. In this context, the determinant relation that commodity money had over symbolic forms of money becomes increasingly negligible if not non-existent.

What are the implications flowing from the above for a Marxian theory of money? Marxian theory must now recognize that in our present post-Bretton Woods/social welfare era, commodity money in its function as the universal equivalent has been extinguished from the capitalist system, and symbolic forms of money now dominate. Floating currencies no longer function as the measure of value of commodities, which means they can still (mal)function (very badly) as a standard of price of commodities. The vast array of symbolic forms of money and derivatives of money – coins, paper notes, bills of exchange, bonds, electronic accounts, secondary share tokens, futures tokens, and so on – no longer operates directly on the basis of the law of value as depicted by Marx, but on the basis of government *fiat* and central bank trust.

The law of value is becoming superseded by a game played with complex rules underwritten by trust among central bankers. According to Ganssmann, such rules may provide:

> sufficient trust in the overall system of international trade and credit, in its stability and the capacity to answer crisis situations by re-negotiating credit arrangements, that the reversion back to real money as defined by Marx, is no longer required or needed.
>
> (Ganssmann 1998: 153)

However, such a perception of the power of trust is contentious, given that agents have very little knowledge as to whether what they hold now or in the future is real or fictitious money. The developing financial crisis in East Asia, concerning which the loudest remonstrations have been blurted out about financial cronyism, corruption and central bank mismanagement (especially by the World Bank and the IMF), suggests that blind hope may be a more precise phrase than trust. Whatever one cares to call it, however, the East Asian crisis demonstrates clearly that there can be little faith in monetary stability in a world devoid of real money.[28]

Notes

I wish to thank Tom O' Gorman and Steve Fleetwood for their helpful comments on an earlier draft of this chapter. I accept Steve Fleetwood's detailed analysis of 'labour', 'commodity' and 'money' as well as the ontological propositions surrounding their derivation outlined by him in Chapter 9. Hence, for purposes of brevity, whenever I make reference to these categories, I presume the reader has referred to the detailed definitions provided by Steve Fleetwood.

1 As I explain later, by 'symbolic' I mean a notion of money which has no value itself, but which can act as the reflex of all other relative values because of the social trust given to that symbol, either through tradition, trial and error and experience, or through the fact that the symbol has been given legal status as money.
2 Since the collapse of the Bretton Woods gold exchange standard in 1973 and the subsequent rush to sell off gold by central banks, Kenneth Gooding can accurately state that: 'Gold has fallen from grace and is now a mere metal and a bad investment' (*Financial Times* 13 December 1997).
3 See the article 'Beholders of Gold Reassert Its Value', by Barry Riley (*Financial Times* 22 March 1995), which refers to the growing, ultimately nostalgic, interest in the properties of gold as real money.
4 According to Paul Kennedy (1994: 51), 90 per cent of the trade which took place daily (approximately $1 trillion) occurred within the leading financial centres of the world and bore no relation to the trading of commodities.
5 Of course symbolic money also pre-dates commodity money in the same way that merchant capitalism pre-dates the developed capitalist relation based on wage labour.
6 It is important to stress that the act of naming an object 'money' is the outcome of it being an expression of social relations and in this sense money *is* a social relation.
7 For Simmel, along with others who see money as 'symbol' of social relations, money does not itself have a use value or utility, it is merely a 'psychic constellation' through which the relative value of other objects of utility is expressed: 'If the economic value of objects is constituted by their mutual relationship of *exchangeability*, then money is the autonomous expression of this relationship' (Simmel 1990: 120, emphasis added). As an autonomous expression, money is 'abstract value', a mere 'visible symbol' of relative values.
8 While Williams (1997) has produced a more complex and nuanced view of money, his overall argument concerning the ontological status of money leads ultimately to a symbolic account of money.
9 For Hegel, 'the state, over and against the sphere of the family and civil society, is an "*external necessity*", an authority, in relation to which "laws" and "interests" are subordinate and dependent' (Marx and Engels 1975: 5).One can include the law of value in this criticism by Marx of the general proposition that the state posits 'laws' externally.
10 This is, in fact, the view of Marxists associated with variants of the regulationist school. It is clear in the work of the originator of regulation theory, Aglietta (1979), and in the subsequent work within this general theoretical framework of Jessop (1988).
11 It is usual to say form and content of value. But one must ask: what is value apart from its form and content? The answer comes back, as it must, to the historically specific social production relations which characterize capitalist society. The common relationship to the means of production, the dispossession of the majority from either control or ownership of the means of

production, with the form of wage labour dominating, establishes a value relation between and within the contending classes (conceptualized here as capital and labour) which arises as a result of the common relationship. The value relation is the objective process of commodity fetishism wherein the contending classes relate socially as individuals only by virtue of the exchange of commodities through the market. Incidentally, from a Marxist perspective, the claim that common relations to the means of production derive *both* value relations and class antagonisms has a fundamental bearing on the nature and evolutionary development of money, because money as the expression of social power is the expression not simply of value and the value relation, but also of class antagonism. This is a perspective which leads to the view that the expressive social power of money as a universal equivalent form is very much open-ended and conjunctural, which is to say that the categories of capitalism are never closed structures, but rather open social processes. This perspective illuminates the ongoing problem of the relationship between structure and agency, and I re-address it later in the chapter.

12 As noted in Chapter 9 by Steve Fleetwood.
13 As McGoun (1997) observes in connection to this, symbolic social relations now dominate much of the social intercourse occurring within the global financial community. Not only this, money is increasingly pursued, not for its capacity to attract material goods, but as a 'sign' in a game of exchange for its own sake.
14 An example of this (highlighted by the British Royal Commission on Industrial Relations of 1968) was the so called 'wage drift' and 'productivity deficit' which characterized British post-Second World War industrial relations: particularly so in the 1970s after the collapse of the Bretton Woods fixed exchange rate regime.
15 For Adam Smith (1933) the control exerted upon agents from the market place to production was so all-embracive, it was as if an 'invisible hand' were conducting and co-ordinating the whole process.
16 These manifestations of value relations were of course personified by Frederick W. Taylor and Henry Ford themselves. For Taylor, the search for the most efficient forms of labour management became a fetish which absorbed his life. Ford celebrated the discipline imposed on human activity by technology.
17 One might ask why gold is 'chosen'. Here there are elements of accident and necessity at work. First, the condition that money must express the twofold nature of labour (concrete and abstract) and that money must be expressed by a material capable of easy division and highly resistant to wear and/or corrosion are *necessary* features which restrict the money object to a very narrow field. At this point, accident and specific conjunctural events take over in the final choice society makes as to which object will express money. In this sense, whether it was, for example, gold or silver becomes a matter of historical contingency. What matters of necessity is that money continues to express the antagonism between itself and commodities, and this can only be done if money is itself a commodity which expresses the twofold nature of labour.
18 For Marx, the rising organic composition of capital (OCC), was, given the nature of capital accumulation, a logical necessity, producing a 'progressive tendency for the rate of profit to fall . . . [which was] . . . just an expression peculiar to the capitalist mode of production of the progressive development of the social productivity of labour' (Marx 1974: 213). A very brief definition of the OCC is required. The OCC constitutes two related parts: the technical composition of capital (TCC) and the value composition of capital (VCC). The VCC is the social measurement of the existing value tied up in machines

and labour, and the current period of expanded value. The TCC is the use value or material/technical side of this process. It measures the relationship between the development of technology and expenditure of labour. The common sense finding is that, as capitalist industry has developed and expanded, the extension of technology (in all its forms) increasingly outstrips that of labour. Under the strict discipline of competitive accumulation, capitalists are compelled to raise the TCC, which, although raising the rate of relative surplus value extracted from living labour power, also, in the long run, raises the rate of growth of VCC. Time and again a situation is reached where the rate of growth of relative surplus value extraction cannot keep up with the rate of growth in the VCC. As a result overaccumulation of capital occurs, leading to pressure on the rate of profit to decline. Such an outcome occurs because the continual raising of TCC (the increase of machinery relative to labour) reduces the source of surplus value (and so profit), labour power (in relative terms to the rise in the composition of capital). The more that individual capitalists are driven to increase TCC in the race to accumulate, the relatively less living labour is required within the system and so the more difficult it becomes to increase aggregate relative surplus value at a rate faster than the increase in aggregate VCC. The result is that profits tend to decline and structural unemployment begins to rise above and beyond a 'reserve army'. Monopoly conditions of accumulation do not alter the problem, what they do is to redistribute the costs in terms of bankruptcy and insolvency to weaker capitalists, while also facilitating the material basis to attempt to arrest the rising OCC amongst the larger capitalists, through control of the market and the institutions of the state.

19 See Marx (1858: 705–6). Marx was neither the first nor the last to make this point a central focus of theoretical reflection and generalization. St Simone before him and Emile Durkheim after him made the social integration of labour and production the central focus of sociological theory and political reflection.

20 I refer the reader to Marx's (1973) extensive notes on the antagonism between fixed and circulating capital in the *Grundrisse*.

21 For Hilferding (1981: 116) 'fictitious capital' referred to the difference between actual capital in use and nominal share capital which the advent of the stock market had facilitated. As Marx put it in the context of the circulation of railway shares:

> Gain and loss through fluctuations in the price of these titles of ownership . . . become by their very nature, more and more a matter of gamble, which appears to take the place of labour as the original method of acquiring wealth and also replaces naked force.
>
> Marx (1974: 478)

'Fictitious' also refers more generally to the development of money capital to the point whereby its function as the circulation of loan capital upon an interest payment, becomes superseded by the circulation of interest-bearing capital upon itself. The point is that both tendencies have increased dramatically over the course of the twentieth century, to the extent that more than 90 per cent of trade is in fictitious symbols of money (Kennedy 1994).

22 There has been a great deal written about the history, politics and economic technicalities of the Bretton Woods Agreement. My aim here is to discuss one particular aspect – the dollar hegemony – as it bears on value relations.

23 Elsewhere (Kennedy 1996) I have characterized the British variant of social welfarism as Labourism, and I keep faith with this term here. 'Commodified labour power' refers to a condition whereby human labour can be bought and

sold in the market place relatively unrestricted, and largely in accord with the criterion of profitability. 'Decommodified labour power' refers to a situation whereby human labour is administered and distributed according to the requirements of production and those of the state. (This occurred in the former Soviet Union and should be distinguished from the Marxist notion of the condition of freely-associated producers.) Therefore the partial decommodified state referred to here is that whereby human labour power is administered and distributed by the requirements of production and those of the state, and only indirectly by the criteria of profitability and competition from external labour markets.
24 Such a victory was clearly discernible in the confidence with which Keynes took to his task of writing and publishing his *General Theory* (1936).
25 The generalized nature of managerial *ad-hocery* is evidenced, for example, in the work of Littler (1982).
26 'Labour' here refers to the Labour Party.
27 In this sense it is not suggested that all aspects of the resulting welfare state are somehow functions of control over the labour movement, although many can be seen in this way. To a large extent the interface of the provision and consumption of mass education, universal health and other public benefits, is a contested terrain, which nevertheless contains the labour movement by narrowing the contestation to one concerned with the *form* that Labourism should take.
28 Ganssmann (1998: 147) also points out that since the detachment of currencies from a fixed point of reference (the gold standard and Bretton Woods) it can no longer be said that symbolic money gravitates back to real money. However, instead of seeing this as the outcome of real developments within the value relation, Ganssmann sees it as evidence of an error in Marx's *theory* of value, in as much as it proves conclusively what was always the case: namely that, 'The Marxian starting point of the theory of money and credit [the law of value] has to be left behind, as do all starting points' (Ganssmann: 153).

References

Aglietta, M. (1979) *A Theory of Capitalist Regulation*, London: Verso.
Beveridge, W. (1944a) *White Paper on Employment*, Cmnd. 6527, London: HMSO.
—— (1944b) *Full Employment in a Free Society*, London: Allen and Unwin.
Ganssmann, H. (1998) *The Emergence of Credit Money*, in R. Bellofiore (ed.) *Marxian Economics: A Reappraisal*, London: Macmillan.
Hilferding, R. (1981) *Finance Capital, A Study of the Latest Phase of Capitalist Development*, London: Routledge and Kegan Paul.
Kennedy, P. (1994) *Preparing For the Twenty-First Century*, London: Fontana.
Keynes, J. M. (1936) *The General Theory of Employment, Interest and Money*, London: Macmillan.
Littler, C. R. (1982) *The Development of the Labour Process in Capatalist Societies*, London: Heinemann.
Marx, K. (1954) *Capital*, vol. I, London: Lawrence and Wishart.
—— (1973) *Grundrisse*, London: Penguin.
—— (1974) *Capital*, vol. III, London: Lawrence and Wishart.
McGoun, E. G. (1997) 'Hypereal Finance', *Critical Perspectives on Accounting* 8: 97–122.
Nivens, M. M. (1967) *Personnel Management*, London.

Pilling, G. (1986) *The Crisis of Keynesian Economics: A Marxist View*, London: Croom Helm.
Rubin, I. I. (1990) *Essays on Marx's Theory of Value*, Montreal: Black Rose.
Simmel, G. (1990) *The Philosophy of Money*, London: Routledge.
Smith, A. (1933) *An Inquiry into the Nature and Causes of the Wealth of Nations*, London: Dent.
Tomlinson, J. (1993) 'Mr Attlee's Supply-Side Socialism', *Economic History Review* 46, 1.
Williams, M. (1997) 'Marx(ists) on Money: Why Money is not Commodity but the Most Autonomous Form of Existence of Value', paper presented at the annual conference of the Eastern Economic Association, Washington D.C., March.

11 Menger's theory of money: some experimental evidence

Peter G. Klein and George Selgin

Introduction

More than a century ago, Karl Menger (1981[1870], 1892) sought to explain how the social institution of money – a generally-accepted medium of exchange – could develop without deliberate design in an economy of self-interested individuals. Rejecting as unhistorical earlier theories treating money as a product of some explicit agreement or edict, Menger portrayed it as a product of spontaneous evolution. Menger's theory ultimately helped to inspire a large modern literature on the spontaneous emergence of exchange media, including contributions by Jones (1976) and Kiyotaki and Wright (1989, 1993).

Despite its originality and enduring value, Menger's theory leaves many questions unanswered. In particular, Menger had little to say about the dynamic process by which one out of many potential commodity monies becomes a universally-acceptable medium of exchange. Modern theories of the evolution of money likewise suffer from a relative lack of attention to evolutionary dynamics.

Here we use computer simulations to elaborate upon Menger's theory, examining both the dynamics of monetary evolution and the robustness of Mengerian convergence to a single money.

Menger's theory

Menger's account begins in a barter economy. A trader wishing to obtain good A may have difficulty trading endowment good B directly for A because the seller of A does not want B. The trader may then try instead to trade indirectly, swapping B for C in order to swap C for A. Good C may have even less use value to the trader than good B, but is assumed to have a higher degree of marketability (*Absatzfähigkeit*) than B.

Under barter, all goods have very limited marketability: the absence of what Jevons termed a 'double coincidence of wants' makes it difficult for any trader to exchange his or her endowment directly for something having a higher use value to that trader. Consequently, a significant difference exists between each good's normal buying price and the sale price it will command if it must be disposed of quickly. This is the bid–ask spread. Still, Menger argues, certain goods are more marketable, and hence exhibit lower bid–ask spreads, than others. Such goods 'can be disposed of . . . at any convenient time' with relatively little loss from their normal purchasing prices (Menger 1892: 244). Any trader intending to trade goods of relatively low marketability will therefore benefit by trading those goods 'not only for such as he happens to be in need' but also for a more marketable good that might be utterly useless to the trader except as a medium that can be exchanged more readily for the goods the trader ultimately wishes to acquire.

At first, Menger argues, only a few traders will recognize the advantages of employing especially marketable goods as media of exchange. However, the success of a small number of innovative traders will spur imitation. As traders begin to employ a particular marketable good as an exchange medium, the demand for that good broadens, and its marketability is further enhanced. Eventually, some good that was once only slightly more widely accepted than other goods becomes money, a *universally* accepted medium of exchange.

In game-theoretic terms, the adoption of a particular good as money can be understood as the solution to a pure co-ordination game: in principle, traders could employ any good as money. The more agents who adopt a particular good, the greater that good's marketability, and the more attractive it becomes in the eyes of other agents. Once a good becomes universally accepted, it normally will not be in any trader's interest to abandon that good in favour of any other less marketable indirect exchange medium.

If the monetary co-ordination game just described has many possible Nash equilibrium solutions – one for each exchangeable commodity – how do agents manage to co-ordinate around one particular equilibrium? To answer this question, Menger appeals to what Thomas Schelling (1960: 57) later referred to as co-ordination-problem 'focal points'. In Menger's account, certain goods are more marketable than others *before* the monetary selection process begins. The greater marketability of these goods makes them more prominent candidates for adoption as indirect exchange media.[1] Monetary equilibria based on these more prominent goods become focal points of the monetary co-ordination game, while other potential equilibria are ignored. In the simplest case, one good is initially more marketable and hence a more prominent candidate for adoption as money than others, so that traders focus on it to the neglect of all other potential candidates. In this way, the economy selects one particular Nash equilibrium solution to the monetary selection game out of numerous potential alternatives.

Shortcomings of Menger's account

Although Menger's theory provided a plausible and enduring answer to the question 'How can money emerge?', the theory leaves many questions unanswered. Several of these questions raise doubts concerning the robustness of Menger's main conclusion that barter will inevitably give way to monetary exchange without need for public interference.

First, Menger's explanation of the origins of money lacks an adequate treatment of the *dynamics* of the monetary selection process. Menger's argument, with its reliance upon a monetary co-ordination game with pre-existing and directly observable focal points, suggests that agents initially assumed to be engaged in barter would 'jump' immediately from barter to a monetary equilibrium upon discovering that one good is more marketable than the rest. Agents should realize at once that the most marketable good is bound to become money, and so proceed immediately to accept that good in exchange. Instead of evolving gradually, as Menger would have it, money emerges in a flash.

Menger himself does not reach this conclusion, because he assumes that many agents hesitate at first to take advantage of the goods' differing degrees of marketability. But this assumption seems patently *ad hoc*: if the goods' varying degrees of marketability are directly observable, why should anyone refrain from immediately putting this knowledge to use? On the other hand, if agents *do not* directly observe goods' varying degrees of marketability, how can convergence upon a particular medium be guaranteed? Clearly, we need to relax Menger's assumption that marketability is directly observable, both to allow for more interesting evolutionary dynamics and to determine whether Menger's main conclusion holds for an economy with imperfectly informed agents.

Menger's assumption that some goods are initially more marketable than others also begs an important question. Suppose that all goods are at first equally marketable. Would such a starting point preclude convergence upon a particular monetary equilibrium?

Finally, we may ask whether the answers to the above questions depend upon the size of the economy being considered, that is, the number of distinct goods and agents. Does it become more difficult (or perhaps impossible) for an economy to select a monetary equilibrium as the number of distinct goods exchanged in the economy increases?

These questions are only a few raised by Menger's original analysis. In this chapter we provide preliminary answers to several of them with the help of computer simulations of the monetary selection process.

The experimental framework

Imagine an economy in which N agents trade J distinct goods. Each agent is endowed with a single unit of one of the J goods, and wishes to consume one unit of some other good. Agents visit a central marketplace on a daily basis, and each encounters another randomly-chosen agent on each visit. An agent can limit him- or herself to direct exchange, trading the endowment good only for the good he or she ultimately wishes to consume, or he or she can offer the good in exchange for *either* the desired consumption good *or* some other good considered to be an effective medium of exchange. We assume that an agent restricts him- or herself to accepting in exchange only a single good (perhaps because it is the only good whose quality he or she can expertly judge) apart from the desired consumption good.

In Menger's analysis, some goods are initially more marketable than others, and agents know goods' degrees of marketability. Applying Schelling's focal point theory, Menger's framework leads to trivial learning dynamics in which the most saleable good would immediately become universally accepted were it not for some agents' (unexplained) hesitation to engage in indirect exchange.

Here we assume that, although all agents are prepared to take advantage of indirect exchange, they are not equipped with perfect knowledge of goods' marketability. Instead, they have very limited knowledge, which they acquire by sampling the market. Before any visit to the marketplace, a trader communicates with some randomly-selected agent (not necessarily the one he or she will encounter in the next trip to the marketplace), and notes which good that agent is willing to receive in exchange for the endowment. If the sampled agent has not yet chosen an indirect exchange medium, that agent's desired consumption good is noted. Otherwise, the agent's desired medium of exchange is noted. Traders then visit the marketplace, willing to accept as an exchange medium the good that appears most saleable according to their market sample.

In this incomplete-information framework, different agents may initially choose different exchange media based on their particular market sampling results: the economy no longer jumps at once to a particular monetary equilibrium. But does the economy *eventually* converge upon a particular monetary equilibrium, and, if so, under what circumstances? Does convergence depend on the presence of a starting focal point, where one good is initially acceptable to more agents than the rest? How is the likelihood or speed of convergence affected by changes in the number of agents or in the variety of goods?

Simulation

To answer the above questions, we programmed a computer to simulate trade interactions in the described environment. The program simulates a 'Polya urn' experiment, named after the famous Stanford mathematician George Polya (1887–1985). For a physical analogy to our economy with N agents and J distinct types of goods, imagine an urn filled with beads. Each bead represents a unit of demand (marketability) for a particular type of good, and each type of good is represented by a distinct colour. The beads are placed in an urn, where the initial number of beads is at least equal to the initial number of agents. Suppose initially there are four agents and four types of goods, yellow, blue, green, and red. If each trader demands one unit of some good with which he or she is not endowed, and no two traders demand the same type of good, the urn will initially contain one bead of each colour only, the market for each type of good consisting of one agent only.

At first, the demand for goods is a consumption demand only. However, each trader will eventually be willing to exchange his or her endowment *either* for the desired consumption good or for an indirect exchange medium. Thus, once each trader has chosen an initial medium of exchange, the total number of beads or 'marketability units' in the urn will be equal to N plus the initial number of beads. After each trader makes an initial selection, the original beads representing consumption demands are removed from the urn, because agents undertaking further market samples inquire what *medium of exchange* a sampled agent is willing to accept, ignoring agents' consumption goods preferences. (We ignore the fact that some agents will not ultimately engage in indirect exchange, because the exchange medium they would select is none other than their preferred consumption good, or because they are initially endowed with what turns out to be the generally-accepted exchange medium.)

The medium of exchange selection process proceeds as follows: an agent planning to visit the marketplace first draws a bead randomly from the urn (samples for information). That colour of good becomes the agent's exchange medium, and the bead is returned *with double replacement*. The extra bead represents the extension of the market for the good by one unit. Eventually every agent chooses an exchange medium, and all the beads which were initially in the urn, representing the consumption demands, are removed. Thereafter the selection process is repeated, with agents taking new market samples, and revising their medium of exchange choices accordingly. As a new exchange medium is selected, and a corresponding bead is added to the urn, a bead representing the previous period's selection is removed. Although the total number of beads in the urn remains equal to the number of traders, the relative marketability of different goods may continue to change. The economy is said to have converged upon a particular monetary steady-state when all the beads in the urn are of one colour.

Our primary goal is to see how changes in initial conditions, the number of agents, the number of goods and the initial prominence of particular goods affect the time needed for convergence to a monetary steady-state. We measure time in 'market days', defined as completed rounds of trading. For example, in a model with twenty agents, the first twenty trades (each agent's initial visit to the market) constitute the first market day, the next twenty trades (each agent's second visit to the market) the second market day, and so on. The simulation continues until the economy has converged on a single medium of exchange.[2] Because two simulations with the same initial conditions may produce very different results, we ran a simulation for each set of initial conditions thirty times, then computed the average time to convergence for those thirty simulations.

Results

Our base simulation represents an economy with ten types of goods and ten agents, with each agent wishing to consume one unit of one type of good (so that all goods are equally prominent). In this and all other simulations we perform, agents' exchange medium choices are based on a single market sample only.

Results of simulating this base model are given in the first column of Table 11.1. The economy converged to a monetary steady-state in every run, although the time to convergence varied widely, ranging from 2.3 to 12.4 market days. The average time to convergence over thirty runs was 4.5 market days (or forty-five total trades), with a standard deviation of 2.1 market days. Thus, even in an extremely simple framework with limited information and no focal point, a simulated economy converges on a universally-accepted medium of exchange in a relatively short period.

To learn more about the convergence pattern, let us consider in detail the run with the median time to convergence. Figure 11.1 shows the convergence pattern by plotting the percentages of beads representing each good for each market day until the economy converges. For ease of exposition, we number the goods *ex post* according to their finish in the simulation: the good that is eventually chosen as the medium of exchange is labelled Good 1, the last good to be eliminated is labelled Good 2, the next-to-last to be eliminated is labelled Good 3, and so on.

Figure 11.1 reveals a striking feature of the convergence process: there is no monotonic increase in the percentage of beads representing the good that eventually becomes the medium of exchange. Indeed, the relative shares of the different beads change unpredictably. For example, Good 2 has 90 per cent of the 'money market' after twenty-seven trades (2.7 market days), but begins to lose market share and eventually drops out. This suggests that, in an economy described by this simple sampling and belief-updating process, a good may be the economy's most widely-accepted medium of exchange at one point, yet not be the good that ultimately becomes a universally-accepted medium of exchange.

Changes in the number of agents, number of goods, and scale

Next we study the effects of changing the number of agents, holding the number of distinct goods constant. The results appear in the second, third, fourth, and fifth columns of Table 11.1. We first return to our base model, with ten agents and ten goods, and then progressively double the number of agents, keeping the number of distinct goods at ten. As seen in Table 11.1, doubling the number of agents roughly doubles the average time to

Table 11.1 Simulation results

	(1) Base model	(2)	(3)	(4)	(5)	(6)	(7)	(8)	(9)	(10)	(11)	(12)
		Changes in number of agents				Changes in number of goods			Changes in scale			
Initial parameters												
Agents	10	10	20	40	80	20	20	20	10	20	40	80
Goods	10	10	10	10	10	5	10	20	10	20	40	80
Simulations	30	30	30	30	30	30	30	30	30	30	30	30
Time to converge (market days)												
Mean	4.5	4.5	10.9	19.2	38.5	8.8	10.8	9.3	4.5	9.3	17.3	34.7
Median	3.9	3.9	9.2	13.2	31.2	7.2	9.2	8.4	3.9	8.4	14.7	32.1
Standard deviation	2.1	2.1	6.7	11.5	15.5	5.8	6.7	4.0	2.1	4.0	7.8	14.5
Minimum	2.3	2.3	3.0	4.9	11.9	1.0	3.0	2.9	2.3	2.9	7.4	13.4
Maximum	12.4	12.4	34.2	49.7	62.5	24.2	34.2	18.5	12.4	18.5	41.5	62.5
Change in mean from first model in set	—	—	2.422	4.267	8.556	—	1.227	1.057	—	2.059	3.845	7.711
Change in median from first model in set	—	—	2.359	3.385	8.000	—	1.278	1.167	—	2.141	3.769	8.231

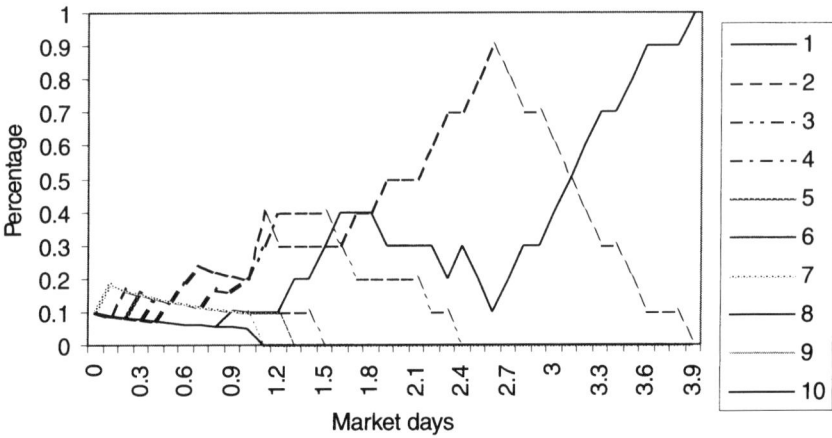

Figure 11.1 Convergence path for base model (ten agents, ten goods)

convergence. (Note that increasing the number of agents also increases the number of trades per market day, so the time to convergence measured in total trades more than doubles as we double the number of agents.) Figure 11.2 summarizes the average, minimum, and maximum time to convergence as a function of the number of agents.

To see how the convergence *pattern* changes as we change the number of agents, we again plot convergence paths for the runs of each model having median convergence times. Figures 11.3a through 11.3c show convergence paths for the models with twenty, forty and eighty agents, each with ten goods. It can be seen that all four models have similar convergence characteristics. In each case, a good can have a majority share of the market in the early rounds yet not end up as the chosen medium of exchange.

For the next set of experiments, we hold constant the number of agents and vary the number of distinct goods. Columns (6), (7), and (8) of Table 11.1 give the results of three sets of simulations, the first for twenty agents and five goods, the second for twenty agents and ten goods, and the third for twenty agents and twenty goods. Surprisingly, variation in the number of goods has little effect on the average time to convergence. With five goods, the mean time to convergence is 8.8 market days. With ten goods, the mean time to convergence increases slightly, to 10.8 market days. With twenty goods, the mean time to convergence falls to 9.3 market days. Figure 11.4 summarizes the average, minimum, and maximum time to convergence as a function of the number of goods.

Figures 11.5a through 11.5c plot the convergence paths for the median time-to-convergence run of each model.[3] Increasing the number of goods has no systematic effect on the convergence path, because goods with low percentages in the early rounds of trading are quickly eliminated from

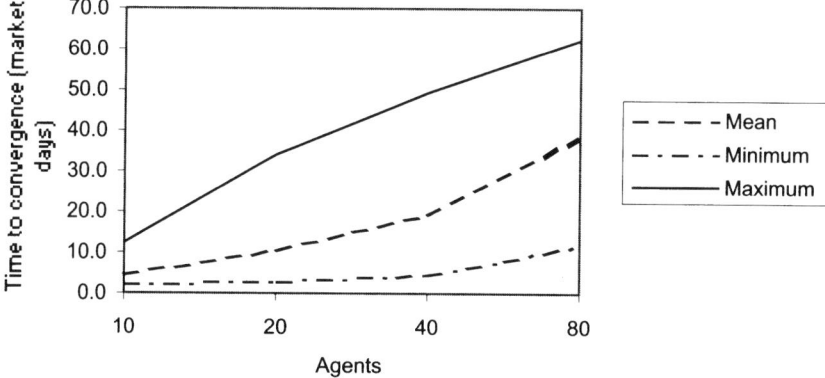

Figure 11.2 Effects of changes in the number of agents

consideration. Thus increasing the initial number of goods has little effect on agents' ability to co-ordinate on a medium of exchange.

Finally, we vary the overall scale of the economy by proportionately increasing the numbers of both agents and distinct goods. Columns (9) to (12) of Table 11.1 reveal the results of four sets of simulations, the first with ten agents and ten goods, the second with twenty agents and twenty goods, the third with forty agents and forty goods, and the fourth with eighty agents and eighty goods. Figure 11.6 summarizes the average, minimum, and maximum time to convergence as a function of scale, and Figures 11.7a through 11.7c plot convergence paths for the median run in each set. As seen in Table 11.1 and Figures 11.7a through 11.7c, a doubling in the scale of the economy leads to an approximate doubling of the average time to convergence. However, as we learned in the previous experiments,

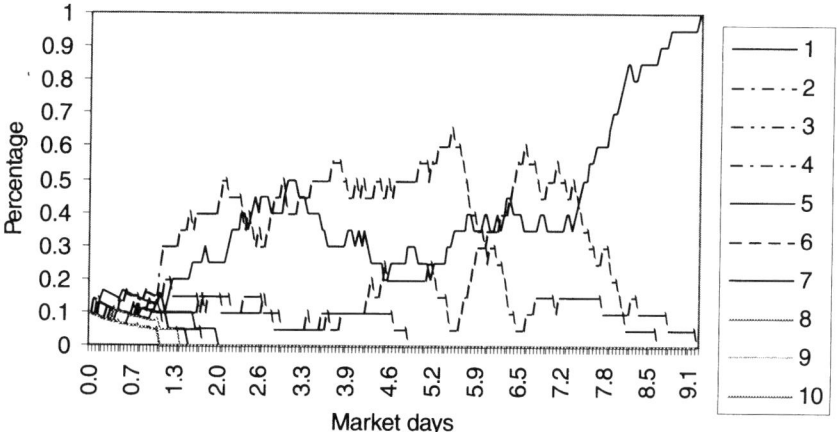

Figure 11.3a Convergence paths with changes in the number of agents (twenty agents, ten goods)

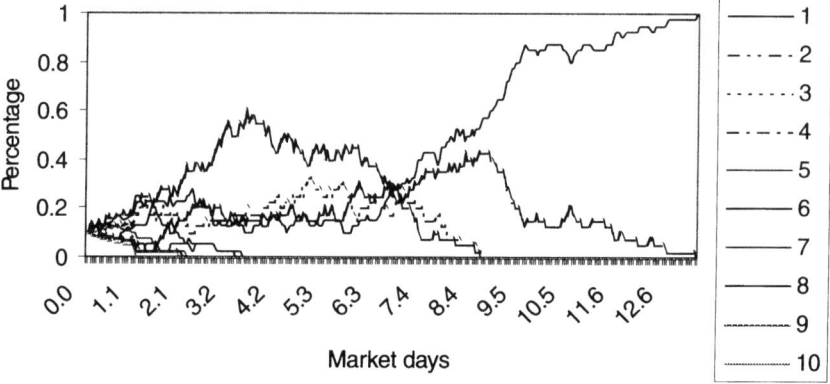

Figure 11.3b Convergence paths with changes in the number of agents (forty agents, ten goods)

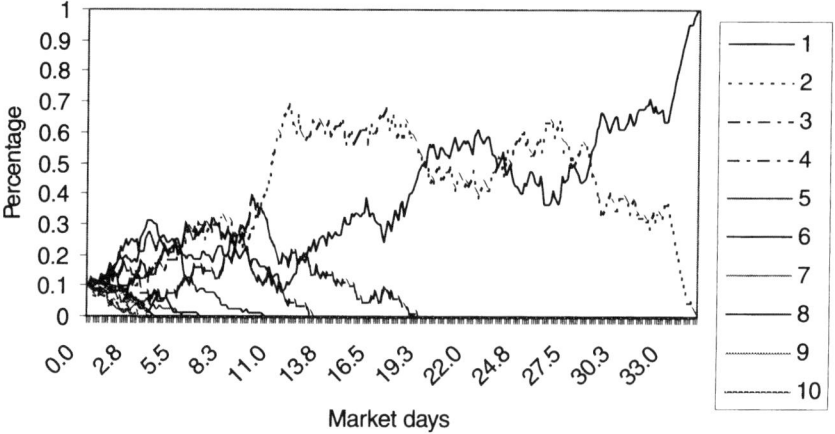

Figure 11.3c Convergence paths with changes in the number of agents (eighty agents, ten goods)

this is primarily due to the effect of increasing the number of agents, not the effect of increasing the number of goods.

Simulating a focal point

In the previous section we showed how, in a very simple model, a universally-accepted medium of exchange can emerge even when all goods are initially equally marketable. As we noted previously, Menger's account of the origins of money assumes that some goods are initially more marketable, thus constituting focal points on which the economy can

Menger's theory of money 227

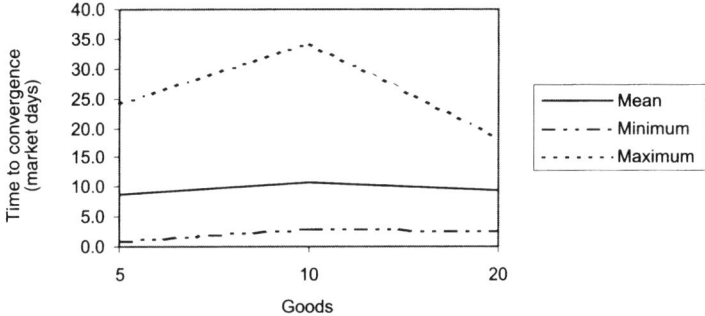

Figure 11.4 Effect of changes in the number of goods

converge. To explore the effects of focal points, we ran sets of simulations in which one good was initially more prominent – that is, had more beads in the urn – than the other goods. The results of these simulations are presented in Table 11.2. The first column of Table 11.2 gives results from thirty simulations of our base model with ten agents and ten equally marketable goods, each represented by a single bead in the urn. The average time to convergence is 4.5 market days. Column (2) reports the result of thirty simulations of a model with ten agents and nine goods, one of which is represented by two beads in the urn. As before, we began with the same number of beads as agents; this time, however, one good was twice as likely to be selected by the first trader as the remaining eight goods.

Surprisingly, making one good initially more marketable than the others had only a fairly small effect on the average time to convergence.

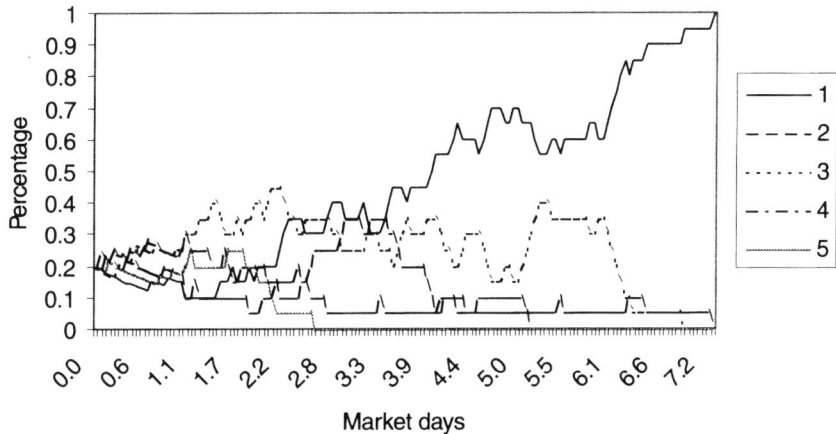

Figure 11.5a Convergence paths with changes in the number of goods (twenty agents, five goods)

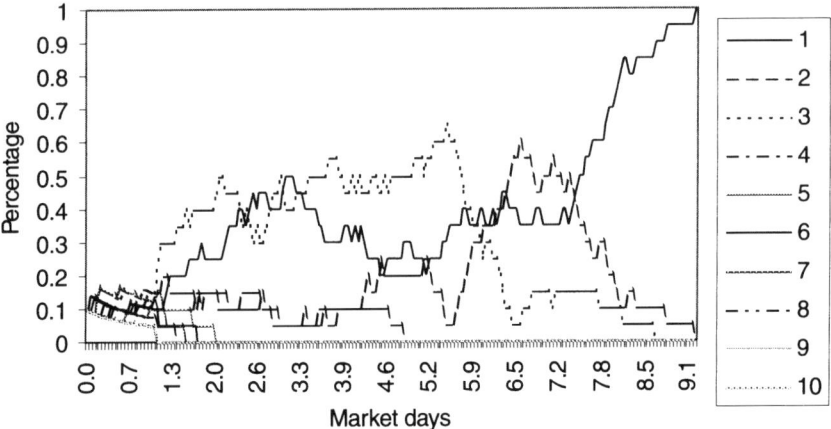

Figure 11.5b Convergence paths with changes in the number of goods (twenty agents, ten goods)

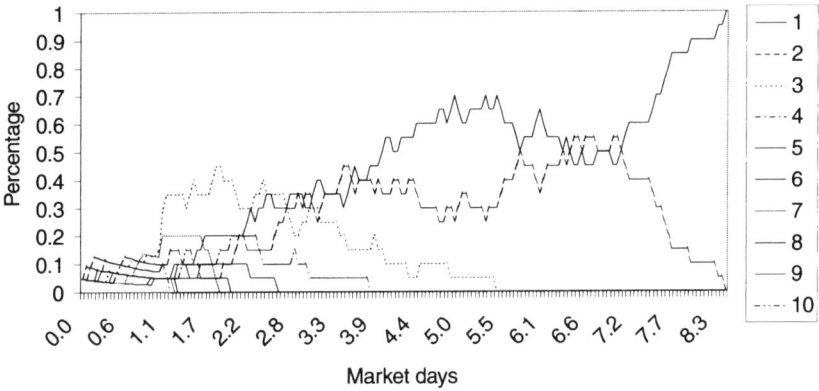

Figure 11.5c Convergence paths with changes in the number of goods (twenty agents, twenty goods)

For the simulations reported in column (2) of Table 11.2, in which the focal good is initially twice as saleable as the other goods, the mean time to convergence is 4.6 market days, essentially the same as that of our base simulation. (The standard deviation is larger, 3.4 to 2.1, since one simulation converged in only 1.5 days.) However, the good that is initially twice as marketable was about twice as likely to end up as the generally-accepted medium of exchange. The last row of Table 11.2 shows the percentage of simulations in which the good that was initially more marketable became the eventual medium of exchange. In our base simulation with ten equally marketable goods, each good should be chosen, on average, three out of thirty times. For the thirty simulations reported in column (2), the good

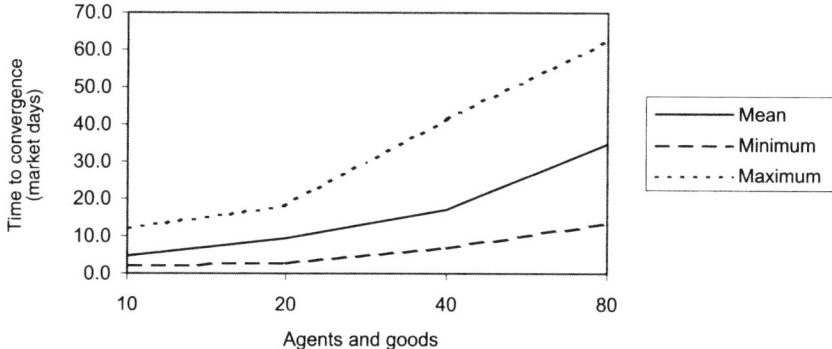

Figure 11.6 Effects of changes in scale

that is initially more marketable is chosen six times. Thus, although it might be assumed that a small initial advantage would bring a substantial *ex post* advantage, in our model increasing the probability that a particular good would be chosen in the early rounds gave only a roughly proportionate increase in the probability that that good will be chosen as the medium of exchange.

Columns (3), (4) and (5) of Table 11.2 report sets of simulations in which we progressively increased the initial probability that a particular good would be chosen: first we gave one good three times as many initial beads as the other goods, then five times as many, then seven times as many. As seen in column (3), giving one good three times as much initial marketability has about the same effect as giving it twice the initial marketability. The mean time to convergence falls slightly, to 4.2 market days, and the initially more marketable good is chosen as the medium of exchange seven times. Increasing the focal good's initial advantage to five

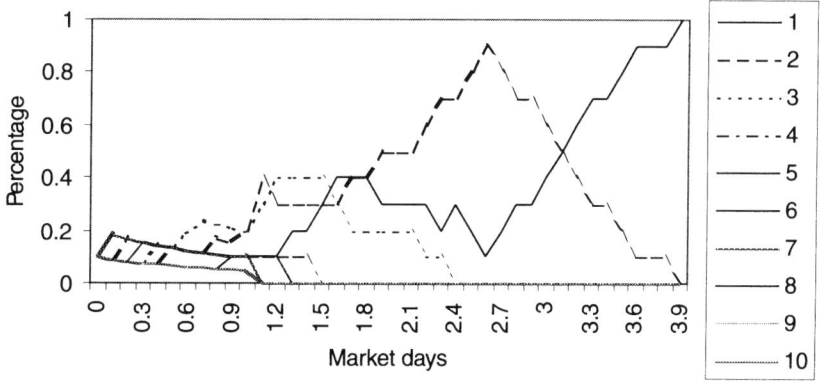

Figure 11.7a Convergence paths with changes in scale (ten agents, ten goods)

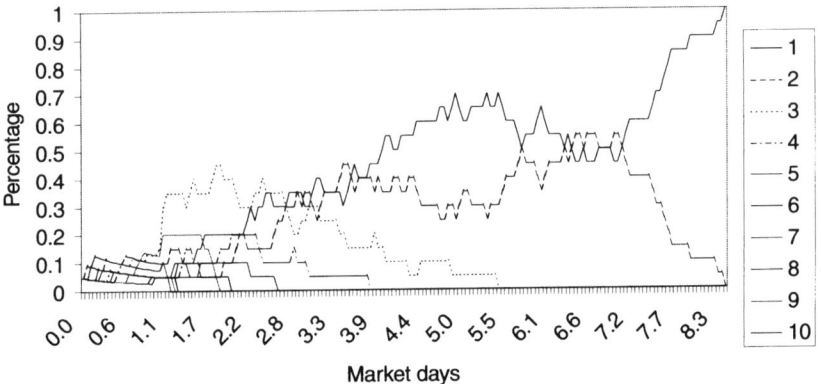

Figure 11.7b Convergence paths with changes in scale (twenty agents, twenty goods)

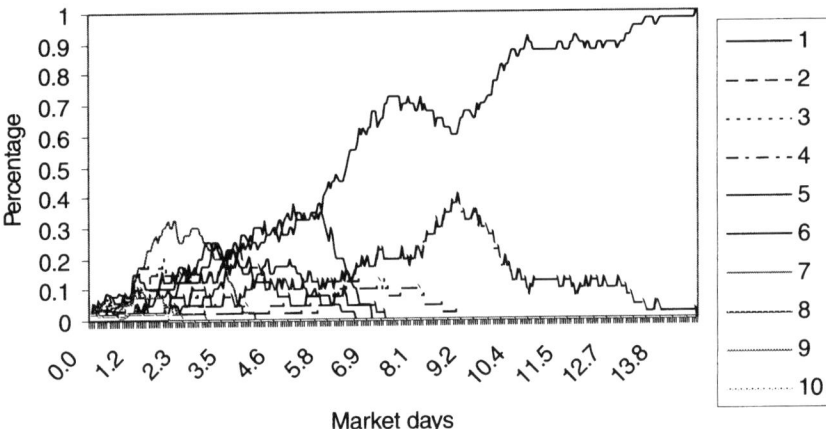

Figure 11.7c Convergence paths with changes in scale (forty agents, forty goods)

times the marketability of the other goods causes a slight increase in the mean time to convergence (4.6 market days), but it again leads to a proportionate increase in the effectiveness of the focal point. The initially more marketable good is chosen as the medium of exchange in fourteen of the thirty simulations, roughly five times the probability of any good's being chosen in the simulations without a focal good.

Figures 11.8 and 11.9 summarize the effects of changes in the strength of the focal point. The horizontal axis measures this strength in terms of the initial share of the focal good. A value of 1 corresponds to the base simulation in which all goods are equally prominent. A value of 2 represents the simulation in which one good has twice the initial share of

Table 11.2 Focal point simulation results

	(1) All goods equally marketable	(2) One good twice as marketable	(3) One good three times as marketable	(4) One good five times as marketable	(5) One good seven times as marketable
Initial parameters					
Agents	10	10	10	10	10
Goods	10	9	8	6	4
Initial beads	10	10	10	10	10
Simulations	30	30	30	30	30
Time to converge (market days)					
Mean	4.5	4.6	4.2	4.6	3.4
Median	3.9	4.1	3.9	3.3	3.2
Standard deviation	2.9	3.4	1.7	3.7	1.7
Minimum	2.3	1.5	2.0	1.1	1.1
Maximum	12.4	20.4	10.1	16.4	6.6
Number of simulations in which focal good is chosen as medium of exchange	—	6	7	14	19

the other goods, and so on through 7, representing a simulation in which one good has seven times the initial share of the other goods. In Figure 11.8, the vertical axis measures the average, minimum, and maximum time to convergence. In Figure 11.9, the vertical axis measures the percentage of simulations, based on the sample of thirty, in which the initially more saleable good was chosen as the medium of exchange.

As the strength of the focal point increases, the mean time to convergence tends to fall. When we increased the initial marketability of the focal good to seven times that of the other goods, the mean time to convergence fell to 3.4 market days, with a standard deviation of 3.2. As the column (5) of Table 11.2 indicates, the fastest time to convergence was 1.1 market days, significantly less than the fastest time without a focal good. Moreover, the initially more marketable good was chosen as the medium of exchange in nineteen of the thirty simulations, roughly seven times the probability of any good's being chosen in the simulations with ten equally marketable goods.

Conclusion

In his treatment of the spontaneous origins of money, Karl Menger argued that different goods under barter have different degrees of marketability. The most marketable goods become adopted as indirect exchange media

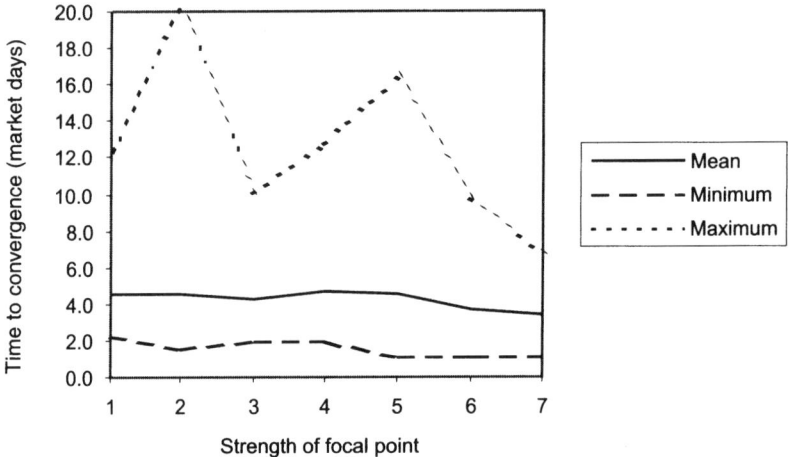

Figure 11.8 Effects of focal point on time to convergence

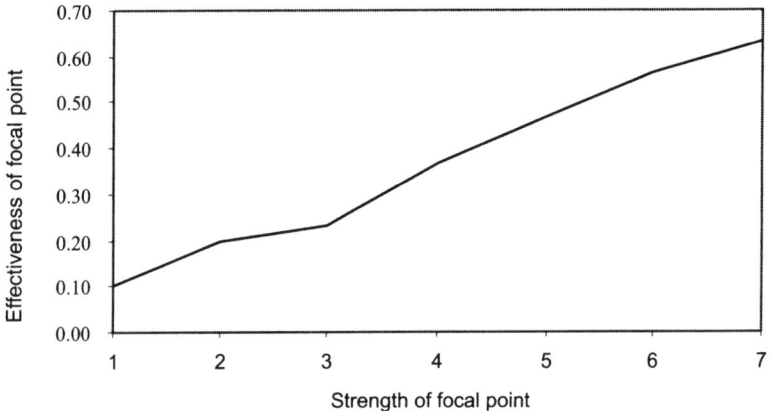

Figure 11.9 Effectiveness of focal point

by a sub-set of traders, thus further enhancing those goods' relative marketability until all traders are willing to trade for them. Money – a universally-accepted exchange medium – is thus an outcome of human action, but not of human design.

We have shown that money can emerge spontaneously even where traders have only a very dim perception of the marketability of distinct goods, based on very limited random sampling, and even where all goods are equally marketable at the onset of the evolutionary process. The assumption of limited information makes for a much more interesting evolutionary process than in Menger's own account, where the only factor preventing an economy from jumping all at once to a particular monetary equilibrium is the assumed hesitation of certain traders to become involved in the monetary selection process. In our framework, agents rely on a single market sample to determine which good is most marketable on any market day. Opinions therefore differ at first, but are drawn together as trade continues. The time required for convergence to a monetary steady state is independent of the number of goods in the economy, but is more or less proportional to the number of agents in the economy.

Although no good has to be particularly marketable or prominent at the onset of a monetary selection process for the process to lead to a monetary steady state, as one would expect, a good's initial prominence has a direct bearing on its likelihood of becoming money. A good that is initially twice as prominent as all other goods is about twice as likely to become money. Still, under limited information, a good may be quite prominent at first and yet may not be chosen as money. Finally, and somewhat counter-intuitively, the initial presence of especially prominent goods does not necessarily result in a more rapid convergence to a monetary equilibrium.

In our endeavour to show how money may evolve even under circumstances where agents have very limited knowledge of goods' relative marketability, we have probably exaggerated the extent of agents' ignorance. A more realistic set of simulations might allow agents to rely upon larger market samples to form opinions concerning goods' relative saleability. Also, while we have assumed an extreme version of adaptive expectations in which agents rely on current sample evidence only and ignore findings from past samples, a more realistic model might allow agents to assign a positive but diminishing weight to earlier sample results. These are just two of many possible changes that might contribute to a more realistic depiction of the monetary selection process. We hope to consider the effects of such changes in later work.

Notes

We thank David Robinson and Lawrence H. White for helpful comments.

1 A good's initial non-monetary marketability, interpreted narrowly as depending on the number of persons wishing to possess the good for value in use, is only one of several factors that may contribute to its degree of prominence in a monetary co-ordination game. A good's physical properties, its durability, portability, divisibility, etc., may also render it more prominent that other goods.
2 To economize on computer resources, we place an upper bound on the total number of trades. The simulation ends either when the economy converges, or when the upper bound has been reached. We used an upper bound of 5000 trades, which was binding in only five of about 400 total simulations.
3 To clarify the pictures, we plot only the ten goods that attain the highest acceptance rates during the process.

References

Jones, R. A. (1976) 'The Origin and Development of Media of Exchange', *Journal of Political Economy* 84, 4: 757–75.

Kiyotaki, N. and Wright, R. (1989) 'On Money as a Medium of Exchange', *Journal of Political Economy* 97, 4: 927–54.

—— (1993) 'A Search-Theoretic Approach to Monetary Economics', *American Economic Review* 83: 63–77.

Menger, K. (1892) 'On the Origin of Money', *Economic Journal* 2: 239–55

—— (1981 [1970]) *Principles of Economics*, trans. J. Dingwall and B. F. Hoselitz, New York: New York University Press.

Schelling, T. C. (1960) *The Strategy of Conflict*, Cambridge, Mass.: Harvard University Press.

12 Dr Freud and Mr Keynes on money and capitalism

Gilles Dostaler and Bernard Maris

Introduction

Keynes's references to Freud are not numerous, but they are important. His letter to the editor of the *Nation and Athenaeum*, 29 August 1925, on 'Freudian Psycho-analysis', contains methodological remarks and an appraisal of Freud's work that looks like a self-appraisal:

> Professor Freud seems to me to be endowed, to the degree of genius, with the scientific imagination which can body forth an abundance of innovating ideas, shattering possibilities, working hypotheses, which have sufficient foundation in intuition and common experience to deserve the most patient and unprejudiced examination, and which contain, in all probability, both theories which will have to be discarded or altered out of recognition and also theories of great and permanent significance.
>
> (Keynes 28: 392)[1]

There is a passage in *A Treatise on Money* (1930) which contains significant references to the Freudian theory of the love of money, as developed by Freud himself as well as his disciples Ferenczi and Jones (Keynes 6: 258–9). Keynes was well acquainted with Freud's work, edited and translated by his friend James Strachey, and published by Leonard and Virginia Woolf's Hogarth Press. Alix and James Strachey were analysed by Freud in Vienna and became two of his principal lieutenants in England. There is, thus, a close relationship between Bloomsbury, Freud and psychoanalysis.

Not only was Keynes convinced of the importance of the psychological element in life, but psychoanalytical concepts can shed light on many aspects of his economic and social vision. The *General Theory* is built on three psychological drives: the propensity to consume, the marginal efficiency of capital and liquidity preference. In his article bearing the same title and published in 1937, Keynes writes that 'this feeling about money . . . operates, so to speak, at a deeper level of our motivation' (Keynes 14: 116). The love of money, the irrational fascination for the gold standard, the drive to accumulation, animal spirits, speculation, uncertainty, all these elements can be analysed with the help of Freudian concepts. As some of these themes predate Keynes's discovery of Freud, we can say that there were similar influences on Freud and on Bloomsbury's vision of the world.

Freud is thus himself, up to a certain point, as much influenced by, as the partial initiator of, this ideological transformation with which the name of Bloomsbury is associated. Freud praised Lytton Strachey for his use of psychological analysis in *Elizabeth and Essex* (1928). But this kind of analysis is also used in Strachey's first great success, *Eminent Victorians* (1918), and in *Queen Victoria* (1921). Keynes was himself a master in this art, and his portrait of President Wilson in *The Economic Consequences of the Peace* (1919) was read by Freud in preparation for his own psychological study of the President, published posthumously in 1967. It is often thought that Strachey influenced Keynes in these kinds of writings, but a closer analysis shows that influences probably ran in both directions. As early as the beginning of the century, the young Keynes was practising this type of analysis, combining historical and psychological considerations.

The beginning of the twentieth century witnessed the emergence of a new vision of the world, the relations between the individual and society, the motivations of human action, and the perception of time and flows of consciousness, in art, literature and science. When Keynes read Freud at the time of his struggle against Victorian morals, his first criticism of *laissez-faire*, his first reflections on money, speculation, thrift and savings, as well as the ideas elaborated in the successive versions of his *Treatise on Probability*, concerning in particular the methods of the 'moral sciences', he thus found some ideas with which he was already familiar. In his 1925 article on Freud, Keynes writes that the argument in favour of Freud's thesis would not be weakened if it were discovered that Freud had invented his case studies, because they are based on intuitions 'and very little indeed upon the so-called inductive verifications' (Keynes 28: 393).

Keynes talks psychology, but Freud talks economics. Freud's reader cannot but be struck by the ease with which the father of psychoanalysis uses economic concepts such as gain and loss, work, enrichment and impoverishment (for example of libido), and the tendency to economize in many of his most important texts.[2] In his analysis of dreams, Freud uses the metaphors of the entrepreneur and capitalist:

> To put it figuratively, it is quite possible that a day-thought plays the part of the *entrepreneur* in the dream; but the *entrepreneur*, who, as we say, has the idea, and feels impelled to realize it, can do nothing without *capital*; he needs a *capitalist* who will defray the expense, and this capitalist, who contributes the psychic expenditure for the dream, is invariably and indisputably, whatever the nature of the waking thoughts *a wish from the unconscious*.
>
> (Freud 1932 [1900]: 527)[3]

Psychology makes use of certain notions that economists would not renounce, such as transfers, exchange and investment. Words such as accumulation, retention, saving, are widely utilized by psychologists in acceptations that would satisfy the Viennese theoreticians of capital and roundabout production. Repression, the refusal to live for the instant and the illusory quest for eternity in infinite accumulation are developed by Max Weber (1958 [1904–5]) who identifies capitalism with the rational moderation of an irrational drive. This drive is a limitless greed, a childish insatiability. As we will show, it finds echoes in Keynes and Marx.

Not much has been written on relations between Freud and Keynes. There are pioneering papers by Winslow (1986, 1990, 1992, 1995), to which must be added the work of Bonnadei (1994), Bormans (1997), Mini (1994) and Parsons (1997). Skidelsky also addresses the relationship in the second volume of his biography of Keynes (Skidelsky 1992). We therefore embark upon a relatively unexplored path, which is why we will begin our paper with a story of the relations between Bloomsbury, psychoanalysis, Freud and Keynes. We will then turn to what we call the Freudo-Keynesian conception of money, by examining two myths, the goose which lays golden eggs, and Midas. The third and final part of our paper will address the analysis of capitalism and, in particular, Keynes's idea of the market as a mob, which is closely linked to the Freudian idea of the mob.

Bloomsbury and Freud

The term Bloomsbury, a geographical area of London, now designates a group of friends who shared certain values and a world view that was radically opposed to the Victorian ideology which still impregnated England at Queen Victoria's death at the beginning of the twentieth century. Five men, who were then at Trinity College, Cambridge, were involved from the outset: Lytton Strachey, Leonard Woolf, Saxon Sydney-Turner, Thoby Stephen and Clive Bell. The Bloomsbury group formally began its existence in London, in 1905, with the reunion of the Cambridge group and two exceptional women, Vanessa and Virginia Stephen, sisters of Thoby, who was to die in 1906. There was another younger brother, Adrian. Vanessa, a painter, married Clive Bell in 1907. Virginia took the name by which she was to be known as one of the greatest English writers of the century, when she married Leonard Woolf in 1912. Soon Keynes, the painter Duncan Grant, art critic Roger Fry, journalist Desmond McCarthy, and others joined the group. The friendships were very intimate. Love relationships were complicated, changing, and anything but conventional. Their personalities were complex, tormented, and usually quite egotistical. The ground was thus propitious for an encounter with psychoanalysis.

Lytton Strachey and Leonard Woolf, like other future members of the Bloomsbury group, were admitted in 1902 to the Cambridge *Conversazione* Society, also known as the Apostles, a secret society established in 1820. In

February 1903 they proposed the election to this group of John Maynard Keynes, who had just come up to Cambridge. Keynes told the story of this part of his life in a paper read in 1938 to the Bloomsbury Memoir Club, entitled 'My Early Beliefs'. In this account, he wrote that before the First World War, he and his Apostle friends, being 'pre-Freudian', had 'completely misunderstood human nature, including our own' (Keynes 10: 448). But Leonard Woolf, criticizing Keynes's account, recounts how Lytton Strachey and Woolf himself had invented and experimented on their friends what they called a 'method' to explore their psyches, and thus to ameliorate interpersonal relationships by rendering them more authentic:

> The 'method' referred to in the conversation had been invented by Lytton and me; it was a kind of third-degree psychological investigation applied to the souls of one's friends. Though it was a long time before we had any knowledge of Freud, it was a kind of compulsory psychoanalysis. It was intended to reveal to us, and incidentally to the victim, what he was really like; the theory was that by imparting to all concerned the deeper psychological truths, personal relationships would be much improved. Its technique was derived partly from Socrates, partly from Henry James, partly from G. E. Moore, and partly from ourselves.
>
> (Woolf 1960: 113)

Freud explained that we can find elements of psychoanalytical theory in art and literature, and this well before their 'rational reconstruction' by the theoreticians of the new discipline. There was thus, in the *Weltanschauung* of what would become Bloomsbury, some elements of the Freudian vision, which we can also find in historical essays written by Keynes when he was at Eton, even before his time at Cambridge: for example, a paper he wrote on the Stuarts.[4] Psychoanalysis and what we can call the culture of Bloomsbury were born in similar contexts, in reaction to the same culture and the same kind of society, and, in particular, in reaction to religious obscurantism and its attendant sexual repression.

A somewhat bizarre organization, the Society for Psychical Research, played a role in the early relations between Freud and Bloomsbury. It was in fact the first port of entry of psychoanalysis in England. It was established in 1882, among others by Henry Sidgwick, who was a close friend of Keynes's father.[5] The society was interested in parapsychological phenomena, such as telepathy. It was also interested in Freud's work. In April 1893, F. W. H. Myers provided the society with an abstract of Freud and Breuer's study on hysteria. Communications on Freud's theories were often read at its meetings, which were attended by James Strachey, Lytton's younger brother, and by Keynes, who joined the society's committee in 1911.[6]

It was Ernest Jones, the first English disciple of Freud and his future biographer, who officially introduced psychoanalysis to England with the foundation in 1913 of the London Psychoanalytic Society, affiliated with the International Psychoanalytic Association established in 1910. Jones was the first person to start practising psychoanalytical therapy in London that same year. In 1914, Freud's *The Psychopathology of Everyday Life* was published in a translation by the American A. A. Brill, whose other translations of Freud had not been considered satisfactory by the author. It is probable that the book was widely read in Bloomsbury. Lytton Strachey wrote a dialogue on Freud in the same year.[7] Leonard Woolf reviewed this book in the June 1914 issue of the *New Weekly*. This paper was the first article on Freud published in England in a non-medical journal. To prepare his review, Leonard also read, in May, *The Interpretation of Dreams*.[8]

In the fourth volume of his autobiography, Leonard Woolf wrote: 'In the decade before 1924 in the so-called Bloomsbury circle there was great interest in Freud and psycho-analysis, and the interest was extremely serious' (Woolf 1967: 164). Four members of the Bloomsbury set would become more closely associated with the psychoanalytical movement. The first was Virginia Woolf's younger brother, Adrian Stephen. After graduating in law from Cambridge he spent several directionless years, but at the end of the war he and his wife Karin Costelloe decided to enrol in a medical course in order to be able to practice psychoanalysis. They started practising in 1926.

James Strachey, who was elected an Apostle in 1906, and was also unclear about his orientation for many years, took the same decision at the end of the war. However he soon abandoned his medical studies, choosing instead to go with his wife, Alix Sargant Florence, to the Mecca of psychoanalysis, Vienna, where Freud himself had agreed to take charge of James's unconscious. Shortly after James began his analysis, Alix decided to follow suit, and Freud agreed to see both of them, contrary to his own orthodoxy.[9] This continued until the spring of 1922, when Alix's analysis was interrupted by illness. Freud was of the opinion that both could practice as analysts, but he suggested to Alix that she continue her analysis, which she did between the autumn of 1924 and 1925, with Karl Abraham in Berlin.[10]

Wishing to preserve his hold on the field, Freud quickly discovered that his new patients could become precious and helpful allies, and a counterforce to Ernest Jones, who dominated the English analytical scene. Jones, who was a member of Freud's close guard, understood this, and his relations with James Strachey would never be perfectly harmonious. Shortly after their arrival, Freud asked the Stracheys to translate one of his papers, 'A Child is Being Beaten'. The translation was published in 1920. A further translation, by James, of *Massenpsychologie und Ich-Analyse* followed in 1922. A much more important task was entrusted to both Alix and James in March 1921 with the translation of the five great case histories, which were to occupy them over the next five years. Freud appreciated the Stracheys' work and called them his 'excellent English translators'. Their new career was launched.

The Strachey's Viennese sojourn provided the occasion for the first indirect exchange between Freud and Keynes. On February 22, 1921, Lytton Strachey wrote to Keynes:

> The enclosed, from James, may amuse you. Apparently your fame in Vienna is tremendous, & Dr Freud says that he has got far more notoriety from a mention of his name by you somewhere than from anything else. He received several letters of congratulations on the occasion. Otherwise he is unknown in Austria.
> (*Keynes Papers*: 45/316)[11]

The mention of Freud's name is probably from chapter three of *The Economic Consequences of the Peace*, in which Keynes draws the portraits of the protagonists of the Paris Peace Conference, and writes, about President Wilson: 'In the language of medical psychology, to suggest to the President that the treaty was an abandonment of his professions was to touch on the raw of a Freudian complex' (Keynes 2: 34). In 1930 Freud himself undertook the writing of a psychological portrait of President Wilson, with the American journalist and diplomat William Bullitt, who first suggested the idea. Sent by the US government to negotiate with Lenin in the newly-born USSR in 1919, Bullitt was also member of the American delegation to the Paris Conference that same year. Like Keynes, he denounced the Versailles Peace Treaty. The book he wrote with Freud, although completed in 1932, was not published until 1967, after the death of the President's second wife (Freud and Bullitt 1967). It is at least a plausible assumption that the reading of Keynes's book played a part in Freud's decision to write on Wilson.

Keynes chaired the annual Apostles' Dinner in June 1921. James wrote to him on 6 June: 'I'm sorry to say that I shan't be back in England in time for the Dinner. It's sickening to miss it – but the Professor's scalpel is still probing the recesses of my *verdrängten Unbewussten* [repressed subconscious]' (*Keynes Papers*: UA/36). Before quoting this letter in his presidential address, Keynes commented that 'James Strachey, who is being disintegrated at the hands of Professor Freud, rendered immortal by Professor [undecipherable], and fitted out with a more than ordinarily complete sex apparatus at the expense of the poorer classes of Vienna, writes as follows'.[12]

Freud had probably read both Keynes and Lytton Strachey before his meeting with James.[13] *Eminent Victorians* (1918), and *Queen Victoria* (1921) inaugurated a new type of psychological biography which might appear to have been influenced by Freud, but in reality Lytton was then somewhat hesitant about Freud's theses, and more seriously influenced by

Dostoevsky. Things changed during the 1920s when he read Freud's *Collected Papers*, and he eventually explicitly applied Freud's ideas in *Elizabeth and Essex*, as did Virginia Woolf a decade later in *Three Guineas*. This prompted Freud to write a long laudatory letter to Lytton Strachey:

> I am acquainted with all your earlier publications, and I have read them with great enjoyment. But the enjoyment was essentially an aesthetic one. This time you have moved me more deeply, for you yourself have reached greater depths. You are aware of what other historians so easily overlook – that it is impossible to understand the past with certainty, because we cannot divine men's motives and the essence of their minds and so cannot interpret their actions. . . . As a historian, then, you show that you are steeped in the spirit of psychoanalysis.
> (Meisel and Kendrick 1985: 332)

The rapprochement between Bloomsbury and the master of Vienna was transformed into a more formal alliance in 1924, in which Leonard Woolf again played a determining role. James Strachey asked him to publish the projected four volumes of the *Collected Papers* of Freud, which he was then translating with others. Published in 1924 and 1925, the volumes were greatly successful.[14] It is in this edition that Keynes and other members of the Bloomsbury group read Freud's most important writings. The debate that the edition launched appeared in the columns of the *Nation and Athenaeum*. Intervening in praise of Freud's work, Keynes's contribution appeared under the signature of 'Siela'. It was at this time that Keynes collected some of the material he would use in his *Treatise on Money* and the *General Theory*. In 1924, Roger Fry published *The Artist and Psycho-Analysis*.

The story of the relationship between Bloomsbury and Freud does not end there. Hogarth Press published all the English translations of Freud's works, as well as all the writings of the Psycho-Analytical Library, associated with the London Institute of Psycho-Analysis: that is, around seventy books. Leonard and Virginia met Freud once, after his arrival in London, on 28 January 1939.[15] After Freud's death, and some difficult negotiations, in particular with Ernest Jones, James Strachey took charge of the edition and translation of Freud's complete works and Hogarth Press was the publisher. The first of twenty-four volumes of what is called the Standard Edition was published in 1953. James, whose physical resemblance to Freud at the end of his life was striking, died in 1967, shortly after the publication of the twenty-third volume. He was about to receive a prize for this monument of erudition.

The Freudo-Keynesian conception of money

It is clear that Keynes, through his own readings and his conversations with his Bloomsbury friends, had a thorough knowledge of Freud's writings.[16] It is also clear that many elements in Bloomsbury and Keynes's vision of the world are similar to those of the founder of psychoanalysis. Thus Keynes found in Freud's thought an understanding of money that was in many ways similar to ideas he had arrived at independently. This is why we can speak of a Freudo-Keynesian conception of money.

Two mythical traditions help understand the double nature of money in Freud. As far as the origin of money is concerned, 'the goose which lays golden eggs' and 'the donkey which makes ducats' both express the anal-erotic character of the genesis of money. On the other hand, as mentioned on different occasions in Keynes's works, the myth of King Midas, who dies when he transforms his food into gold, expresses the morbid character of the love of money.[17] But let us not be misled: the goose with golden eggs and Midas represent two sides of the same coin.

The goose which lays golden eggs

'The human body is a kind of biological household', writes Borneman (1976: 31). The four moments of nutritive life – ingestion, digestion, retention and excretion of food – can be made to correspond with acquisition, investment, savings and hoarding, and sale. In particular, 'the oral nature of financial acquisition is hardly open to doubt' (ibid.: 32). According to the Freudian theory, the child learns about gift, exchange, value, price, wealth, savings – in short, political economy – in his coprophylic exchange relations with his parents. This is why the human being is, according to Georg Simmel, 'in the first place an exchanging animal' (Viderman 1992: 40). Freud (1908) and then Ferenczi (1914, 1916) easily recognize the faecal character of money in language and popular tales: in addition to 'the goose that lays golden eggs' and 'the donkey which makes ducats', there is also 'to do one's business', or the expression 'money doesn't smell', attributed to the Roman emperor Vespasian, inventor of public urinals (Borneman 1976: 50). They express reality by antiphrasis, or are 'euphemistic reversal' (Ferenczi 1916: 98).

Although it appears earlier in his correspondence, Freud first expounded his thesis on the anal character of money in 1908, in 'Character and Anal Erotism'. There he describes as 'especially *orderly, parsimonious* and *obstinate*' those class of individuals who 'took a comparatively long time to overcome their infantile *incontinenta alvi*' (Freud 1908: 73–4). According to Freud this is one of the origins of the tendency to money hoarding. Ferenczi follows up with 'The Ontogenesis of the Interest in Money' (1914), in which he writes that 'the character of capitalism, however, not purely practical and utilitarian, but libidinous and irrational, is betrayed in this stage also: the child decidedly enjoys the collecting in itself' (Ferenczi 1914: 85). The enjoyment of money contains an important irrational element. Ferenczi concludes that 'the capitalistic instinct thus contains, according to our conception, an egoistic and an anal-erotic component' (ibid.: 88). In his paper, Ferenczi also links anal-eroticism with artistic activity, the compulsion to collect and even hypochondria which 'is really a fermentation-product of anal-erotism' (ibid.: 89). For Ferenczi, following Freud, 'aesthetics in general has its principal root in repressed anal-erotism' (ibid.: 84–5).

Keynes explicitly uses Freudian concepts in *A Treatise on Money*, in a section entitled '*Auri Sacra Fames*', where he writes: 'Dr. Freud relates that there are peculiar reasons deep in our subconsciousness why gold in particular should satisfy strong instincts and serve as a symbol' (Keynes 6: 258). To this passage he appended a note with references to the texts just quoted by Freud and Ferenczi, to which he adds a reference to Ernest Jones. Of the latter, he quotes the following prophecy, as an example of the success of the psychoanalytical method:

> The ideas of possession and wealth, therefore, obstinately adhere to the idea of 'money' and gold for definite psychological reasons. This superstitious attitude will cost England in particular many sacrifices after the war, when efforts will probably be made at all costs to reintroduce a gold currency.
>
> (Jones 1917: 172, quoted in Keynes: 6: 259)

This is indeed a remarkable prophecy.

Reading Freud and his disciples, Keynes discovered the foundations for several ideas he had already come to independently. The theme of the irrational love of money and of its psychological roots is already present in his first reflections on money, written in the first decade of the century. This love is both irrational and fundamental in explaining the functioning of capitalism. In a normal world, 'money is only important for what it will procure' (Keynes 4: 1). Love of money *per se*, accumulation of gold, coins, papers or any other form of liquid wealth is irrational. But this propensity is fundamental to capitalism. Very critical of the Bolshevik Soviet Union, Keynes also praised it for the elimination of the money motive as a fundamental drive to action. Of course, this psychological reality has important economic consequences: 'Unemployment develops, that is to say, because people want the moon; – men cannot be employed when the object of desire (i.e., money) is something which cannot be produced and the demand for which cannot be readily choked off' (Keynes 7: 235). And this problem has endured for many centuries:

> That the world after several millennia of steady individual saving, is so poor as it is in accumulated capital-assets, is to be explained, in my opinion, neither by the improvident propensities of mankind, nor even by the destruction of war, but by the high liquidity-premiums formerly attaching to the ownership of land and now attaching to money.
>
> (Keynes 7: 242)

Keynes personally earned a lot of money, mainly through speculation, and particularly by speculation on money. He rationalized this activity on two grounds. First, it permitted him to avoid 'salaried drudgery' (Harrod 1951: 297) and thus to concentrate his energy on greater tasks. Second, it permitted him to acquire beautiful objects, of which he was a great collector, in particular rare books and pictures. Like his father, Keynes was a compulsive collector. He started early with stamps. He kept detailed lists of his belongings and activities, and he threw away very few papers, however insignificant they might be. It is interesting to note that Keynes shared many of the character traits described by Freud and Ferenczi. We could thus link together his compulsion for collections, for compilations, his relation to art, to money, and even to hypochondria, which he also inherited from his father. With regard to money, hoarding (retention) was for him hoarding of the useless (which translated into a compulsion for collection). At the same time, money must be spent (in theory), if possible on works of art (in practice); and also in gifts and rents to his friends (Strachey, Duncan Grant, Wittgenstein). Of course, we must be very careful in this kind of *a posteriori* psychoanalysis.

Midas

Accepting the Freudian ideas of the link of money to the unconscious, and of the psychological roots of the love for money, Keynes goes further to berate the desire for gold for itself, which he frequently associates with the myth of King Midas:

> Of late years the *auri sacra fames* has sought to envelop itself in a garment of respectability as densely respectable as was ever met with, even in the realms of sex or religion. Whether this was first put on as a necessary armour to win the hard-won fight against bimetallism and is still worn, as the gold-advocates allege, because gold is the sole prophylactic against the plague of fiat moneys, or whether it is a furtive Freudian cloak, we need not be curious to inquire.
>
> (Keynes 9: 162)

This quotation shows the perfect knowledge that Keynes had of the theory of repression. We find even more clearly the morbid character of the desire for gold for itself in this sentence of 'Economic Possibilities for our Grandchildren':

> The love of money as a possession – as distinguished from the love of money as a means to the enjoyments and realities of life – will be recognised for what it is, a somewhat disgusting morbidity, one of those semi-criminal, semi-pathological propensities which one hands over with a shudder to the specialists in mental disease.
>
> (Keynes 9: 329)

Disgusting morbidity, semi-pathological propensities, shudder, mental disease. It could not be clearer.

Midas helps us to understand the fascination of the master of Cambridge for the master of Vienna. Midas's insatiability is infantile, as is the desire for money. One could add that capitalism is itself infantile, unfinished, insatiable. Capitalism is a system that has not succeeded in dealing with death, like the child, or which refuses to do so. That is why capitalism is transitional; it can only exist in accumulation and movement. The paradox of Midas is that his fear of death, which leads him to desire more and more power over things through wealth, leads to his death. The miser dies on his pile of gold, the *rentier* drowns in his liquidity. Liquidity preference, which is a denial of the future, results in kicking off our future. Midas is also a metaphor for liquidity preference, 'the fetish of liquidity' (Keynes 7: 155). The fetish, in Freud, is a means to negate reality in its most threatening aspect. Is there a more threatening event than death? Money gives us an illusory immortality:

> The 'purposive' man is always trying to secure a spurious and delusive immortality for his acts by pushing his interest in them forward into time. He does not love his cat, but his cat's kittens; nor, in truth, the kittens, but only the kittens' kittens, and so on forward for ever to the end of catdom. For him jam is not jam unless it is a case of jam tomorrow and never jam today. Thus by pushing his jam always forward into the future, he strives to secure for his act of boiling it an immortality.
>
> (Keynes 9: 330)

'*In the long run* we are all dead', declared Keynes (4: 65). Infantility is a fear of the future. What better protection against the hazards of the future than the possession of money? '*For the importance of money essentially flows from it being a link between the present and the future*' (Keynes 7: 293, original emphasis). Death is ineluctable. And money, the bridge between the present and the future, is the vain shield protecting against the inevitable. Desiring liquidity for itself, I deny my future. I die, as did Midas, from the fear of death. In the end, the only way to achieve immortality is not to live. But what makes us believe that we are immortal, if not our unconscious, which, as Freud taught, ignores time, space and death? From whichever angle we consider it, the Keynesian theory of money echoes the Freudian conception of money.

> He that loveth silver shall not be satisfied with silver; nor he that loveth abundance with increase: this is also vanity.
>
> (Ecclesiastes: 5.10)

Midas, the *rentier*, the miser, is guilty not only of killing himself, but also of killing the society to which he denies the circulation of his money. The hoarder perverts all exchanges in the community of human beings by hiding the money that enlivens the relations in it. The euthanasia of the *rentier* called for by Keynes is preventive. It is a question of public safety. Here Keynes is approaching Marx, a thinker for whom he couldn't care less.[18] The capitalist is but one piece of the mechanism in the service of social progress.

We should note that Midas is irrational. This is why economists have difficulty understanding Keynes beyond the budgetary macroeconomics of communicating vessels or IS–LM mechanics, which do not engage the question of rationality. To read Freud in Keynes is to admit that our relation to money is impulsive and unconscious. It implies a radical criticism of economic science since Walras and even before, founded on the pillar of individual economic rationality. To ignore Freud, which means to ignore the relativity of reason in human sciences, is similar to ignoring Einstein in physics. Orthodox economics wanted to create a science that ignored money (the 'neutrality of money') and postulated a rational individual. Keynes took the opposite position to this strange view which is much like talking about matter with the assumption that matter does not exist. The irrational and impulsive motives for liquidity detention belong to an infantile regression: as a means of exchange, money is kept for itself, as symbol. The regression of individuals corresponds to the depression of society, another Freudian concept. Freud's discoveries challenge the triumph of reason in science, and Keynes's discoveries challenge rationality in economics. In both, there is no opposition between the libidinal and the rational spheres.

In the Keynesian theory of consumption we encounter the King Midas myth once again, through two images, one attenuated and one strong:

> To me, regarded historically, the most extraordinary thing is the complete disappearance of the theory of the demand and supply for output as a whole, i.e. the theory of employment, *after* it had been for a quarter of a century the most discussed thing in economics. One of the most important transitions for me, after my *Treatise on Money* had been published, was suddenly realising this. It only came after I had enunciated to myself the psychological law that, when income increases, the gap between income and consumption will increase, – a conclusion of vast importance to my own thinking but not apparently, expressed just like that, to anyone else's. Then, appreciably later, came the notion of interest as being the measure of liquidity preference, which became quite clear in my mind the moment I thought of it. And last of all, after an immense lot of muddling and many drafts, the proper definition of the marginal efficiency of capital linked up one thing with another.
>
> (Keynes 14: 85)

The attenuated image of Midas concerns this desire for savings which grows with wealth: the richer I am, the less I want to spend. The strong image is that of liquidity preference. As we stated earlier, liquidity preference reveals our fear of the future, of uncertainty, of precariousness, in short, our disquietude: 'The possession of actual money lulls our disquietude; and the premium which we require to make us part with money is the measure of the degree of our disquietude' (Keynes 14: 116). The interest rate is thus an index of fear. Keynes considers his vision of the interest rate as a monetary phenomenon linked to conventions and expectations as one of his major achievements, and he was very careful, after the publication of the *General Theory*, to stress the irreducibility of his vision to the classical or loanable funds theory of interest.

Capitalism and the market

His theory and philosophy of human behaviour allowed Keynes to elaborate an economic theory, a social theory and a political philosophy, contained in the *General Theory*. Let us summarize. The economic theory reveals itself in what he calls the 'three fundamental psychological laws', the propensity to consume, the marginal efficiency of capital and liquidity preference. This is closely linked to the idea of 'animal spirits'. Thus, the social theory defines the market (the 'society') not as a sum of individuals, but as a mob, in the Freudian meaning of the word, in total opposition to the Walrasian understanding of the market.[19] Thus, society looks very much like a person, subject to manias, panics, and depression.

'Animal spirits', the speculator, and the capitalist

What are these 'animal spirits'? Keynes describes them as 'a spontaneous urge to action rather than inaction' (Keynes 7: 161). They generate 'waves of irrational psychology', linked to the psyche and physiology: 'in estimating the prospects of investment, we must have regard, therefore, to the nerves and hysteria and even the digestions and reactions to the weather of those upon whose spontaneous activity it largely depends' (ibid.: 162). Note here the term 'hysteria', of which Freud analysed the sexual connotations and origins. Sexual drive or libido is a major component of animal spirits, as are also the closely-linked aggression and sadism:

> Moreover, dangerous human proclivities can be canalised into comparatively harmless channels by the existence of opportunities for money-making and private wealth, which, if they cannot be satisfied in this way, may find their outlet in cruelty, the reckless pursuit of personal power and authority, and other forms of self-aggrandisement. It is better that a man should tyrannise over his bank balance than over

his fellow-citizens; and whilst the former is sometimes denounced as being but a means to the latter, sometimes at least it is an alternative.
(Keynes 7: 374)

Thus Keynes suggests that speculation and capital accumulation constitute excellent outlets – sublimation – for the 'abundant libido' of certain individuals. This idea is already clearly expressed in a review of a book by H. G. Wells published in 1927: that is, well before the elaboration of the theoretical structure of the *General Theory*, but after Keynes had read Freud:

Why do practical men find it more amusing to make money than to join in open conspiracy? . . . That is why, unless they have the luck to be scientists or artists, they fall back on the grand substitute motive, the perfect *ersatz*, the anodyne for those who, in fact, want nothing at all – money. . . . Clissold and his brother Dickon, the advertising expert, flutter about the world seeking for something to which they can attach their abundant *lidido*. But they have not found it. They would so like to be apostles. But they cannot. They remain business men.
(Keynes 9: 319–20)

Do we have to oppose the speculator and the capitalist? Keynes warns against the fact that 'as the organisation of investment markets improves, the risk of the predominance of speculation does, however, increase' (Keynes 7: 158). But the risk of seeing entrepreneurs transformed into speculators shows clearly that their motivations are identical. They are of the same race, unlike the *rentiers*. Both are gamblers and players. They play with the future, which terrorizes the common run of people. Their animal spirits are opposed to Midas. Their myth is rather that of Hermes, the god of players (who invented, among other things, the game of knucklebones), of thieves, of merchants and of wanderers. The speculator is a magician.

That we play with the future, as speculator or entrepreneur, implies that we ignore it. 'We do not know'. The uncertainty is radical. This radical uncertainty corresponds to a particular understanding of the market. The market is an irrational mob of speculators. 'The irrational exuberance of markets', to quote Alan Greenspan, comes under the Keynesian conception of market.

The market as a mob

The *General Theory* opens with a radical rejection of Say's Law of markets, which is the assertion of the constant realization of equilibrium. Walras's general equilibrium model extends and formalizes this result. The Keynesian theory of the market is the opposite of the Walrasian theory.[20] The Keynesian market is a collective object in itself. It does not result from the addition of individuals, nor from the law of supply and demand. It is the mob, blind, sheeplike, ignorant, stupid, liable to panic and sensitive to all its own movements, to all wild rumours. The theory of the market-mob is expressed in chapter twelve of the *General Theory*, and the reference to the beauty contest describes a situation in which everyone is 'unduly interested in discovering what average opinion believes average opinion to be' (Keynes 7: 159). We are confronted with radical uncertainty:

> Knowing that our own individual judgment is worthless, we endeavour to fall back on the judgment of the rest of the world which is perhaps better informed. That is, we endeavour to conform with the behaviour of the majority or the average.
>
> (Keynes 14: 114)

Confronted with radical uncertainty, speculators and businesspeople are compelled to adopt the only possible behaviour, which Keynes designates as 'convention', that is to act as if the past was repeating itself, as if the state of affairs would perpetuate itself. But is this not the attitude of denying the future? The loop is looped. The denial of the future by the consumer (Midas) corresponds to the denial of uncertainty by the speculator (Hermes).

This theory of the market-mob, the mimetic theory of human behaviour, by which the other's desire moulds our own desire, is Freudian. Freud removes the opposition between individual psychology and social psychology:

> It is clearly perilous for him to put himself in opposition to it, and it will be safer to follow the example of those around him and perhaps even 'hunt with the pack'. In obedience to the new authority he may put his former 'conscience' out of action, and so surrender to the attraction of the increased pleasure that is certainly obtained from the removal of inhibitions.
>
> (Freud 1955 [1921]: 85)

Or again: 'the individual gives up his ego ideal and substitutes for it the group ideal' (Freud 1955 [1921]: 129). Keynes says: 'Wordly wisdom teaches that it is better for reputation to fail conventionally than to succeed unconventionally' (Keynes 7: 158). These two quotations say practically the same thing.

The 'depressed' society and radical uncertainty

Society is not a sum of individuals, but an autonomous entity, led by irrational drives and capable of 'depressions', 'manias', and 'cyclothymia'. Capitalism displays a sort of organic unity which complies with these drives. Capitalism is unachieved, 'infantile'. Economic agents act in the fear of uncertainty, like children. Finally, the political philosophy demands the euthanasia of the *rentier* for lack of Midas's psychoanalytical cure and the submission of economy, not to politics and to the state, as we might too easily think, but to aesthetics.

The rejection of determinism, the conviction that movement is the essence of social and human reality, the belief in the transitory nature of states of life and states of mind, in the precariousness of all human and social realizations, are themes at the root of Keynes's vision from the beginning of his career, as they are at the root of Bloomsbury's culture. The future is unknown and we can never know precisely the results of our decisions. This is a central message of the *General Theory*, as Keynes recalled in his 1937 *Quarterly Journal of Economics* article:

> Actually, however, we have, as a rule, only the vaguest idea of any but the most direct consequences of our acts. . . . The whole object of the accumulation of wealth is to produce results, or potential results, at a comparatively distant, and sometimes at an *indefinitely* distant, date.
> (Keynes 14: 113)

This is where money enters the scene. In 1933, Keynes wrote that he was trying to build a theory of a monetary economy, which he opposed to a real-exchange economy that 'uses money but uses it merely as a neutral link between transactions in real things and real assets and does not allow it to enter into motives and decisions' (Keynes 13: 408). In his *QJE* article, he stresses that the difference between his view and the classical view, overlooked by his critics, is particularly important in the treatment of money. The classical economist cannot answer the question 'why should anyone outside a lunatic asylum wish to use money as a store of wealth?' (Keynes 14: 115–6). The reason is that:

> partly on reasonable and partly on instinctive grounds, our desire to hold money as a store of wealth is a barometer of the degree of our distrust of our own calculations and conventions concerning the future. Even though this feeling about money is itself conventional or instinctive, it operates, so to speak, at a deeper level of our motivation. It takes charge at the moments when the higher, more precarious conventions have weakened.
> (Keynes 14: 116)

Thus the passage from the individual to the collective in Keynes has Freudian characteristics. What is society, embodied as it is in the market as a crowd of individuals, if not a collective individual, subject to the drives and depressions of the human being, denying death in the morbid desire for liquidity, or sublimating it in unending accumulation? What is mass psychology if not, in great part, a transposition of individual psychology?

Are not the collective beings that interested Freud, such as the church and the army, liable to be analysed, with concepts such as the unconscious, with all proper reservations?[21] We must return here to the Freudian theory of money, which finds echoes in the Marxian vision of the accumulating capitalist as 'personified capital . . . Fanatically bent upon the expansion of value, he relentlessly drives human beings to production for production's sake' (Marx 1933: 650–1). Here again, the capitalist *per se* is innocent. For Marx, as for Keynes, it is the hoarder who is immoral and guilty.[22] Is the capitalist *élan* only an *élan vital*, for Keynes as it is for Marx? The answer is clearly no. Unlimited saving and investment are both against what the Cambridge master reveres most, civilization:

> There grew round the non-consumption of the cake all those instincts of puritanism which in other ages has withdrawn itself from the world and has neglected the arts of production as well as those of enjoyment. And so the cake increased; but to what end was not clearly contemplated. . . . Saving was for old age or for your children; but this was only in theory – the virtue of the cake was that it was never to be consumed, neither by you nor by your children after you
>
> (Keynes 2: 12)

Neglect of productive as well as recreative arts, accumulation for accumulation, profits for profits, work for work. Marx welcomes this capitalist, because he gives birth to the communist paradise. For Keynes, he is sick and neurotic, with the very castrating neurosis that we find in Freud's *Civilization and its Discontents*, and foreshadowing Reich, Marcuse, and the aesthetic and sexually liberating philosophy with which we can associate the name of Keynes.

Conclusion

In his *Treatise on Money*, Keynes defines money as 'that by delivery of which debt contracts and price contracts are *discharged*, and in the shape of which a store of general purchasing power is held' (Keynes 5: 3). Shortly after, he adds: 'by the mention of contracts and offers, we have introduced law or custom, by which they are enforceable; that is to say, we have introduced the State or the community' (ibid.: 4). Money is thus co-extensive with society, and 'like certain other essential elements in civilisation, is a far more ancient institution than we were taught to believe some few years ago' (ibid.: 11–12). Money has been an object of reflection for many great philosophers and scientists, as far back as Aristotle. Money cannot be analysed in isolation from one's vision, not only of the functioning of the economy but of the whole of social life, including its psychological components. Money is a fundamental element in Keynes's world, and we have shown that his vision of money is very closely linked to the Freudian conception of money.

The expression the 'Keynesian revolution' has not been usurped. Human humility can be associated with three names: Galileo, who said that the earth is not the centre of the universe; Darwin, who affirmed that his ancestor was a monkey; Freud, who submitted the reasoning reason to the unconscious. Keynes adds that the project of accumulation is vain and:

> the day is not far off when the economic problem will take the back seat where it belongs, and that the arena of the heart and head will be occupied, or reoccupied, by our real problems – the problems of life and of human relations, of creation and behaviour and religion.
> (Keynes 9: xviii)

The Keynesian theory of money is destructive, in two senses. First, it bases the desire for money on unconscious and infantile drives, and second, it negates the very principle of accumulation, which satisfied the Victorian bourgeois as well as Marxists – who consider bourgeois accumulation as a necessary state – and other socialists, 'Keynesians' included. Keynes's vision of the market is opposed to the Walrasian vision, based as it is on individual rationality and equilibrium. Not only are individuals sanguine because they are led by drives, not only is market equilibrium a delusion, but the market itself is a mob. If there is an economist for whom methodological individualism is an aberration, it is Keynes.

Do other economists talk psychology? Undoubtedly. Orthodox economists, for example, use the word 'confidence', out of which Arrow (1974) made a sort of ether meant to facilitate exchanges. Some even formalized this in a new microeconomics built around insurance concepts such as 'moral hazard' or 'adverse selection'. It is no exaggeration to say that the theory of incentives and the new industrial economics constitute attempts to model the psychological relations of confidence between employers and employees, principals and agents, merchants and customers. But this does not preclude the radical rejection of psychology by contemporary economics. Such behaviour can probably be accounted for, somewhat ironically, by the very concept of repression and guilt.

Keynes is one of the very few economists to have claimed openly and fully the importance of psychology, and particularly of Freudian psychoanalysis. He tackled the psychological dimension head on, often writing that it was the principal dimension of human and social problems, before the political and economic dimensions. He was probably influenced, among others, by the founder of the Cambridge school, his teacher Alfred Marshall, who said to his wife, Mary Paley, shortly before his death: 'If I had to live my life over again, I should have devoted it to Psychology. Economics has too little to do with ideals' (Groenewegen 1995: 729). But the Victorian Marshall probably never read Freud, and would surely have reacted strongly against the Freudian theses. Veblen, on the contrary, tended to use psychological analysis akin to Freud.[23] Veblen most probably influenced Keynes, even if he is never mentioned in the latter's work.[24] Others, like Pareto, also borrowed from psychology, but Keynes, taking advantage of the close relations between Bloomsbury and Freud, borrowed 'consciously and without complex' from the latter. Moreover, like his Bloomsbury friends, he developed some of his own Freudian-like ideas before he got to know Freud. This is why we can speak of a Freudo-Keynesian conception of money, of accumulation, and even of capitalism

Notes

The *Unpublished Writings of J. M Keynes* are © The Provost and Scholars of King's College, Cambridge, 1999. The Society of Authors as agents of the Strachey Trust have kindly granted us permission to quote unpublished letters from James Strachley and Lytton Strachley to J. M. Keynes.

We acknowledge grants from the Social Sciences and Humanities Research Council of Canada and from the Fonds pour la Formation des Chercheurs et l'Aide à la Recherche (FCAR, Québec).

We thank Hélène Jobin for her research assistance. We are grateful, for their comments on a previous version of this paper, to Brad Bateman, Bob Dimand, Crauford Goodwin, Ric Holt, Kari Polanyi-Levitt, Patrick Raines, John Smithin and Ted Winslow.

1. Volume numbers refer to the thirty volumes of *The Collected Writings of John Maynard Keynes* (Keynes 1971–89)
2. It is interesting to note here that the young Freud had translated some essays of John Stuart Mill.
3. Unless otherwise indicated, the emphases in quotations are in the original texts.
4. See Dostaler (1996).
5. The young Keynes was admitted to this father's discussions with his friends.
6. On this see Moggridge (1992: 59) and Skidelsky (1983: 264).
7. Unpublished until 1974 (Levy 1974: 111–20).
8. According to Quentin Bell, Woolf was very impressed by these books 'and it is possible that, if he had read Freud two years earlier, Virginia's medical history might have been different' (Bell 1976 [1972]: 19) James Strachey thought that Leonard should have forced Virginia to follow psychoanalytical therapy. Such was not the opinion of his wife Alix, who considered that the literary *oeuvre* of Virginia Woolf was fed by her phantasms and her madness: 'It may be preferable to be mad and be creative than to be treated by analysis and become ordinary' (Noble 1972: 116, quoted in Meisel and Kendrick 1985: 309).
9. James wrote to his brother Lytton, on 6 November 1920, that the Professor became 'fascinated, partly by her case, & partly by the effect of the actions & re-actions caused by his taking both of us at once. (He had in fact begun by thinking it a technical impossibility)' (Meisel and Kendrick 1985: 6). In the same letter, he describes Freud, whom he calls 'the Prof', as 'most affable and as an artistic performer dazzling' and the psychoanalytical session as 'an organic aesthetic whole'.
10. This is the origin of the correspondence collected in Meisel and Kendrick (1985).
11. The reference is to the archive's catalogue number.
12. James Strachey is one of the sexual partners whose name Keynes noted for the

years 1906, 1907 and 1908 (Keynes Papers, PP/20A, see also Moggridge 1992: 838–9). We can thus guess that Freud himself had a more intimate knowledge of Keynes's life than many others.
13 This might explain why Freud accepted James as a patient and charged him less than his usual fee.
14 The first volume had been printed in Germany rather than by Hogarth. A fifth volume was published much later, in 1950.

15   Nearly all famous men are disappointing or bores, or both. Freud was neither; he had an aura, not of fame, but of greatness. . . . There was something about him as of a half-extinct volcano, something sombre, suppressed, reserved. He gave me the feeling which only a very few people whom I have met gave me, a feeling of great gentleness, but behind the gentleness, great strength.

(Woolf 1967: 168–9)

To Virginia, he offered ceremoniously a narcissus. See also Virginia's more reserved judgment in Woolf 1977–8 5: 202). But she then started in earnest to read Freud and wrote, shortly before her suicide, that this reading enlarged the circumference of her ideas (2 December 1940).
16 On Freud, psychoanalysis and money, the reader can consult Borneman (1976), a collection of the seminal papers on the psychoanalytical theory of money, Reiss-Schimmel (1993), and Viderman (1992). Some ideas in this section were originally presented in Dostaler (1997) which compares Friedman and Keynes on money.
17 See, for example, Keynes (7: 219, 9: 248, 11: 235, 12: 763, 21: 71–2).
18 'For Marx it is the hoarder who is immoral and guilty . . . the capitalist is innocent' (Vidermann 1992: 41).
19 The standard edition of Freud translated '*massenpsychologie*' as 'group psychology'. Freud indicated to Ernest Jones that he would have preferred 'mass psychology'. But 'mob' seems nearer to the mark of what, in French, Le Bon, who inspired Freud, called *Psychologie des Foules* (1895).
20 On this see Maris (1995).
21 Concerning, in particular, the notion of collective unconscious.
22 'Enrichment, accumulation of wealth could be considered, in the order of general economy, as in free economy also, as a sort of equivalent of that antientropic force that is life itself' (Viderman 1992: 105).
23 See Schneider (1948).
24 But he is mentioned in Keynes's lists of readings.

References

Arrow, K. (1974) *The Limits of Organization*, New York: Norton.
Bell, Q. (1976 [1972]) *Virginia Woolf: A Biography*, vol. 2, *Mrs Woolf: 1912–1941*, St. Albans, Herts: Triad/Paladin.
Bonadei, R. (1994) 'John Maynard Keynes: Contexts and Methods', in A. Marzola and F. Silva (eds) *John Maynard Keynes: Language and Method*, Aldershot: Edward Elgar.
Bormans, C. (1997) 'De la 'vision' à la 'révolution' Keynésienne: l'hypothèse Freud', paper presented to the Journées d'étude sur la pensée Keynésienne, Amiens, Université de Picardie–Jules Verne, May.
Borneman, E. (ed.) (1976) *The Psychoanalysis of Money*, New York: Urizen.
Dostaler, G. (1996) 'The Formation of Keynes's Vision', *History of Economics Review* 25: 14–31.

—— (1997) 'Keynes and Friedman on Money', in A. J. Cohen, H. Hagemann and J. Smithin (eds) *Money, Financial Institutions and Macroeconomics*, Boston: Kluwer.

Ferenczi, S. (1914) 'The Ontogenesis of the Interest in Money', *Internationale Zeitschrift für ärtzliche Psychoanalyse* 2: 506–13, reprinted in Bornemann 1976.

—— (1916) 'Pecunia – olet', *Internationale Zeitschrift für ärztliche Psychonanalyse* 4: 327, reprinted in Bornemann 1976.

Freud, S. (1932 [1900]) *The Interpretation of Dreams*, London: Allen and Unwin.

—— (1908) 'Character and Anal Erotism', *Psychiatrisch–neurologische Wochenschrift* 9: 465–7, reprinted in Bornemann 1976.

—— (1955 [1921]) *Group Psychology and the Analysis of the Ego*, in the Standard Edition.

—— (1949 [1930]) *Civilization and its Discontents*, London: Hogarth Press and the Institute of Psychoanalysis.

—— (1953–74) *Standard Edition of the Complete Psychological Works of Sigmund Freud*, ed. J. Strachey, London: Hogarth Press and the Institute of Psychoanalysis, 24 vols.

Freud, S. and Bullitt, W. (1967) *Thomas Woodrow Wilson, Twenty-Eighth President of the United States: A Psychological Study*, Boston: Houghton Mifflin.

Groenewegen, P. (1995) *A Soaring Eagle: Alfred Marshall, 1842–1924*, Aldershot: Edward Elgar.

Harrod, R. F. (1951) *The Life of John Maynard Keynes*, London: Macmillan.

Jones, E. (1951 [1917]) 'The Theory of Symbolism', in *Papers on Psychoanalysis*, London: Bailliere, Tindall and Cox.

Keynes, J. M. (unpublished) *Keynes Papers*, King's College Library, Cambridge.

—— (1930) *A Treatise on Money*, 2 vols., London: Macmillan.

—— (1971–89), *The Collected Writings of John Maynard Keynes*, London: Macmillan for the Royal Economic Society, 30 vols.

Levy, P. L. (1974) *Lytton Strachey: The Really Interesting Question and Other Papers*, London: Capricorn.

Maris, B. (1995) 'Les figures du marché et le champ de l'économie des conventions', *Cahiers d'Économie Politique* 26: 183–209.

Marx, K. (1933) *Capital*, London: Dent.

Meisel, P. and Kendrick, W. (eds) (1985) *Bloomsbury/Freud: The Letters of James and Alix Strachey, 1924–25*, New York: Basic Books.

Mini, P. V. (1994) *John Maynard Keynes: A Study in the Psychology of Original Work*, London: Macmillan.

Moggridge, D. E. (1992) *Maynard Keynes: An Economist's Biography*, London: Routledge.

Noble, J. R. (ed.) (1972) *Recollections of Virginia Woolf*, London: Peter Owen.

Parsons, W. (1997) *Keynes and the Quest for a Moral Science: A Study of Economics and Alchemy*, Cheltenham: Edward Elgar.

Reiss-Schimmel, I. (1993) *La psychanalyse de l'argent*, Paris: Odile Jacob.

Schneider, L. (1948) *The Freudian Psychology and Veblen's Social Theory*, New York: King's Crown Press.

Skidelsky, R. (1983) *John Maynard Keynes*, vol. 1, *Hopes Betrayed: 1883–1920*, London: Macmillan.

—— (1992) *John Maynard Keynes*, vol. 2, *The Economist as Saviour: 1921–1937*, London: Macmillan.

Viderman, S. (1992) *De l'srgent: en psychanalyse et su-delà*, Paris: Presses universitaires de France.

Weber, M. (1958 [1904–5]) *The Protestant Ethic and the Spirit of Capitalism*, New York: Scribner.

Winslow, E. G. (1986) 'Keynes and Freud: Psychoanalysis and Keynes's Account of the 'Animal Spirits' of Capitalism', *Social Research* 53, 4: 549–78.

—— (1990) 'Bloomsbury, Freud, and the Vulgar Passions', *Social Research* 57, 4: 785–819.

—— (1992) 'Psychoanalysis and Keynes's Account of the Psychology of the Trade Cycle', in B. Gerrard and J. Hillard (eds) *The Philosophy and Economics of J. M. Keynes*, Aldershot: Edward Elgar, 212–30.

—— (1995) 'Uncertainty and Liquidity-Preference', in S. C. Dow and J. Hillard (eds) *Keynes, Knowledge and Uncertainty*, Aldershot: Edward Elgar.

Woolf, L. (1960) *Sowing: An Autobiography of the Years 1890 to 1904*, London: Hogarth Press.

—— (1967) *Downhill all the Way: An Autobiography of the Years 1919 to 1939*, New York: Harcourt Brace Jovanovich.

Woolf, V. (1977–84) *The Diary of Virginia Woolf*, ed. A. O. Bell and A. McNeillie, London: Hogarth Press, 5 vols.

13 The disappearance of Keynes's nascent theory of banking between the *Treatise* and the *General Theory*

Colin Rogers and T. K. Rymes

Introduction

In this paper we advance work which we have previously undertaken (Rymes 1998). We argue that if Keynes had rewritten his *General Theory*, he would have shown, first, that real classical theory was special in that it presumed automatic equilibration at full employment, and second, that classical monetary theory was special in that it had 'nominal anchors' determining nominal (and real) magnitudes.

In the *Treatise* Keynes argued it was not the existence of an exogenous nominal magnitude called money which determined the level of nominal magnitudes, but the policy of the monetary authority. By contrast, classical monetary theory can be interpreted as saying that, given some anchor, the level of nominal magnitudes would automatically be determined at full employment levels. Additionally, Patinkin (1965) demonstrated that, with real balance effects, the existence of a nominal anchor automatically enabled the determination of both full employment and the price level. Keynes's double-barrelled destruction of the two pillars of classical economics rested on his finding that nominal exogenous anchors no longer existed in a modern banking system. In such a context, automaticity without discretion was empty of content.

In the *Treatise*, the pure theory of banking applies to a world in which the anchor provided by a nominal exogenous 'money' had vanished. In the *General Theory*, Keynes obscured this point because he wished to establish his multiple real equilibria story. Nevertheless, in his *General Theory*, it was monetary policy which helped to determine real magnitudes and the long-run non-neutrality of money. Unfortunately the third volume, which might have been entitled the *General Theory of Real and Nominal Magnitudes*, was never written.[1] The key is Keynes's realization that monetary theory had progressed from a world where real and nominal anchors existed, to a world where anchors had been replaced by the banking system, which itself rested on the bedrock of discretionary monetary policy.

The format of the chapter is as follows. The first section outlines some elements of modern banking theory. Then we examine Keynes's rejection of this banking theory, and outline his claim that bank rate remains effective irrespective of reserve ratios, coefficients of expansion, and the like. The next two sections deal with the characteristics of a Keynesian banking system and the determination of nominal magnitudes in such a system. Finally we consider the disappearance of Keynes's banking theory between the *Treatise* and the *General Theory* and conclude with some conjectures about the implications of Keynes's ideas for monetary theory.

Banking theory and the effectiveness of the bank rate

There is a long history of debate in literature on the effectiveness of bank rate as a constraint on the expansion of the banking system. One line of argument was that, to be effective, the bank rate would have to exceed the banks' loan rate by a margin, dependent on the reserve ratio, so as to make borrowing reserves from the central bank unprofitable for the commercial banks.

Assume a single commercial bank borrows reserves from the central bank to expand its overdrafts to borrowers. The increase in its overdrafts L is given by: $L = \lambda L + \lambda r L = R_B$, where λ is the 'coefficient of reflux' or the fraction of deposits created by the overdraft (loan) which the bank retains, r is the desired reserve to deposit ratio, and R_B are the borrowed reserves. The bank's 'coefficient of expansion' is then simply $L/R_B = 1/[1- \lambda(1 - r)]$. If $\lambda = 0$, the zero reflux case, the coefficient of expansion of a single bank is unity. Similarly, if $\lambda = 1$ we have the entire banking system (or the case of the central bank and a monopoly bank) and the coefficient of expansion is $1/r$. Note also that if $r = 1$ the coefficient of expansion is again unity, while if $r = 0$ the coefficient of expansion becomes very large.[2]

If $\lambda = 0$ the commercial bank's overdrafts increase one for one with its borrowing from the central bank ($L/R_B = 1$) but provided that the interest rate charged by the central bank exceeds the overdraft rate it will not be profitable for the commercial bank to borrow reserves to expand its overdrafts. However, if $\lambda = 1$, the case of the entire banking system or a monopoly bank, then $L/R = 1/r$ and it would appear that the bank rate would have to be $1/r$ times the overdraft rate to make borrowing from the central bank unprofitable. If i_{Br} is the bank rate, and i_0 the overdraft rate, the profits made by the bank would be $\pi = i_0 - i_{Br}R_B$ which, in the case of a monopoly bank, reduces to $\pi = i_0 (R_B/r) - i_{Br}R_B = (i_0/r - i_{Br})R_B$. So long as $(i_0/r > i_{Br})$ it would appear be profitable for the monopoly bank (or the banking system as a whole) to borrow from the central bank to expand its overdrafts (loans).

A similar argument is found in the modern literature in the form of the liquidity management model for banks. Assume a system in which a central bank acts as a clearing house for a group of competitive banks. The central bank charges a penalty rate on negative clearings but does not pay interest on positive clearings or reserves. The basic liquidity management model

(Baltensperger 1980) suggests that the liquidity costs of a bank are given by:

$$C = iR + \rho \int_{R}^{0} (X - R) f(X) \, dX \qquad (1)$$

where R is the value of the positive clearings or reserves held by a commercial bank with the central bank on which no interest is paid, $f(X)$ is the stochastic normal distribution of the bank's negative clearing balances, X, with the central bank and ρ is the penalty rate imposed by the central bank when negative entries exceed the bank's reserves, R. A system with $R > 0$ can be thought of as a fractional reserve system in which R may be a legal requirement. Thus, the higher a bank's positive clearings the more earnings it foregoes, at the opportunity cost rate i (called hereafter the overnight rate), but the less it experiences negative clearings and the need to pay a penalty rate to the central bank. Minimizing liquidity costs with respect to R yields:

$$i = \rho_R \int_{R}^{\infty} f(X) \, dX = 0 \qquad (2)$$

The assumption of a normal distribution implies $\int_{0}^{\infty} f(X) \, dX = 1/2$ and so the infamous 'two for one' rule comes into play, namely $\rho = 2i$.

Thus, if the penalty rate is twice the overnight rate, the commercial bank would be content with its portfolio position if R were equal to zero. If $\rho > 2i$, then the bank would want to hold positive reserves, would be selling off loans or overdrafts and running up deposits, whereas if $\rho < 2i$, it would want to be in a negative settlement balance position with the central bank, and running an opposite portfolio policy.

Imagine a competitive bank whose overdraft (loan) and deposit policies, its portfolio policy, are such that it expects to be in a zero net clearings position with the central bank. It considers expanding its overdrafts by $1 to earn i. Marginally, it expects all states with positive settlement balances to be down by $1, but, since it receives no interest on positive settlement balances, it loses no interest and the expected loss is zero. However, it expects all states with negative settlement balances to be up by $1, so that its expected costs are $1/2\rho$, where ρ is the penalty rate the central bank charges on all negative clearing balances. Thus, if $\rho = 2i$, the marginal gain equals the marginal loss and the profit maximizing (liquidity cost minimizing) portfolio is the current balance in overdrafts and deposits. Similarly, should the bank see its deposits expand by $1 and should i be the rate paid on deposits, then a bank loses i on the marginal deposits, gains nothing from the fact that all states of nature which involve the bank experiencing positive settlement balances which are up by $, but does gain from the fact all negative settlement balances would be down by $1, saving on the penalty charged by the central bank. To summarize, preventing banks from borrowing from the central bank at bank rate would seem to depend, both theoretically and empirically, upon the penalty rate imposed by the commercial bank being substantially in excess of the commercial bank's opportunity cost of funds.[3]

Keynes on the effectiveness of the bank rate

The ideas outlined in the previous section were examined by Keynes and found to be theoretically wanting. In short, the 'two for one' rule is a fallacy. It repeats an invalid argument that Keynes brilliantly exposed in his discussion on banking in his *Treatise on Money*.

In his emancipation from the quantity theory of money, Keynes can be interpreted as developing an argument that the only anchor for nominal magnitudes in a monetary economy is the policy of the central bank. There is no base, exogenous or endogenous, to nominal magnitudes in the economy to determine nominal magnitudes.

In his *Treatise on Money*, Keynes developed the beginnings of what we call the Keynesian theory of banking. Among the many problems Keynes addressed was the question of how effective bank rate was if, in fact, banks could profitably borrow reserves from the central bank. This is the same question addressed by the 'coefficient of expansion' analysis of Lawrence and Phillips, and the 'two for one' rule. The argument Keynes sought to put to rest was that by Lawrence, for example, who argued there was 'some sanction in authority for the supposition that a bank may expand its loans by several times the amount of the advance which it receives from its own reserve bank' (Lawrence 1928: 329), and:

> If a bank can extend multiple loans on the basis of a given advance from the central bank then the rate that the latter charges within ordinary limits is a man of straw so far as the attempts to control credit is concerned.
>
> (Lawrence 1928: 362–3)

Also, assuming a legal reserve requirement of, for example, 10 per cent behind deposits for all banks, 'when they all expand equally, the central bank would, theoretically, have to charge a discount rate equal to ten times the rate charged by banks to their own clients' (ibid.: 368).

These claims by Lawrence reflect the analysis outlined in the previous section for the case where $\lambda = 1$ so that the coefficient of expansion equals $1/r$, unless r, the reserve ratio, is 1. For the banking system as a whole, where the reflux is complete, if r were 10 per cent the central bank would have to impose a penalty rate of ten times the overnight rate on the commercial banks who are borrowing reserves to make overdrafts. Similarly, if the Baltensperger story were adjusted for significantly-sized banks, the bank, at a zero reserve position, would expect to see its positive settlement balance fall by less and its negative settlement balances rise by less than the overdraft amount. The formula for the penalty rate holding the portfolio policy of the bank unchanged would be $2r/(1-\lambda) = \rho$ so that if $0 < \lambda < 1$, the penalty rate would have to be more than twice the overnight rate.

It seems that when the number of banks is large, any one bank's coefficient of expansion would be small. However, when the number of banks is small, it will become profitable for the banks to borrow from the central bank and the coefficient of expansion will become large. There is no problem in the case of a large number of banks because that makes the reflux parameter small. At the limit a small competitive bank for which the reflux ratio is zero would have a coefficient of expansion of 1, so that if bank rate were only marginally higher than the overnight rate, it would be unprofitable for a bank to borrow from the central bank. Bank rate is then effective. But in the case of a few large banks or a closed banking system as a whole, the Lawrence argument comes into play, particularly if the banks move in step. As Keynes wrote, 'Moreover, if all the banks are acting in step in response to the same stimulus, the net result is as great as in the case of a single bank' (Keynes 6: 227).

Keynes offered two arguments against the Lawrence analysis. First, he argued that banks would not borrow from the central bank but would find it more profitable to 'steal away the reserve balances of other member banks then to borrow itself from the Reserve Bank'. 'Steal' is Keynes's word for the fact that the banks would offer higher deposit rates, forcing other banks into negative positions with the central bank.

Second, and more significantly, we would argue that Keynes supplied the *coup de grace* to the whole question when he concluded:

> the central bank would still have weapons at its disposal in the shape of open-market policy – so long as it possesses suitable ammunition. For if the member banks start borrowing from it above the market rate, *the central bank can make a tiresome profit at their expense by selling all its open-market assets at the market rate, and so forcing the member banks to borrow back from it the equivalent of these at above the market rate*. Thus the assumption that the official rate is effective if it is in touch with the market rate need not be abated.
>
> (Keynes 6: 224, emphasis added)

What is so extraordinary about this passage is that, fully understood, which we have no doubt Keynes did (the word tiresome is very illustrative), coefficients of expansion or reserve ratios do not matter for monetary control. Any combination of them, which might supposedly make bank rate ineffective, is no longer of any concern. The required reserve ratio could be zero and Keynes's argument still holds, namely, that bank rate could be set marginally above the bank's loan rate. If $\lambda = 1$ and $r = 0$, the coefficient of expansion for any individual bank (in this case each bank acting as if it were the banking systems with no legal reserve requirement) would be infinitely great. It appears that bank rate would then be a thing of straw, as Lawrence argued. Keynes saw that the whole argument is otiose. Individual banks could borrow reserves at bank rate until they were 'blue in the face'. It would be necessary only for the central bank to counter automatically each dollar borrowed by the banks, by means of open-market sales.

If one defines bank rate as the instrument of monetary policy, it remains effective regardless of the legally-required reserve ratio and the reflux experience of individual banks. It remains effective even if the legally-required reserve ratio is zero and a pure credit system is in operation. In this respect, Keynes also pointed out in his *Treatise* that increasingly transactions were exercised not just through deposits but by means of overdraft facilities. He wrote for the UK:

> In the case of large and well-organized firms, the tendency is for their cash accounts to tend on the average (reckoning cash deposits plus and overdrafts minus) towards zero, or, at any rate a very low figure, partly by the use of the overdraft and partly by investing temporary surplus balances in bills or in loans to the money market. If the minimum balances, maintained in pursuit of an agreement for the remuneration of the bank, be subtracted, the average cash discounts of big business (reckoned as above) bear a very small promotion to the volume of the cheques passing through the accounts. But private individuals also are making an ever-increasing use of overdraft facilities.
> (Keynes 5: 37)

Keynes went on to argue that it was the commitment to overdrafts, not necessarily just exercised overdrafts, which were the variable of concern. Things have not changed much since. When Keynes allowed for these overdraft privileges in 1930, there was, as now, 'no statistical record whatever' (Keynes 5: 37).

Keynes's banking system

What matters for our purpose is that the Keynesian monetary system is one in which banks provide individuals and firms with intertemporal transaction services, and that, on balance, the values of overdrafts (loans) and deposits net out for all. For the representative transactor the net position with his or her bank will be zero. Similarly for the representative bank, it will be carrying neither positive nor negative reserves with the central bank, because as Keynes argued, the control of the central bank over the total amounts of overdrafts and deposits in the system is a function of the effectiveness of bank rate, not a function of cash reserve ratios and the like. Thus, there is a pure Keynesian system with no anchor, no positive base money on which the system rests. The total level of overdrafts and deposits, the indication of the total flow of the intertemporal transaction services provided by the banks, will be regulated not by the non-existent base money but by the bank rate policy of the central bank.

Of course this is a highly stylised version of the Keynesian banking system, but it captures the essence of a position which can be derived from his *Treatise*. As we have already indicated, the practical world he was concerned with would have positive reserves, bank notes would be part of the monetary base issued by central banks, there would be problems associated with the foreign balances and so forth. The pure system we have unearthed in Keynes seems to us to represent the best of what we call Keynesian banking theory. The bank rate becomes the price of the services of liquidity which the central bank is providing. When the central bank wishes to restrict the flow of liquidity services, it raises bank rate and may reinforce with drawdowns or open market policies. Banks respond by raising their overdraft rates relative to deposit rates and the price of banking services rises. When it wishes to expand the flow of liquidity services, the central bank lowers bank rate. The spread of overdraft and deposit rates charged by the banks narrows, and the relative price of liquidity services provided by the central bank and the bank falls. This is why central banks always have real effects.

It is now well known that effective monetary policy can be exercised without any reserve base, which is so much of a 'fifth wheel on the coach' of monetary control (Goodhart 1987). Modern monetary systems are rapidly approaching Keynes's conception of a banking system. Iindeed, one can argue that they are just logical extensions of the ideas set out in his *Treatise*.

In a Keynesian banking equilibrium, no exogenous entity called money is required. All that is required is a set of contractual relationships between the central bank and the commercial banks, and between the latter and the non-bank agents using the banks for the execution of intertemporal transactions. The positive settlement balances, which those banks who hold them will be attempting to reduce, are just matched by those who hold negative settlement balance and who will also be attempting to eliminate them. Stochastically it would be a fluke, but in a deterministic model, each bank would be running its overdrafts and deposits policies so that it was holding a zero position with the central bank. No high-powered or *fiat* money would be required. Similarly, some private agents might find that their debits and credits were currently running up, their positions with the banks showing as increases in deposits or declines in overdrafts. Others would experience deficits, their overdrafts would rise and their deposits fall. One might be tempted to call deposits money but what, as Keynes asked, does one call the overdrafts (Keynes 5: 36)? Both are just ways in which private agents are financing discontinuities in intertemporal transactions by employing the services supplied by the banks.

It is not just that 'money' is endogenous. The crux is that the banking system has evolved to the point where no exogenous 'money' is required to determine nominal magnitudes. All one observes is the debits and credits (overdrafts and deposits) offered by the banks as they supply intertemporal transaction services to firms and households. Similarly, the banks are using the intertemporal transaction services offered by the central bank. One observes positive and negative settlement balances. No deposit or positive settlement balance counts as money, any more or any less than does an overdraft or a negative settlement balance. No reserves exist. There is no base.

Indeterminate nominal magnitudes

This modern system is characterized by potential indeterminacy with respect to the level of nominal magnitudes (including a CPI). Pinning down the level of nominal magnitudes is the responsibility of the central bank. Should the bank believe that there is upward pressure on nominal magnitudes, it raises bank rate and enforces it by operations which put the banks as a whole into a negative settlement balance position. Endeavouring to eliminate such negative settlement balances, the banks will in general behave so that interest rates on deposits and overdrafts will be higher, leading non-bank agents to attempt to save more and to accumulate less. There is nothing the commercial banks can do to eliminate their negative settlement balances with the central bank until the central bank acts to restore their accounts.

It is the central bank which finally eliminates the negative settlement balances the banks tried vainly to eliminate. Before the central bank acts to eliminate the asymmetry, the commercial banks constrain firms and households to take surplus positions in the hope that they will be then in a similar positive position, and able to correct their negative settlement balance positions with the central bank. As the direct clearers seek to contract, so do overdrafts and deposits, as well as total nominal and real expenditures in the economy. There is no limit to the reduction in nominal magnitudes, as in Keynes's famous banana plantation parable. Should the central bank, for example the Bank of Canada, initiate expansionary monetary policy by redepositing government accounts with the banks, the banks would endeavour to escape the costs of holding positive settlement balances with the Bank of Canada by trying to expand overdrafts and loans. Rates of interest on overdrafts and deposits would be lower, expenditures would be greater and overdrafts and deposits higher. There is also no upper limit to nominal magnitudes, until the central bank reverses the step by which it imposed an asymmetry onto the system.

The essence of the banana plantation parable in Keynes's *Treatise* is that there is an equilibrium in which investment is equal to savings and the price level is unchanging. There is a strength and weakness to Keynes's argument. An increase in savings, an increase in the attempt on the part of consumers to save, appears as a reduction in the demand for bananas, and as an increase in the demand for bank deposits or a reduction in overdrafts. If there is not a corresponding increase on the part of the entrepreneurs to add to the productive capacity of the plantations (bananas, like Marshall's fish, are perishable) and to give up deposits or to incur overdrafts, the price of bananas should fall and the build-up of deposits (or the run-down of overdrafts) by consumers will be matched exactly by a decline in the deposits (or an increase in overdrafts) of the entrepreneurs. As Keynes says:

> Thus the increased saving has not increased in the least the aggregate wealth of the community; it has simply caused a transfer of wealth from the pockets of the entrepreneurs into the pockets of the general public. The savings of the consumers will be required, either directly or through the intermediary of the banking system, to make good the losses of the entrepreneurs.
>
> (Keynes 5: 159)

The entrepreneurs will then cut back on banana harvesting and lay off hands in an attempt to rebuild their depleted deposits or decrease their unwarranted accumulation of overdrafts. Wages fall. The entrepreneurs, in attempting to rebuild their deposits or reduce their overdrafts, can only be successful, however, in running down the deposits of consumers (with some now unemployed, which tends to damp the savings) or running up unwarranted overdrafts. Prices fall again and the process generates a Wicksellian cumulative deflation. So long as bank deposits and overdrafts fall, the process has no limit. There is, as in Wicksell's pure credit economy, no reason for the process to stop. Nor is there in Keynes. In Wicksell the point is theoretical; in Keynes, we would argue, the point is both theoretical and immediately practical. This is true not only, to a limited extent, in Keynes's time, but in our world, the world which Keynes's analysis foreshadows. There is also a weakness in Keynes's analysis. If there is no nominal anchor in the banana plantation parable, the price level is arbitrary. Variations in investment and saving may start it moving, but it is the essential indeterminacy in its level which matters.

If there were a monetary base in the banana plantation, such as notes issued by a monetary authority, then as overdrafts, deposits, prices and wages contracted, there would come a point where the real value of the notes put a limit to the cumulative deflation. Consider the process as involving lower and lower levels of wages and prices. As the banks came to hold larger and larger balances of notes relative to their deposits and overdrafts, they would lower rates of interest on overdrafts and the Wicksellian process would come to an end as money rates fell below real rates. The indeterminacy of the price level does not hold. The same analysis would hold for reserves held by the banks with the monetary authorities (this is sometimes referred to as the 'Keynes effect'). If banks held reserves with the monetary authority, the same argument could be made (assuming the authority does not contract the reserve base of the banks). Indeed, from Keynes's *Tract*, one sees, in the case where falling prices could be associated with falling money deposits and overdrafts but rising real reserves, that the appropriate action of the authorities is to increase, not to contract, nominal reserves.

In the case of falling money wages and prices, all interest rates would adjust to lower levels such that real interest rates would be unchanged. The analysis for *fiat* money can be augmented to include positive or negative rates of change in the nominal money supply such that prices might be steadily rising or steadily falling. *Ceteris paribus*, steadily rising prices, as compared with zero inflation, cause the excess demand for money to be negative, and a one-off overall increase in prices such that agents will hold smaller real stocks of fiat money in equilibrium. Keynes discussed this case in the *Tract on Monetary Reform*, so the argument that real *fiat* money balances would vary inversely with the rate of inflation was known to him. Thus, if prices were falling, the excess demand for real money balances would be positive and there would be an one-off fall in the price level such that real *fiat* money balances would be higher. If the one-off fall in the price level caused the expected rate of deflation to be greater, then the stability of the demand for real money balances would be in question. If the demand for real *fiat* money balances were globally stable, the rate of change of prices would stabilize at that dictated by the central bank and the level of prices would be such that full monetary equilibrium would apply.

In modern central banking, the central bank sets a bank rate, the rate it charges on negative settlement balances, and a lower rate, say bank rate minus fifty basis points, which it pays on positive settlement balances. The spread will be greater than that set by a clearing house. A commercial bank which experiences a negative settlement balance will be able to finance it in-house since, unless the central bank takes action, the negative settlement balance must be matched by positive settlement balances for the other banks. However if the central bank puts the banking system as a whole into negative settlement balances, they must end up 'in the bank'. Thus when the central bank raises its bands, it signals to all the banks that if overnight rates do not increase, it will put the banking system into negative settlement balances. The enforcement threat will be sufficient to see a rise in overnight rates. Overnight rates are thus determined by the central bank.

Without banknotes, a banking equilibrium which involves zero nominal anchors means that price levels are indeterminate without central bank activity. This is the point now formally modelled in the modern literature in terms of a central bank reaction function which pins down the nominal price level or inflation rate (McCallum 1981, Edey 1989, 1990).

Conclusion

If we move the banana plantation parable and banking theory of the *Treatise* to the *General Theory*, what would we have? We would still have the fundamental idea that the economic system would equilibrate at levels of output involving less than full employment. However, rather than having the rate of interest determined by the demand and supply of some given stock of money, it would be much clearer that the central bank played a role in determining 'the' rate of interest. However, the possibility of falling or lower money wages and prices performing an equilibrating role, the so-called Keynes effect, extended to the Pigou effect, would have played an even weaker role. In the limit of the non-existent anchor, it would have played no role at all. It would be clear that, even at full employment, it would be necessary for the central bank to determine nominal and real magnitudes. Should there be a shortfall in aggregate demand, for the reasons Keynes set out in the banana plantation parable, the central bank would have to act to prevent a shortfall in real and nominal magnitudes. In some sense, the argument would be novel in the sense that a central bank would be charged with ensuring the maintenance of real and not just nominal magnitudes. We would still have the argument that there was a non-cyclical less than full employment equilibrium. We would have avoided the argument that the central bank cannot affect real magnitudes but should direct itself to nominal magnitudes only. There would be no optimum money supply literature, and so forth.

What would have been the price? We think that Keynes would have had to reformulate his theory of the rate of interest with greater care. In the *General Theory*, a rate of interest comes into existence even when in Keynes's sense there is a base or *fiat* money which earns no explicit pecuniary rate of interest whatsoever. If there is no money which earns only a liquidity premium, there is no reason for Keynes to ask why would anybody hold non-interest-bearing money. It would not be the money *per se* but rather the fact that the central bank set higher rates on negative balances than on positive settlement balances. Keynes would have had to deal with the argument that it is the policy of the central bank, the spread the central bank sets, the difference between such rates, which constitute the liquidity premia.

However, if the central bank sets bank rate and a lower rate on positive settlement balances, so that the spread is fixed at (say) fifty basis points, then the idea of the central bank's spread determining just the liquidity premiums appears weak indeed. When the central bank raises the bank rate, it also raises the rate it pays on positive settlement balance. These rates indicated to the banks that an unchanging portfolio policy invites higher penalties on negative settlements balance and higher returns on positive settlement balance, which will lead the banks to tilt their portfolio policy away from overdrafts toward deposits.

The banks are attempting to constrain the general public to shift their portfolio policies towards savings away from investment. If the central bank lowers the bank rate, it runs the risk that with a fixed spread, the rate it pays on positive settlement balances will become zero. It could be argued that the house would still pay some positive rate on positive settlement balances, and it could continue to be argued that the spread is the price of liquidity so that the central bank is attempting to encourage the system to expand by lowering the spreads, lowering the price of liquidity, and increasing the supply of liquidity services provided by the central bank and indirectly the commercial banks. Thus, it is clear that the spread may stand for the 'price' of the supply of liquidity of the central bank, but it should always be remembered that the central bank can change the spread.

This is a further way the central bank can operate on the relative price of transaction services it supplies to the general public through the commercial banks. When the central bank increases the spread, the price of banking services rises for the general public holding overdrafts, while it also rises for those holding deposits. What has to be examined is how the rise in the price of banking services affects the composition and volume of output of the transaction and intermediate services provided by the banks.

If this conjecture is correct, and if Keynes had incorporated fully his thoughts on banking in the *Treatise* into the *General Theory*, he would have had a theory of how banking affected not only the level of output but also the growth rate of the economy. If, however, his banking theory had developed in the direction to which we suggest it leads, it would mean that in determining the real rate of interest, not only would his theory of liquidity preference have still prevailed in the sense that the central bank and the commercial banks provide liquidity services, but the real rate of growth of the economy, as affected by the transaction and intermediate services provided by the central bank and commercial banks, would have to be worked out as well. This was perhaps too tall an order for the 1930s, but think of what we would have experienced. In the negative sense, we would have been spared the doctrine that money has no real effects simply because nominal anchors had vanished in the *Treatise*, and we would have progressed with working out how the level and growth of banking output, partly determined by the central bank, affects the real rate of interest.

Notes

We would like to record special indebtedness to Jong Bibow whose papers, particularly on the loanable funds fallacy, are most insightful.

1 For some attempts see Harcourt and Riach (1997).
2 See Lawrence (1928) and Phillips (1924).
3 For an illustration of the influence of the 'two for one' rule on the actual implementation of Canadian monetary policy with respect to paper clearings, see Clinton (1997).

References

Baltensberger, A. (1980) 'Alternative Approaches to the Theory of the Banking Firm', *Journal of Monetary Economics* 6: 1–37.

Clinton, K. (1997) 'Implementation of Monetary Policy in a Regime with Zero Reserve Requirements', Bank of Canada Working Paper 97-8.

Edey, M. (1989) 'Monetary Policy Instruments: A Theoretical Analysis', in *Studies in Money and Credit*, Reserve Bank of Australia.

—— (1990) 'Operating Objectives for Monetary Policy', Research Discussion Paper 9007, Reserve Bank of Australia.

Goodhart, C. A. E.(1987) 'Monetary Base', in the *New Palgrave*, London: Macmillan.

Keynes, J. M. (1930) *A Treatise on Money* (2 vols.) London: Macmillan.

—— (1936) *The General Theory of Employment, Interest and Money*, London: Macmillan.

—— (1971–89), *The Collected Writings of John Maynard Keynes*, London: Macmillan, 30 vols.

Lawrence, J. S. (1928) *Stabilization of Prices: A Critical Study of the Various Plans Proposed for Stabilization*, New York: Macmillan.

McCallum, B. T. (1981) 'PriceLevel Determinacy with an Interest Rate Policy Rule and Rational Expectations', *Journal of Monetary Economics* 8: 319–29.

Patinkin, D. (1965) *Money, Interest and Prices: An Integration of Monetary and Value Theory*, 2nd edn, New York: Harper and Row.

Phillips, C. A. (1924) *Bank Credit*, London: Macmillan.

Rogers, C. and Rymes, T. K. (1997) 'Keynes's Monetary Theory of Value and Modern Banking', in G. C. Harcourt and P. A. Riach (eds) *The Second Edition of the General Theory*, London: Routledge.

Rymes, T. K. (1998) 'Keynes and Anchorless Banking', *Journal of the History of Economic Thought* 20, 1: 71–82.

Index

Abraham, K. 239
account, unit of 12–3
accounting services 114
Adler, B. E. 78
Aglietta, M. 212
Alchian, A. A. 74
analysis, economic 2–3; real and monetary 2–3
Andrewes, A. 69
Angell 38
arbitrage 149–50
Aristotle 10, 157–73, 251
Arrow 35, 76
Arthur, C. 191
Asimakopulos, A. 132
Austrian school 4
Axilrod, S. H. 91

Bagehot, W. 90–2, 98
Bailey, M. J. 75
Bailly, J. L. 108
balance of payments *see* budget, fiscal policy
bank: creation of money by 19, 28, 51–2, 55, 79, 85, 88, 101, 117; creditworthiness of 108, 145–8; provision of credit by 103, 112, 134–5; rate 12, 258–62
Bank of England 38; Monetary Policy Committee 38
banking: Keynes and effectiveness of bank rate 260–3; Keynes's banking system 262–4; theory and effectiveness of bank rate 11, 258–60
banks, role of 8
banks, state central 7, 12, 38, 54–9, 69–70, 79, 89–92, 111, 118, 140, 262–4
Banking Law Journal 13

Barbon 28
barter: barter-exchange theory 9, 72–3, 76, 84, 113; barter systems 3–4, 20–1, 24–5, 43, 69, 141–2, 157, 217–18
base money 6
Baxter, W. T. 35
Begg, D. 34
Bell, C. 237
Bell, S. 118, 120
Bell, Q. 253
Betz, E. 8
Beveridge, W. 208
Bibow, J. 268
bill of exchange 28
Bloomfield, A. I. 38
Bloomsbury group 237–41
Bogaert, R. 87
Bonar 165
bonds, government 60, 92, 118–19, 133
Bonnadei, R. 237
Bormans, C. 237
Borneman, E. 242, 254
Boulding, K. 61
Boyer-Xambeu, M. T. 18, 22, 28
Bretton Woods 151, 203, 205–7, 210–12, 214
Breuer 238
Brill, A. A. 241
British Institute of Management (BIM) 209
Bryan, W. J. 36
budget, balancing of 8, 10, 58–68
bullion 73
Bullitt, W. 240
Bushaw, D. W. 126

Campbell, M. 190

Cannan, E. 165–6
Capital (Marx) 178
Carling, A. 176, 182, 190–1
Carruthers, B. G. 30, 37–8
cashless society 1
Cencini, A. 129, 136–7
Chantraine, H. 87
Character and Anal Eroticism (Freud) 242
chartalist approach 6, 7, 21, 26, 28–30, 47–59
Chick, V. 9, 117–8, 128, 132, 137
Child is Being Beaten, A 239
circuit theory of money 8–9, 10, 101–20, 130–2
Civilisation and its Discontents 251
Clark, S. R. L. 172
classical economics 72–4
Clinton, K. 268
Clower, R. W. 5, 22, 113–14, 126
Coase, R. H. 141
coinage 26, 28, 42, 44–7, 144–6
Committee on Industrial Productivity 209
commodity market 94; *see also* market
commodity theory of money 11, 174–90, 194–211
consumer spending 127
Contribution to the Critique of Political Economy (Marx) 172, 178
conversion rate 50
convertibility 145–6; *see also* gold
Cook, R. M. 46, 64
Costelloe, K. 239
Cowen, T. 5, 35
Crawford, M. 64
credit: banks 87; -based systems, drawbacks of, 6; control 3; economy 6, 105–7; money 26, 202; rationing 78; theory 80–9, 101–20
Cripps, S. 209
curency crises 3
Currency and Credit (Hawtrey) 34
cycles, economic 2–3, 8, 95–6

Dalton, G. B. 43, 69
Dalton, H. 209
Dalziel, P. 117
Darwin, C. 252
Dasgupta 35, 37
Davies, G. 26, 36, 47, 103, 106
De Cecco, M. 38
De Partibus Animalium (Aristotle) 160–1

Debreu, G. 74, 76
debts, creation of 8–9, 44, 57, 82; role of 93, 101–3
deficits *see* budget
deflation 62
Deleplace, G. 8
demand curve 124
Demsetz, H. 71, 74
Depression, Great 2, 206
dereguation 5
devalation 96, 206–7
Dickson 30
Dodd, N. 22, 24
Doge of Venice 139–40
Dornbusch, R. 34
Dostaler, G. 1, 11, 254
Douglas, M. 30, 38
Dow, S. C. 4, 6, 127, 135–7
Dowd, K. 9, 10–11, 155–6
Durkheim, E. 7, 36

Economic Consequences of the Peace 236, 240
Economic Possibilities for our Grandchildren 244
Edey, M. 266
Edgeworth 18
effective demand 9, 124–37; *see also* Post Keynesian theory
Einstein 246
Einzig, P. 36, 102
Einaudi, L. 28
Elizabeth and Essex 236
Elson, D. 193
Eminent Victorians 236, 240
employer of last resort 8, 62
Employment Policy, white paper on (1944) 208
endogeneity *see* money
Epstein, R. A. 75
equilibrium theory 16–17, 32, 74, 263
ethics: and economics 169–72
Ethics (Aristotle) 159, 164, 167, 171–2
euro (currency) 3
European Central Bank 38
exchange: of goods 1-2, 20–6 (*see also* barter); rates 152; ratios 24
exogeneity *see* money

fairs *see* markets
Ferenczi, S. 235, 242–4
financial institutions *see* banks
financial struments 148; *see also* bonds
Finley, M. L. 169

fiscal policy 59–63; *see also* taxes
Fischer, S. 34
Fisher, I. 74
Fitzgibbons, A. 172
Fleetwood, S. 10–11, 190, 212–13
Florence, A. S. 239
Ford, H. 213
Freeman, D. B. 103
Friedman, M. 3, 76, 254
Freud, S. 11, 235–7, 239–40, 242–3, 245, 251–4; Freudian theory 238, 245, 247, 249–51, 253
Freudo-Keynsian conception of money 11, 241–4
Fry, R. 237
functional finance approach 8
Furness, W. H. 63
Full Employment in a Free Society 208

Galileo 252
Gambetta 37
Ganssman, H. 29, 194, 211, 215
General Theory (Keynes) 2, 9, 12, 64, 117, 126, 235, 247–50, 257–68
Genovese, F. C. 98
German school 25
Giddens, A. 38
Glasner, D. 156
Gnos, C 109
gold 6, 48, 50–1, 92, 142–50, 187; anchor 150; as embodiment of wealth 1, 142; standard 49, 148–50, 206–7 (*see also* Bretton Woods); *see also* coinage
Goldsmith, R. W. 26–7, 36
Goodhart, C. A. E. 32, 50, 64, 98, 141, 263
Gooding, K. 212
Gordon, W. 62
Grant, D. 237, 244
Graziani, A. 8, 104, 114, 127, 129–32
Greenfield, R. L. 5
Greenspan, A. 248
Grierson, P. 25, 27, 35–6, 63
Groenewegen, P. 252
Gurley, J. G. 114
Guttman, R. 36

Hahn, F. H. 16, 21, 35–6, 76, 114
Harcourt 268
Hart, K 22, 37
Harrod, R. F. 244
Harvey, P. 62
Hawtrey, R. 34, 83, 85, 90–1, 98

Hayek, F. A. von 3, 113–14
Hecksher 35
Hegel, G.W. F. 197, 212
Heinsohn, G. 8, 35, 64, 67, 69, 101–2, 106
Hermes 248–9
Hicks, J. R. 3, 6, 18, 20–1, 23–4, 29–30, 35, 80, 131, 135, 137
Hilferdine, R. 214
History of Economic Analysis 2
Hogarth Press 254
Hoover, K. D. 4–5, 20, 24–5, 32
horizontalist model 9, 116–17
housing/house purchase 135–6
Howells, P. G. A. 127, 135
Hudson, M. 63
Hume, D. 35
Humphrey, T. M. 98

Ilyenkov, E. 190
inflation 76, 95–6; *see also* cycle, business; deflation
Ingham, G. 3, 4, 7, 16–17, 20, 22, 24, 27–8, 33–5, 37–8, 193
Innes, A. M. 13, 44, 46–7, 64, 101, 106
Institute of Industrial Administration 209
Institute of Personnel Management 209
Interpretation of Dreams 239
interest 9, 44, 67–97, 158; rate of 4, 12, 60–1, 110, 117, 119, 125, 266–7
international monetary systems 151–2
International Monetary Fund (IMF) 211
investment, industrial 19, 80–1, 107–10, 116, 118, 126–30
'invisible hand' 9, 139–56

Jackson, K. 28, 35–6
Jaffee, D. 78
James, H. 238
Jessop 212
Jevons, W. S. 113
Jones, E. 235, 239, 243, 254
Jones, R. A. 4, 20

Kaldor, N. 9, 116, 131, 132
Kasecklan 118
Kanatas, G. 77, 78
Kendrick, W. 253
Kennedy, P. 10–11, 190, 212, 214
Keynes, J. M. 2–4, 7, 9, 11–12, 16, 18–19, 21, 23–9, 31–2, 34–8, 42,

47–8, 53–8, 61–4, 84–7, 91, 96, 109, 116–18, 120, 125–7, 129, 132–5, 168–9, 215, 235–8, 240–54, 257–68; eclipse of theories 2–3
Keynesianism 2, 4, 8–11, 16, 29, 33–4, 36, 72, 78–81, 90, 104, 115–17, 119, 124–5, 127, 129–33, 135, 207, 245–7, 249, 252–3, 258, 262–3; finance motive debate 126–7; functional finance approach 8
Kindleberger, C. 34
Kiyotaki, N. 4
Klein, P. G. 9, 11
Knapp, G. F. 7, 26, 29, 31, 34, 36–7, 46, 48, 50–5, 57, 64, 120
Knies 36
Koopmans, J. G. 114
Kroszner, R. 5, 35

labouring activity 175–8
Labourism 207–10
Laidler, D. E. W. 5
laissez-faire approach 42, 139–56
Lane 28, 35
Laufer, N. K. A. 8, 97
Laum, B. 69
Lawrence, J. S. 260–2, 268
Laws (Plato) 163, 166, 172
Lavoie, M. 9, 116, 120, 129
Lawson, T. 190
Le Bon 254
Leijonhufvud, A. 16
Leonard, J. 110
Lerner, A. P. 8, 58–60
Leyshon, A. 22, 32
Libecap, G. D. 74
Littler 215
Lloyd, C. L. 126
Lopex 34
Lopokova, L. 34
Luhmann, N. 37

MacDonald, G. 47, 64
McGoun, E. G. 213
McIntosh, M. K. 64
Maier, C. 32
Malinowski, B. 43, 69
Marcuse, H. 251
Maris, B. 1, 11, 254
market: economy 26, 161; historical 18, 32, 44, 157–8; inter-bank 12; simulation of 220–31
Marshall, A. 71, 172, 252, 265; Marshallian economics 117

Marx, K. 10–11, 72, 95, 168, 172, 174, 180–2, 185, 187–202, 205, 212–14, 246, 251, 254
Marxian(ism) 10–11, 212–13, 215, 251–2; relationship between commodity money and symbolic money 194–211; theory of commodity money 174–193
Massenpsychologie und Ich–Analyse (Freud) 239
McCallum, B. T. 266
McCarthy, D. 237
medium of final settlement 6
Meisel, P. 253
Melitz, J. 35, 37
Menger, K. 3, 11, 20, 26, 35–6, 113, 142; theory of money 217–233
Midas 242, 244–247, 249
Miekle, S. 10, 190
Mill, J. S. 1, 17, 172, 253
Millet, P. 172
Mini, P. V. 237
Minsky, H. P. 17, 32, 34, 56–57, 62, 64, 136
Mirowski, P. 38
Mises, L. von 26
Mitchell, B. 62
modelling of monetary function 5
Moggridge, D. E. 253–4
Mohun S. 191–2
monetarism 5, 30–1
monetary circuit (TMC) 8–9, 10, 101–120; neo–chartalist approach 118–120; Post Keynesian 115–118
monetary standard 30
monetary system: collapse of 107; control over 6; development of bank currency 144–5; development of deposit banking 145; evolution of 139; evolution of coinage 144; bank safety 146–8; indirect exchange 141–2; international dimensions 151–2; development of *laissez-faire* 149–50, 152–5; replacement of gold anchor 150–1; unit of account 142–4
money: of account 4, 18, 22, 24–6, 42, 53, 84–92, 94–9; barter 113–14 (*see also* barter); base *see* base money; brief history 23–4, 43–47, 102–3; - changers 22; commodity 23, 54–5, 106, 114, 182–8, 194–5; chartalist approach 47–59 (*see also* chartalist); creation of 4, 78–80; credit-based

theory of 13, 18, 27, 101–20; definition of 104–5; endogenously created money 32, 56, 103, 115, 127–29; exogenous money 32, 80, 115, 257; existence, explained 19–20; *fiat* money 54, 89–93; financing working capital 129–130; historical origins 23–33; means of payment 20–1, 26–31; medium of exchange 5, 17–19, 20–1, 114; medium of final settlement 6, 28; nature of, in monetary circuit 102–4; neutral 7; orthodox economic analysis 17–23; policy implications of chartalist approach 59–63; Post Keynesian approach 130–2; property theory 67–97; psychological aspects 11; role as medium of exchange 3–4, 17–19; role of firms 107–10; role of the state 86, 110–113 (*see also* bank, state central); social relation of 4, 22–23; sociological origins 23–31, 42; stability of 33; store of abstract value 5, 20–2, 26–31; supply 5 (xogeneity or endogeneity of 3, 6, 32, 56, 120, 125); triple analysis of 5–6; valuata *see* valuata; 'virtual money' 1
Moore, B. J. 9, 116–7, 127, 131–2, 137
Moore, G. E. 238
Moseley, F. 190
Mosler, W. 112, 118
Muldrew 30
Muller, A. 37
Murray, P. 190
Myers, F. W. H. 238

Nature and Significance of Economic Science 170
Neale, W. C. 43
Nell, E. S. 8, 109
neochartalist school 7, 118–20
neoclassical economics 2, 9, 20, 28, 73–8, 80, 84, 113–20, 124, 139
New Palgrave Dictionary of Economics and the Law 75
New Theory of Money (Muller) 37
Nivens, M. M. 209
Noble, J. R. 253
North, D. C. 74
numismatics 16

Oeconomica 169

Of Money (Hume) 35
O'Gorman, T. 212
Ontogenesis of the Interest in Money 242
Orwell, G. 209
Ostroy, J. M. 114
overdrafts 131, 258–9, 262

Paley, M. 252
paper money 49, 53, 73, 88, 149; *see also* bank money
Pareto 253
Parguez, A. 3, 6, 8–9, 108–9, 114, 129–30, 135
Parsons, W. 237
Patinkin, D. 114, 115, 257;
payments systems 12
Pheidon of Argos 44
Phillips, C. A. 260, 268
Pilling, G. 190, 208
Pistor, K. 74
Plato 163, 166, 172
Polanyi, K. 34, 43
Politics (Aristotle) 158–64, 166, 172
Pollin 32
Polya, G. 220
Poor Law Act (1834) 208
Post-Keynesian school/theory 4, 9, 16, 115–18, 124–7; horizontalist version 9, 116–17
Production Efficiency Board (PES) 209
profit 94, 109, 117
property, private: encumbered 8, 74–5, 83, 93, 96–7; premium 67, 82–4; role of 8, 72
property theory 67–97; distinctive characteristics 81–2
Psychopathology of Everyday Life 239
public sector, role of 10, 110–12, 125, 132; *see also* state theory

Quarterly Journal of Economics 250
Queen Victoria 236, 240

Radford, R. A. 143
Ray, A. S. 103
Realfonzo, R. 114
Redish, A. 46
Reich 251
Reiss-Schimmel I. 254
Renaud, J. F. 109
reserve assets, nature of 6; provision of 89–90, 145–8, 260–2
Reuten, G. 175

Rhetoric (Aristotle) 159
Riach 268
Ricardo, D. 1, 71, 73, 190
Riemersma 35
Riese, H. 78, 97
Riley, B. 212
Robbins, L. 170
Robertson, D. H. 18
Robinson, D. 233
Rochon, L. P. 9, 116
Rogers, C. 2, 12, 17
Roll, E. 164
Roover, de 28
Ross 165, 166
Rossi, S. 129, 137
Roy, T. 8, 97
Rubin, I. I. 190, 198, 199
Rymes, T. K. 2, 12, 257

SteCroix, G. E. M. de 169
Samuelson, P. 5, 21, 35, 42, 63
saving, role of 133
Sayer, D. 190
Sayers, R. S. 98
Schapiro 30
Schelling, T. C. 218
Schmitt, B. 129, 130, 132
Schneider, L. 254
Schumpeter, J. A. 2, 4, 16–17, 19, 23–4, 27, 29–30, 34, 37, 79–80, 157, 171
Schmartz, A. J. 98
Seccareccia, M. 8–9, 108, 114, 118
Selgin, G. 5, 9, 11, 63
Sen, A. 171
share capital 133
Shaw, E. S. 114
Sidgwick, H. 238
Simmel, G. 7, 22–4, 29, 36–7, 196, 212, 242
Skidelsky, R. 237, 253
Smith, A. 1, 47–9, 52, 57, 71–2, 98, 168, 171, 213
Smith, T. 190
Smithin, J. 2–3,, 6, 12, 17, 19–20, 23–4, 27, 34, 38
Social Insurance Act (1943) 208
social security reforms (1911) 208
sociologists (attitude to money of) 7, 16–17
Socrates 238
Solon 106
speculation 135–6, 247–8
Spufford, P. 28

Stadermann, H. J. 87, 91, 98
stagflation 2
state theory of money 50–2, 54–5
Starr, R. M. 69, 114
Steiger, O. 8, 35, 64, 67, 87, 98, 101–3, 106
Stephen, A. 237, 239
Stephen, T. 237
Stephen, Vanessa 237
Stephen, Virginia 237
Steuart, J. 88, 89, 98
Stiglitz, J. 78
stock transactions, financing of 135–6
Strachey, A. 253
Strachey, J. 235, 238–40, 244, 253
Strachey, L. 236–40, 253
Studart, R. 128, 132
Swedberg, R. 25
Sydney-Turner, S. 237

taxes, payment/role of 9, 44, 48, 57–9, 111, 118; *see also* fiscal policy
'taxes drive money' approach 7; *see also* chartalist approach
Taylor, F. W. 208, 209, 213
Thomas, R. P. 74
Thrift, N. 22, 32
title, property and possessional 81–2, 84, 96–7
TMC *see* monetary circuit
tobacco as medium of exchange 25
Tobin, J. 5, 64, 87
Tomlinson, J. 209
Trade and Markets in the Early Empires 34
Treatise on Probability 236
Treatise on Money 12, 16, 34, 109, 235, 243, 246, 251, 260, 263, 268
Trevithick, J. A. 131–2

Ullman-Margalit, A. 140
Unemployed Workman's Act (1905) 208
unemployment 61–2, 87
Unemployment Act (1934) 208
Usher 28
usury 158
Utlitarianism 170

Vallageas, B. 109
valuata money 6, 12, 53,
value, Marxist theory of 179–86, 195–200
Veblen, T. 63, 253
Viderman, S. 242, 254

wages 94–5
Wallich, H. C. 91
Walras, L. 71, 246; Walrasian theory 76, 247–8, 252
Walsh, C. E. 5
Weber, M. 7, 28, 29, 32–3, 35, 37–8, 237
Wells, H. G. 248
wergeld 25, 43
What is Money? (Innes) 12
White, L. H. 5, 25, 63, 143, 233
Wicksell 3, 6, 114, 265
Wicksteed 165
Williams, M. 170, 175, 190–2, 194, 197, 212
Wilson, H. 190
Wilson, President W. 236, 240
Winslow, E. G. 237
Wittfogel, K. 102, 244
Woolf, L. 235, 237–9, 253–4
Woolf, V. 235, 237, 239, 253–4
Woolsey, W. W. 156
World Bank 211
Wray, L. R. 6, 7, 28, 32, 35, 64, 101, 117–20
Wright, R. 4

Yeager, L. B. 1, 2, 5, 156

Zeleny, J. 190

Printed in Great Britain
by Amazon